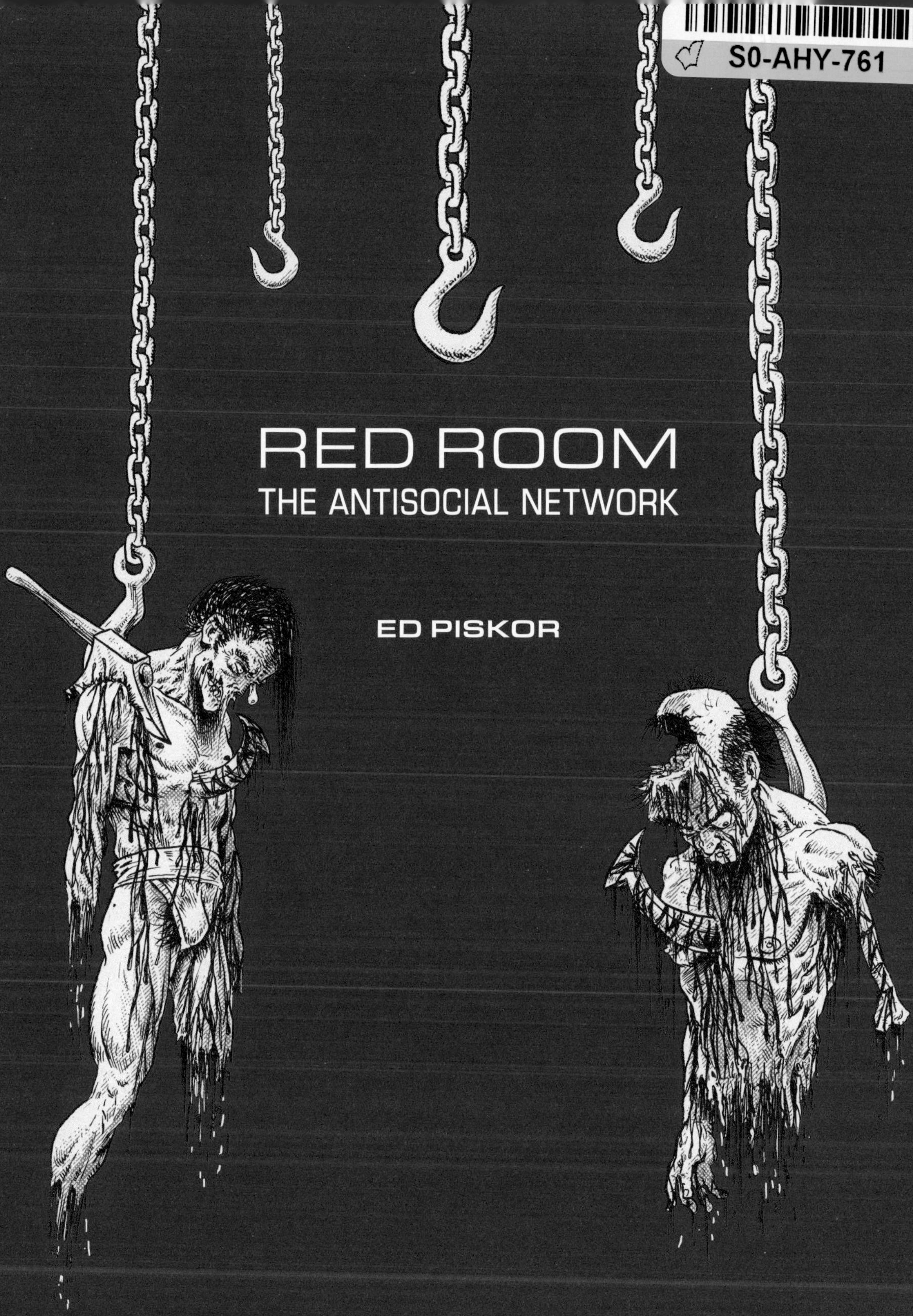

RED ROOM
THE ANTISOCIAL NETWORK

ED PISKOR

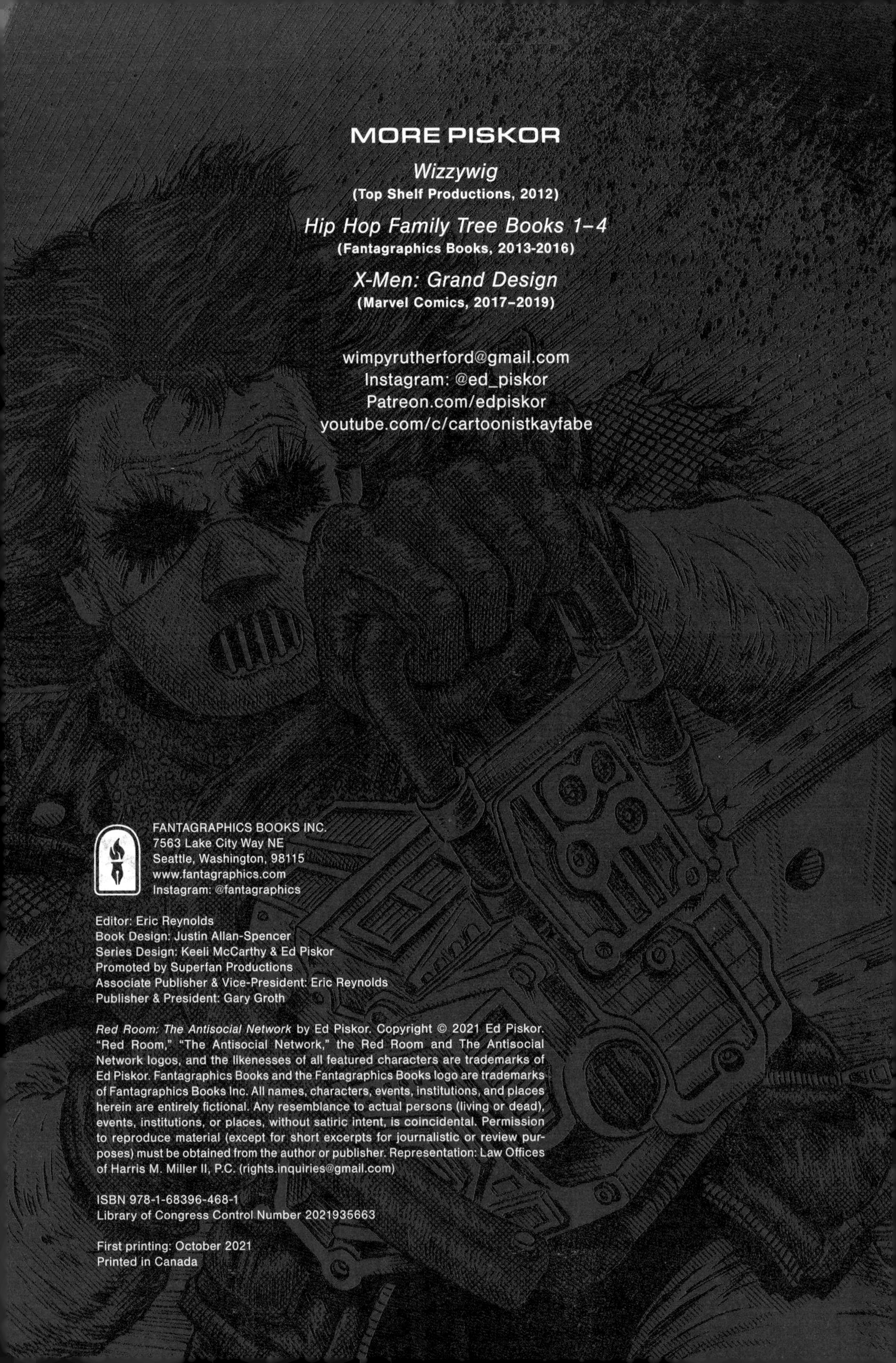

MORE PISKOR

Wizzywig
(Top Shelf Productions, 2012)

Hip Hop Family Tree Books 1–4
(Fantagraphics Books, 2013-2016)

X-Men: Grand Design
(Marvel Comics, 2017–2019)

wimpyrutherford@gmail.com
Instagram: @ed_piskor
Patreon.com/edpiskor
youtube.com/c/cartoonistkayfabe

FANTAGRAPHICS BOOKS INC.
7563 Lake City Way NE
Seattle, Washington, 98115
www.fantagraphics.com
Instagram: @fantagraphics

Editor: Eric Reynolds
Book Design: Justin Allan-Spencer
Series Design: Keeli McCarthy & Ed Piskor
Promoted by Superfan Productions
Associate Publisher & Vice-President: Eric Reynolds
Publisher & President: Gary Groth

ISBN 978-1-68396-468-1
Library of Congress Control Number 2021935663

First printing: October 2021
Printed in Canada

FANTAGRAPHICS
BOOKS INC

RED ROOM

ED PISKOR

MEDIEVAL_ON_DAT_ASS(JUDAS).WMV

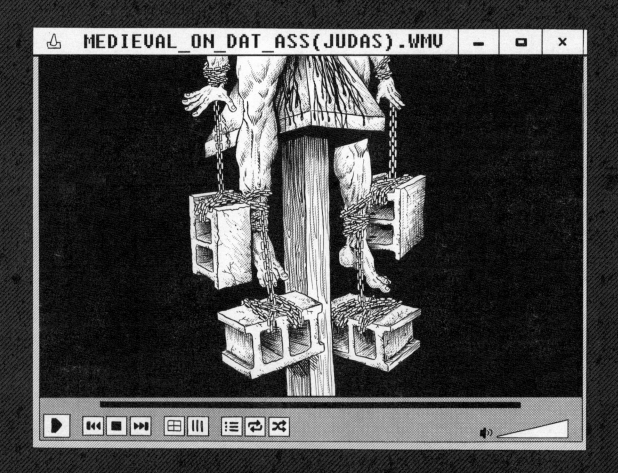

CONTENTS

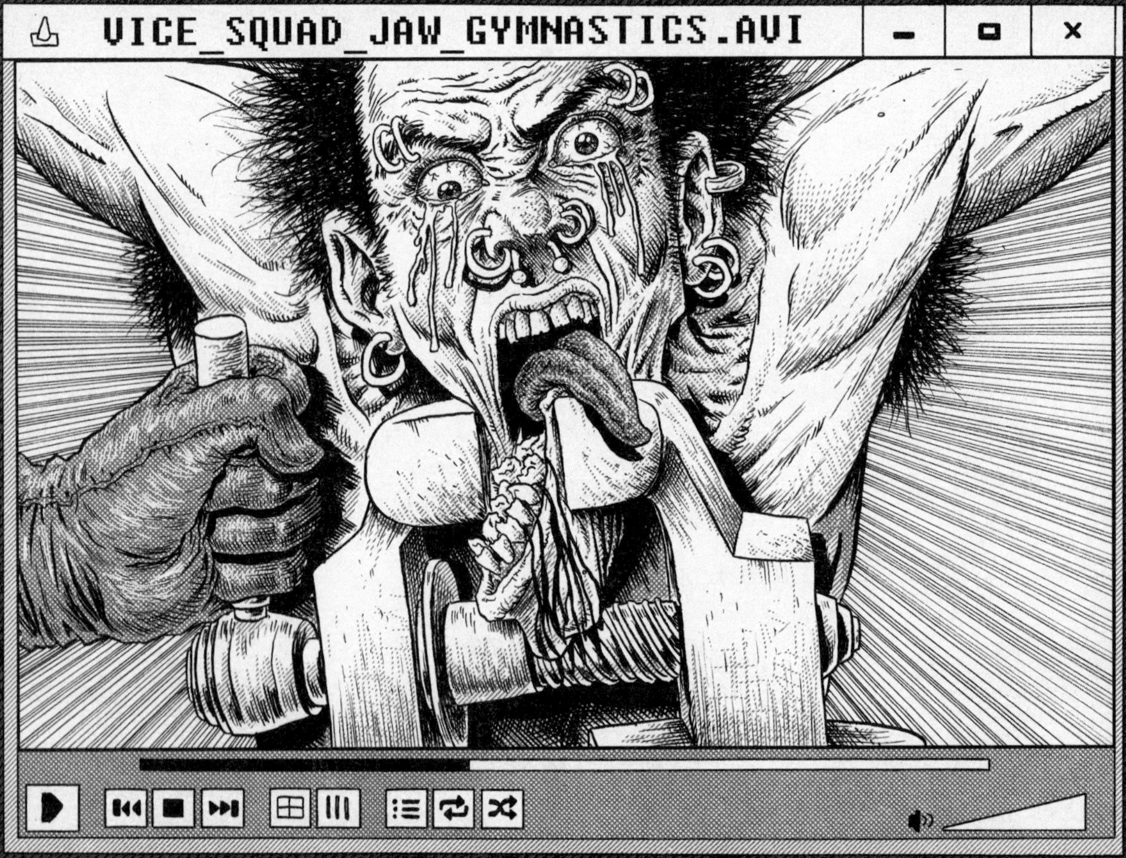
VICE_SQUAD_JAW_GYMNASTICS.AVI

FOREWORD

2020 was supposed to be a production year for me anyhow, and the emergence of Covid-19 made damn sure I was gonna be getting some comics done during that calendar year so long as I didn't catch the bug. All of the comic material here was done with that germy albatross around my neck and I think the work is weirdly better for it. I was so fucking uneasy, anxious, and thinking loops and loops of dark thoughts. Weren't we all, though?

Red Room was something I was planning to launch into after Book 4 of *Hip Hop Family Tree* but a detour through the X-Men kept the project in my mind's eye for three years longer than anticipated. I'm really glad for that. It's good to let ideas percolate for a while before committing pen to paper. The project turned into something completely different than what I was originally intending it to be. I think my initial pitch was more procedural whodunnit with a "theater of the mind" approach, where all the fun stuff happens off camera. Fuck that noise. Vulgarity is my default setting. Can't fight who I am.

I honestly think I've put together enough of a body of work that I can probably be profiled down to the year and month of my birth at this point. The material from my mental compost heap that *Red Room* employs is that of the kid who grew up with mom and pop video rental stores every two blocks, each containing robust horror sections that I'd completely pillage for a decade-and-a-half before online piracy and Netflix killed those enterprises. Blood, guts, exploitation, pot-boilers, and pulp. A hearty brew served straight-to-video and into the mind of a boy with a very overactive imagination. It just took 20 years to bloom into this piece of pulp you're holding in your hands.

Growing up during the inertia of Stephen King's powers in the '80s and early '90s also provided an insane amount of other very cheap, secondhand, paperback horror novels to comb through, all with unforgettable, provocative cover art! Books by people like Clive Barker, Richard Laymon, Jack Ketchum, J.R. Lansdale, John Skipp, and Rex Miller. Not to mention that when the HBO *Tales From The Crypt* TV show went live in the early 1990s, the EC reprints began showing up in the (honest-to-goodness) grocery store and I was able to enjoy those comics at eight years-old the same way a kid in 1953 would have. How could a work like *Red Room* not exist with such formative influences?

I spent a lot of time working on *X-Men: Grand Design* listening through King's bibliography via audiobook. It's something I recommend. Sissy Spacek reads *Carrie*! C'mon! His 1981 thesis, *Danse Macabre*, was a huge influence in shaping *Red Room* as it very cogently marries multimedia examples of horror with the social fears and anxieties from which those works were created. I immediately began thinking about what cool horror possibilities were out there today that really haven't been explored in a satisfactory way for me. The dark net was the first thing that came to mind. The idea of an untraceable internet where drug smugglers, gun runners, human traffickers, pedophiles, and hitmen reside with impunity is the perfect stuff for my horror fiction purposes.

Hip Hop Family Tree was a world building exercise on rails using real life to help set the pieces in motion. *X-Men: Grand Design* was world building with some fictional wiggle room to play with. World building is something I wanted to bring into *Red Room* and that would have been a tough approach in the graphic novel zeitgeist. *Red Room* needed to be a classic pamphlet comic.

It's not a controversial opinion to suggest that the classic pamphlet comic format has been grossly misused for maybe 20 years or so. The stories are spread so thin in order to compile six issues of content into expensive trade paperbacks that they don't provide very satisfying reading experiences for the price point. Rather than complain, I figured I'd do the opposite of all the things I dislike about the abuse of my favorite artistic medium and try to make some monthly comics that you'd be happy to trek to the comics shop to scoop up every four weeks or so. That said, I also want to make this book collection its own satisfying experience on top of that. Lots of spinning plates in this comic book game.

The visual approach to *Red Room* has its foundation rooted in a visual approach that burned like a supernova in the 1980s and early '90s. Gritty, outlaw, black-and-white comics work by the likes of James O'Barr, Tim Vigil, Tim Tyler, Guy Davis, Vince Locke, Michael Zulli, Kevin Eastman, Eric Talbot, and more. Duotone grayscaling was a piece of connective tissue that links all of these raw and organic artists. The subject matter they often chose to draw echoes the *Red Room* vibe as well.

This is not a graphic novel you're holding in your hands. It's a collection of four comic books that each tell their own tale but if you read them all you will see the bigger world I'm developing. Much like our own world, we're not given a clear map of how everything works. We get drips and drabs of intelligence along the way and that's how the *Red Room* comics operate. Stick with me and you'll get a very clear picture of the whole ecosystem of murder on the dark web for fun and profit.

This is also a very self-aware creation. Your humble author isn't trying to woo librarians and academics. No Eisner award-bait here. I'm just looking to make you a little uneasy, to freak you out a bit, and if I have to resort to some gross-outs to get the results I want, you'll clearly see that I'm not above that in the very least.

Ed Piskor, June 2021
Dixmont State Hospital
for the Criminally
Insane

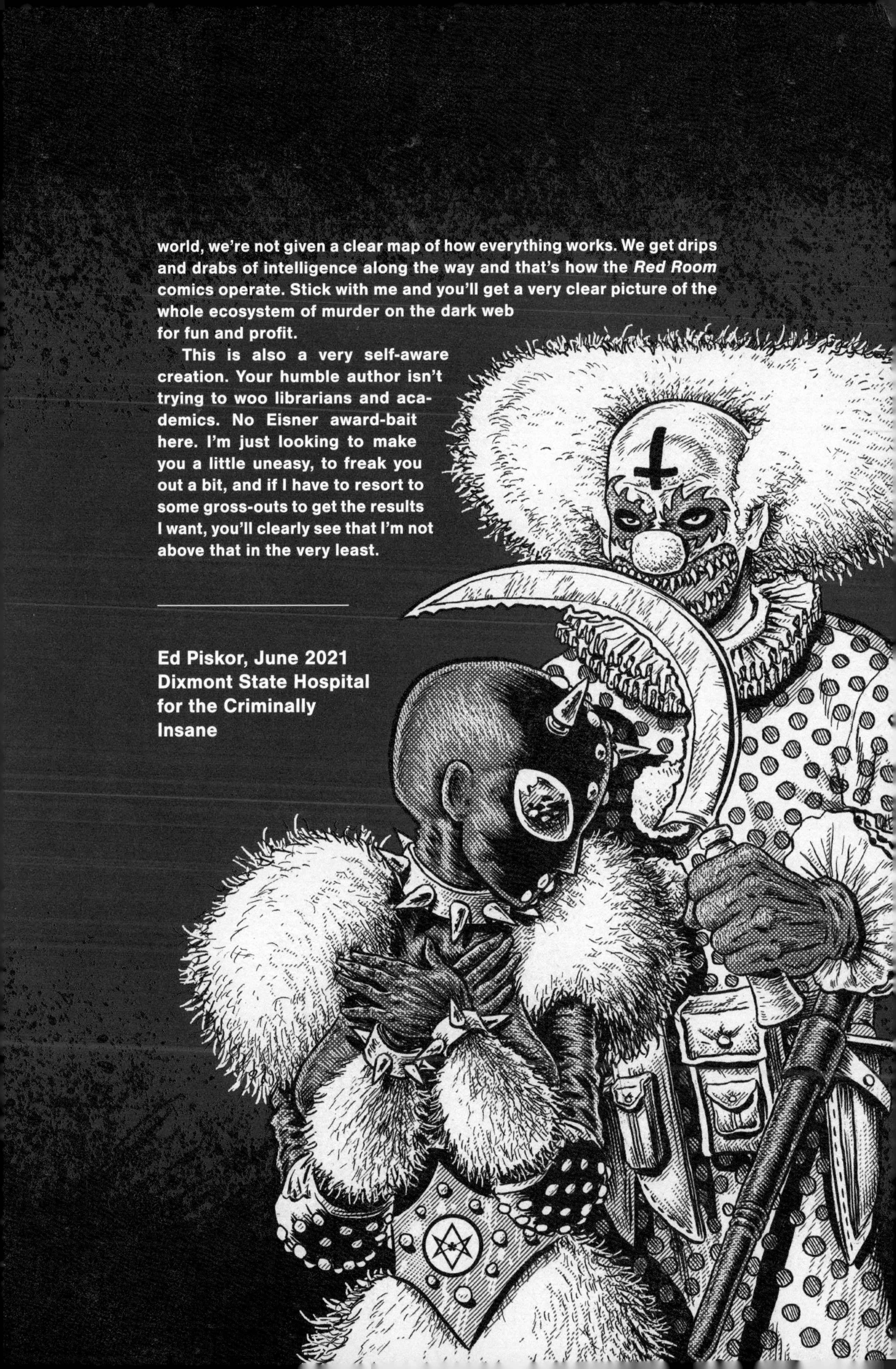

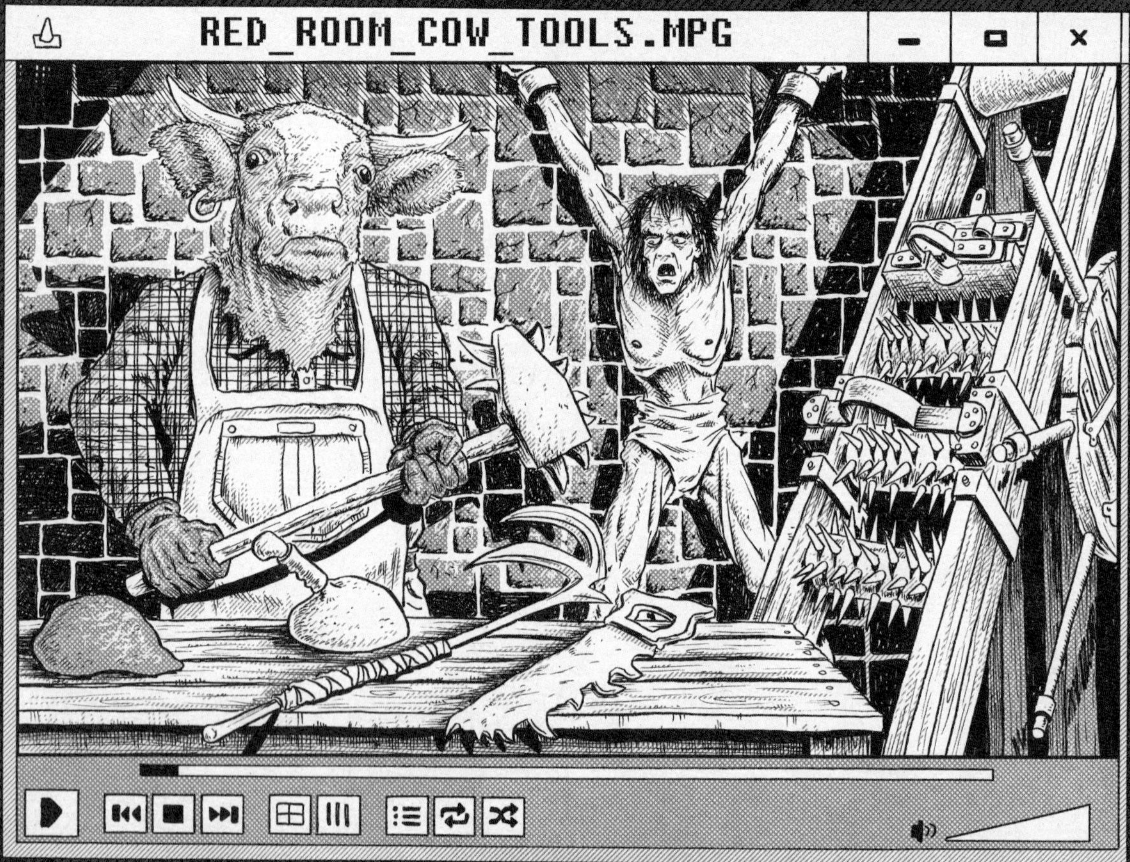
RED_ROOM_COW_TOOLS.MPG

ONE

BLOODY BAPTISM

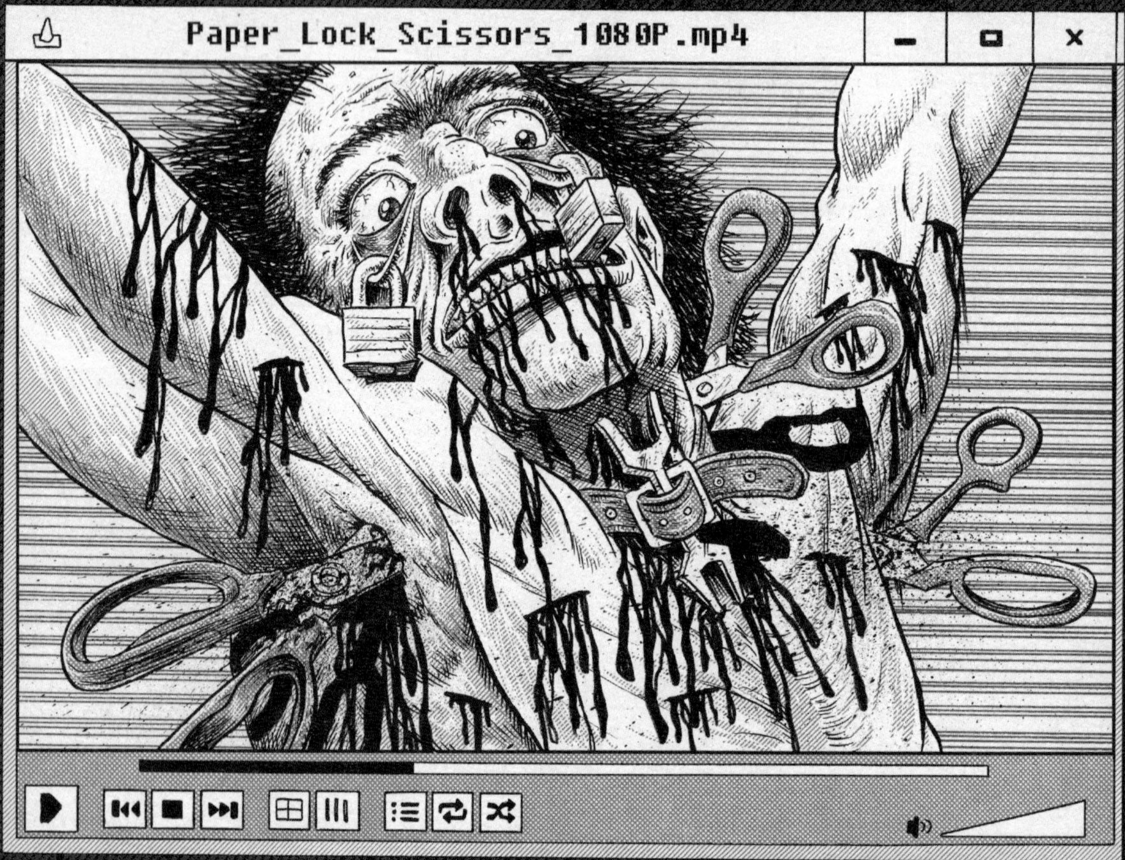
Paper_Lock_Scissors_1080P.mp4

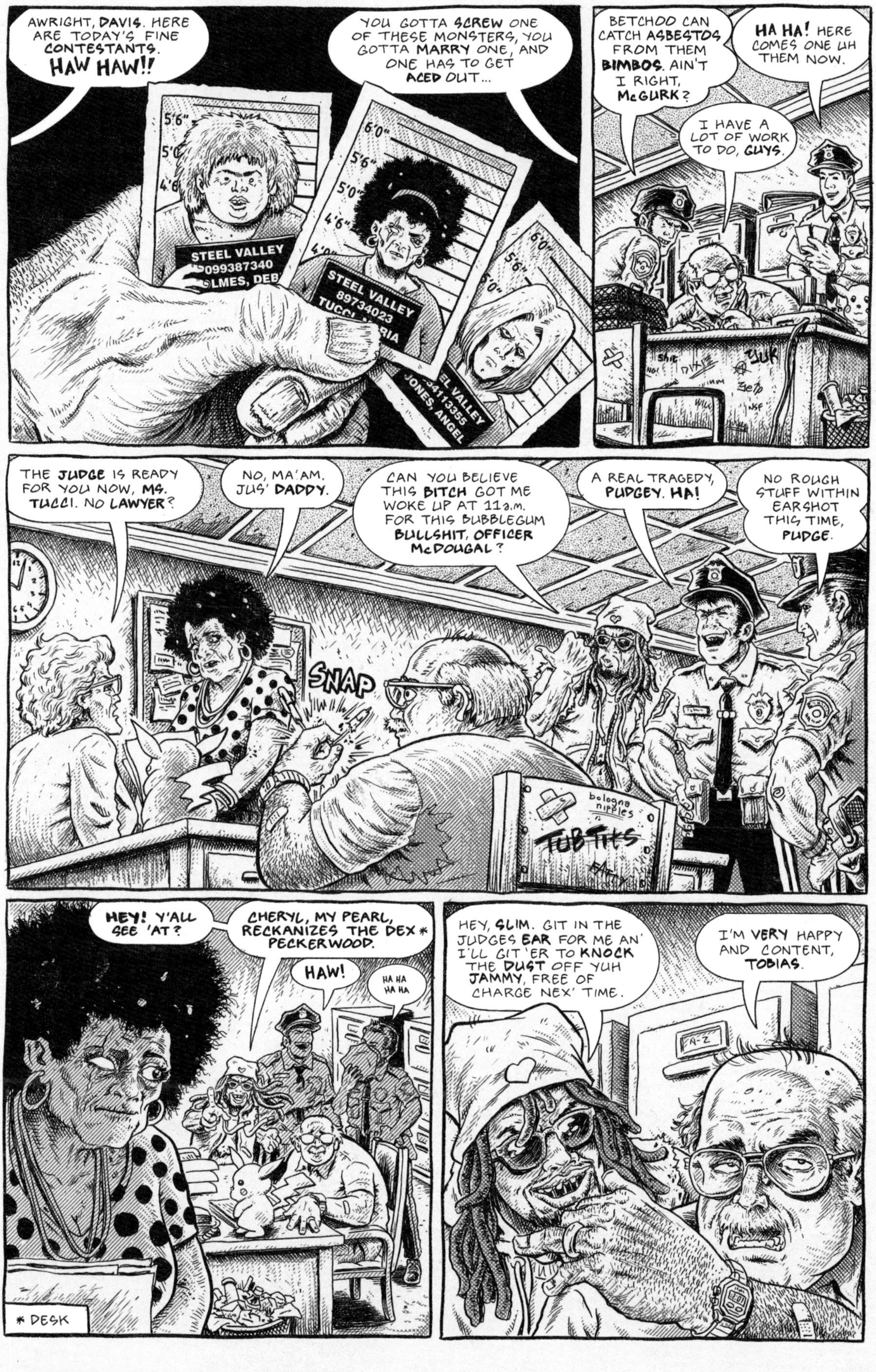

AWRIGHT, DAVIS. HERE ARE TODAY'S FINE CONTESTANTS. HAW HAW!!
YOU GOTTA SCREW ONE OF THESE MONSTERS, YOU GOTTA MARRY ONE, AND ONE HAS TO GET ACED OUT...
STEEL VALLEY
STEEL VALLEY
89734023
BETCHOO CAN CATCH ASBESTOS FROM THEM BIMBOS. AIN'T I RIGHT, McGURK?
HA HA! HERE COMES ONE UH THEM NOW.
I HAVE A LOT OF WORK TO DO, GUYS.
THE JUDGE IS READY FOR YOU NOW, MS. TUCCI. NO LAWYER?
NO, MA'AM. JUS' DADDY.
CAN YOU BELIEVE THIS BITCH GOT ME WOKE UP AT 11a.m. FOR THIS BUBBLEGUM BULLSHIT, OFFICER McDOUGAL?
A REAL TRAGEDY, PUDGEY. HA!
NO ROUGH STUFF WITHIN EARSHOT THIS TIME, PUDGE.
SNAP
bologna nipples
TUB TITS
HEY! Y'ALL SEE 'AT?
CHERYL, MY PEARL, RECKANIZES THE DEX* PECKERWOOD.
HAW!
HA HA HA HA
*DESK
HEY, SLIM. GIT IN THE JUDGES EAR FOR ME AN' I'LL GIT 'ER TO KNOCK THE DUST OFF YUH JAMMY, FREE OF CHARGE NEX' TIME.
I'M VERY HAPPY AND CONTENT, TOBIAS.
A-Z

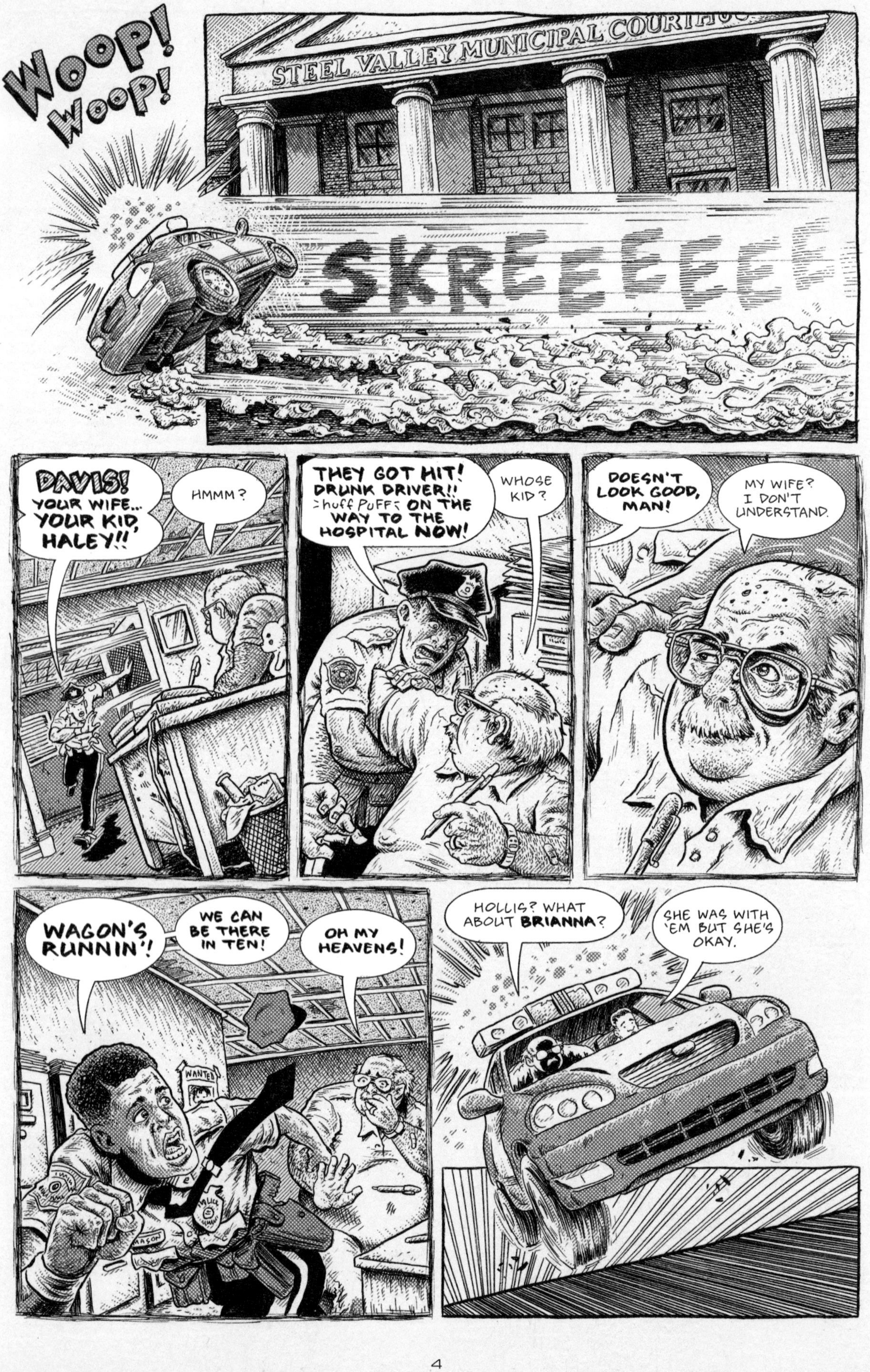
WOOP! WOOP!
STEEL VALLEY MUNICIPAL COURTHO
SKREEEEEE
DAVIS! YOUR WIFE... YOUR KID, HALEY!!
HMMM?
THEY GOT HIT! DRUNK DRIVER!! =huff PUFF= ON THE WAY TO THE HOSPITAL NOW!
WHOSE KID?
DOESN'T LOOK GOOD, MAN!
MY WIFE? I DON'T UNDERSTAND.
WAGON'S RUNNIN'!
WE CAN BE THERE IN TEN!
OH MY HEAVENS!
WANTED
HOLLIS? WHAT ABOUT BRIANNA?
SHE WAS WITH 'EM BUT SHE'S OKAY.

DELORES FAIRFIELD

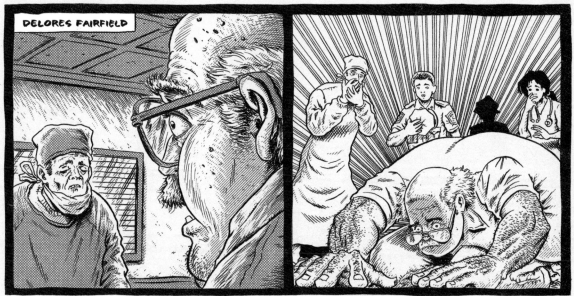

HAYLEY FAIRFIELD

MR. FAIRFIELD, MY NAME IS **BEVERLY CHASTAIN**. I'LL BE YOUR SOCIAL WORKER FOR THIS MATTER.

BEFORE ANYTHING ELSE, THERE IS **ONE**, VERY IMPORTANT, TIME-SENSITIVE ISSUE THAT WE MUST ADDRESS...

AS **HAYLEY'S** SOLE LIVING GUARDIAN...

WHERE DO YOU STAND ON THE SUBJECT OF **ORGAN DONATION**?

BRIANNA FAIRFIELD

OH **BREE-BREE**. DOES IT HURT, BABY?

DADDY... THEY JUST TOLD ME ABOUT MOMMY... THESE SHOTS THEY'RE GIVING ME... THEY ARE HELPING... WITH THAT PAIN, TOO...

WE GOT YOUR PRESCRIPTION FILLED... IT'S... IN MOMMY'S BAG... DID SHE GIVE THEM TO YOU? OH YEAH... NEVERMIND...

5

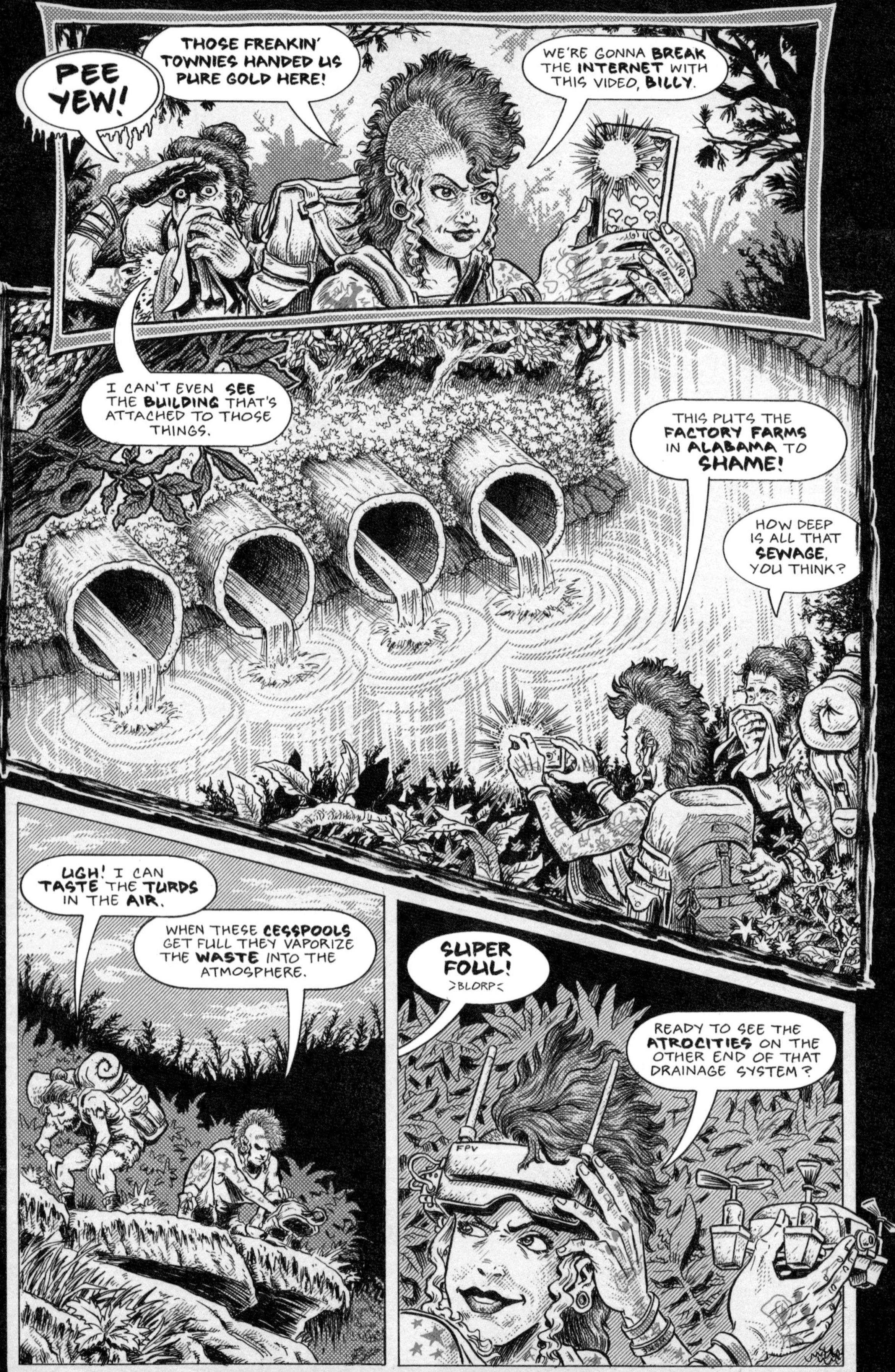
PEE YEW!
THOSE FREAKIN' TOWNIES HANDED US PURE GOLD HERE!
WE'RE GONNA BREAK THE INTERNET WITH THIS VIDEO, BILLY.
I CAN'T EVEN SEE THE BUILDING THAT'S ATTACHED TO THOSE THINGS.
THIS PUTS THE FACTORY FARMS IN ALABAMA TO SHAME!
HOW DEEP IS ALL THAT SEWAGE, YOU THINK?
UGH! I CAN TASTE THE TURDS IN THE AIR.
WHEN THESE CESSPOOLS GET FULL THEY VAPORIZE THE WASTE INTO THE ATMOSPHERE.
SUPER FOUL!
>BLORP<
READY TO SEE THE ATROCITIES ON THE OTHER END OF THAT DRAINAGE SYSTEM?
FPV

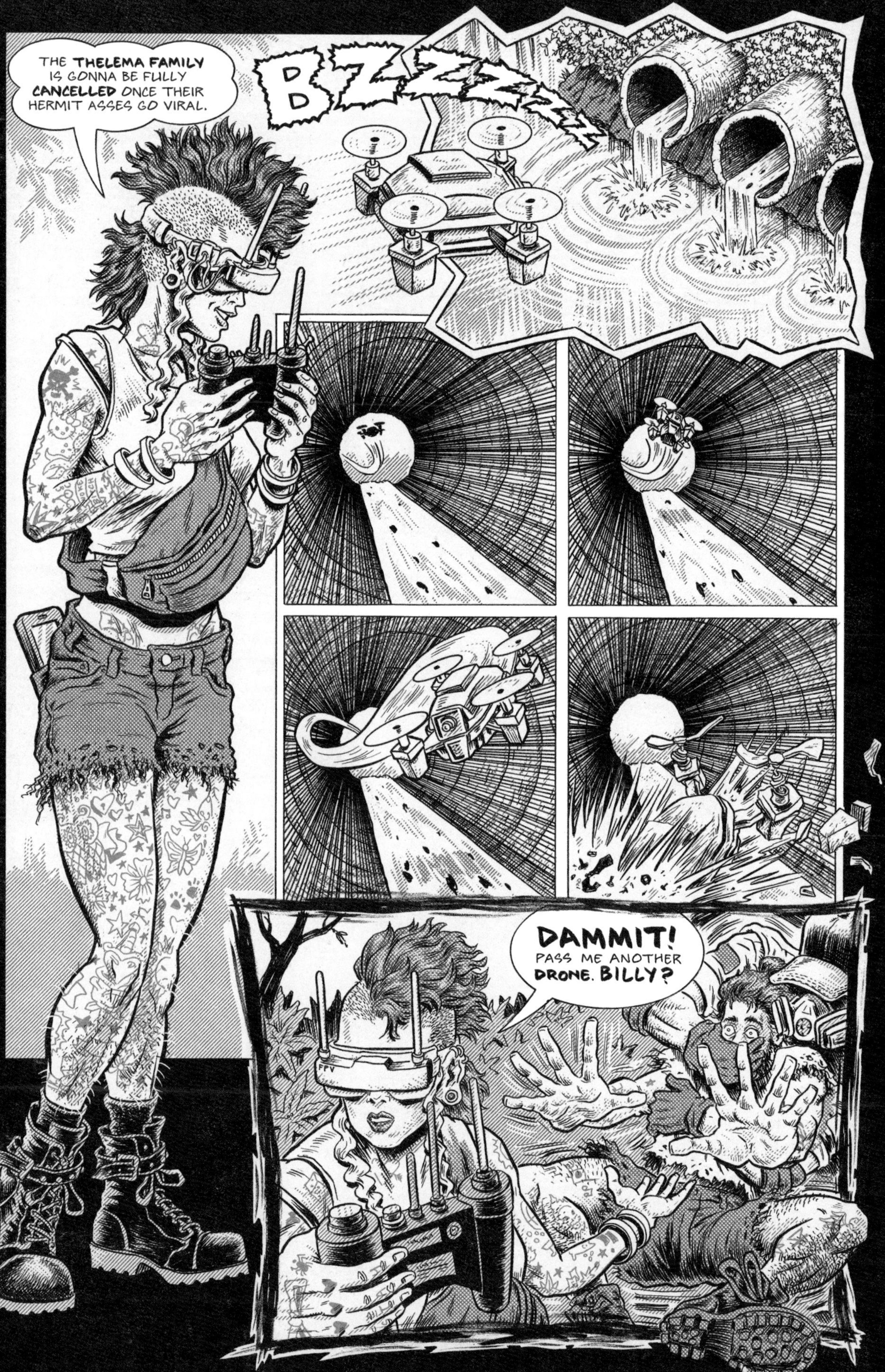
THE **THELEMA FAMILY** IS GONNA BE FULLY **CANCELLED** ONCE THEIR HERMIT ASSES GO VIRAL.
BZZZZZ
FPV
DAMMIT! PASS ME ANOTHER **DRONE. BILLY?**

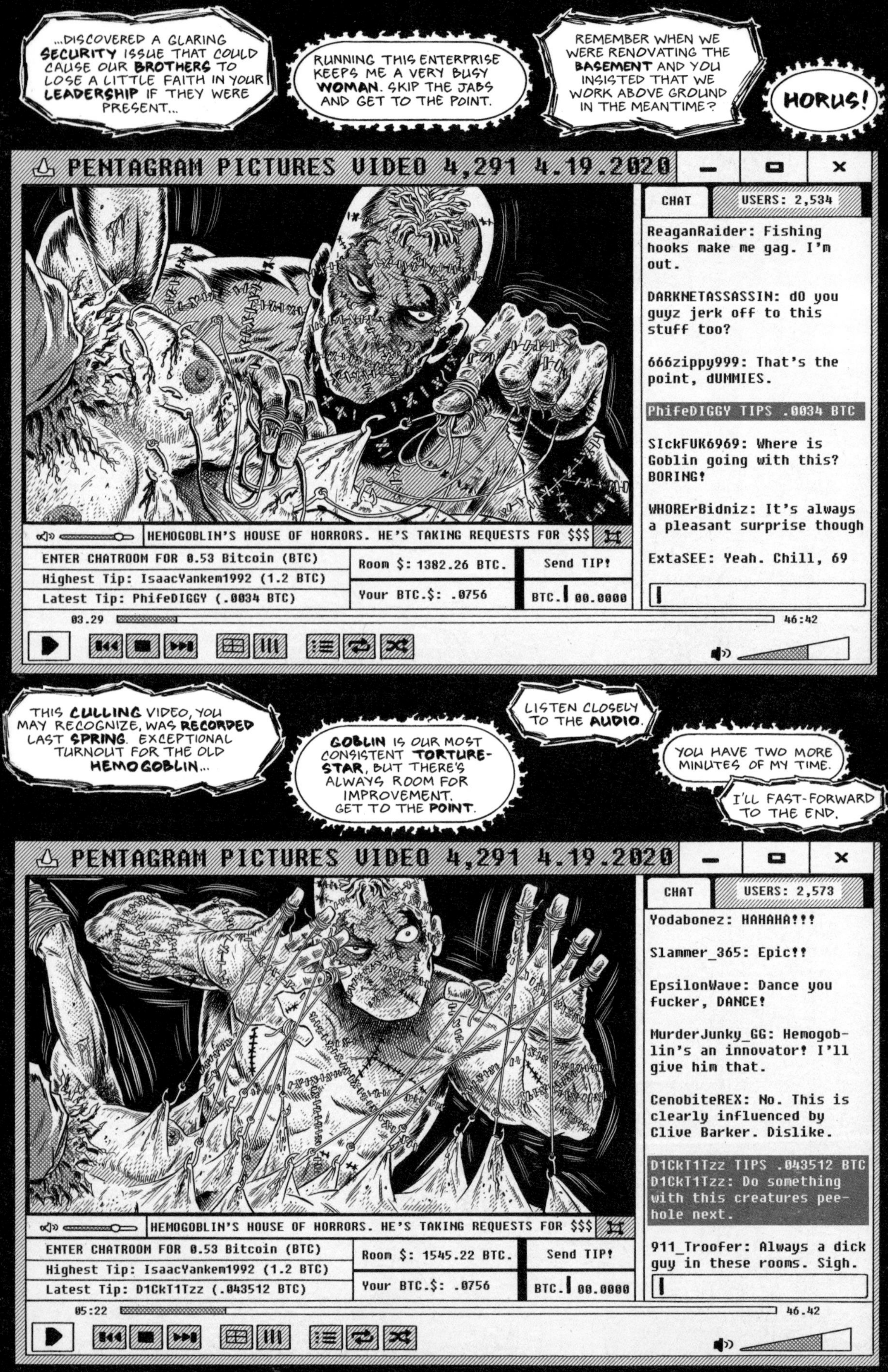
...DISCOVERED A GLARING SECURITY ISSUE THAT COULD CAUSE OUR BROTHERS TO LOSE A LITTLE FAITH IN YOUR LEADERSHIP IF THEY WERE PRESENT...
RUNNING THIS ENTERPRISE KEEPS ME A VERY BUSY WOMAN. SKIP THE JABS AND GET TO THE POINT.
REMEMBER WHEN WE WERE RENOVATING THE BASEMENT AND YOU INSISTED THAT WE WORK ABOVE GROUND IN THE MEANTIME?
HORUS!
PENTAGRAM PICTURES VIDEO 4,291 4.19.2020
CHAT
USERS: 2,534
ReaganRaider: Fishing hooks make me gag. I'm out.
DARKNETASSASSIN: d0 you guyz jerk off to this stuff too?
666zippy999: That's the point, dUMMIES.
PhifeDIGGY TIPS .0034 BTC
SIckFUK6969: Where is Goblin going with this? BORING!
WHORErBidniz: It's always a pleasant surprise though
ExtaSEE: Yeah. Chill, 69
HEMOGOBLIN'S HOUSE OF HORRORS. HE'S TAKING REQUESTS FOR $$$
ENTER CHATROOM FOR 0.53 Bitcoin (BTC)
Highest Tip: IsaacYankem1992 (1.2 BTC)
Latest Tip: PhifeDIGGY (.0034 BTC)
Room $: 1382.26 BTC.
Your BTC.$: .0756
Send TIP!
BTC. 00.0000
03.29
46:42
THIS CULLING VIDEO, YOU MAY RECOGNIZE, WAS RECORDED LAST SPRING. EXCEPTIONAL TURNOUT FOR THE OLD HEMOGOBLIN...
GOBLIN IS OUR MOST CONSISTENT TORTURE-STAR, BUT THERE'S ALWAYS ROOM FOR IMPROVEMENT. GET TO THE POINT.
LISTEN CLOSELY TO THE AUDIO.
YOU HAVE TWO MORE MINUTES OF MY TIME.
I'LL FAST-FORWARD TO THE END.
PENTAGRAM PICTURES VIDEO 4,291 4.19.2020
CHAT
USERS: 2,573
Yodabonez: HAHAHA!!!
Slammer_365: Epic!!
EpsilonWave: Dance you fucker, DANCE!
MurderJunky_GG: Hemogob-lin's an innovator! I'll give him that.
CenobiteREX: No. This is clearly influenced by Clive Barker. Dislike.
D1CkT1Tzz TIPS .043512 BTC
D1CkT1Tzz: Do something with this creatures pee-hole next.
911_Troofer: Always a dick guy in these rooms. Sigh.
HEMOGOBLIN'S HOUSE OF HORRORS. HE'S TAKING REQUESTS FOR $$$
ENTER CHATROOM FOR 0.53 Bitcoin (BTC)
Highest Tip: IsaacYankem1992 (1.2 BTC)
Latest Tip: D1CkT1Tzz (.043512 BTC)
Room $: 1545.22 BTC.
Your BTC.$: .0756
Send TIP!
BTC. 00.0000
05:22
46.42

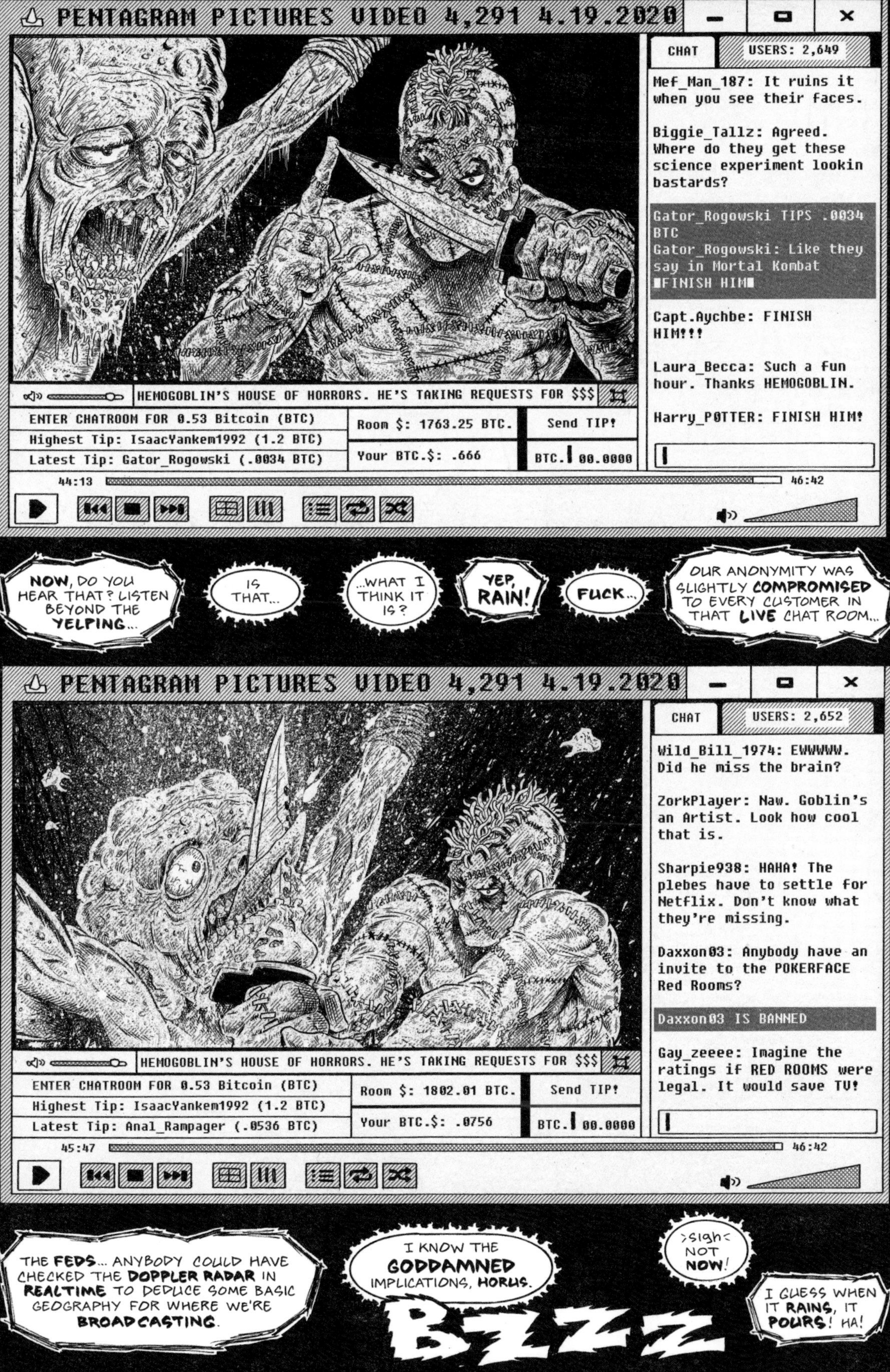
PENTAGRAM PICTURES VIDEO 4,291 4.19.2020
CHAT
USERS: 2,649
Mef_Man_187: It ruins it when you see their faces.
Biggie_Tallz: Agreed. Where do they get these science experiment lookin bastards?
Gator_Rogowski TIPS .0034 BTC
Gator_Rogowski: Like they say in Mortal Kombat ■FINISH HIM■
Capt.Aychbe: FINISH HIM!!!
Laura_Becca: Such a fun hour. Thanks HEMOGOBLIN.
Harry_P0TTER: FINISH HIM!
HEMOGOBLIN'S HOUSE OF HORRORS. HE'S TAKING REQUESTS FOR $$$
ENTER CHATROOM FOR 0.53 Bitcoin (BTC)
Highest Tip: IsaacYankem1992 (1.2 BTC)
Latest Tip: Gator_Rogowski (.0034 BTC)
Room $: 1763.25 BTC.
Your BTC.$: .666
Send TIP!
BTC. 00.0000
44:13
46:42
NOW, DO YOU HEAR THAT? LISTEN BEYOND THE YELPING...
IS THAT...
...WHAT I THINK IT IS?
YEP, RAIN!
FUCK...
OUR ANONYMITY WAS SLIGHTLY COMPROMISED TO EVERY CUSTOMER IN THAT LIVE CHAT ROOM...
PENTAGRAM PICTURES VIDEO 4,291 4.19.2020
CHAT
USERS: 2,652
Wild_Bill_1974: EWWWWW. Did he miss the brain?
ZorkPlayer: Naw. Goblin's an Artist. Look how cool that is.
Sharpie938: HAHA! The plebes have to settle for Netflix. Don't know what they're missing.
Daxxon03: Anybody have an invite to the POKERFACE Red Rooms?
Daxxon03 IS BANNED
Gay_zeeee: Imagine the ratings if RED ROOMS were legal. It would save TV!
HEMOGOBLIN'S HOUSE OF HORRORS. HE'S TAKING REQUESTS FOR $$$
ENTER CHATROOM FOR 0.53 Bitcoin (BTC)
Highest Tip: IsaacYankem1992 (1.2 BTC)
Latest Tip: Anal_Rampager (.0536 BTC)
Room $: 1802.01 BTC.
Your BTC.$: .0756
Send TIP!
BTC. 00.0000
45:47
46:42
THE FEDS... ANYBODY COULD HAVE CHECKED THE DOPPLER RADAR IN REALTIME TO DEDUCE SOME BASIC GEOGRAPHY FOR WHERE WE'RE BROADCASTING.
I KNOW THE GODDAMNED IMPLICATIONS, HORUS.
>sigh< NOT NOW!
I GUESS WHEN IT RAINS, IT POURS! HA!
BZZZ

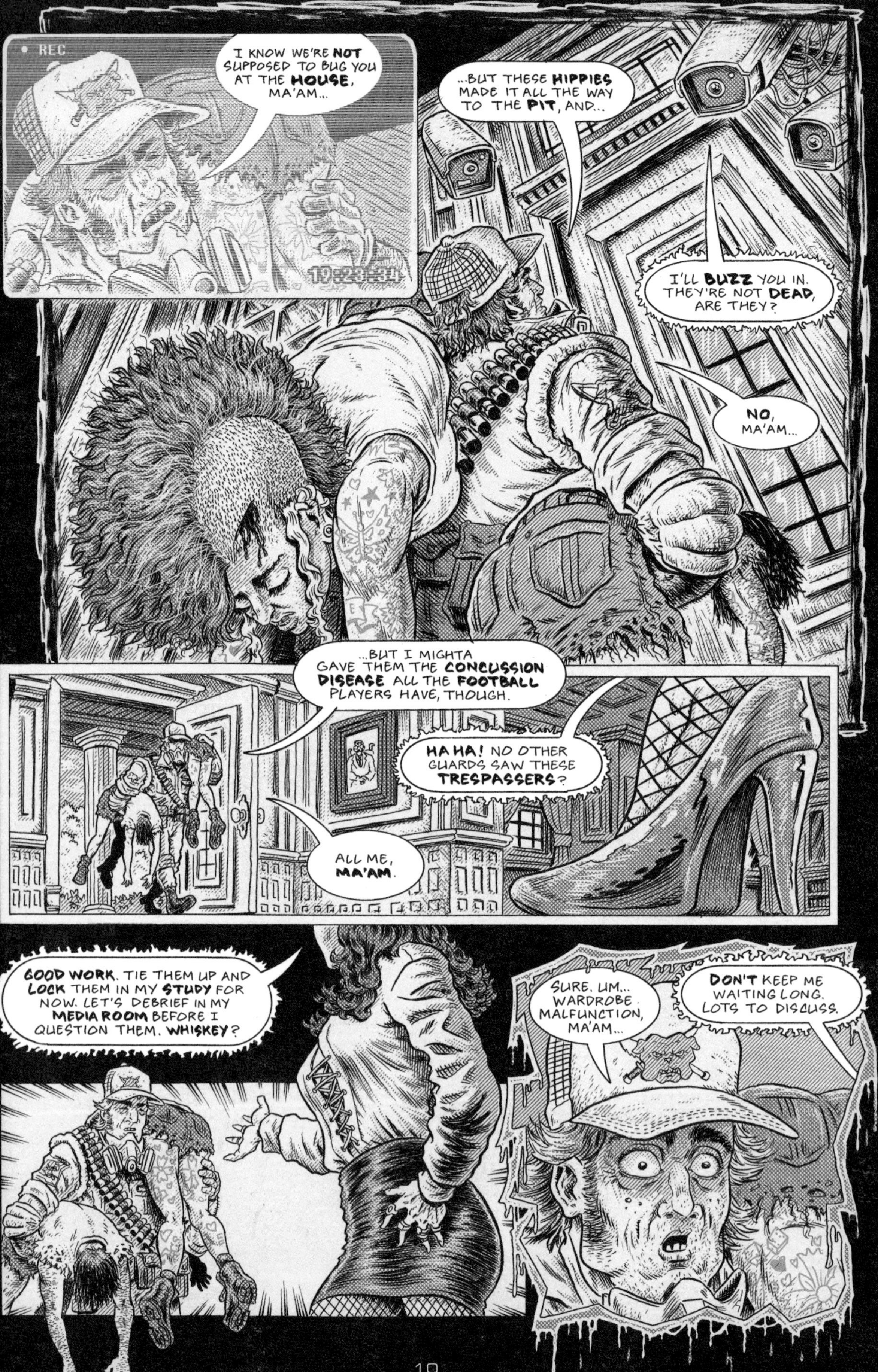
REC
I KNOW WE'RE NOT SUPPOSED TO BUG YOU AT THE HOUSE, MA'AM...
...BUT THESE HIPPIES MADE IT ALL THE WAY TO THE PIT, AND...
I'LL BUZZ YOU IN. THEY'RE NOT DEAD, ARE THEY?
NO, MA'AM...
...BUT I MIGHTA GAVE THEM THE CONCUSSION DISEASE ALL THE FOOTBALL PLAYERS HAVE, THOUGH.
HA HA! NO OTHER GUARDS SAW THESE TRESPASSERS?
ALL ME, MA'AM.
GOOD WORK. TIE THEM UP AND LOCK THEM IN MY STUDY FOR NOW. LET'S DEBRIEF IN MY MEDIA ROOM BEFORE I QUESTION THEM. WHISKEY?
SURE. UM... WARDROBE MALFUNCTION, MA'AM...
DON'T KEEP ME WAITING LONG. LOTS TO DISCUSS.

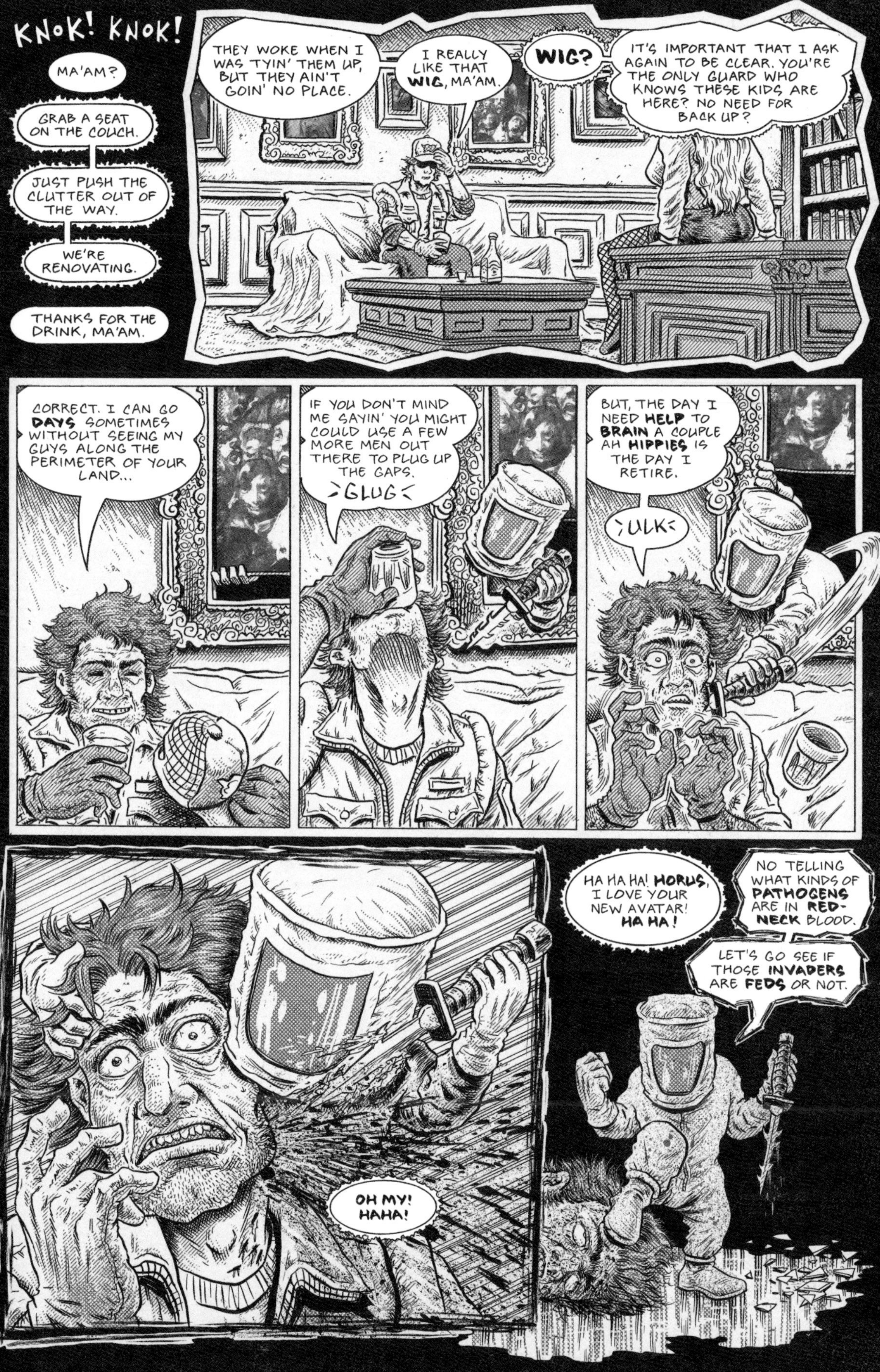
KNOK! KNOK!
MA'AM?
GRAB A SEAT ON THE COUCH.
JUST PUSH THE CLUTTER OUT OF THE WAY.
WE'RE RENOVATING.
THANKS FOR THE DRINK, MA'AM.
THEY WOKE WHEN I WAS TYIN' THEM UP, BUT THEY AIN'T GOIN' NO PLACE.
I REALLY LIKE THAT WIG, MA'AM.
WIG?
IT'S IMPORTANT THAT I ASK AGAIN TO BE CLEAR. YOU'RE THE ONLY GUARD WHO KNOWS THESE KIDS ARE HERE? NO NEED FOR BACK UP?
CORRECT. I CAN GO DAYS SOMETIMES WITHOUT SEEING MY GUYS ALONG THE PERIMETER OF YOUR LAND...
IF YOU DON'T MIND ME SAYIN' YOU MIGHT COULD USE A FEW MORE MEN OUT THERE TO PLUG UP THE GAPS.
GLUG
BUT, THE DAY I NEED HELP TO BRAIN A COUPLE AH HIPPIES IS THE DAY I RETIRE.
ULK
OH MY! HAHA!
HA HA HA! HORUS, I LOVE YOUR NEW AVATAR! HA HA!
NO TELLING WHAT KINDS OF PATHOGENS ARE IN RED-NECK BLOOD.
LET'S GO SEE IF THOSE INVADERS ARE FEDS OR NOT.

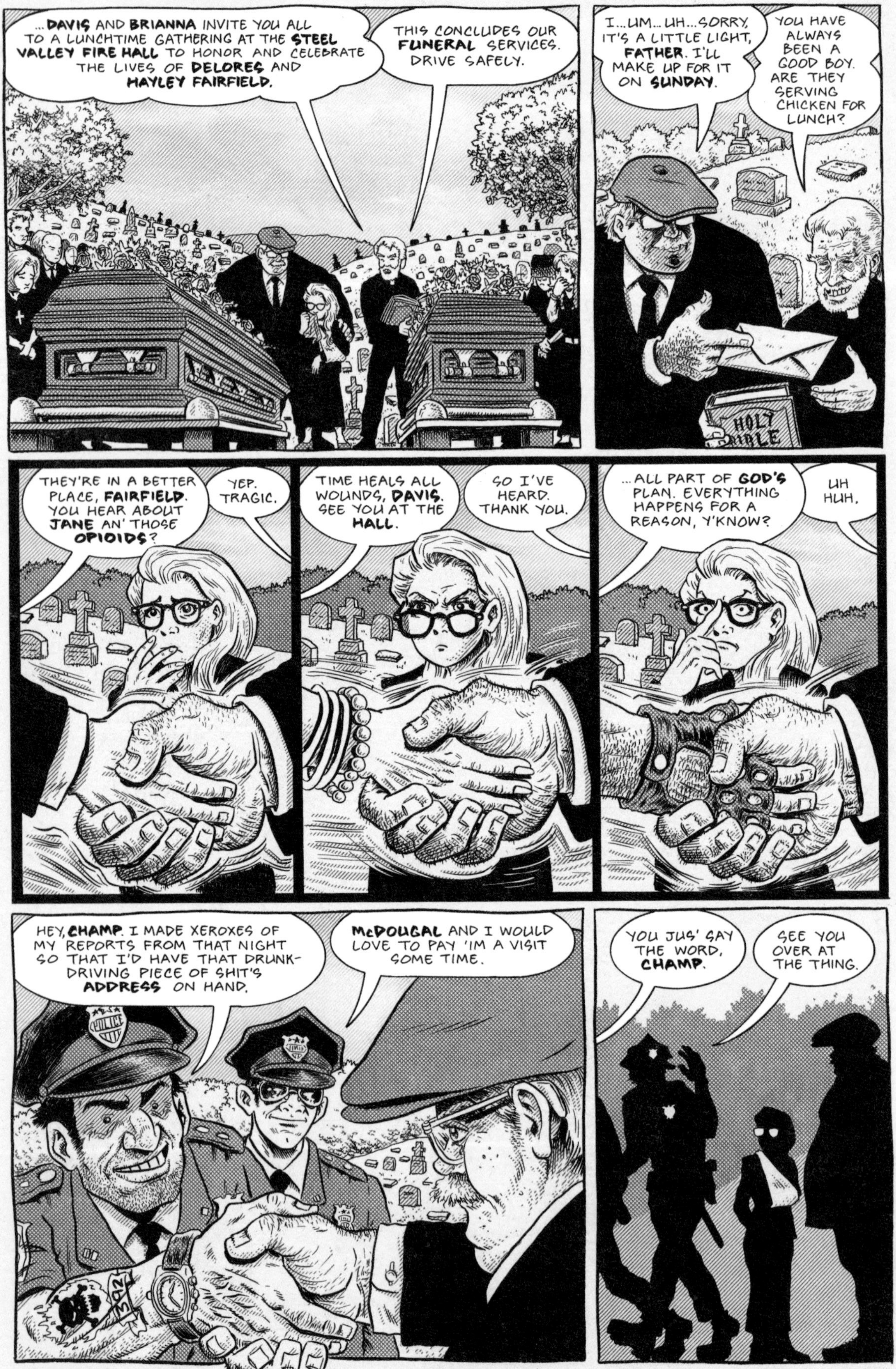
...DAVIS AND BRIANNA INVITE YOU ALL TO A LUNCHTIME GATHERING AT THE STEEL VALLEY FIRE HALL TO HONOR AND CELEBRATE THE LIVES OF DELORES AND HAYLEY FAIRFIELD.
THIS CONCLUDES OUR FUNERAL SERVICES. DRIVE SAFELY.
I...UM...UH...SORRY, IT'S A LITTLE LIGHT, FATHER. I'LL MAKE UP FOR IT ON SUNDAY.
YOU HAVE ALWAYS BEEN A GOOD BOY. ARE THEY SERVING CHICKEN FOR LUNCH?
HOLY BIBLE
THEY'RE IN A BETTER PLACE, FAIRFIELD. YOU HEAR ABOUT JANE AN' THOSE OPIOIDS?
YEP. TRAGIC.
TIME HEALS ALL WOUNDS, DAVIS. SEE YOU AT THE HALL.
SO I'VE HEARD. THANK YOU.
...ALL PART OF GOD'S PLAN. EVERYTHING HAPPENS FOR A REASON, Y'KNOW?
UH HUH.
HEY, CHAMP. I MADE XEROXES OF MY REPORTS FROM THAT NIGHT SO THAT I'D HAVE THAT DRUNK-DRIVING PIECE OF SHIT'S ADDRESS ON HAND.
McDOUGAL AND I WOULD LOVE TO PAY 'IM A VISIT SOME TIME.
YOU JUS' SAY THE WORD, CHAMP.
SEE YOU OVER AT THE THING.

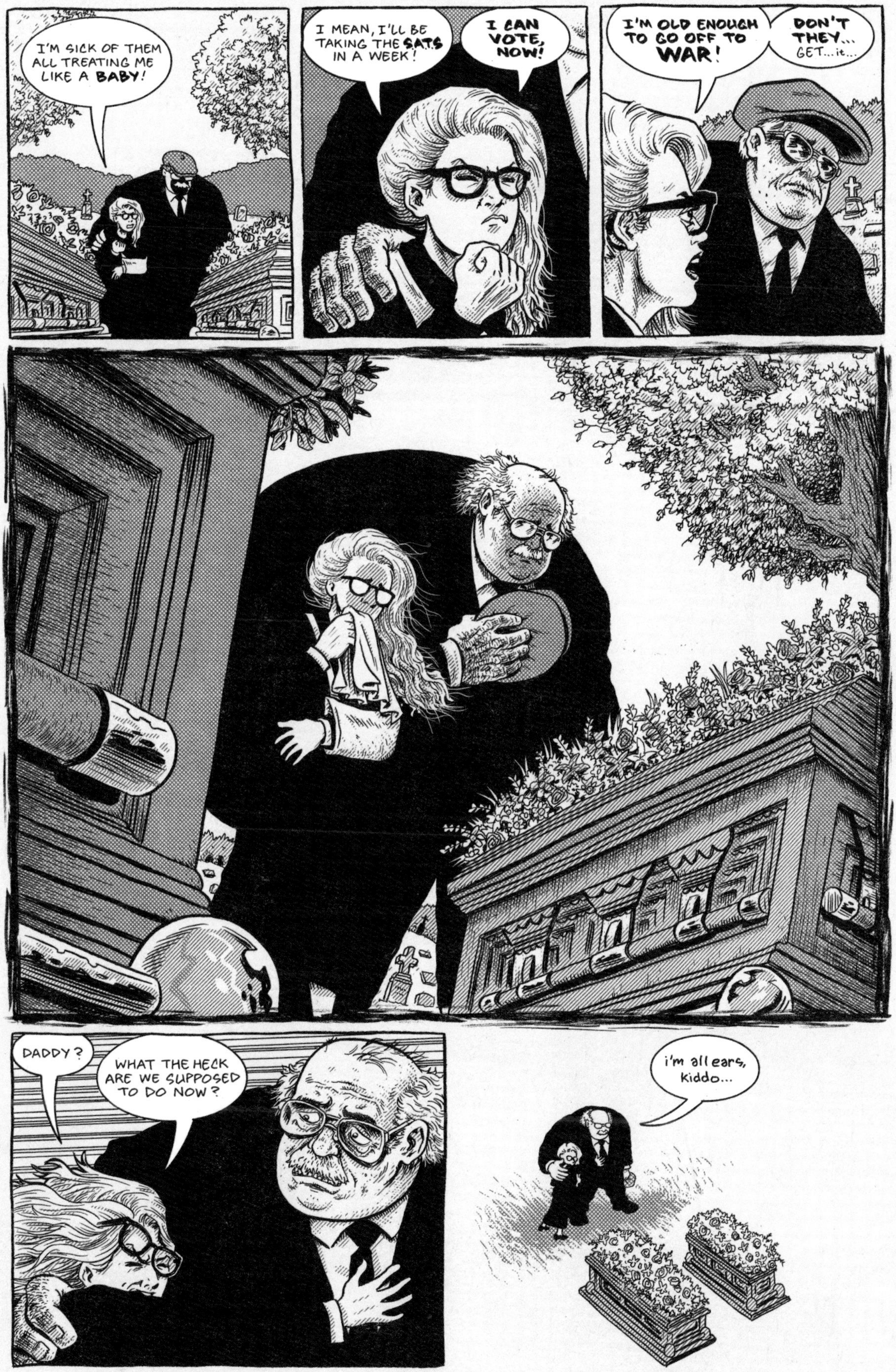
I'M SICK OF THEM ALL TREATING ME LIKE A BABY!
I MEAN, I'LL BE TAKING THE SATS IN A WEEK!
I CAN VOTE, NOW!
I'M OLD ENOUGH TO GO OFF TO WAR!
DON'T THEY... GET...it...
DADDY?
WHAT THE HECK ARE WE SUPPOSED TO DO NOW?
i'm all ears, kiddo...

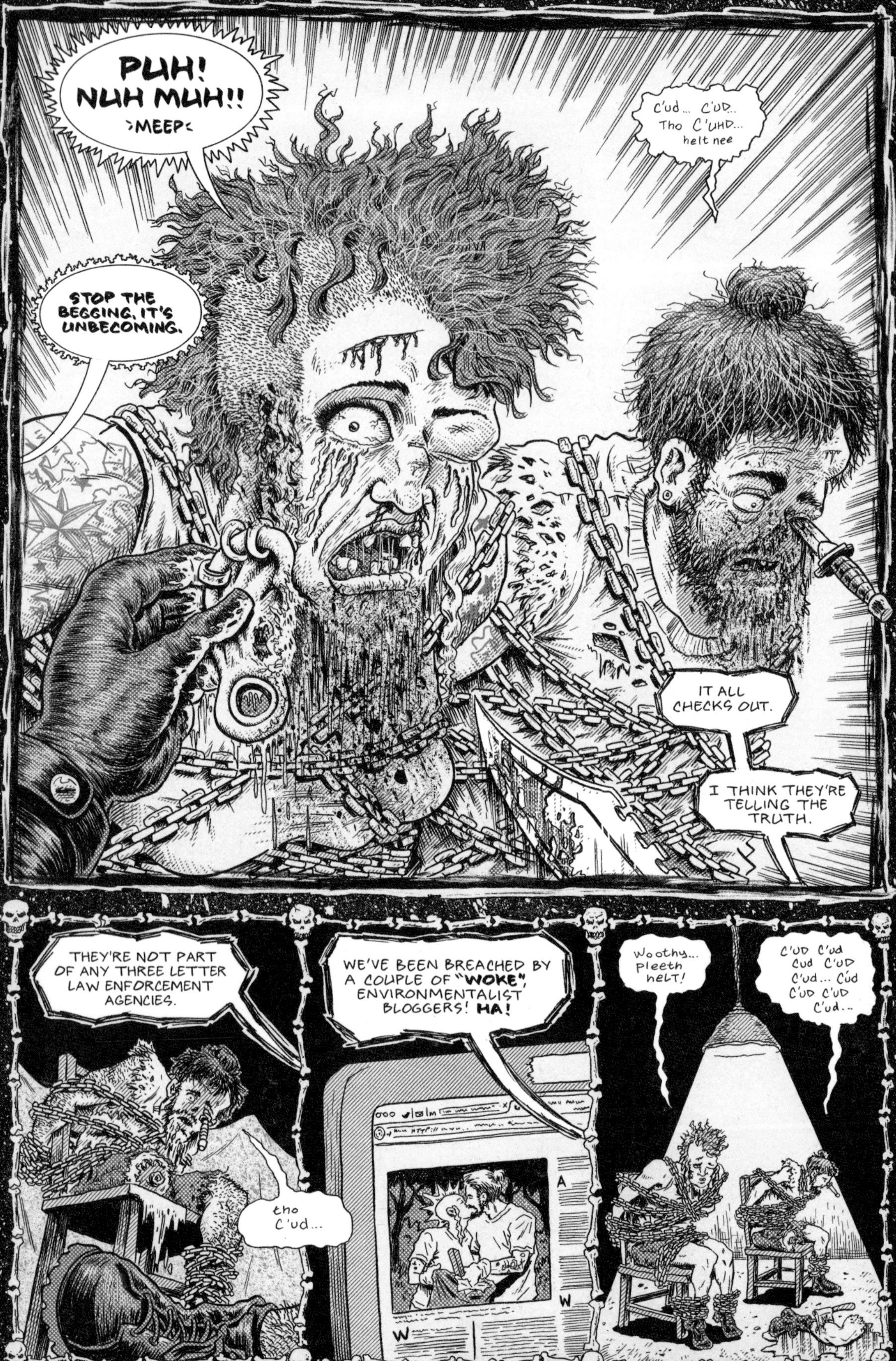
PUH! NUH MUH!!
>MEEP<
C'ud... C'UD.. Tho C'UHD... helt nee
STOP THE BEGGING, IT'S UNBECOMING.
IT ALL CHECKS OUT.
I THINK THEY'RE TELLING THE TRUTH.
THEY'RE NOT PART OF ANY THREE LETTER LAW ENFORCEMENT AGENCIES.
tho C'ud...
WE'VE BEEN BREACHED BY A COUPLE OF "WOKE", ENVIRONMENTALIST BLOGGERS! HA!
Woothy... pleeth helt!
C'UD C'ud Cud C'UD C'ud... Cúd C'UD C'UD C'ud...

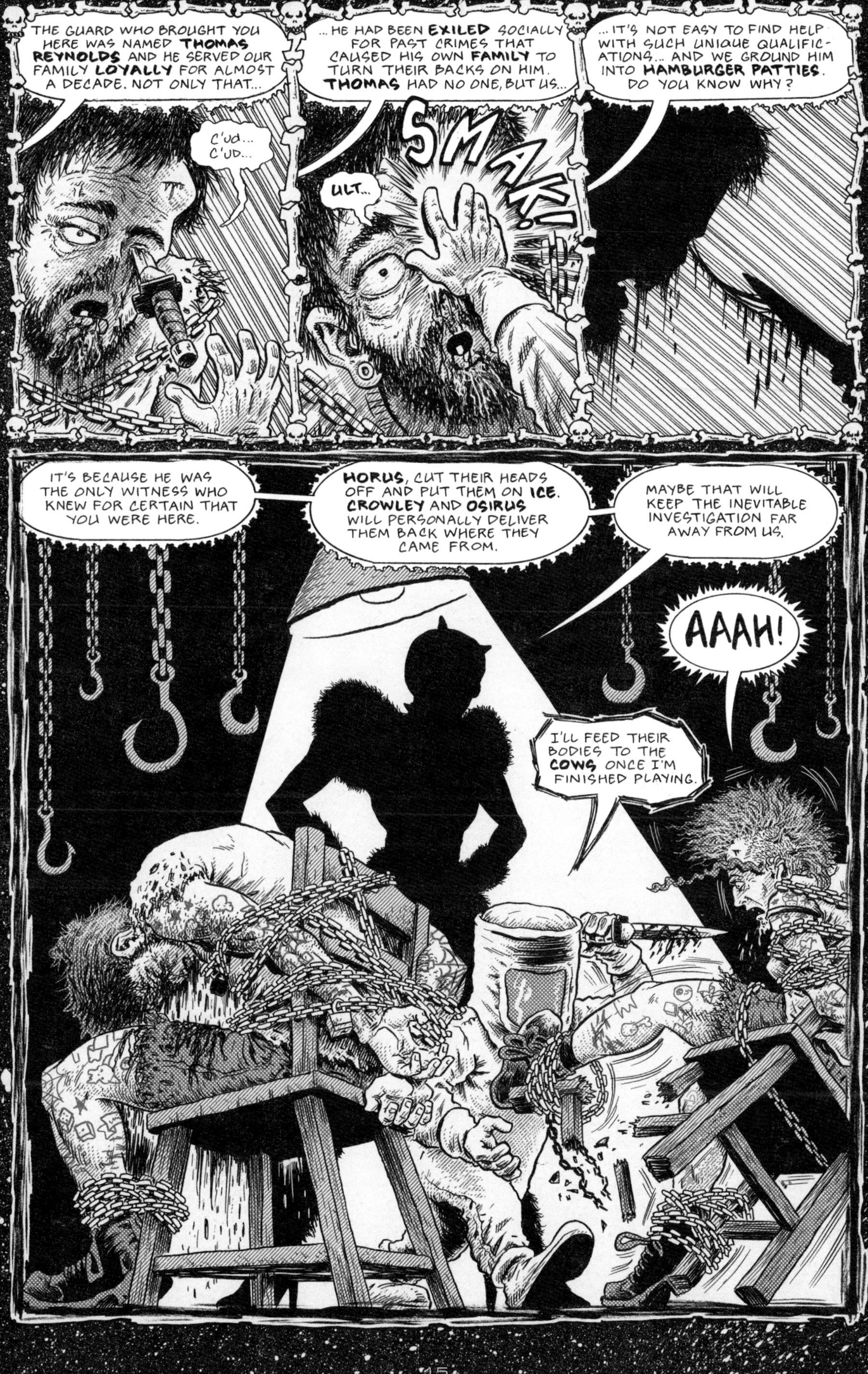
THE GUARD WHO BROUGHT YOU HERE WAS NAMED THOMAS REYNOLDS AND HE SERVED OUR FAMILY LOYALLY FOR ALMOST A DECADE. NOT ONLY THAT...
C'UD... C'UD...
...HE HAD BEEN EXILED SOCIALLY FOR PAST CRIMES THAT CAUSED HIS OWN FAMILY TO TURN THEIR BACKS ON HIM. THOMAS HAD NO ONE, BUT US...
SMAK!
ULT...
...IT'S NOT EASY TO FIND HELP WITH SUCH UNIQUE QUALIFIC-ATIONS... AND WE GROUND HIM INTO HAMBURGER PATTIES. DO YOU KNOW WHY?
IT'S BECAUSE HE WAS THE ONLY WITNESS WHO KNEW FOR CERTAIN THAT YOU WERE HERE.
HORUS, CUT THEIR HEADS OFF AND PUT THEM ON ICE. CROWLEY AND OSIRUS WILL PERSONALLY DELIVER THEM BACK WHERE THEY CAME FROM.
MAYBE THAT WILL KEEP THE INEVITABLE INVESTIGATION FAR AWAY FROM US.
AAAH!
I'LL FEED THEIR BODIES TO THE COWS ONCE I'M FINISHED PLAYING.

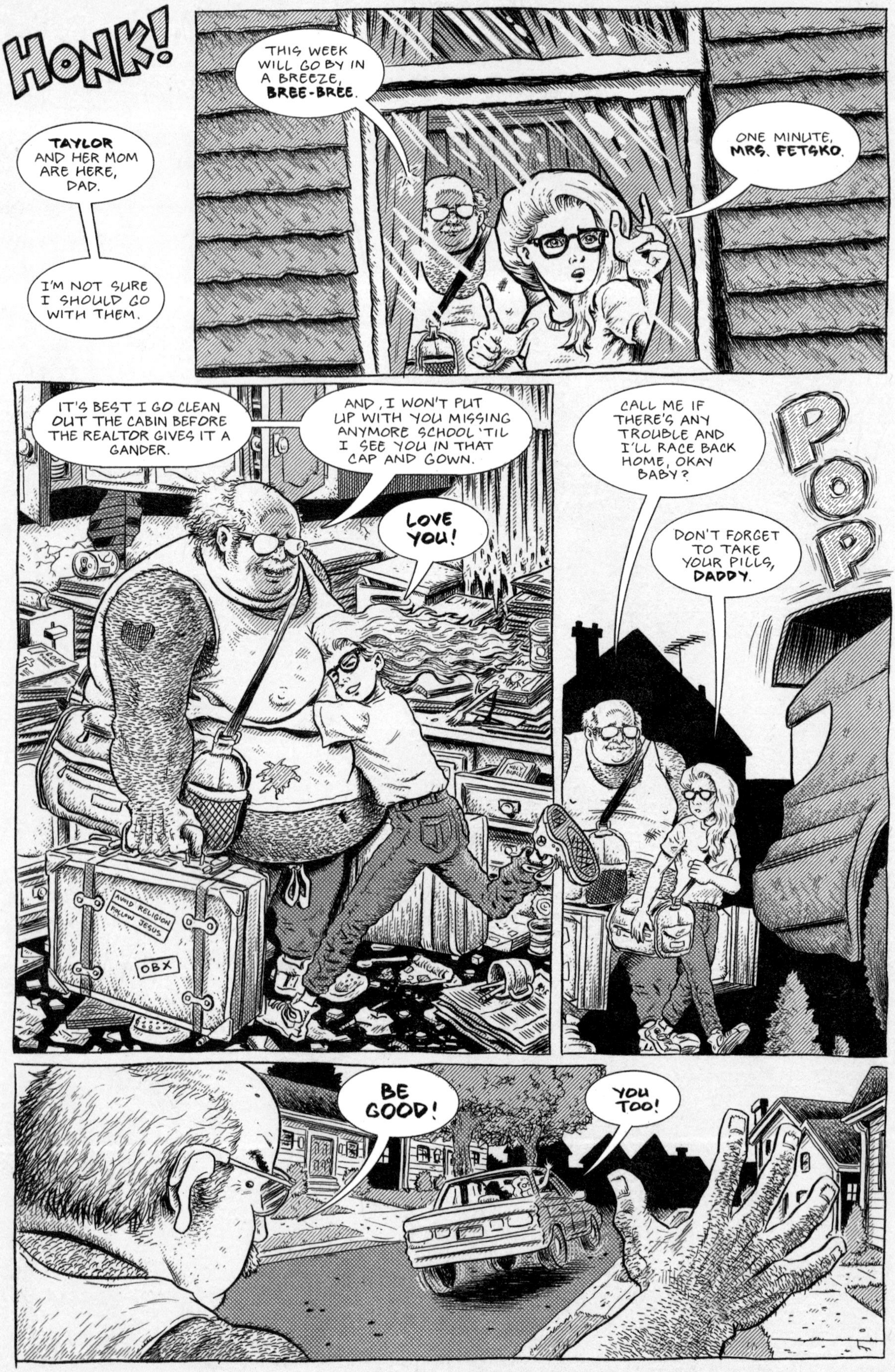
HONK!
THIS WEEK WILL GO BY IN A BREEZE, BREE-BREE.
TAYLOR AND HER MOM ARE HERE, DAD.
I'M NOT SURE I SHOULD GO WITH THEM.
ONE MINUTE, MRS. FETSKO.
IT'S BEST I GO CLEAN OUT THE CABIN BEFORE THE REALTOR GIVES IT A GANDER.
AND, I WON'T PUT UP WITH YOU MISSING ANYMORE SCHOOL 'TIL I SEE YOU IN THAT CAP AND GOWN.
LOVE YOU!
AVOID RELIGION FOLLOW JESUS
OBX
HOLY BIBLE
CALL ME IF THERE'S ANY TROUBLE AND I'LL RACE BACK HOME, OKAY BABY?
DON'T FORGET TO TAKE YOUR PILLS, DADDY.
POP POP
BE GOOD!
YOU TOO!

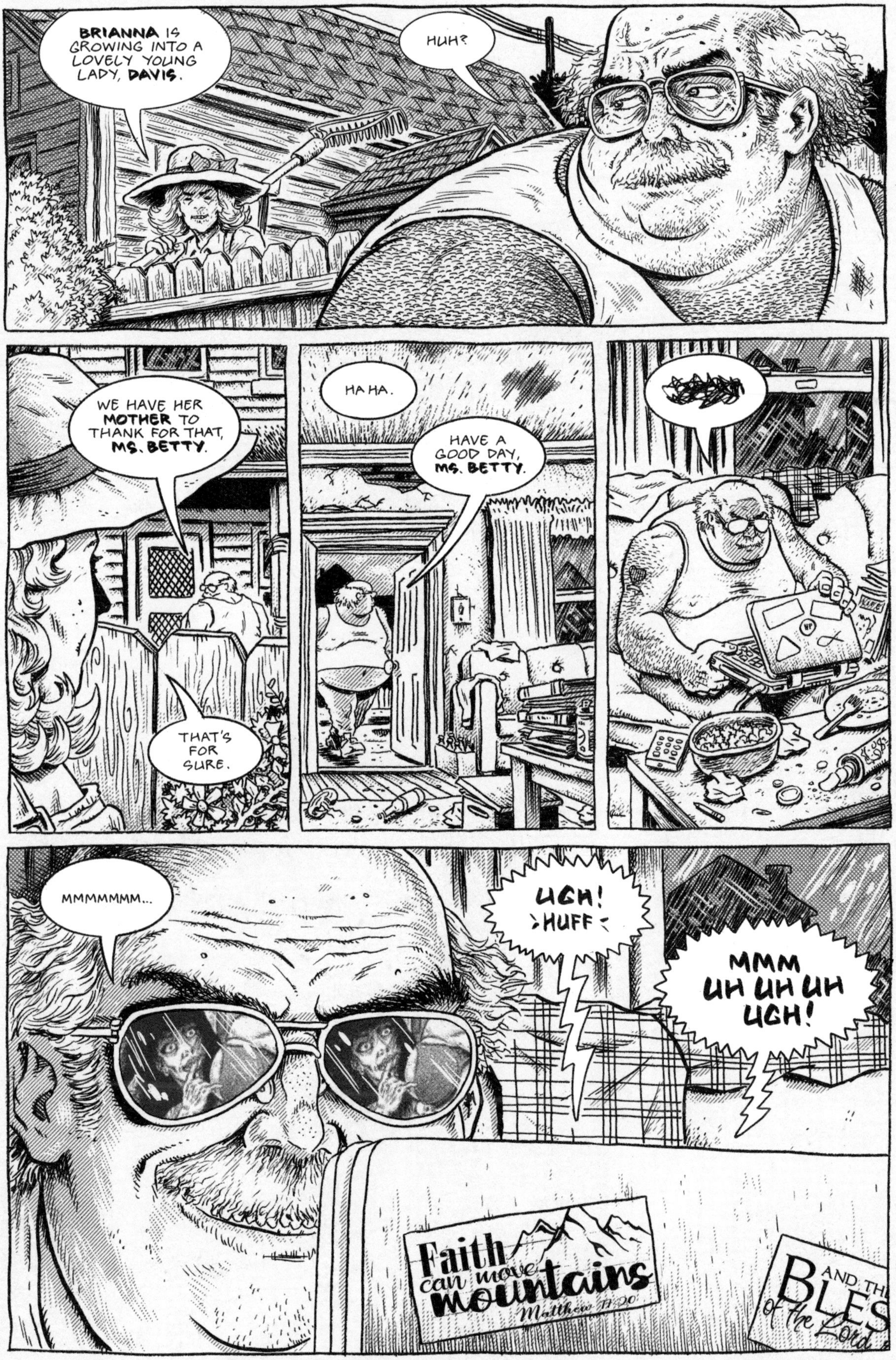
BRIANNA IS GROWING INTO A LOVELY YOUNG LADY, DAVIS.
HUH?
WE HAVE HER MOTHER TO THANK FOR THAT, MS. BETTY.
THAT'S FOR SURE.
HA HA.
HAVE A GOOD DAY, MS. BETTY.
MMMMMMM...
UGH! HUFF
MMM UH UH UH UGH!
Faith can move mountains Matthew 17:20
AND TH BLES of the Lord

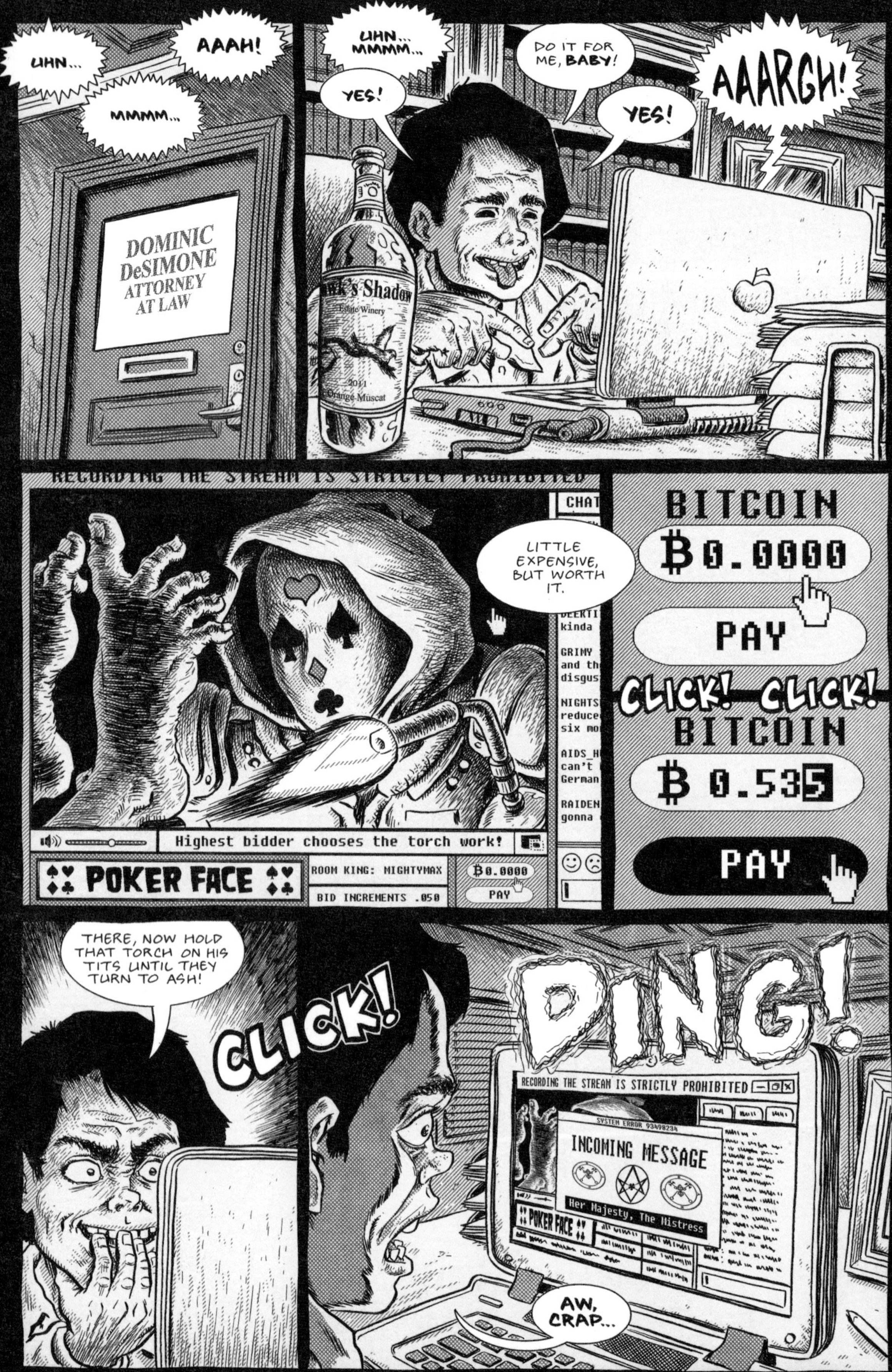
UHN...
AAAH!
MMMM...
DOMINIC DeSIMONE ATTORNEY AT LAW
UHN... MMMM...
YES!
DO IT FOR ME, BABY!
YES!
AAARGH!
Estate Winery
2011
Orange Muscat
LITTLE EXPENSIVE, BUT WORTH IT.
CHAT
Highest bidder chooses the torch work!
POKER FACE
ROOM KING: MIGHTYMAX
BID INCREMENTS .050
฿0.0000
PAY
BITCOIN
฿0.0000
PAY
CLICK! CLICK!
BITCOIN
฿0.535
PAY
THERE, NOW HOLD THAT TORCH ON HIS TITS UNTIL THEY TURN TO ASH!
CLICK!
DING!
RECORDING THE STREAM IS STRICTLY PROHIBITED
INCOMING MESSAGE
Her Majesty, The Mistress
POKER FACE
AW, CRAP...

UM... UH... HELLO, MISTRESS.
YOU HAVEN'T BEEN TO ONE OF OUR... EVENTS IN SOME TIME, DOMINIC. IS THE HONEYMOON OVER?
OH, NO, MISTRESS. I'M JUST... UH... CURBING THE HABIT... I MEAN HOBBY A LITTLE TO SAVE SOME MONEY FOR THE HOLIDAYS.
I'LL GET TO THE POINT. WHAT NEWS DO YOU HAVE FOR ME ABOUT THE CASE THAT WE'RE SO HANDSOMELY PAYING YOU TO REPRESENT?
MOST OF THE EVIDENCE AGAINST THE KID IS SEALED, BUT, I SHOULD HAVE A BETTER UNDERSTANDING OF THINGS WHEN I VISIT HIM
IN ... UP NEX...
BRUMMMM
DO YOU LIVE NEAR A HIGHWAY, MISTRESS?
SHUT UP!!
LASTLY, I'M EXPECTING THAT NEW TROJAN HORSE VIRUS ... THE ONE FROM YOUR RECENT SEXTORTION CASE. IT'S TIME TO GO PHISHING.
SURE. WE CAN MERGE IT WITH YOUR SOFTWARE AND DISTRIBUTE IT IN A BANNER AD ON THE DARK WEB ANYTIME YOU WISH.
DELIVER ME SOME EXCITING PROSPECTS AND THERE WILL BE A HEFTY COMMISSION IN YOUR BITCOIN PURSE.
WE'RE FINISHED. YOU CAN GO BACK TO WASTING YOUR BITCOIN IN POKER FACE'S RED ROOM.
ULP!

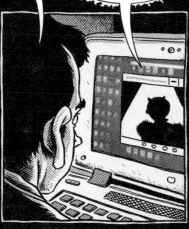

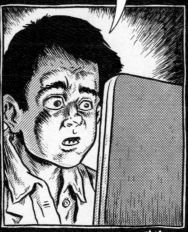

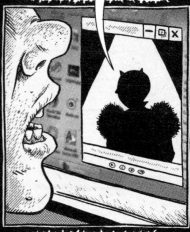

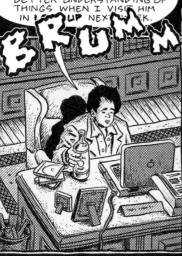

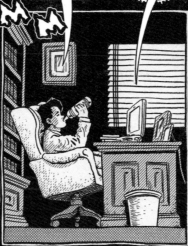

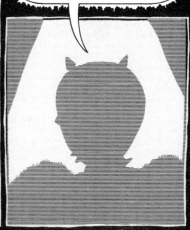

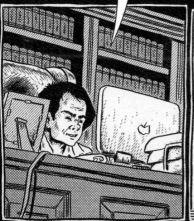

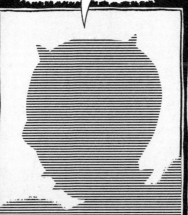

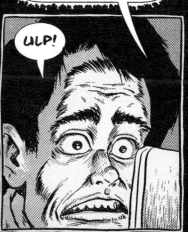

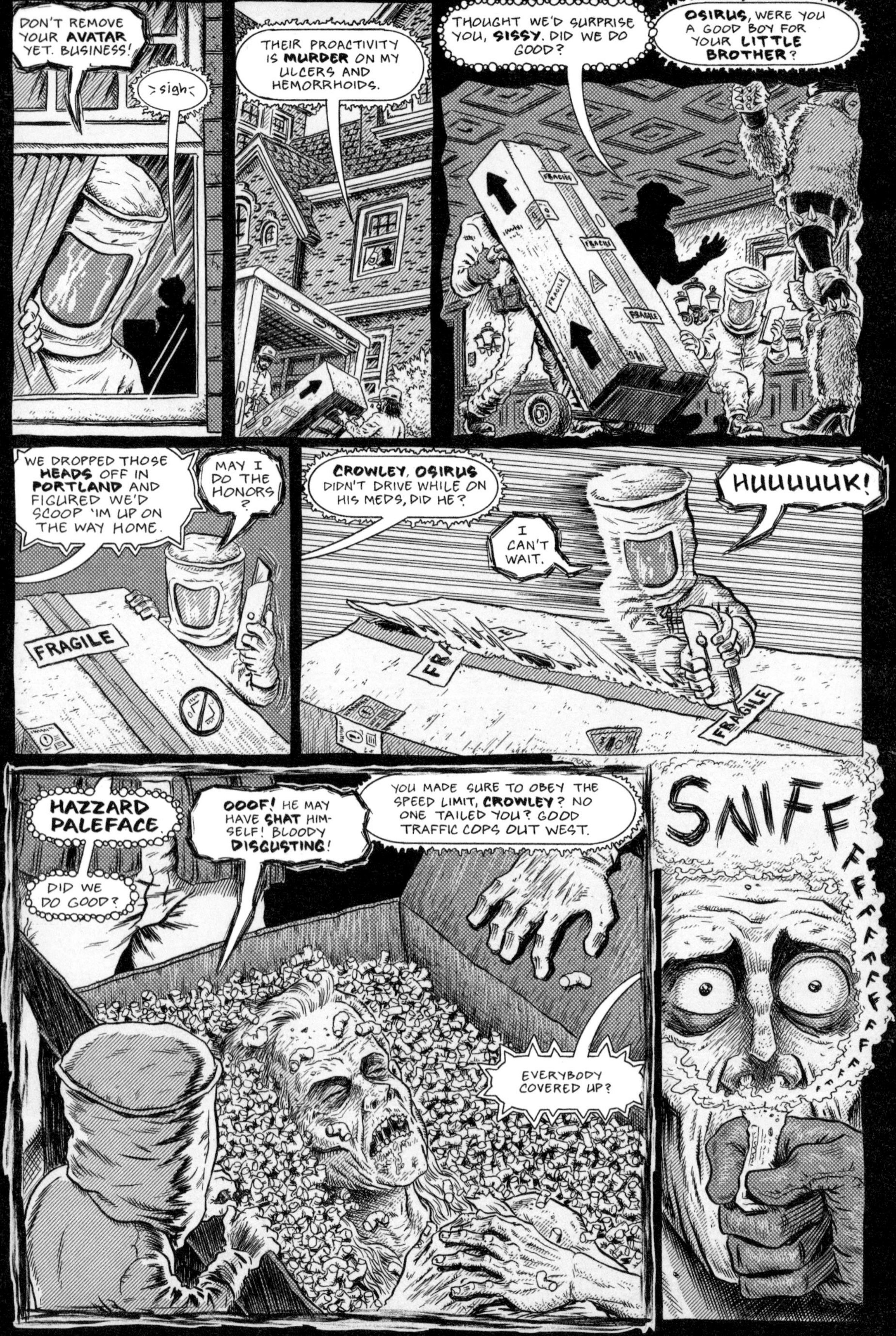

DON'T REMOVE YOUR AVATAR YET. BUSINESS!
>sigh<
THEIR PROACTIVITY IS MURDER ON MY ULCERS AND HEMORRHOIDS.
THOUGHT WE'D SURPRISE YOU, SISSY. DID WE DO GOOD?
OSIRUS, WERE YOU A GOOD BOY FOR YOUR LITTLE BROTHER?
FRAGILE
WE DROPPED THOSE HEADS OFF IN PORTLAND AND FIGURED WE'D SCOOP 'IM UP ON THE WAY HOME.
MAY I DO THE HONORS?
FRAGILE
CROWLEY, OSIRUS DIDN'T DRIVE WHILE ON HIS MEDS, DID HE?
I CAN'T WAIT.
HUUUUUK!
FRAGILE
HAZZARD PALEFACE.
DID WE DO GOOD?
OOOF! HE MAY HAVE SHAT HIMSELF! BLOODY DISGUSTING!
YOU MADE SURE TO OBEY THE SPEED LIMIT, CROWLEY? NO ONE TAILED YOU? GOOD TRAFFIC COPS OUT WEST.
EVERYBODY COVERED UP?
SNIFFFFFFFFFFFFF

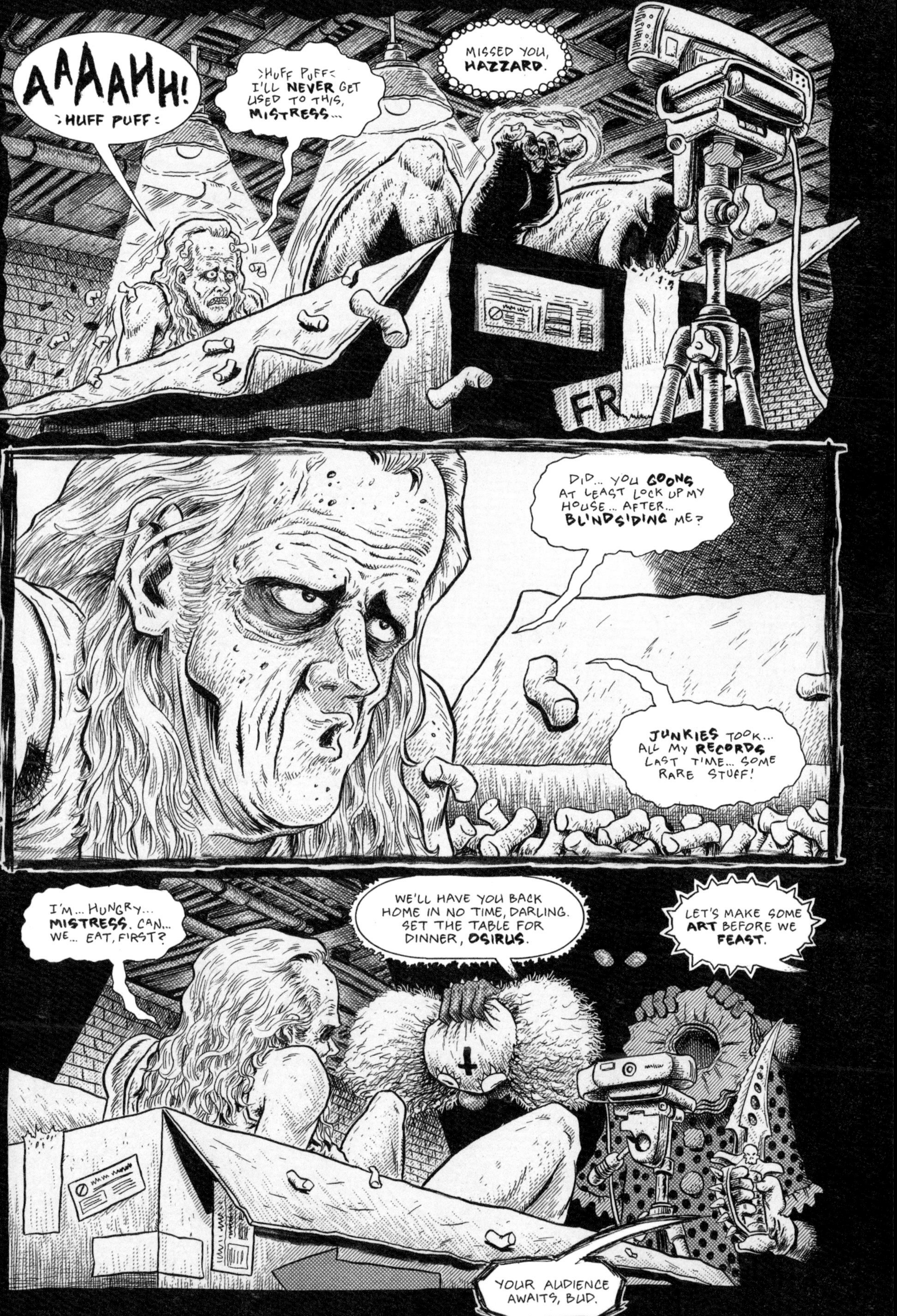
AAAAHH!
>HUFF PUFF<
>HUFF PUFF< I'LL NEVER GET USED TO THIS, MISTRESS...
MISSED YOU, HAZZARD.
FR
DID... YOU GOONS AT LEAST LOCK UP MY HOUSE... AFTER... BLINDSIDING ME?
JUNKIES TOOK... ALL MY RECORDS LAST TIME... SOME RARE STUFF!
I'M... HUNGRY... MISTRESS. CAN... WE... EAT, FIRST?
WE'LL HAVE YOU BACK HOME IN NO TIME, DARLING. SET THE TABLE FOR DINNER, OSIRUS.
LET'S MAKE SOME ART BEFORE WE FEAST.
YOUR AUDIENCE AWAITS, BUD.

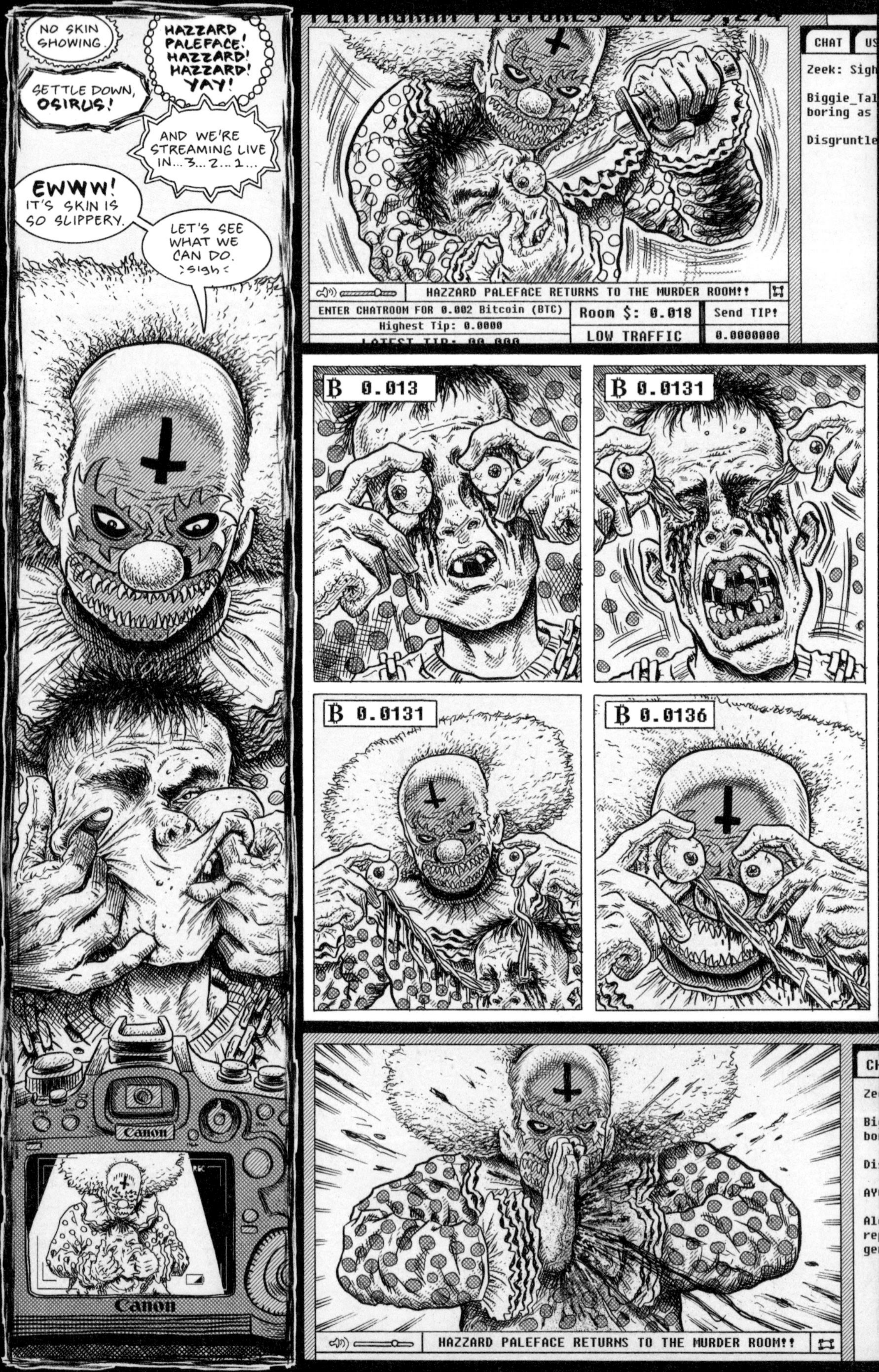

NO SKIN SHOWING.
HAZZARD PALEFACE! HAZZARD! HAZZARD! YAY!
SETTLE DOWN, OSIRUS!
AND WE'RE STREAMING LIVE IN...3...2...1...
EWWW! IT'S SKIN IS SO SLIPPERY.
LET'S SEE WHAT WE CAN DO. >sigh<
Canon
Canon
CHAT
Zeek: Sigh
Biggie_Tal
boring as
Disgruntle
HAZZARD PALEFACE RETURNS TO THE MURDER ROOM!!
ENTER CHATROOM FOR 0.002 Bitcoin (BTC)
Highest Tip: 0.0000
Room $: 0.018
LOW TRAFFIC
Send TIP!
0.0000000
B 0.013
B 0.0131
B 0.0131
B 0.0136
HAZZARD PALEFACE RETURNS TO THE MURDER ROOM!!

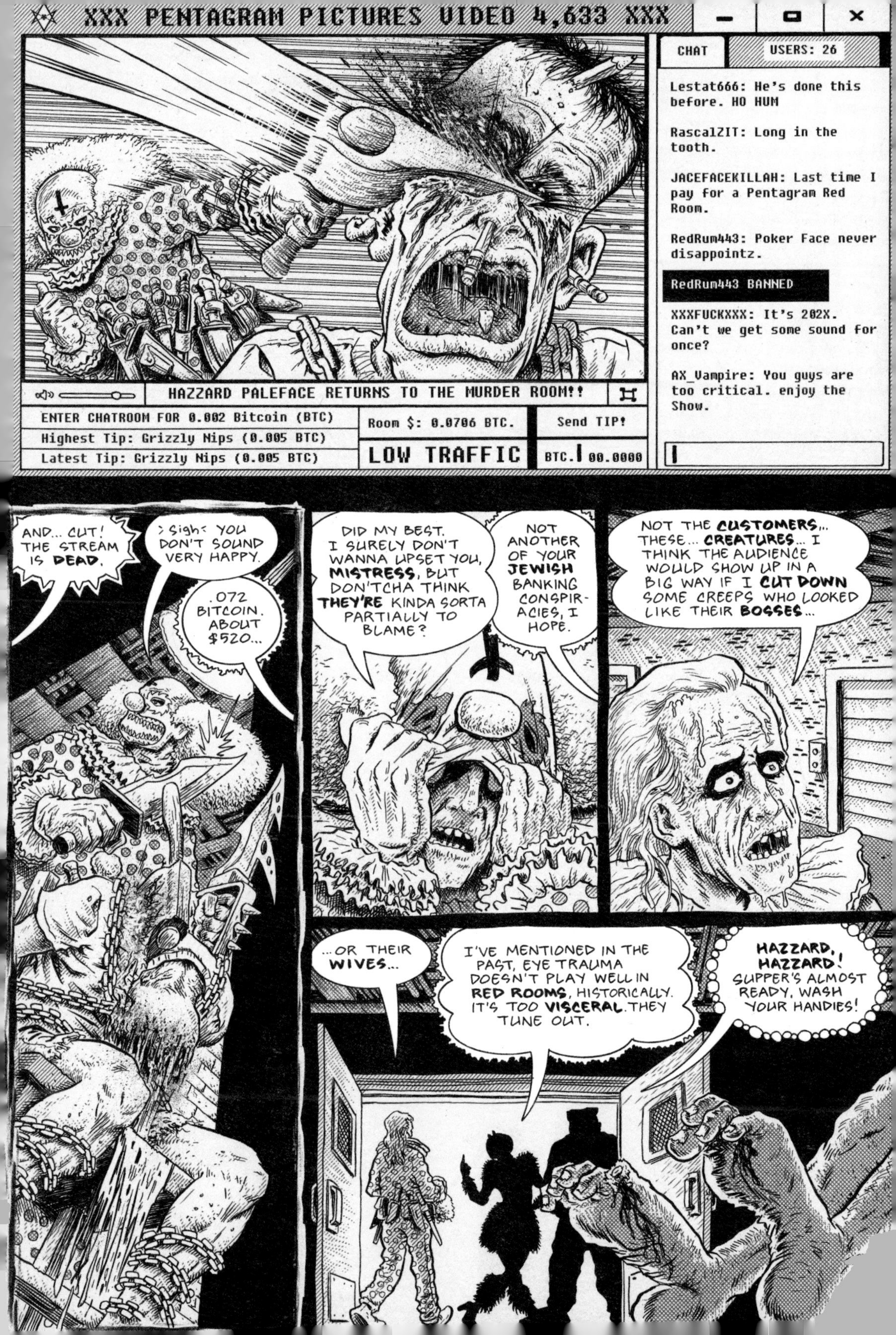
XXX PENTAGRAM PICTURES VIDEO 4,633 XXX
CHAT
USERS: 26
Lestat666: He's done this before. HO HUM
RascalZIT: Long in the tooth.
JACEFACEKILLAH: Last time I pay for a Pentagram Red Room.
RedRum443: Poker Face never disappointz.
RedRum443 BANNED
XXXFUCKXXX: It's 202X. Can't we get some sound for once?
AX_Vampire: You guys are too critical. enjoy the Show.
HAZZARD PALEFACE RETURNS TO THE MURDER ROOM!!
ENTER CHATROOM FOR 0.002 Bitcoin (BTC)
Highest Tip: Grizzly Nips (0.005 BTC)
Latest Tip: Grizzly Nips (0.005 BTC)
Room $: 0.0706 BTC.
LOW TRAFFIC
Send TIP!
BTC. 00.0000
AND... CUT! THE STREAM IS DEAD.
>Sigh< YOU DON'T SOUND VERY HAPPY.
.072 BITCOIN. ABOUT $520...
DID MY BEST. I SURELY DON'T WANNA UPSET YOU, MISTRESS, BUT DON'TCHA THINK THEY'RE KINDA SORTA PARTIALLY TO BLAME?
NOT ANOTHER OF YOUR JEWISH BANKING CONSPIRACIES, I HOPE.
NOT THE CUSTOMERS... THESE... CREATURES... I THINK THE AUDIENCE WOULD SHOW UP IN A BIG WAY IF I CUT DOWN SOME CREEPS WHO LOOKED LIKE THEIR BOSSES...
...OR THEIR WIVES...
I'VE MENTIONED IN THE PAST, EYE TRAUMA DOESN'T PLAY WELL IN RED ROOMS, HISTORICALLY. IT'S TOO VISCERAL. THEY TUNE OUT.
HAZZARD, HAZZARD! SUPPER'S ALMOST READY. WASH YOUR HANDIES!

REMEMBER WHEN **PALEFACE** WAS A TOP EARNER? SIX FIGURES A LIVE-STREAM!

OUR BUSINESS OPERATES MUCH LIKE MAINSTREAM **PORNOGRAPHY**, AND OLD PERFORMERS LOSE **VALUE**.

CAN'T WE JUST PUT 'IM IN A NEW **OUTFIT** AND GIMMICK?

WE'VE DONE THAT A FEW TIMES WITH HIM BUT THE AUDIENCE DOESN'T BUY IT ANYMORE.

THE ARTIST IS STILL THE ARTIST...

...AND I SAID "WRECKED 'IM? IT NEARLY KILLED 'IM."

HA HA HA HA HAW HA HA!

I DON'T GET IT...

:SIGH: **SISSY**, I WISH WE COULD COME UP WITH A SAFER WAY TO **RETIRE** THESE OLD DOGS.

YOU'RE GOING TO BREAK **OSIRUS'S** FRAGILE HEART.

IT NEEDS TO LOOK LIKE A **HEROIN OVERDOSE** WHEN YOU DROP HIM OFF, **CROWLEY**.

AND, **HORUS**, IF **OSIRUS** DISCOVERS THE **TRUTH**, I'LL USE YOUR **CORPSE** AS A BARRIER BETWEEN ME AND HIM. LET'S HEAD DOWN.

OOOF!

...BUT, I STILL THINK YOU'RE SO FUNNY, **HAZZARD**.

HA HA! YOU'RE THE **BESTEST**!

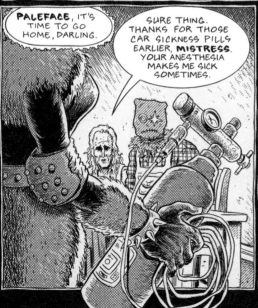

PALEFACE, IT'S TIME TO GO HOME, DARLING.

SURE THING. THANKS FOR THOSE CAR SICKNESS PILLS EARLIER, **MISTRESS**. YOUR ANESTHESIA MAKES ME SICK SOMETIMES.

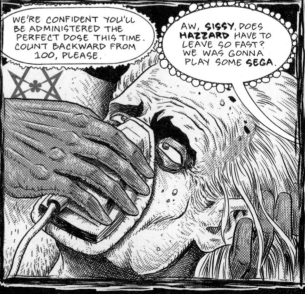

WE'RE CONFIDENT YOU'LL BE ADMINISTERED THE PERFECT DOSE THIS TIME. COUNT BACKWARD FROM 100, PLEASE.

AW, **SISSY**, DOES **HAZZARD** HAVE TO LEAVE SO FAST? WE WAS GONNA PLAY SOME **SEGA**.

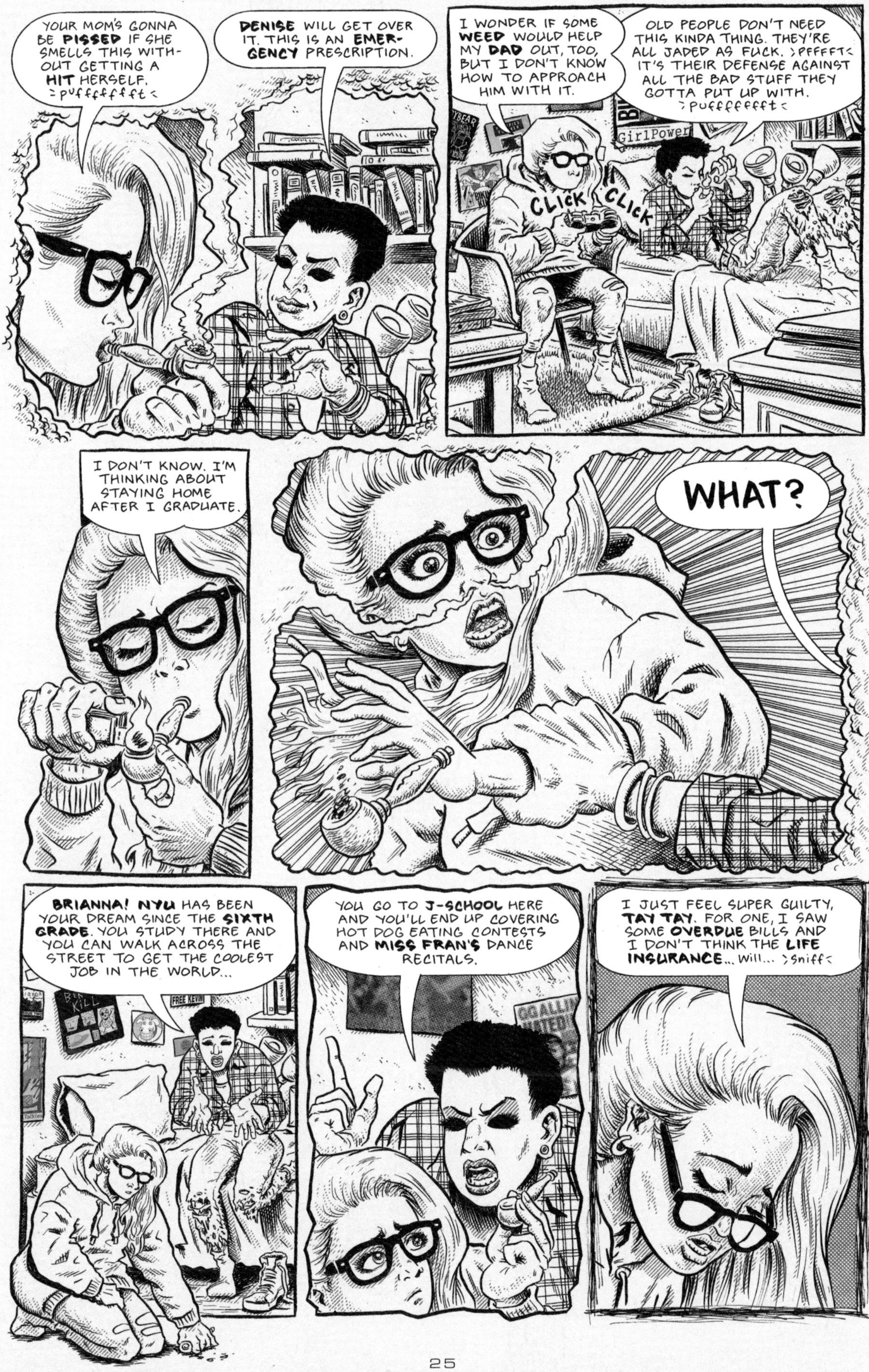
YOUR MOM'S GONNA BE **PISSED** IF SHE SMELLS THIS WITH-OUT GETTING A **HIT** HERSELF. >pufffffft<
DENISE WILL GET OVER IT. THIS IS AN **EMER-GENCY** PRESCRIPTION.
I WONDER IF SOME **WEED** WOULD HELP MY **DAD** OUT, TOO, BUT I DON'T KNOW HOW TO APPROACH HIM WITH IT.
OLD PEOPLE DON'T NEED THIS KINDA THING. THEY'RE ALL JADED AS FUCK. >PFFFFT< IT'S THEIR DEFENSE AGAINST ALL THE BAD STUFF THEY GOTTA PUT UP WITH. >pufffffft<
GirlPower
CLICK
CLICK
I DON'T KNOW. I'M THINKING ABOUT STAYING HOME AFTER I GRADUATE.
WHAT?
BRIANNA! NYU HAS BEEN YOUR DREAM SINCE THE **SIXTH GRADE**. YOU STUDY THERE AND YOU CAN WALK ACROSS THE STREET TO GET THE COOLEST JOB IN THE WORLD...
FREE KEVIN
YOU GO TO **J-SCHOOL** HERE AND YOU'LL END UP COVERING HOT DOG EATING CONTESTS AND **MISS FRAN'S** DANCE RECITALS.
I JUST FEEL SUPER GUILTY, **TAY TAY**. FOR ONE, I SAW SOME **OVERDUE** BILLS AND I DON'T THINK THE **LIFE INSURANCE**... Will... >sniff<

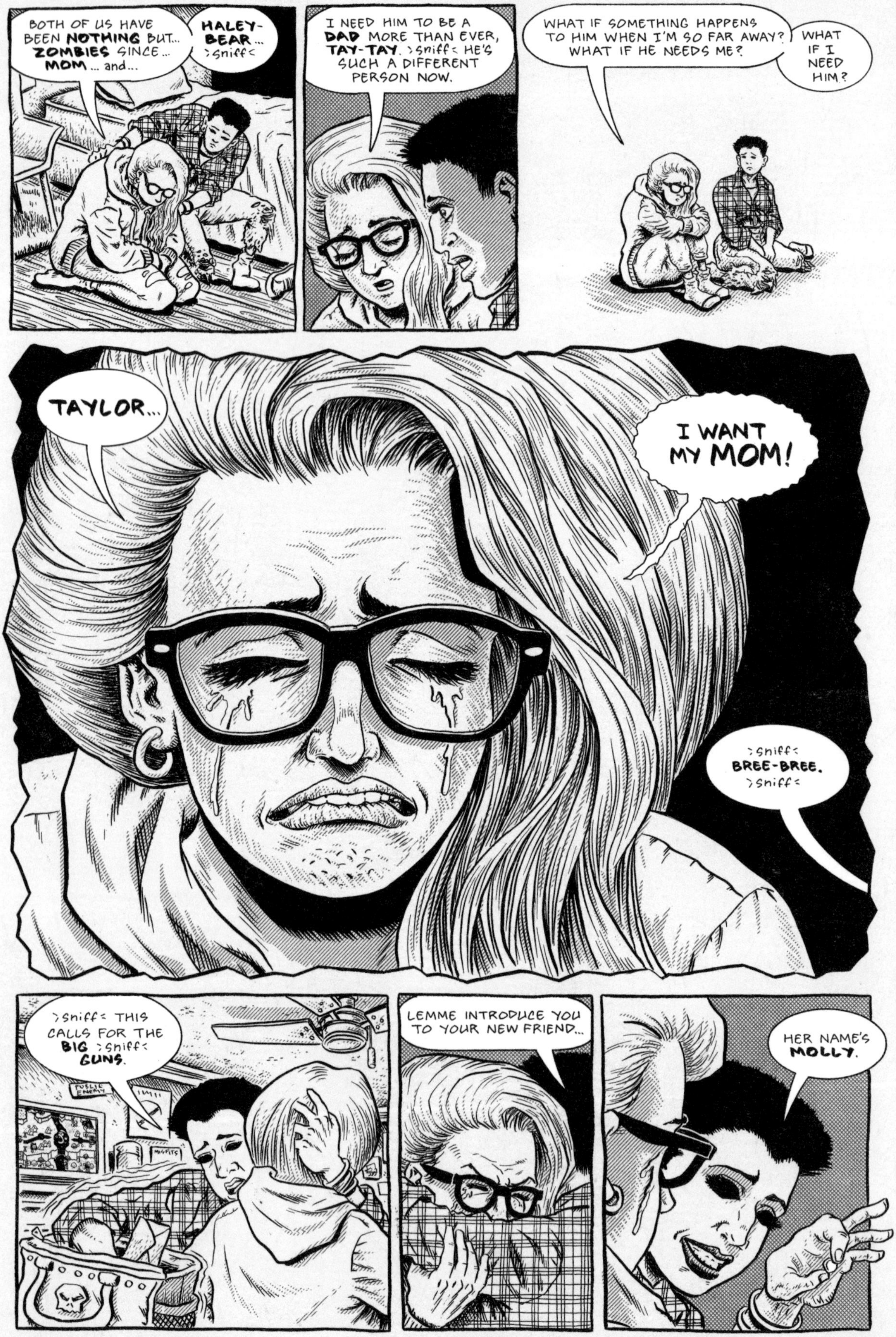
BOTH OF US HAVE BEEN NOTHING BUT... ZOMBIES SINCE... MOM ... and...
HALEY-BEAR... >sniff<
I NEED HIM TO BE A DAD MORE THAN EVER, TAY-TAY. >sniff< HE'S SUCH A DIFFERENT PERSON NOW.
WHAT IF SOMETHING HAPPENS TO HIM WHEN I'M SO FAR AWAY? WHAT IF HE NEEDS ME?
WHAT IF I NEED HIM?
TAYLOR...
I WANT MY MOM!
>sniff< BREE-BREE. >sniff<
>sniff< THIS CALLS FOR THE BIG >sniff< GUNS.
PUBLIC ENEMY
MISFITS
LEMME INTRODUCE YOU TO YOUR NEW FRIEND...
HER NAME'S MOLLY.

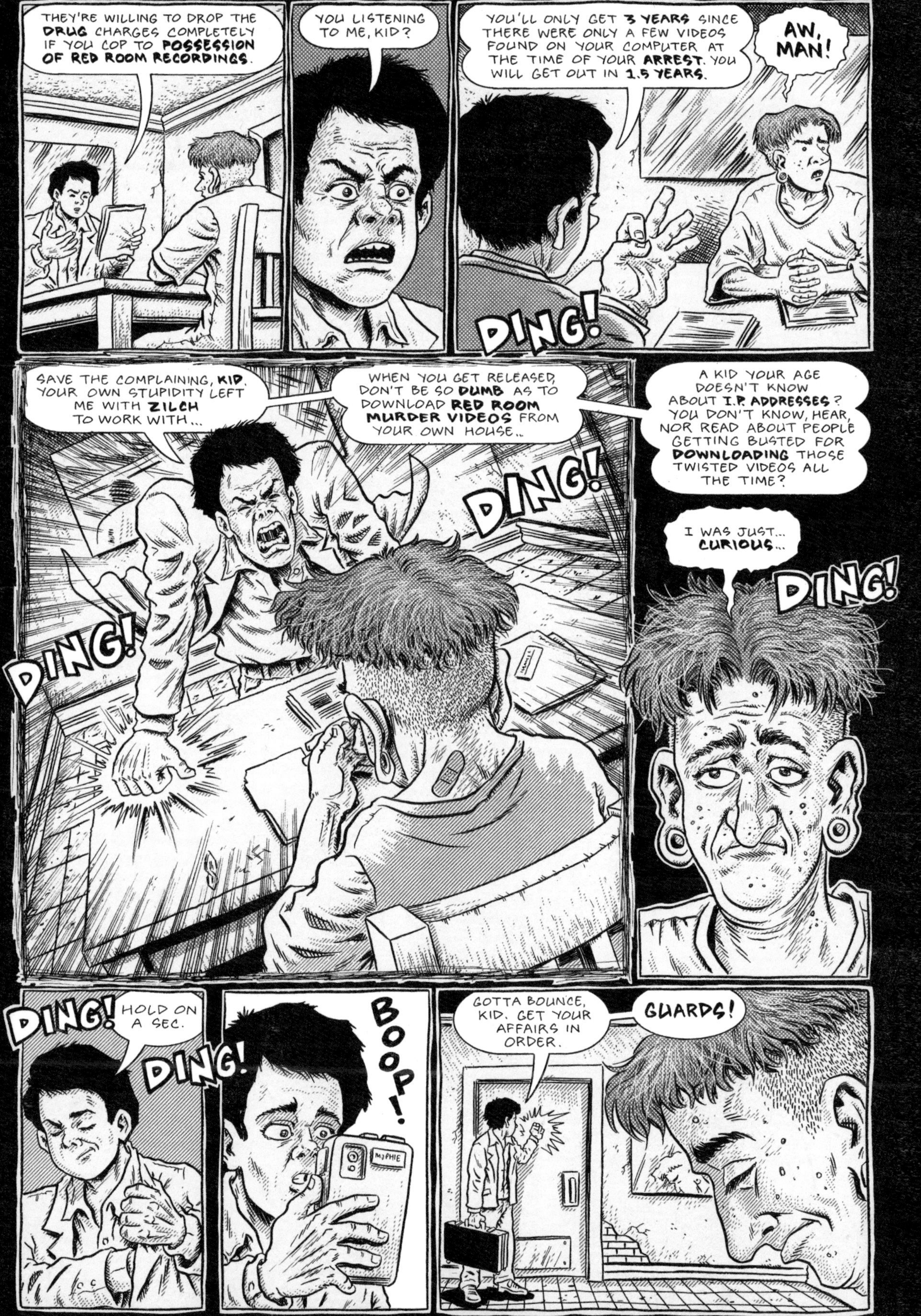
THEY'RE WILLING TO DROP THE DRUG CHARGES COMPLETELY IF YOU COP TO POSSESSION OF RED ROOM RECORDINGS.
YOU LISTENING TO ME, KID?
YOU'LL ONLY GET 3 YEARS SINCE THERE WERE ONLY A FEW VIDEOS FOUND ON YOUR COMPUTER AT THE TIME OF YOUR ARREST. YOU WILL GET OUT IN 1.5 YEARS.
AW, MAN!
DING!
SAVE THE COMPLAINING, KID. YOUR OWN STUPIDITY LEFT ME WITH ZILCH TO WORK WITH...
WHEN YOU GET RELEASED, DON'T BE SO DUMB AS TO DOWNLOAD RED ROOM MURDER VIDEOS FROM YOUR OWN HOUSE..
A KID YOUR AGE DOESN'T KNOW ABOUT I.P. ADDRESSES? YOU DON'T KNOW, HEAR, NOR READ ABOUT PEOPLE GETTING BUSTED FOR DOWNLOADING THOSE TWISTED VIDEOS ALL THE TIME?
DING!
DING!
I WAS JUST... CURIOUS...
DING!
DING!
HOLD ON A SEC.
DING!
BOOP!
MOPHIE
GOTTA BOUNCE, KID. GET YOUR AFFAIRS IN ORDER.
GUARDS!

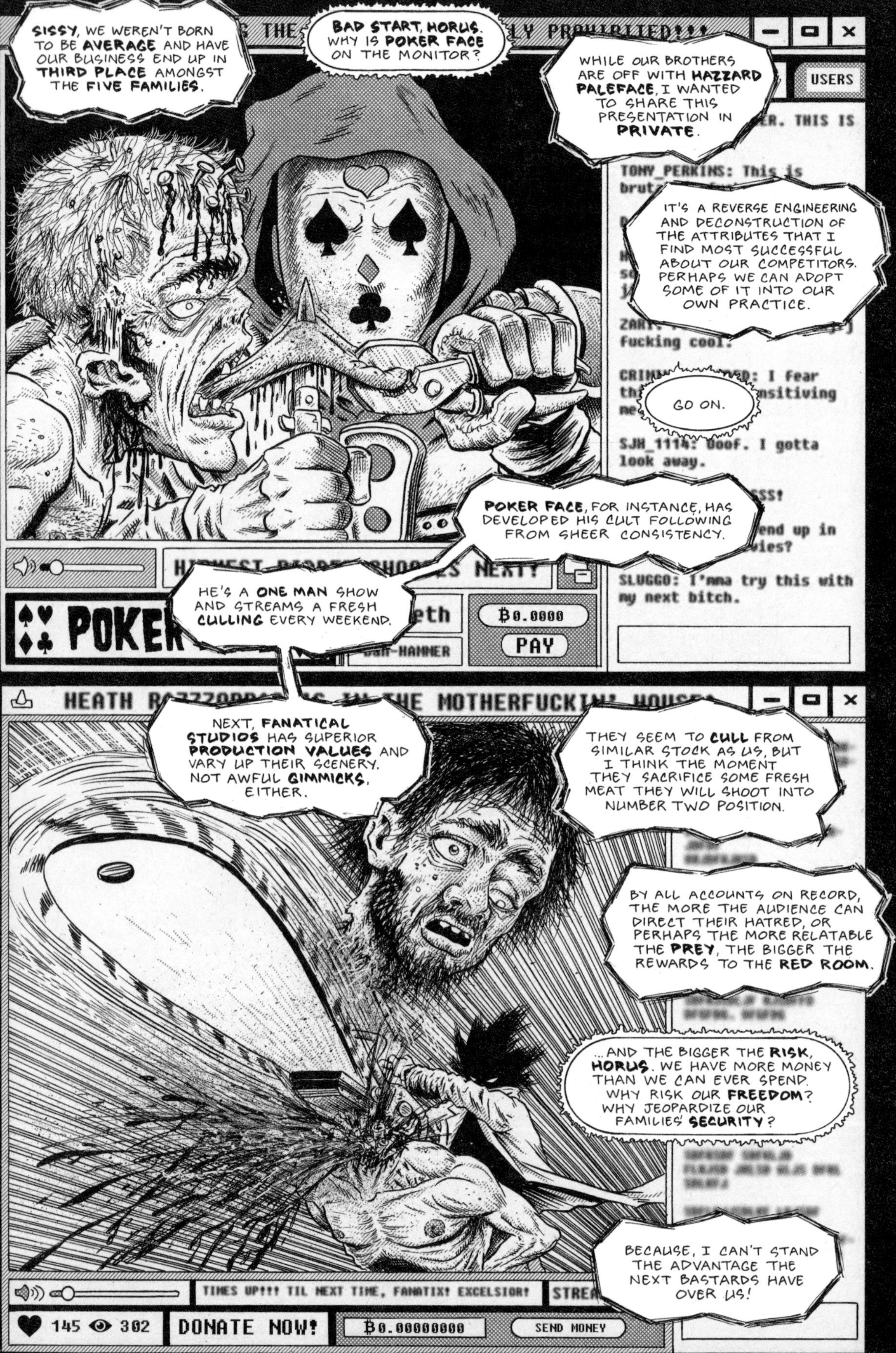
SISSY, WE WEREN'T BORN TO BE AVERAGE AND HAVE OUR BUSINESS END UP IN THIRD PLACE AMONGST THE FIVE FAMILIES.
BAD START, HORUS. WHY IS POKER FACE ON THE MONITOR?
WHILE OUR BROTHERS ARE OFF WITH HAZZARD PALEFACE, I WANTED TO SHARE THIS PRESENTATION IN PRIVATE.
USERS
TONY_PERKINS: This is
IT'S A REVERSE ENGINEERING AND DECONSTRUCTION OF THE ATTRIBUTES THAT I FIND MOST SUCCESSFUL ABOUT OUR COMPETITORS. PERHAPS WE CAN ADOPT SOME OF IT INTO OUR OWN PRACTICE.
fucking cool.
GO ON.
SJH_1114: Oof. I gotta look away.
POKER FACE, FOR INSTANCE, HAS DEVELOPED HIS CULT FOLLOWING FROM SHEER CONSISTENCY.
SLUGGO: I'mma try this with my next bitch.
HE'S A ONE MAN SHOW AND STREAMS A FRESH CULLING EVERY WEEKEND.
₿0.0000
PAY
NEXT, FANATICAL STUDIOS HAS SUPERIOR PRODUCTION VALUES AND VARY UP THEIR SCENERY. NOT AWFUL GIMMICKS, EITHER.
THEY SEEM TO CULL FROM SIMILAR STOCK AS US, BUT I THINK THE MOMENT THEY SACRIFICE SOME FRESH MEAT THEY WILL SHOOT INTO NUMBER TWO POSITION.
BY ALL ACCOUNTS ON RECORD, THE MORE THE AUDIENCE CAN DIRECT THEIR HATRED, OR PERHAPS THE MORE RELATABLE THE PREY, THE BIGGER THE REWARDS TO THE RED ROOM.
...AND THE BIGGER THE RISK, HORUS. WE HAVE MORE MONEY THAN WE CAN EVER SPEND. WHY RISK OUR FREEDOM? WHY JEOPARDIZE OUR FAMILIES' SECURITY?
BECAUSE, I CAN'T STAND THE ADVANTAGE THE NEXT BASTARDS HAVE OVER US!
TIMES UP!!! TIL NEXT TIME, FANATIX! EXCELSIOR!
145
302
DONATE NOW!
₿0.00000000
SEND MONEY

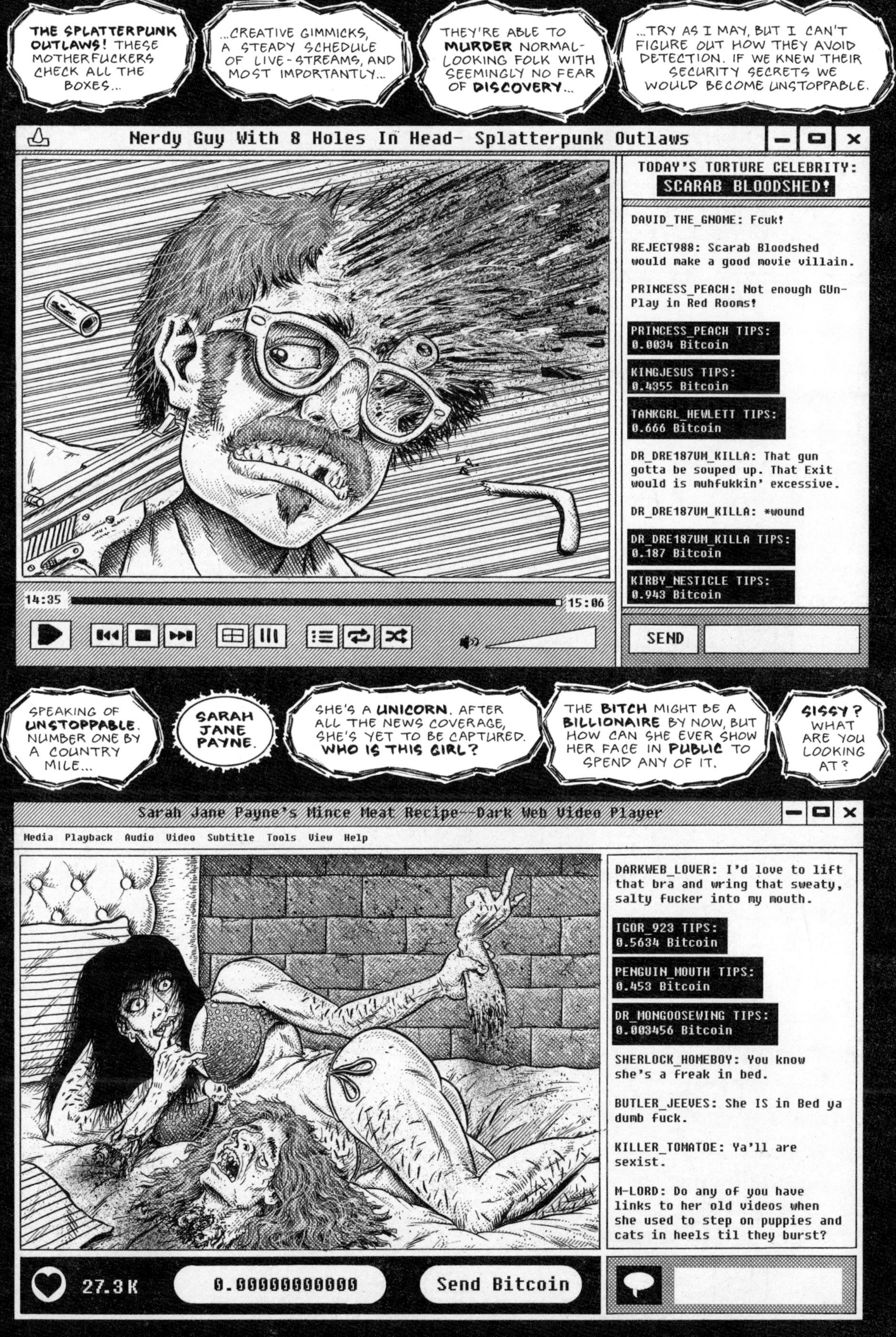
THE SPLATTERPUNK OUTLAWS! THESE MOTHERFUCKERS CHECK ALL THE BOXES...
...CREATIVE GIMMICKS, A STEADY SCHEDULE OF LIVE-STREAMS, AND MOST IMPORTANTLY...
THEY'RE ABLE TO MURDER NORMAL-LOOKING FOLK WITH SEEMINGLY NO FEAR OF DISCOVERY...
...TRY AS I MAY, BUT I CAN'T FIGURE OUT HOW THEY AVOID DETECTION. IF WE KNEW THEIR SECURITY SECRETS WE WOULD BECOME UNSTOPPABLE.
Nerdy Guy With 8 Holes In Head- Splatterpunk Outlaws
TODAY'S TORTURE CELEBRITY:
SCARAB BLOODSHED!
DAVID_THE_GNOME: Fcuk!
REJECT988: Scarab Bloodshed would make a good movie villain.
PRINCESS_PEACH: Not enough GUn-Play in Red Rooms!
PRINCESS_PEACH TIPS: 0.0034 Bitcoin
KINGJESUS TIPS: 0.4355 Bitcoin
TANKGRL_HEWLETT TIPS: 0.666 Bitcoin
DR_DRE187UM_KILLA: That gun gotta be souped up. That Exit would is muhfukkin' excessive.
DR_DRE187UM_KILLA: *wound
DR_DRE187UM_KILLA TIPS: 0.187 Bitcoin
KIRBY_NESTICLE TIPS: 0.943 Bitcoin
14:35
15:06
SEND
SPEAKING OF UNSTOPPABLE. NUMBER ONE BY A COUNTRY MILE...
SARAH JANE PAYNE.
SHE'S A UNICORN. AFTER ALL THE NEWS COVERAGE, SHE'S YET TO BE CAPTURED. WHO IS THIS GIRL?
THE BITCH MIGHT BE A BILLIONAIRE BY NOW, BUT HOW CAN SHE EVER SHOW HER FACE IN PUBLIC TO SPEND ANY OF IT.
SISSY? WHAT ARE YOU LOOKING AT?
Sarah Jane Payne's Mince Meat Recipe--Dark Web Video Player
Media Playback Audio Video Subtitle Tools View Help
DARKWEB_LOVER: I'd love to lift that bra and wring that sweaty, salty fucker into my mouth.
IGOR_923 TIPS: 0.5634 Bitcoin
PENGUIN_MOUTH TIPS: 0.453 Bitcoin
DR_MONGOOSEWING TIPS: 0.003456 Bitcoin
SHERLOCK_HOMEBOY: You know she's a freak in bed.
BUTLER_JEEVES: She IS in Bed ya dumb fuck.
KILLER_TOMATOE: Ya'll are sexist.
M-LORD: Do any of you have links to her old videos when she used to step on puppies and cats in heels til they burst?
27.3 K
0.00000000000
Send Bitcoin

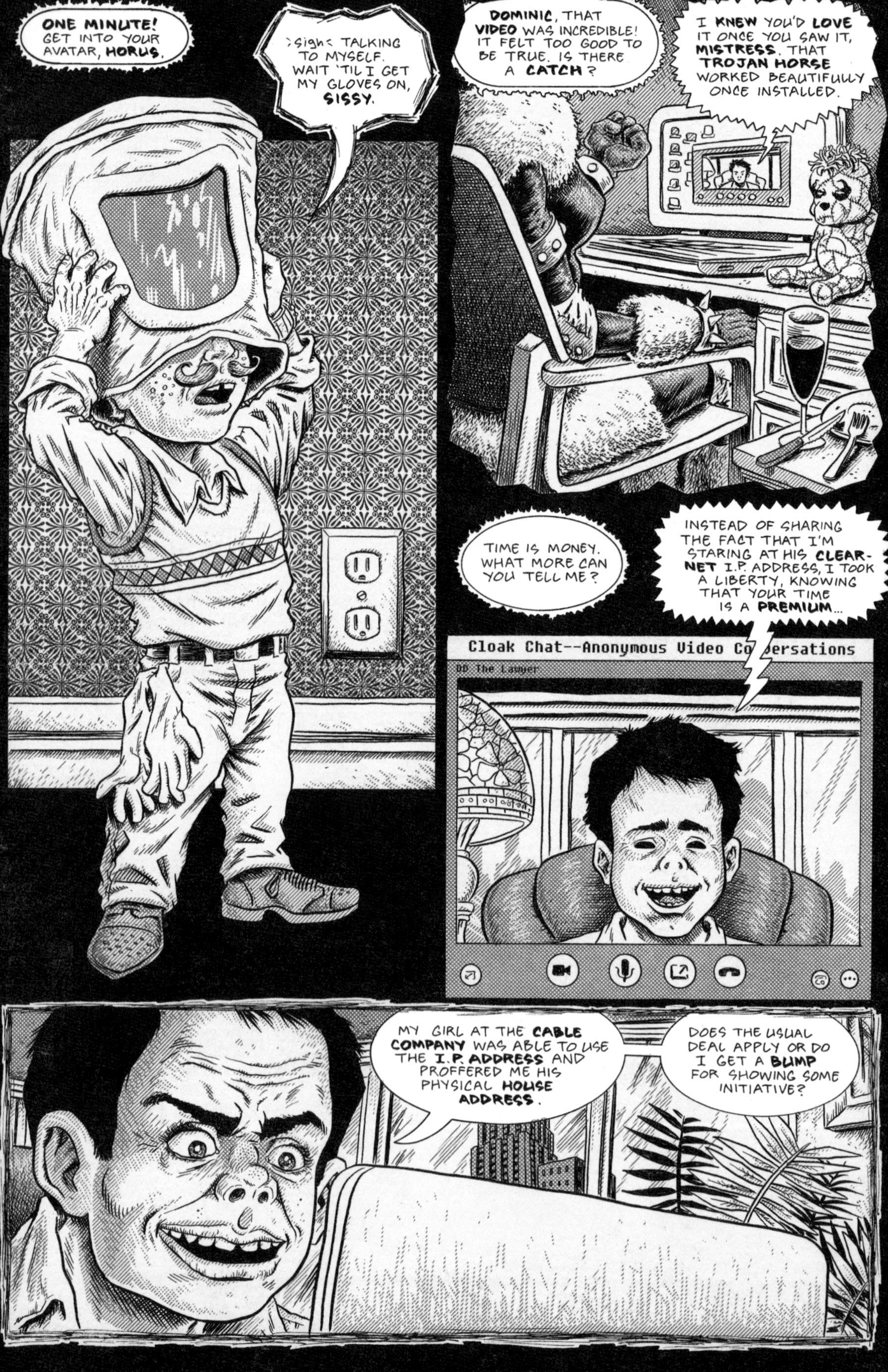
ONE MINUTE! GET INTO YOUR AVATAR, HORUS.
>SIGH< TALKING TO MYSELF. WAIT 'TIL I GET MY GLOVES ON, SISSY.
DOMINIC, THAT VIDEO WAS INCREDIBLE! IT FELT TOO GOOD TO BE TRUE. IS THERE A CATCH?
I KNEW YOU'D LOVE IT ONCE YOU SAW IT, MISTRESS. THAT TROJAN HORSE WORKED BEAUTIFULLY ONCE INSTALLED.
TIME IS MONEY. WHAT MORE CAN YOU TELL ME?
INSTEAD OF SHARING THE FACT THAT I'M STARING AT HIS CLEAR-NET I.P. ADDRESS, I TOOK A LIBERTY, KNOWING THAT YOUR TIME IS A PREMIUM...
Cloak Chat--Anonymous Video Conversations
DD The Lawyer
MY GIRL AT THE CABLE COMPANY WAS ABLE TO USE THE I.P. ADDRESS AND PROFFERED ME HIS PHYSICAL HOUSE ADDRESS.
DOES THE USUAL DEAL APPLY OR DO I GET A BUMP FOR SHOWING SOME INITIATIVE?

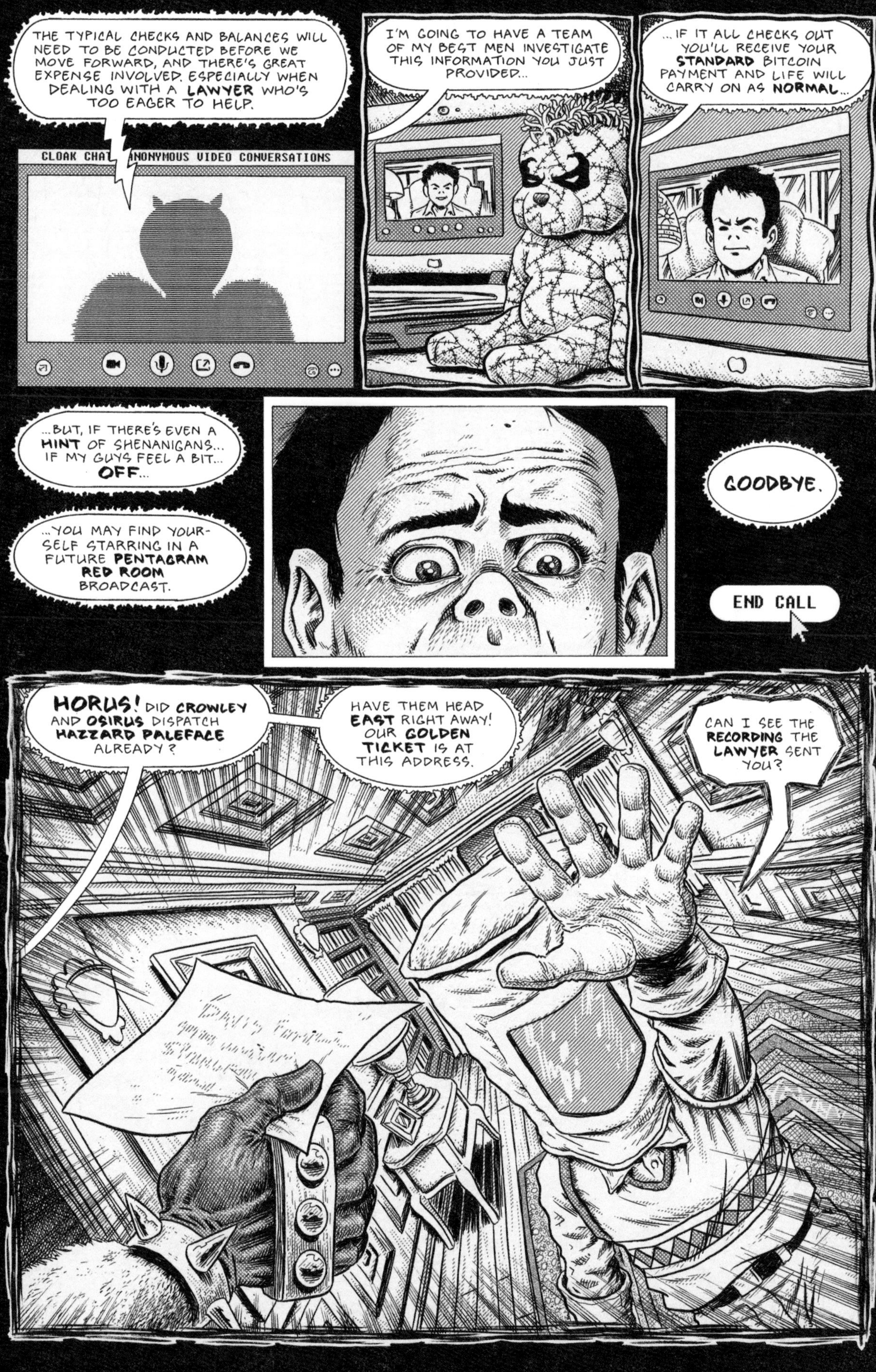
THE TYPICAL CHECKS AND BALANCES WILL NEED TO BE CONDUCTED BEFORE WE MOVE FORWARD, AND THERE'S GREAT EXPENSE INVOLVED. ESPECIALLY WHEN DEALING WITH A **LAWYER** WHO'S TOO EAGER TO HELP.
CLOAK CHAT ANONYMOUS VIDEO CONVERSATIONS
I'M GOING TO HAVE A TEAM OF MY BEST MEN INVESTIGATE THIS INFORMATION YOU JUST PROVIDED...
...IF IT ALL CHECKS OUT YOU'LL RECEIVE YOUR **STANDARD** BITCOIN PAYMENT AND LIFE WILL CARRY ON AS **NORMAL**...
...BUT, IF THERE'S EVEN A **HINT** OF SHENANIGANS... IF MY GUYS FEEL A BIT... **OFF**...
...YOU MAY FIND YOURSELF STARRING IN A FUTURE **PENTAGRAM RED ROOM** BROADCAST.
GOODBYE.
END CALL
HORUS! DID **CROWLEY** AND **OSIRUS** DISPATCH **HAZZARD PALEFACE** ALREADY?
HAVE THEM HEAD **EAST** RIGHT AWAY! OUR **GOLDEN TICKET** IS AT THIS ADDRESS.
CAN I SEE THE **RECORDING** THE **LAWYER** SENT YOU?

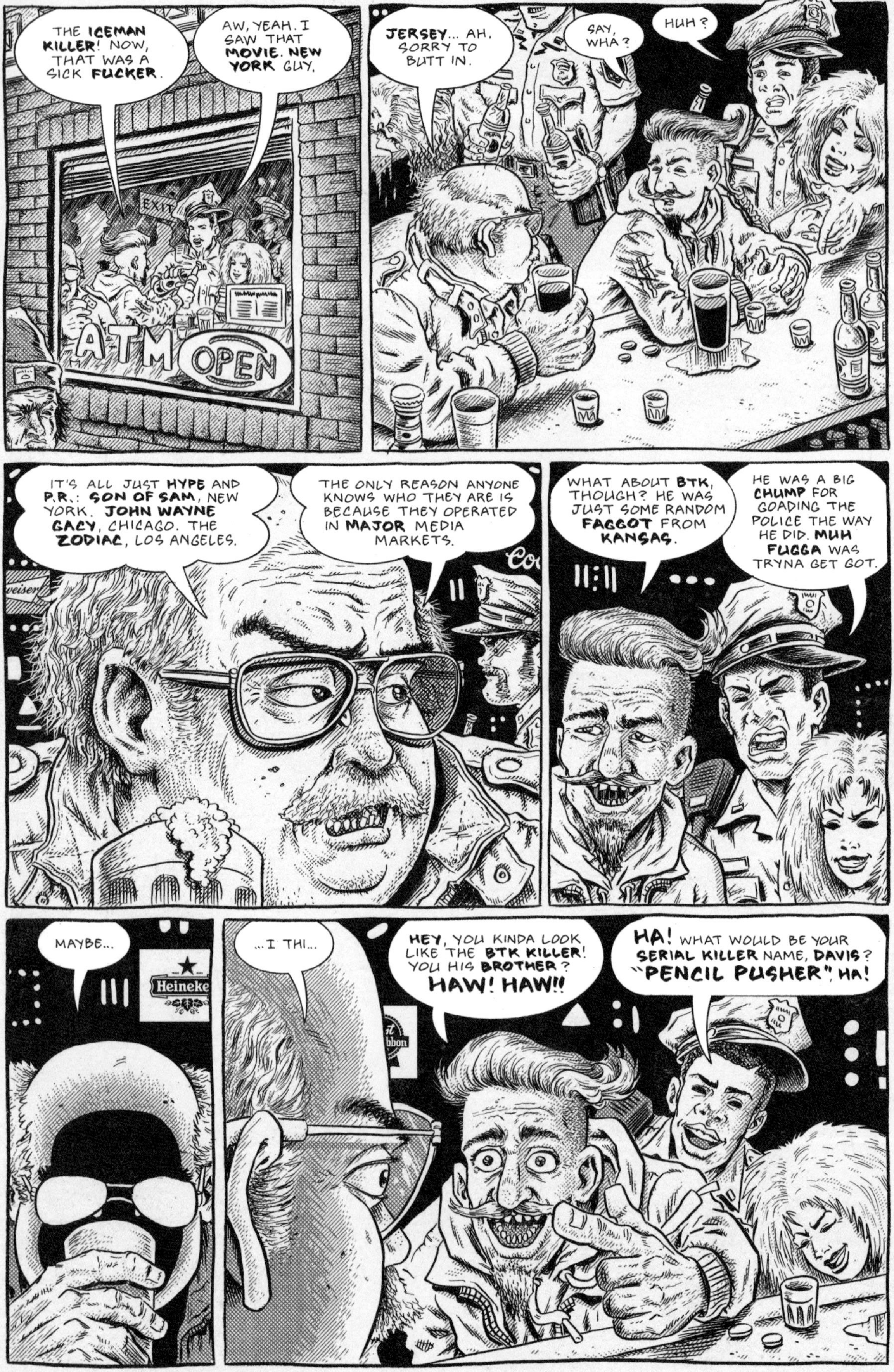
THE ICEMAN KILLER! NOW, THAT WAS A SICK FUCKER.
AW, YEAH. I SAW THAT MOVIE. NEW YORK GUY.
EXIT
ATM
OPEN
JERSEY... AH, SORRY TO BUTT IN.
SAY, WHA?
HUH?
IT'S ALL JUST HYPE AND P.R.: SON OF SAM, NEW YORK. JOHN WAYNE GACY, CHICAGO. THE ZODIAC, LOS ANGELES.
THE ONLY REASON ANYONE KNOWS WHO THEY ARE IS BECAUSE THEY OPERATED IN MAJOR MEDIA MARKETS.
WHAT ABOUT BTK, THOUGH? HE WAS JUST SOME RANDOM FAGGOT FROM KANSAS.
HE WAS A BIG CHUMP FOR GOADING THE POLICE THE WAY HE DID. MUH FUGGA WAS TRYNA GET GOT.
MAYBE...
Heineken
...I THI...
HEY, YOU KINDA LOOK LIKE THE BTK KILLER! YOU HIS BROTHER? HAW! HAW!!
HA! WHAT WOULD BE YOUR SERIAL KILLER NAME, DAVIS? "PENCIL PUSHER", HA!

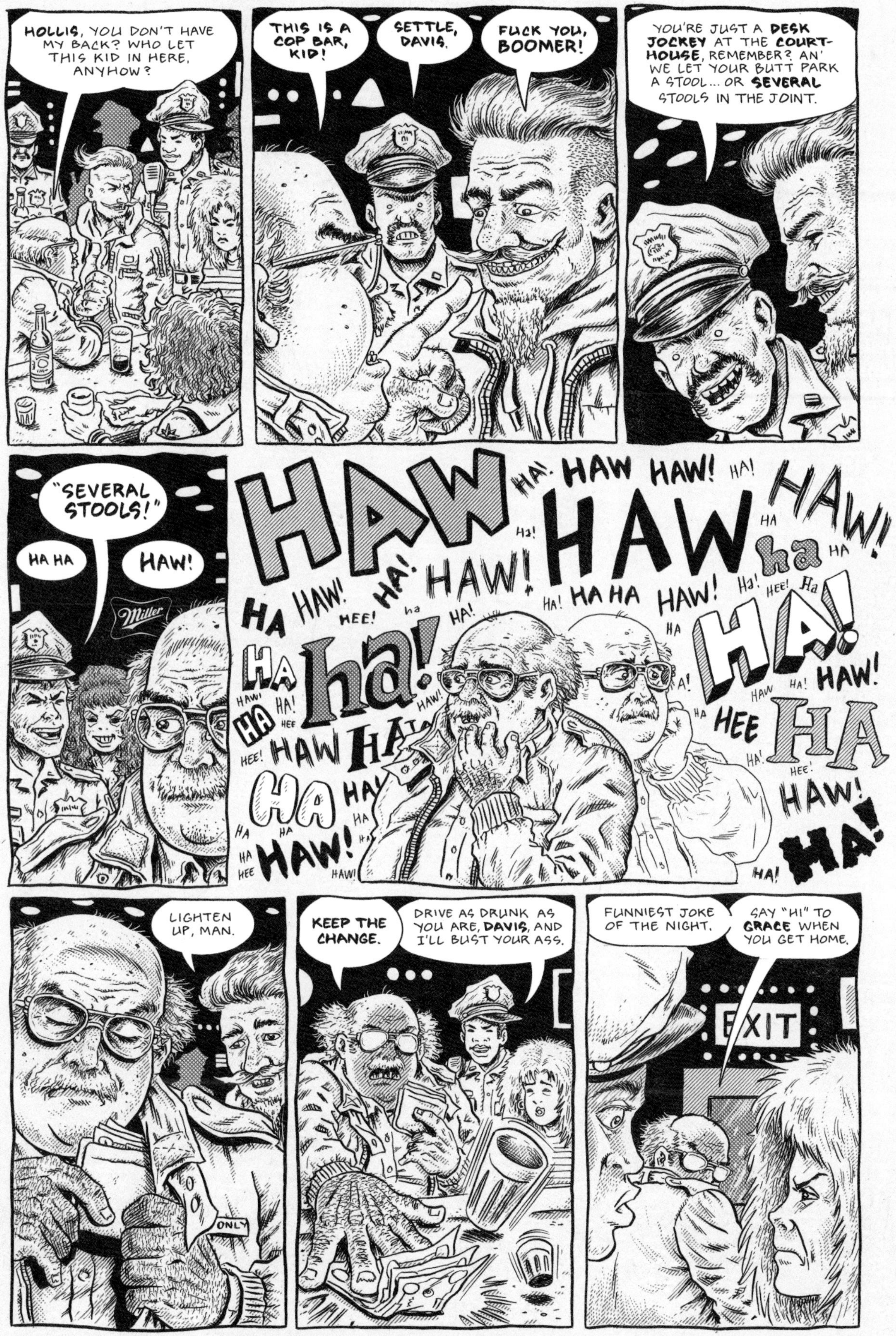
HOLLIS, YOU DON'T HAVE MY BACK? WHO LET THIS KID IN HERE, ANYHOW?
THIS IS A COP BAR, KID!
SETTLE, DAVIS.
FUCK YOU, BOOMER!
YOU'RE JUST A DESK JOCKEY AT THE COURT-HOUSE, REMEMBER? AN' WE LET YOUR BUTT PARK A STOOL... OR SEVERAL STOOLS IN THE JOINT.
"SEVERAL STOOLS!"
HA HA
HAW!
Miller
HAW HA! HAW HAW! HA! HAW! HAW HAW ha HA HA HAW! HA! HAW! HA! HA HA HAW! HA! HEE! Ha
HA HEE! ha HA! HA ha! HA! HA! HAW!
HA HAW HA! HEE HAW HA HEE HA HA HAW!
HA HA HEE HAW! HAW! HA! HA!
LIGHTEN UP, MAN.
ONLY
KEEP THE CHANGE.
DRIVE AS DRUNK AS YOU ARE, DAVIS, AND I'LL BUST YOUR ASS.
FUNNIEST JOKE OF THE NIGHT.
SAY "HI" TO GRACE WHEN YOU GET HOME.
EXIT

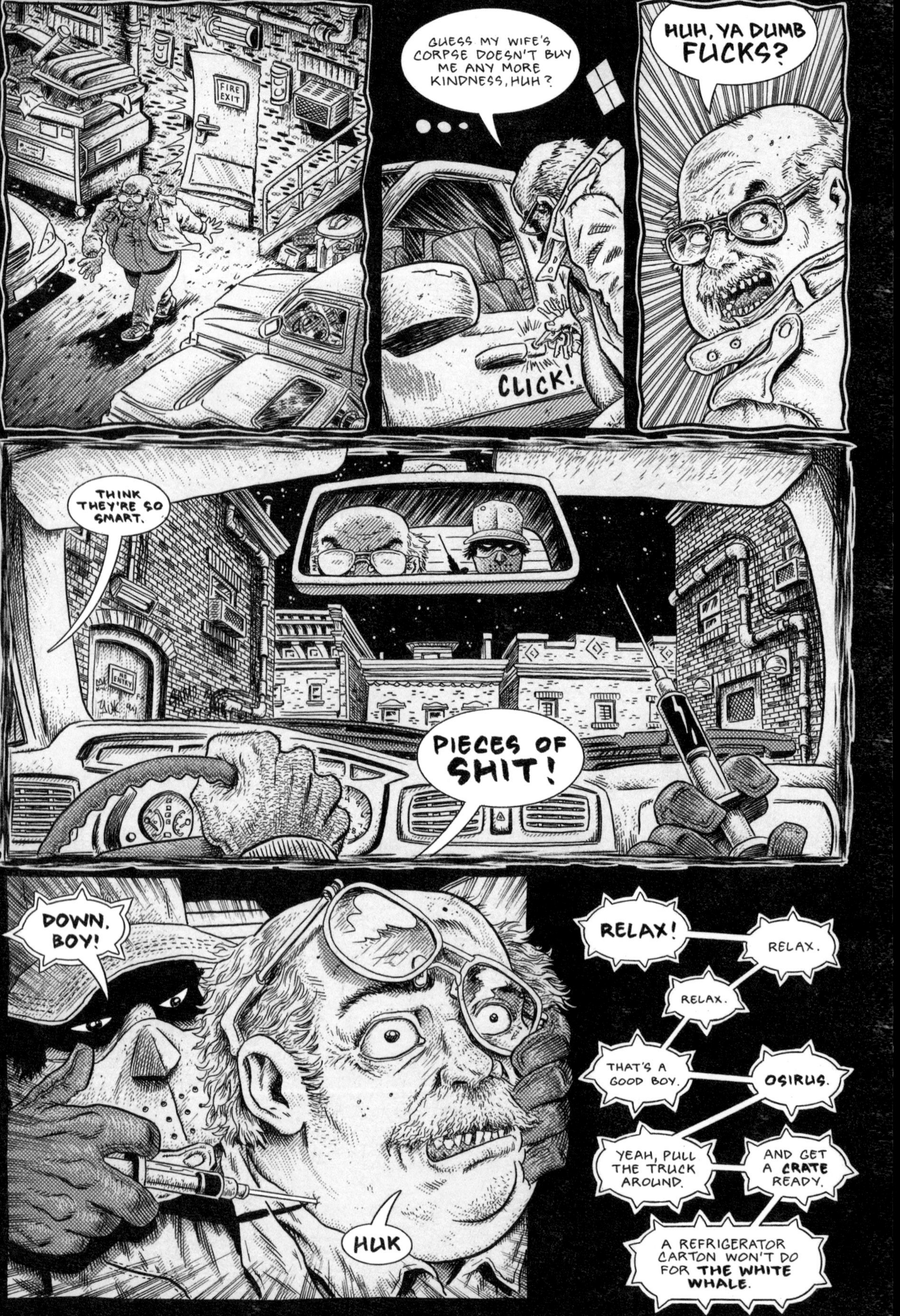
FIRE EXIT
...
GUESS MY WIFE'S CORPSE DOESN'T BUY ME ANY MORE KINDNESS, HUH?
CLICK!
HUH, YA DUMB FUCKS?
THINK THEY'RE SO SMART.
NO ENTRY
PIECES OF SHIT!
DOWN. BOY!
HUK
RELAX!
RELAX.
RELAX.
THAT'S A GOOD BOY.
OSIRUS.
YEAH, PULL THE TRUCK AROUND.
AND GET A CRATE READY.
A REFRIGERATOR CARTON WON'T DO FOR THE WHITE WHALE.

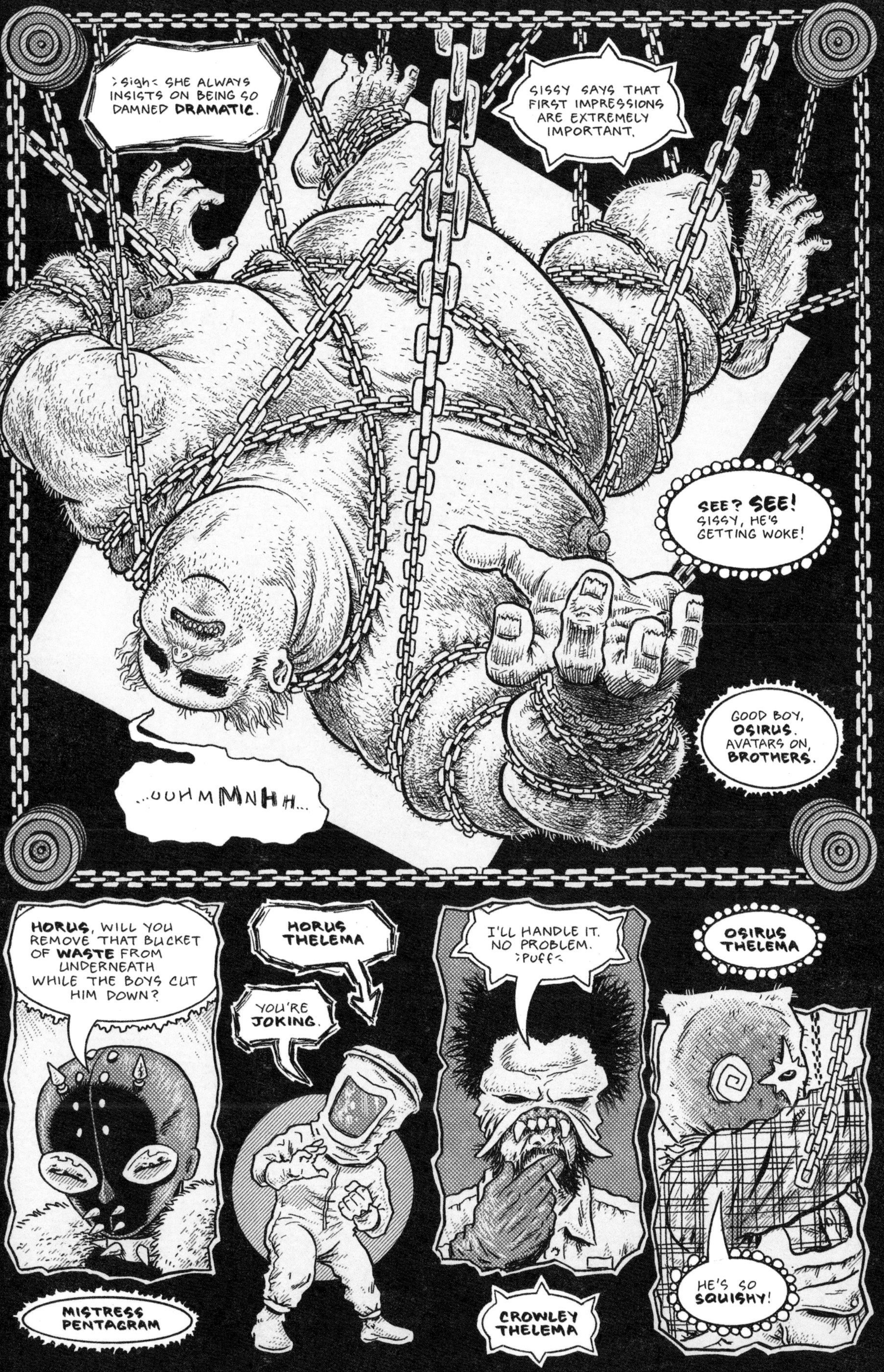
>sigh< SHE ALWAYS INSISTS ON BEING SO DAMNED DRAMATIC.
SISSY SAYS THAT FIRST IMPRESSIONS ARE EXTREMELY IMPORTANT.
SEE? SEE! SISSY, HE'S GETTING WOKE!
GOOD BOY, OSIRUS. AVATARS ON, BROTHERS.
...UUHMMMNHH...
HORUS, WILL YOU REMOVE THAT BUCKET OF WASTE FROM UNDERNEATH WHILE THE BOYS CUT HIM DOWN?
MISTRESS PENTAGRAM
HORUS THELEMA
YOU'RE JOKING.
I'LL HANDLE IT. NO PROBLEM. >PUFF<
CROWLEY THELEMA
OSIRUS THELEMA
HE'S SO SQUISHY!

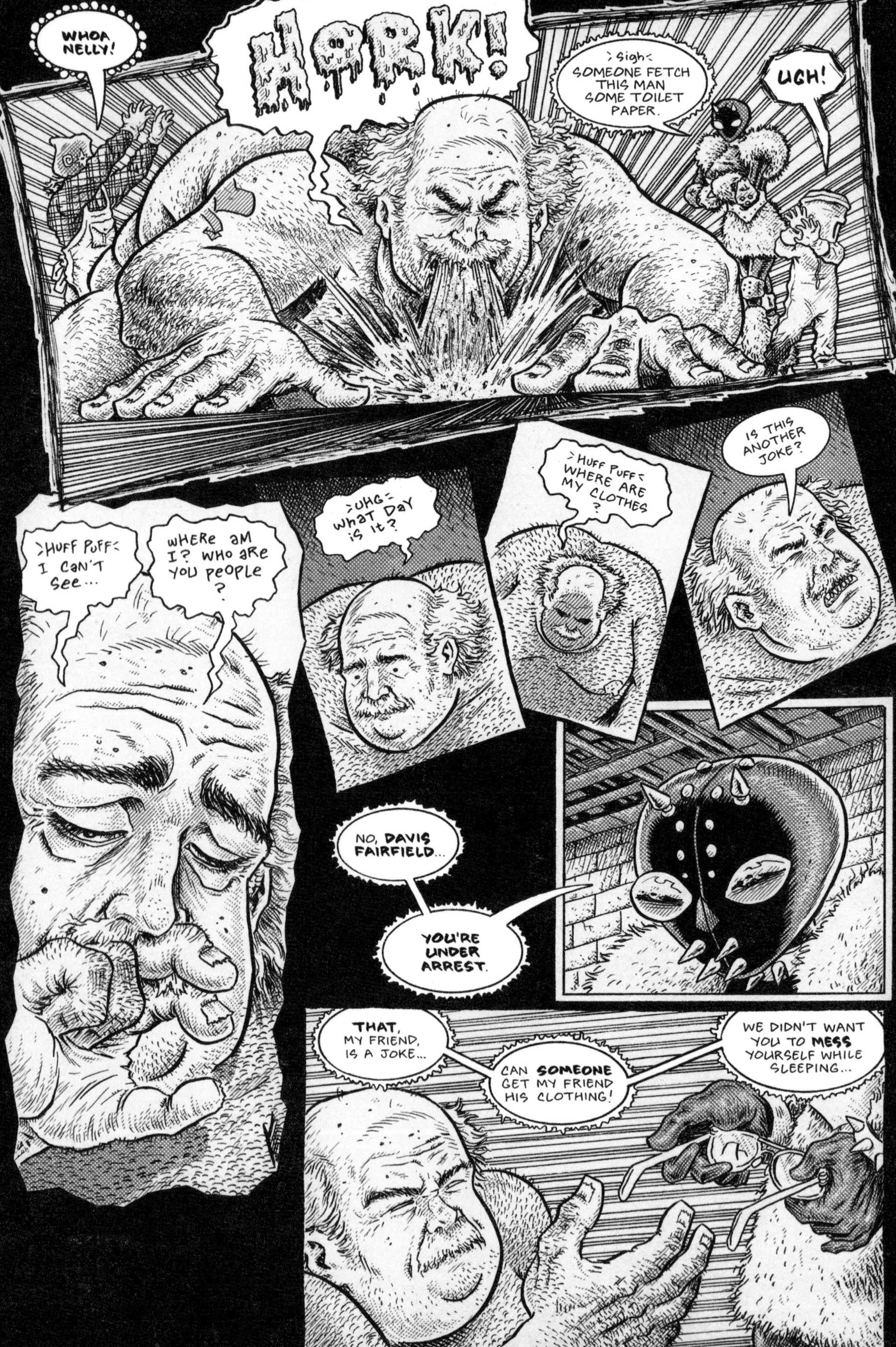
WHOA NELLY!
HORK!
>sigh< SOMEONE FETCH THIS MAN SOME TOILET PAPER.
UGH!
>HUFF PUFF< I CAN'T SEE...
WHERE AM I? WHO ARE YOU PEOPLE?
>UHG< WHAT DAY IS IT?
>HUFF PUFF< WHERE ARE MY CLOTHES?
IS THIS ANOTHER JOKE?
NO, DAVIS FAIRFIELD...
YOU'RE UNDER ARREST.
THAT, MY FRIEND, IS A JOKE...
WE DIDN'T WANT YOU TO MESS YOURSELF WHILE SLEEPING...
CAN SOMEONE GET MY FRIEND HIS CLOTHING!

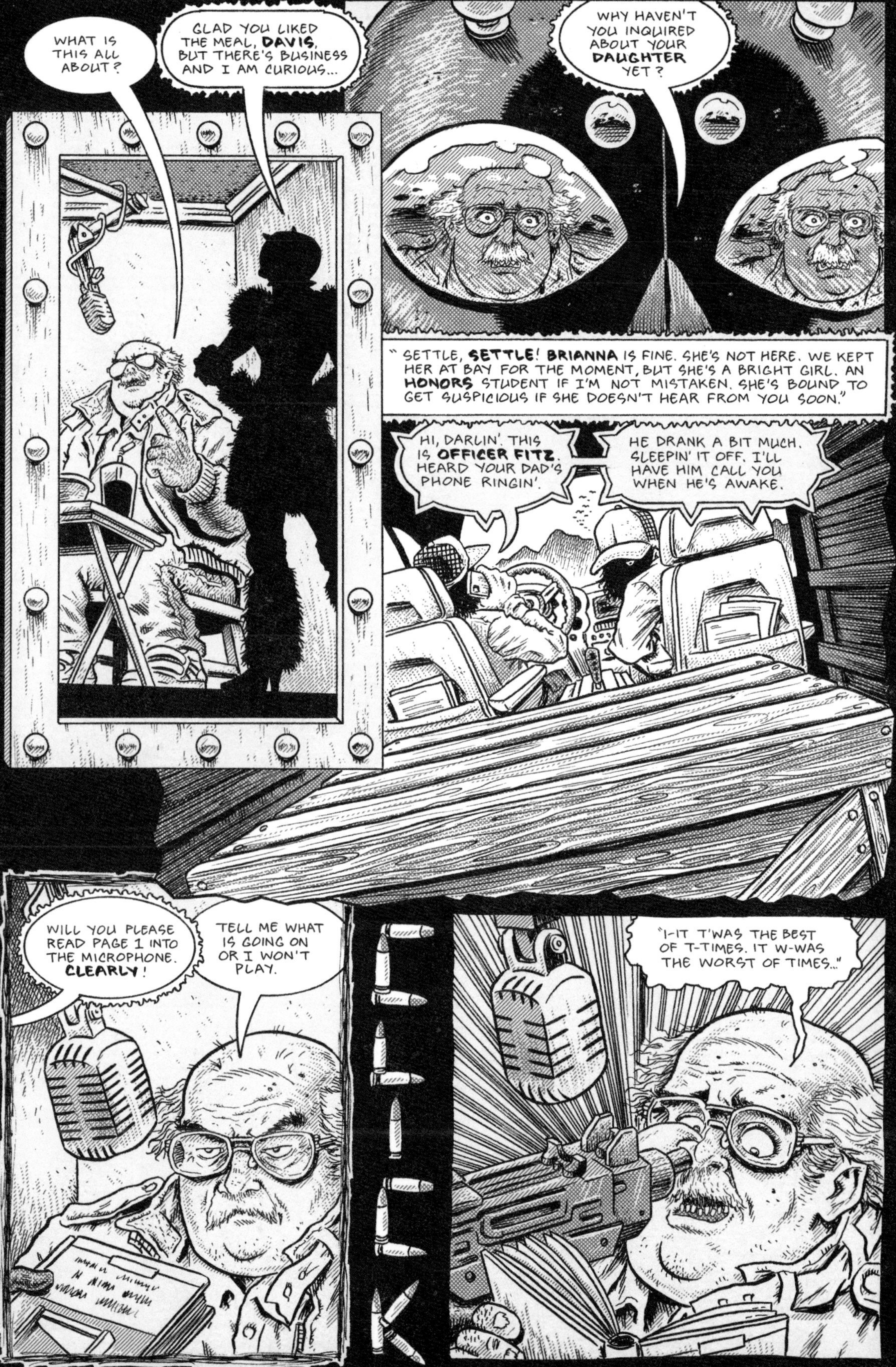
WHAT IS THIS ALL ABOUT?
GLAD YOU LIKED THE MEAL, **DAVIS**, BUT THERE'S BUSINESS AND I AM CURIOUS...
WHY HAVEN'T YOU INQUIRED ABOUT YOUR **DAUGHTER** YET?
"SETTLE, **SETTLE**! **BRIANNA** IS FINE. SHE'S NOT HERE. WE KEPT HER AT BAY FOR THE MOMENT, BUT SHE'S A BRIGHT GIRL. AN **HONORS** STUDENT IF I'M NOT MISTAKEN. SHE'S BOUND TO GET SUSPICIOUS IF SHE DOESN'T HEAR FROM YOU SOON."
HI, DARLIN'. THIS IS **OFFICER FITZ**. HEARD YOUR DAD'S PHONE RINGIN'.
HE DRANK A BIT MUCH. SLEEPIN' IT OFF. I'LL HAVE HIM CALL YOU WHEN HE'S AWAKE.
WILL YOU PLEASE READ PAGE 1 INTO THE MICROPHONE. **CLEARLY**!
TELL ME WHAT IS GOING ON OR I WON'T PLAY.
"I-IT T'WAS THE BEST OF T-TIMES. IT W-WAS THE WORST OF TIMES..."

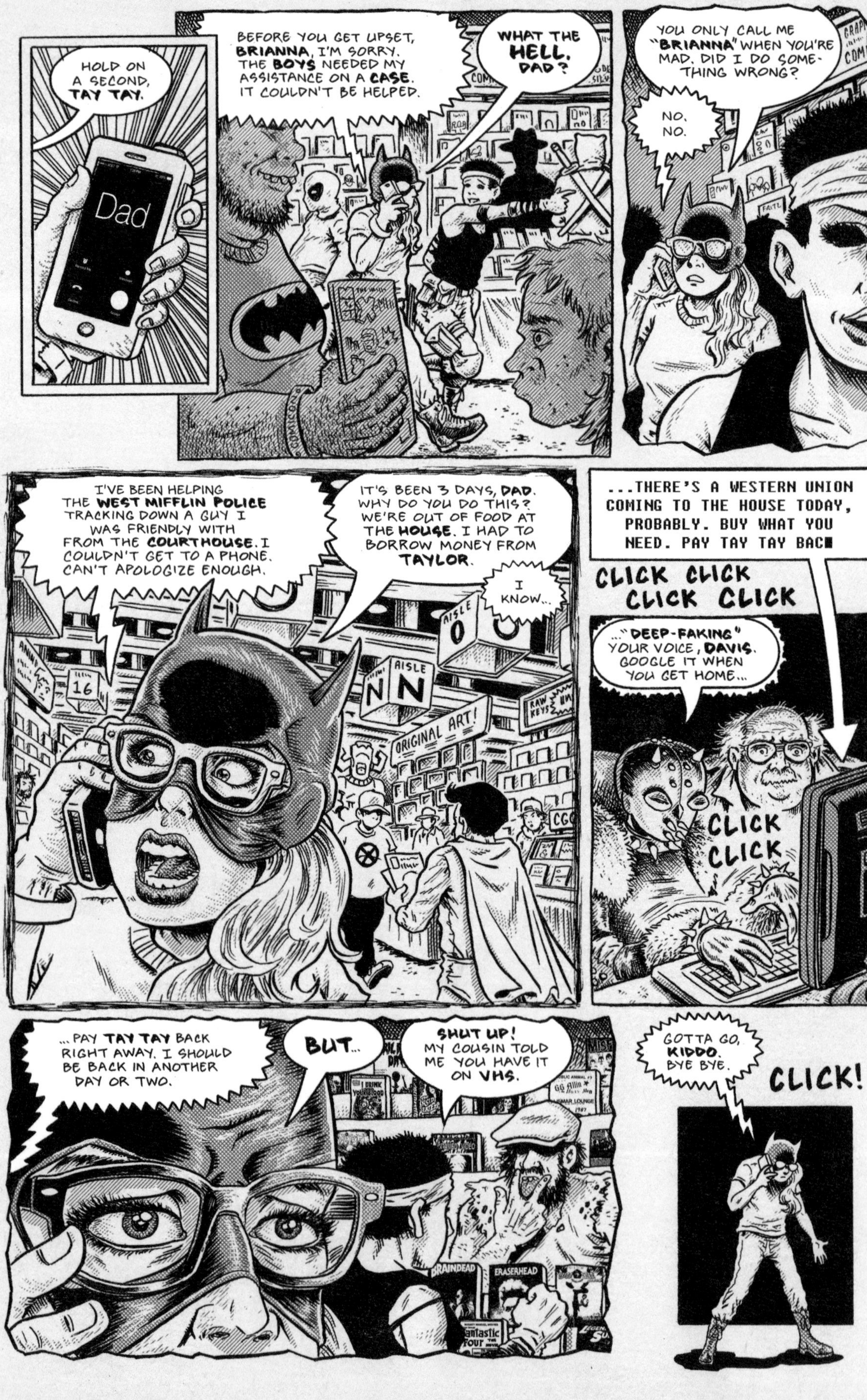
HOLD ON A SECOND, TAY TAY.
Dad
BEFORE YOU GET UPSET, BRIANNA, I'M SORRY. THE BOYS NEEDED MY ASSISTANCE ON A CASE. IT COULDN'T BE HELPED.
WHAT THE HELL, DAD?
YOU ONLY CALL ME "BRIANNA" WHEN YOU'RE MAD. DID I DO SOMETHING WRONG?
NO, NO.
I'VE BEEN HELPING THE WEST MIFFLIN POLICE TRACKING DOWN A GUY I WAS FRIENDLY WITH FROM THE COURTHOUSE. I COULDN'T GET TO A PHONE. CAN'T APOLOGIZE ENOUGH.
IT'S BEEN 3 DAYS, DAD. WHY DO YOU DO THIS? WE'RE OUT OF FOOD AT THE HOUSE. I HAD TO BORROW MONEY FROM TAYLOR.
I KNOW...
AISLE O
AISLE NN
16
ORIGINAL ART!
RAW KEYS
...THERE'S A WESTERN UNION COMING TO THE HOUSE TODAY, PROBABLY. BUY WHAT YOU NEED. PAY TAY TAY BAC
CLICK CLICK CLICK CLICK
..."DEEP-FAKING" YOUR VOICE, DAVIS. GOOGLE IT WHEN YOU GET HOME...
CLICK CLICK
...PAY TAY TAY BACK RIGHT AWAY. I SHOULD BE BACK IN ANOTHER DAY OR TWO.
BUT...
SHUT UP! MY COUSIN TOLD ME YOU HAVE IT ON VHS.
BRAINDEAD
ERASERHEAD
Fantastic Four
GOTTA GO, KIDDO. BYE BYE.
CLICK!

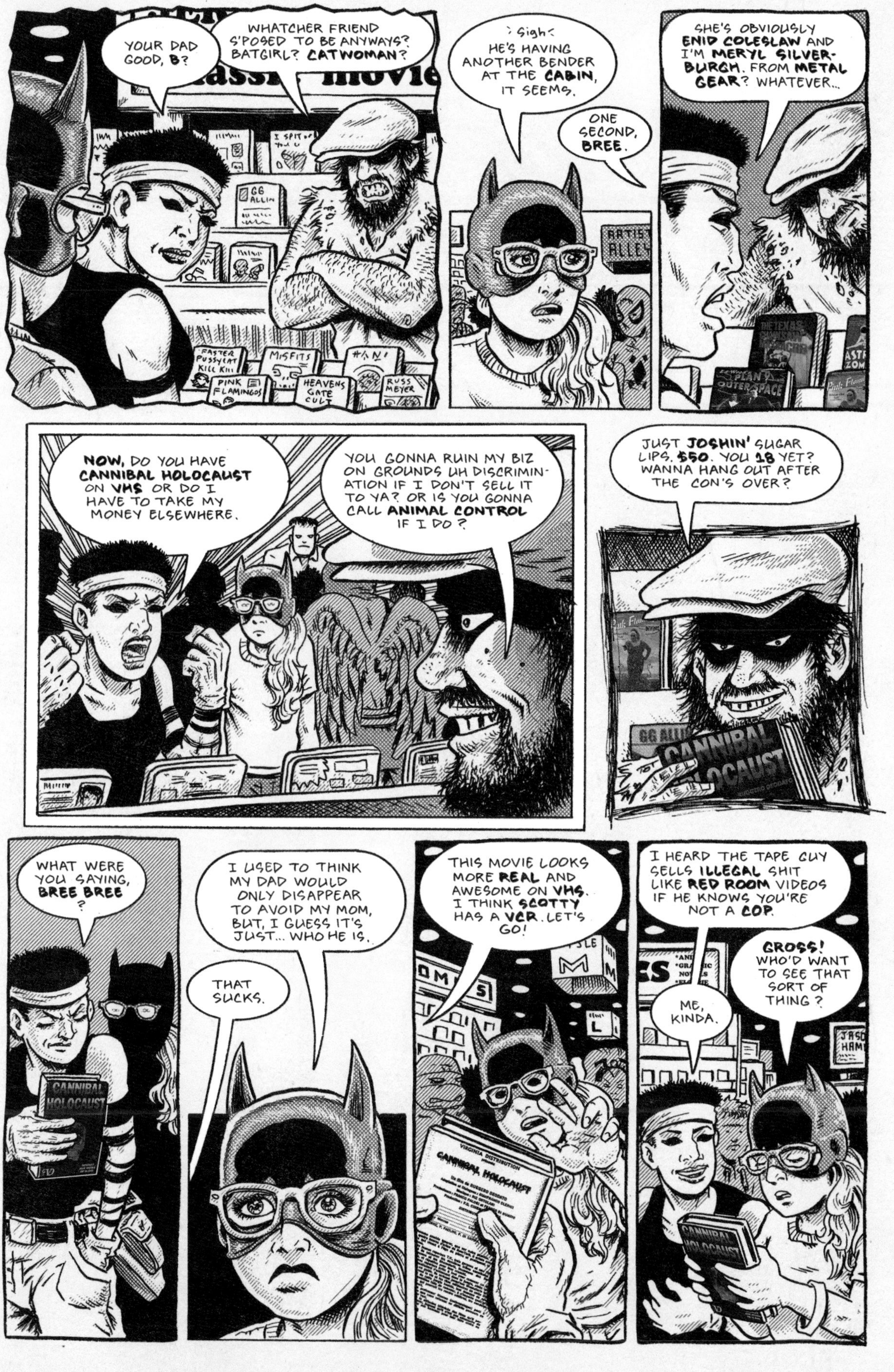
YOUR DAD GOOD, B?
WHATCHER FRIEND S'POSED TO BE ANYWAYS? BATGIRL? CATWOMAN?
GG ALLIN
FASTER PUSSYCAT KILL KILL
PINK FLAMINGOS
MISFITS
HEAVENS GATE CULT
RUSS MEYER
:Sigh: HE'S HAVING ANOTHER BENDER AT THE CABIN, IT SEEMS.
ONE SECOND, BREE.
ARTIST ALLEY
SHE'S OBVIOUSLY ENID COLESLAW AND I'M MERYL SILVERBURGH. FROM METAL GEAR? WHATEVER...
NOW, DO YOU HAVE CANNIBAL HOLOCAUST ON VHS OR DO I HAVE TO TAKE MY MONEY ELSEWHERE.
YOU GONNA RUIN MY BIZ ON GROUNDS UH DISCRIMINATION IF I DON'T SELL IT TO YA? OR IS YOU GONNA CALL ANIMAL CONTROL IF I DO?
JUST JOSHIN' SUGAR LIPS. $50. YOU 18 YET? WANNA HANG OUT AFTER THE CON'S OVER?
CANNIBAL HOLOCAUST
WHAT WERE YOU SAYING, BREE BREE?
CANNIBAL HOLOCAUST
I USED TO THINK MY DAD WOULD ONLY DISAPPEAR TO AVOID MY MOM, BUT, I GUESS IT'S JUST... WHO HE IS.
THAT SUCKS.
THIS MOVIE LOOKS MORE REAL AND AWESOME ON VHS. I THINK SCOTTY HAS A VCR. LET'S GO!
CANNIBAL HOLOCAUST
I HEARD THE TAPE GUY SELLS ILLEGAL SHIT LIKE RED ROOM VIDEOS IF HE KNOWS YOU'RE NOT A COP.
GROSS! WHO'D WANT TO SEE THAT SORT OF THING?
ME, KINDA.
CANNIBAL HOLOCAUST

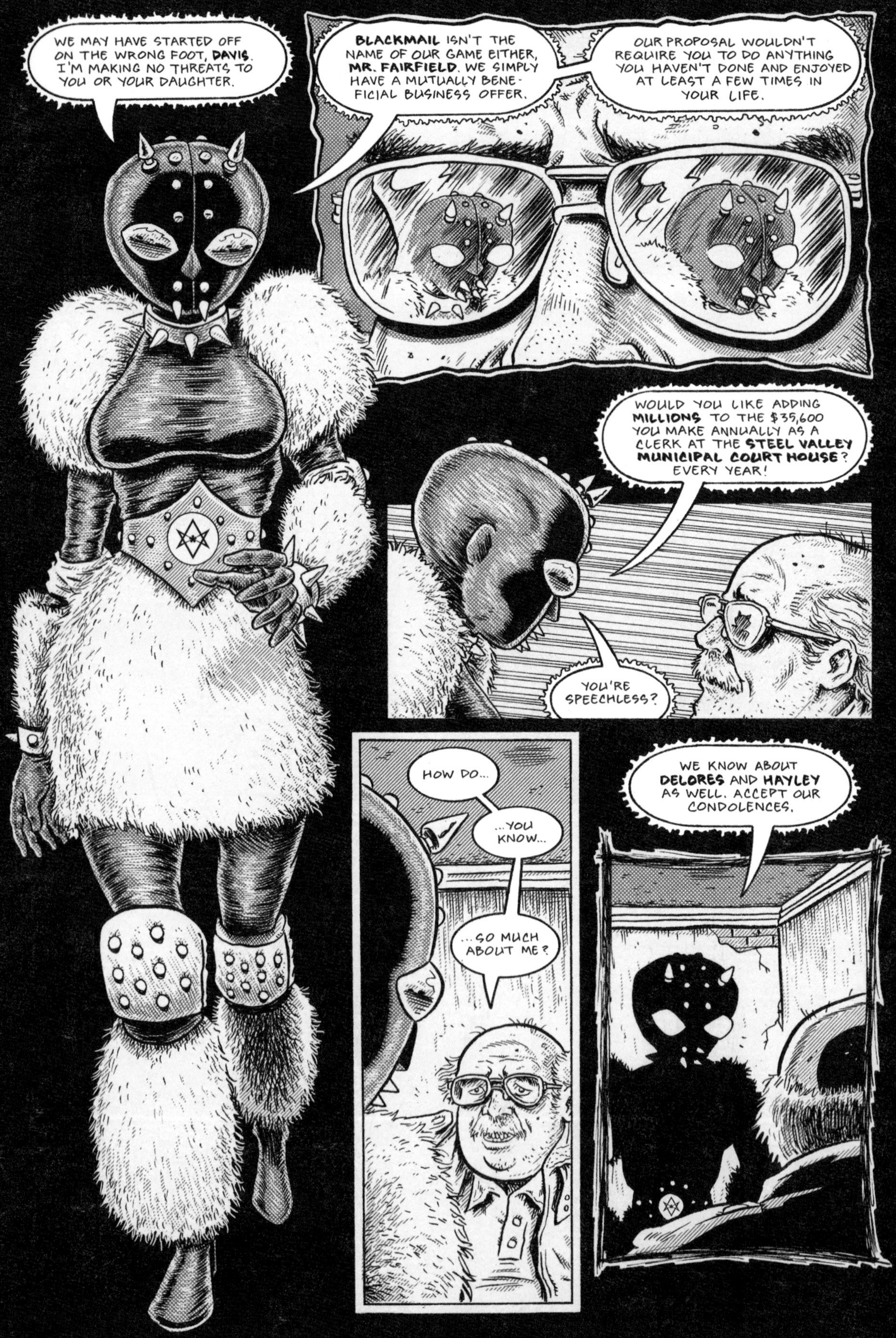
WE MAY HAVE STARTED OFF ON THE WRONG FOOT, DAVIS. I'M MAKING NO THREATS TO YOU OR YOUR DAUGHTER.
BLACKMAIL ISN'T THE NAME OF OUR GAME EITHER, MR. FAIRFIELD. WE SIMPLY HAVE A MUTUALLY BENE-FICIAL BUSINESS OFFER.
OUR PROPOSAL WOULDN'T REQUIRE YOU TO DO ANYTHING YOU HAVEN'T DONE AND ENJOYED AT LEAST A FEW TIMES IN YOUR LIFE.
WOULD YOU LIKE ADDING MILLIONS TO THE $35,600 YOU MAKE ANNUALLY AS A CLERK AT THE STEEL VALLEY MUNICIPAL COURT HOUSE? EVERY YEAR!
YOU'RE SPEECHLESS?
HOW DO...
...YOU KNOW...
...SO MUCH ABOUT ME?
WE KNOW ABOUT DELORES AND HAYLEY AS WELL. ACCEPT OUR CONDOLENCES.

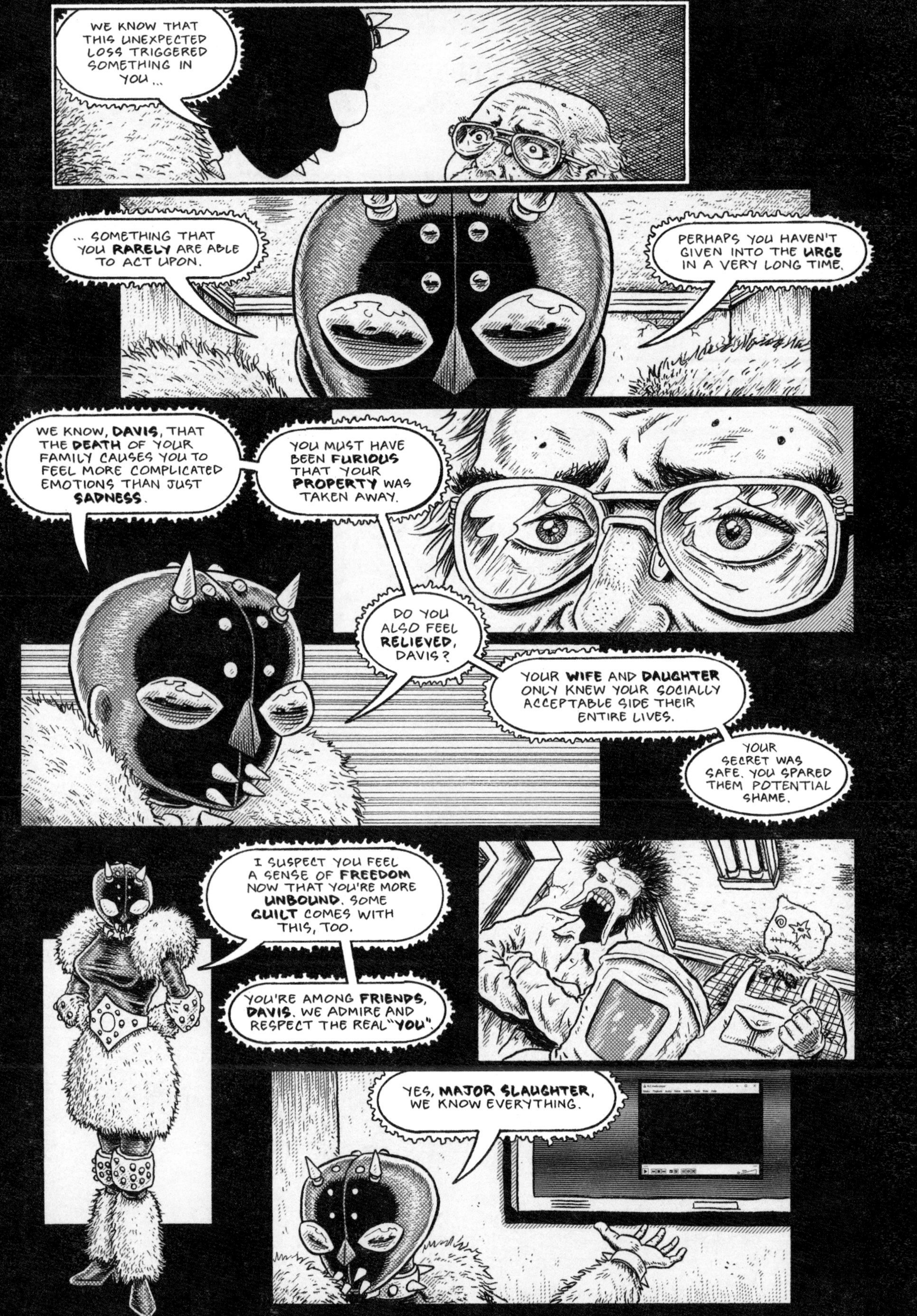
WE KNOW THAT THIS UNEXPECTED LOSS TRIGGERED SOMETHING IN YOU...
... SOMETHING THAT YOU RARELY ARE ABLE TO ACT UPON.
PERHAPS YOU HAVEN'T GIVEN INTO THE URGE IN A VERY LONG TIME.
WE KNOW, DAVIS, THAT THE DEATH OF YOUR FAMILY CAUSES YOU TO FEEL MORE COMPLICATED EMOTIONS THAN JUST SADNESS.
YOU MUST HAVE BEEN FURIOUS THAT YOUR PROPERTY WAS TAKEN AWAY.
DO YOU ALSO FEEL RELIEVED, DAVIS?
YOUR WIFE AND DAUGHTER ONLY KNEW YOUR SOCIALLY ACCEPTABLE SIDE THEIR ENTIRE LIVES.
YOUR SECRET WAS SAFE. YOU SPARED THEM POTENTIAL SHAME.
I SUSPECT YOU FEEL A SENSE OF FREEDOM NOW THAT YOU'RE MORE UNBOUND. SOME GUILT COMES WITH THIS, TOO.
YOU'RE AMONG FRIENDS, DAVIS. WE ADMIRE AND RESPECT THE REAL "YOU".
YES, MAJOR SLAUGHTER, WE KNOW EVERYTHING.

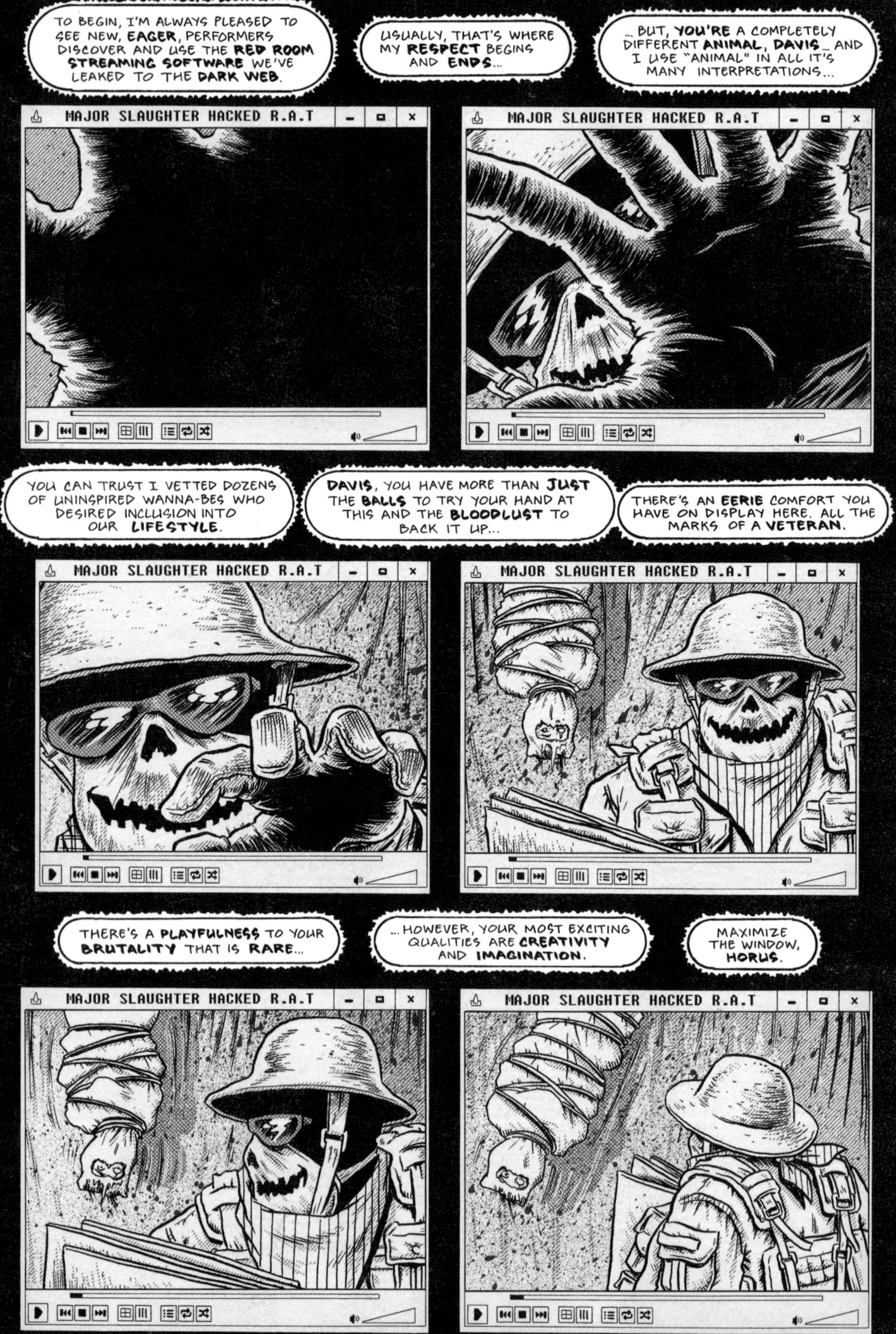
TO BEGIN, I'M ALWAYS PLEASED TO SEE NEW, EAGER, PERFORMERS DISCOVER AND USE THE RED ROOM STREAMING SOFTWARE WE'VE LEAKED TO THE DARK WEB.
USUALLY, THAT'S WHERE MY RESPECT BEGINS AND ENDS...
...BUT, YOU'RE A COMPLETELY DIFFERENT ANIMAL, DAVIS... AND I USE "ANIMAL" IN ALL IT'S MANY INTERPRETATIONS...
MAJOR SLAUGHTER HACKED R.A.T
MAJOR SLAUGHTER HACKED R.A.T
YOU CAN TRUST I VETTED DOZENS OF UNINSPIRED WANNA-BES WHO DESIRED INCLUSION INTO OUR LIFESTYLE.
DAVIS, YOU HAVE MORE THAN JUST THE BALLS TO TRY YOUR HAND AT THIS AND THE BLOODLUST TO BACK IT UP...
THERE'S AN EERIE COMFORT YOU HAVE ON DISPLAY HERE. ALL THE MARKS OF A VETERAN.
MAJOR SLAUGHTER HACKED R.A.T
MAJOR SLAUGHTER HACKED R.A.T
THERE'S A PLAYFULNESS TO YOUR BRUTALITY THAT IS RARE...
...HOWEVER, YOUR MOST EXCITING QUALITIES ARE CREATIVITY AND IMAGINATION.
MAXIMIZE THE WINDOW, HORUS.
MAJOR SLAUGHTER HACKED R.A.T
MAJOR SLAUGHTER HACKED R.A.T

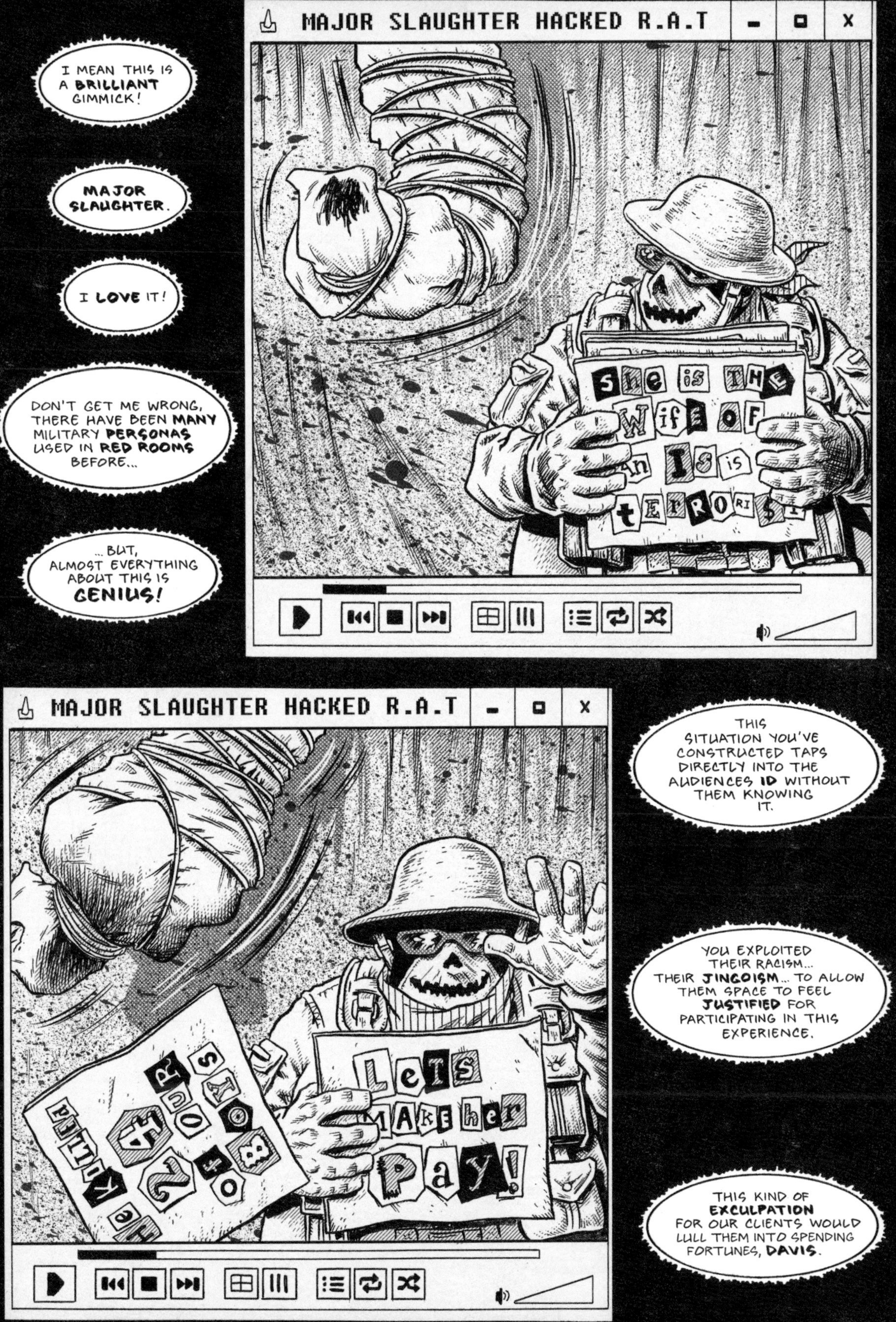

I MEAN THIS IS A **BRILLIANT** GIMMICK!
MAJOR SLAUGHTER.
I **LOVE** IT!
DON'T GET ME WRONG, THERE HAVE BEEN **MANY** MILITARY **PERSONAS** USED IN **RED ROOMS** BEFORE...
...BUT, ALMOST EVERYTHING ABOUT THIS IS **GENIUS!**
MAJOR SLAUGHTER HACKED R.A.T
She is THE WifE OF An IS is terRORI$T
MAJOR SLAUGHTER HACKED R.A.T
He Killed
24 OuR
of BoYS
Lets MAKE her Pay!
THIS SITUATION YOU'VE CONSTRUCTED TAPS DIRECTLY INTO THE AUDIENCES **ID** WITHOUT THEM KNOWING IT.
YOU EXPLOITED THEIR RACISM... THEIR **JINGOISM**... TO ALLOW THEM SPACE TO FEEL **JUSTIFIED** FOR PARTICIPATING IN THIS EXPERIENCE.
THIS KIND OF **EXCULPATION** FOR OUR CLIENTS WOULD LULL THEM INTO SPENDING FORTUNES, **DAVIS**.

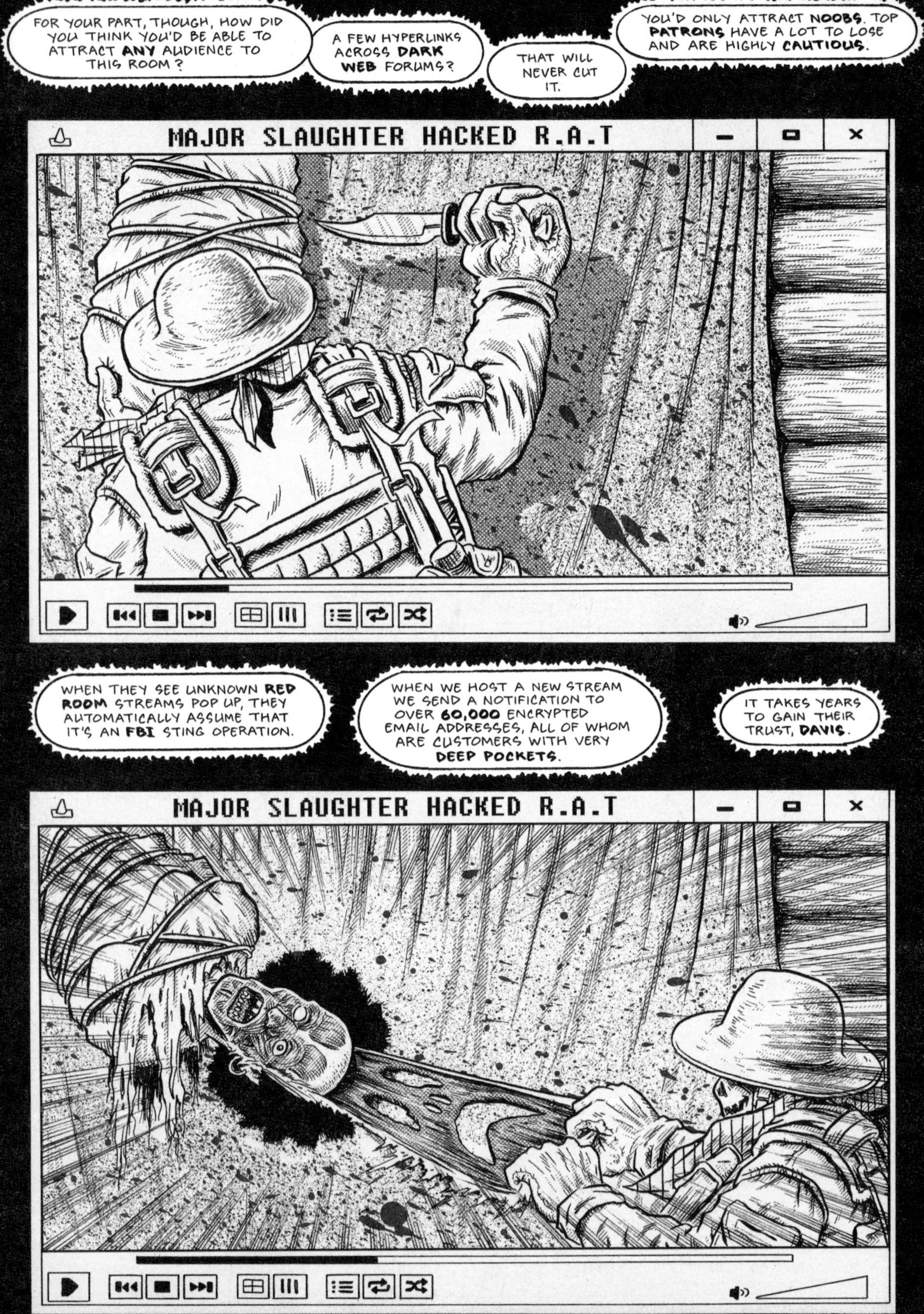
FOR YOUR PART, THOUGH, HOW DID YOU THINK YOU'D BE ABLE TO ATTRACT ANY AUDIENCE TO THIS ROOM?
A FEW HYPERLINKS ACROSS DARK WEB FORUMS?
THAT WILL NEVER CUT IT.
YOU'D ONLY ATTRACT NOOBS. TOP PATRONS HAVE A LOT TO LOSE AND ARE HIGHLY CAUTIOUS.
MAJOR SLAUGHTER HACKED R.A.T
WHEN THEY SEE UNKNOWN RED ROOM STREAMS POP UP, THEY AUTOMATICALLY ASSUME THAT IT'S AN FBI STING OPERATION.
WHEN WE HOST A NEW STREAM WE SEND A NOTIFICATION TO OVER 60,000 ENCRYPTED EMAIL ADDRESSES, ALL OF WHOM ARE CUSTOMERS WITH VERY DEEP POCKETS.
IT TAKES YEARS TO GAIN THEIR TRUST, DAVIS.
MAJOR SLAUGHTER HACKED R.A.T

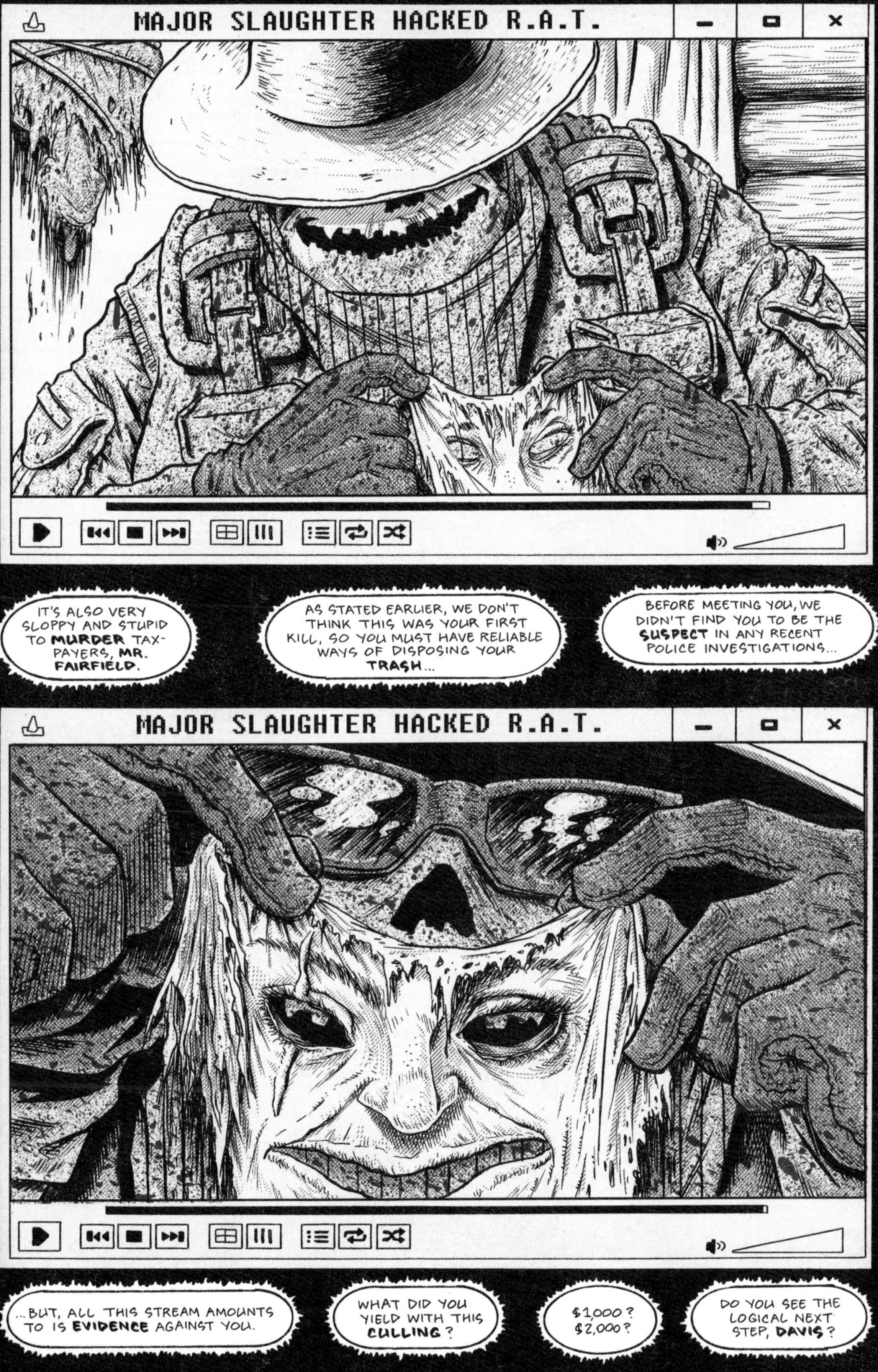
MAJOR SLAUGHTER HACKED R.A.T.
IT'S ALSO VERY SLOPPY AND STUPID TO MURDER TAX-PAYERS, MR. FAIRFIELD.
AS STATED EARLIER, WE DON'T THINK THIS WAS YOUR FIRST KILL, SO YOU MUST HAVE RELIABLE WAYS OF DISPOSING YOUR TRASH...
BEFORE MEETING YOU, WE DIDN'T FIND YOU TO BE THE SUSPECT IN ANY RECENT POLICE INVESTIGATIONS...
MAJOR SLAUGHTER HACKED R.A.T.
...BUT, ALL THIS STREAM AMOUNTS TO IS EVIDENCE AGAINST YOU.
WHAT DID YOU YIELD WITH THIS CULLING?
$1,000? $2,000?
DO YOU SEE THE LOGICAL NEXT STEP, DAVIS?

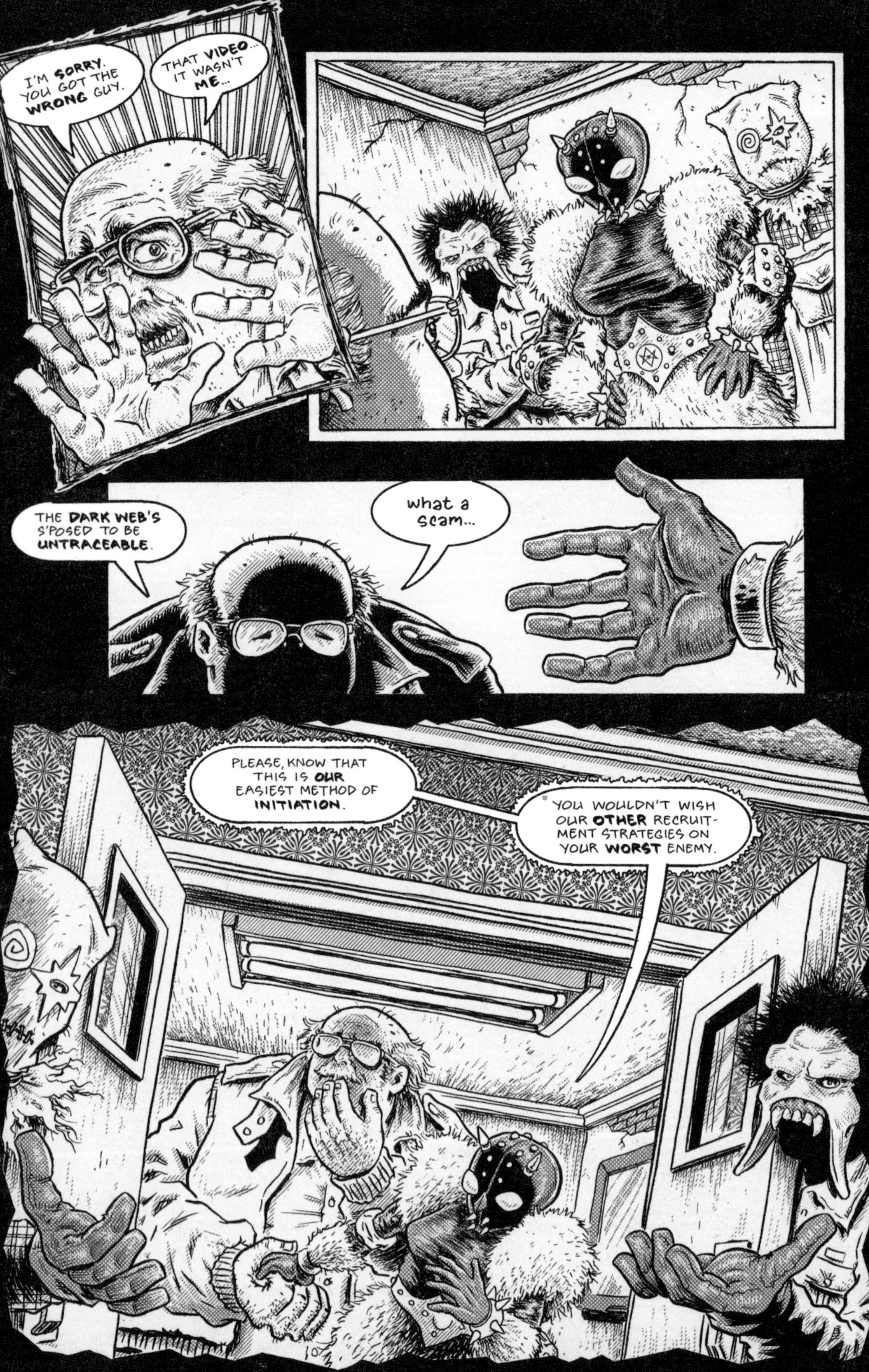

I'M SORRY. YOU GOT THE WRONG GUY.
THAT VIDEO... IT WASN'T ME...
THE DARK WEB'S S'POSED TO BE UNTRACEABLE.
what a scam...
PLEASE, KNOW THAT THIS IS OUR EASIEST METHOD OF INITIATION.
YOU WOULDN'T WISH OUR OTHER RECRUIT- MENT STRATEGIES ON YOUR WORST ENEMY.

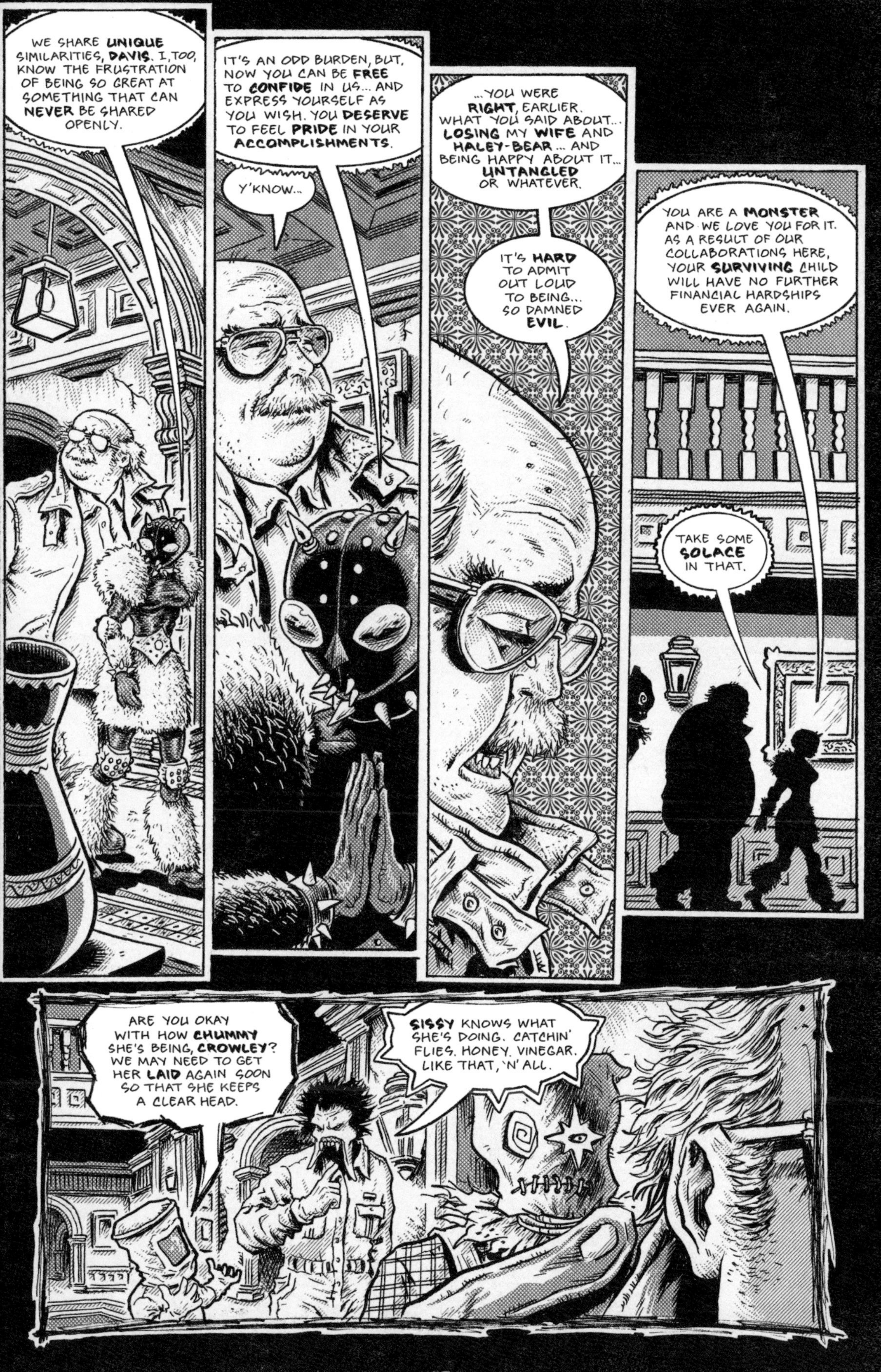
WE SHARE UNIQUE SIMILARITIES, DAVIS. I, TOO, KNOW THE FRUSTRATION OF BEING SO GREAT AT SOMETHING THAT CAN NEVER BE SHARED OPENLY.
IT'S AN ODD BURDEN, BUT, NOW YOU CAN BE FREE TO CONFIDE IN US... AND EXPRESS YOURSELF AS YOU WISH. YOU DESERVE TO FEEL PRIDE IN YOUR ACCOMPLISHMENTS.
Y'KNOW...
...YOU WERE RIGHT, EARLIER. WHAT YOU SAID ABOUT... LOSING MY WIFE AND HALEY-BEAR... AND BEING HAPPY ABOUT IT... UNTANGLED OR WHATEVER.
IT'S HARD TO ADMIT OUT LOUD TO BEING... SO DAMNED EVIL.
YOU ARE A MONSTER AND WE LOVE YOU FOR IT. AS A RESULT OF OUR COLLABORATIONS HERE, YOUR SURVIVING CHILD WILL HAVE NO FURTHER FINANCIAL HARDSHIPS EVER AGAIN.
TAKE SOME SOLACE IN THAT.
ARE YOU OKAY WITH HOW CHUMMY SHE'S BEING, CROWLEY? WE MAY NEED TO GET HER LAID AGAIN SOON SO THAT SHE KEEPS A CLEAR HEAD.
SISSY KNOWS WHAT SHE'S DOING. CATCHIN' FLIES. HONEY. VINEGAR. LIKE THAT, 'N' ALL.

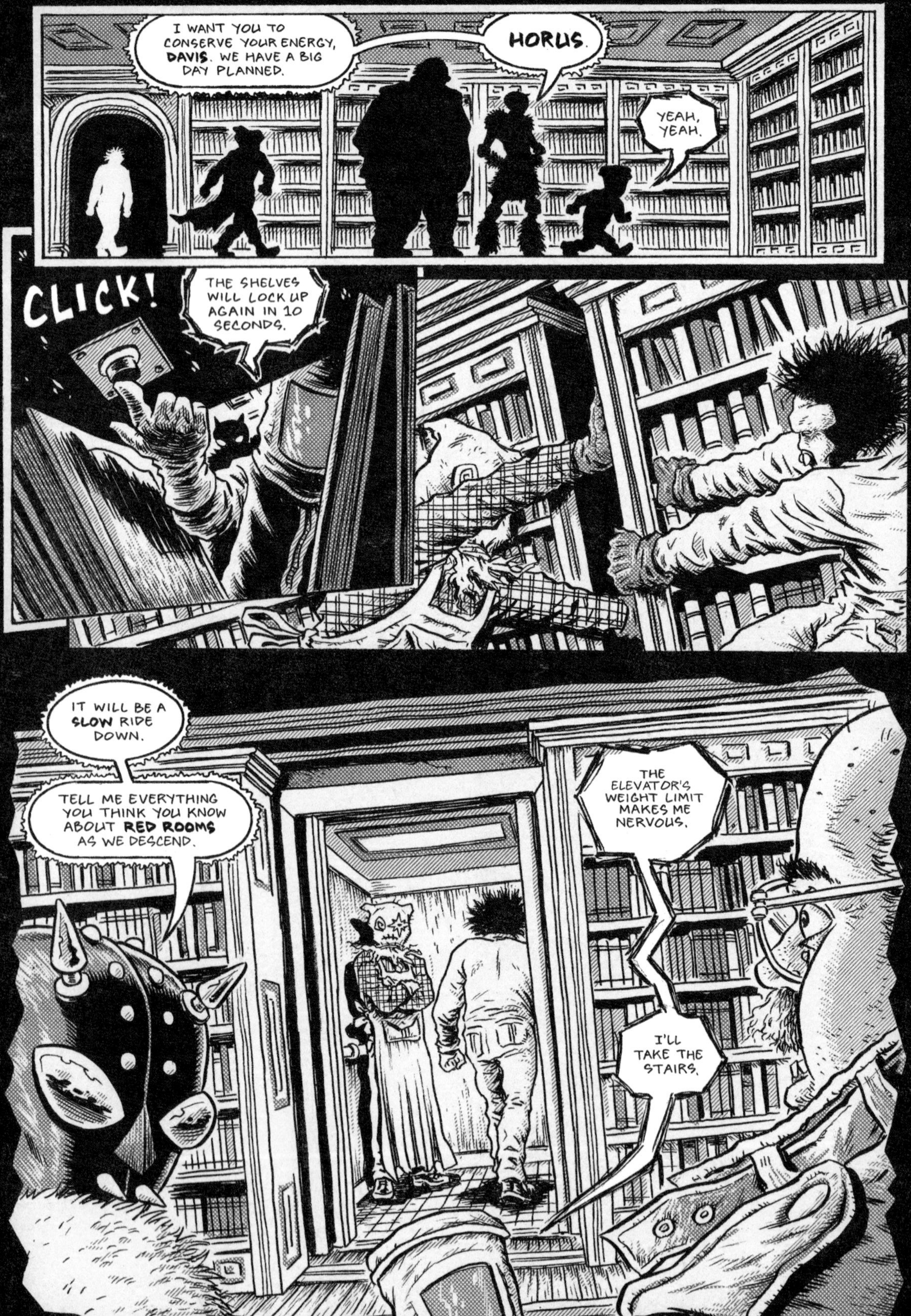
I WANT YOU TO CONSERVE YOUR ENERGY, DAVIS. WE HAVE A BIG DAY PLANNED.
HORUS.
YEAH, YEAH.
CLICK!
THE SHELVES WILL LOCK UP AGAIN IN 10 SECONDS.
IT WILL BE A SLOW RIDE DOWN.
TELL ME EVERYTHING YOU THINK YOU KNOW ABOUT RED ROOMS AS WE DESCEND.
THE ELEVATOR'S WEIGHT LIMIT MAKES ME NERVOUS.
I'LL TAKE THE STAIRS.

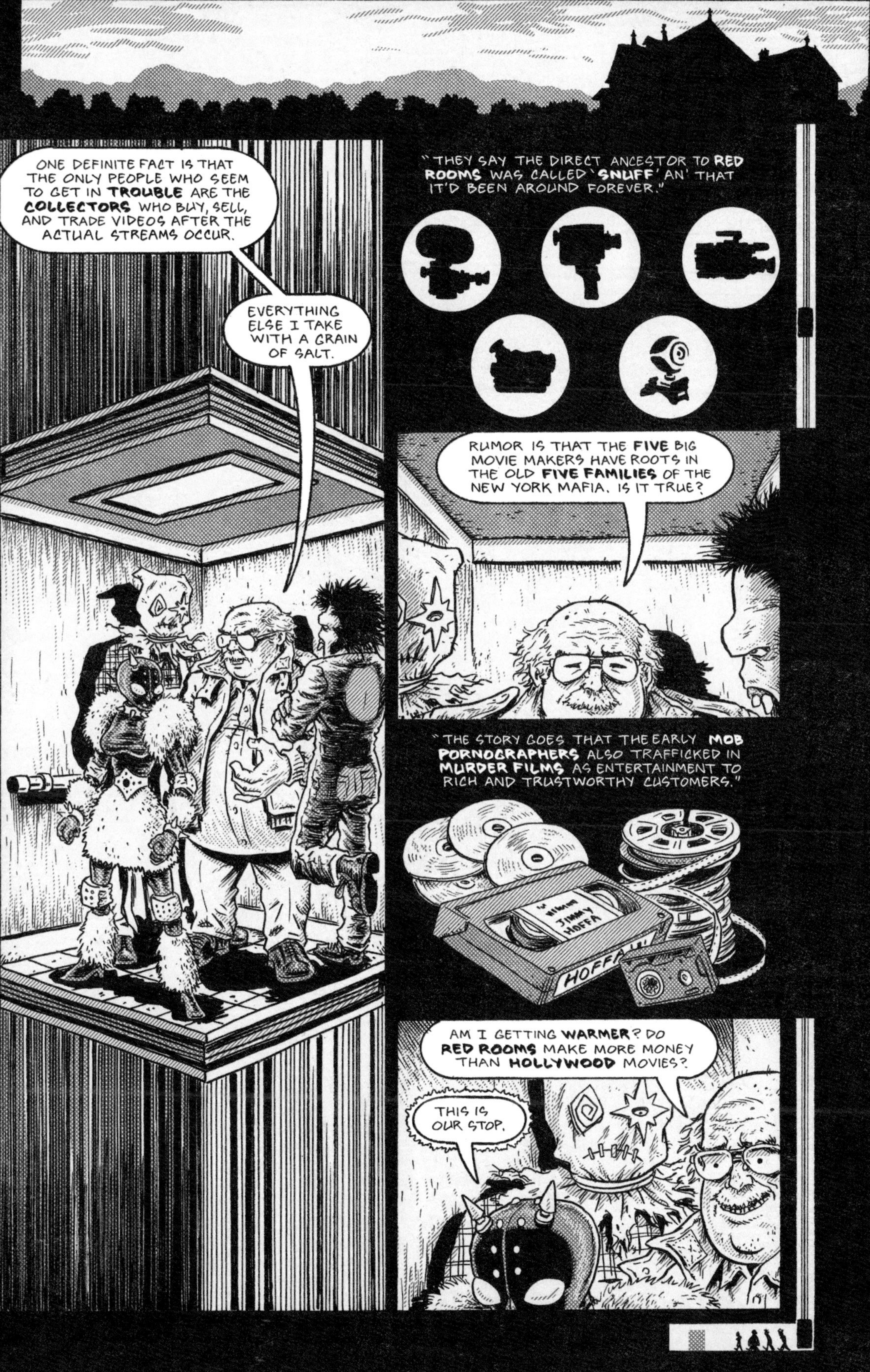

ONE DEFINITE FACT IS THAT THE ONLY PEOPLE WHO SEEM TO GET IN TROUBLE ARE THE COLLECTORS WHO BUY, SELL, AND TRADE VIDEOS AFTER THE ACTUAL STREAMS OCCUR.
EVERYTHING ELSE I TAKE WITH A GRAIN OF SALT.
"THEY SAY THE DIRECT ANCESTOR TO RED ROOMS WAS CALLED 'SNUFF' AN' THAT IT'D BEEN AROUND FOREVER."
RUMOR IS THAT THE FIVE BIG MOVIE MAKERS HAVE ROOTS IN THE OLD FIVE FAMILIES OF THE NEW YORK MAFIA. IS IT TRUE?
"THE STORY GOES THAT THE EARLY MOB PORNOGRAPHERS ALSO TRAFFICKED IN MURDER FILMS AS ENTERTAINMENT TO RICH AND TRUSTWORTHY CUSTOMERS."
JIMMY HOFFA
HOFFA
AM I GETTING WARMER? DO RED ROOMS MAKE MORE MONEY THAN HOLLYWOOD MOVIES?
THIS IS OUR STOP.

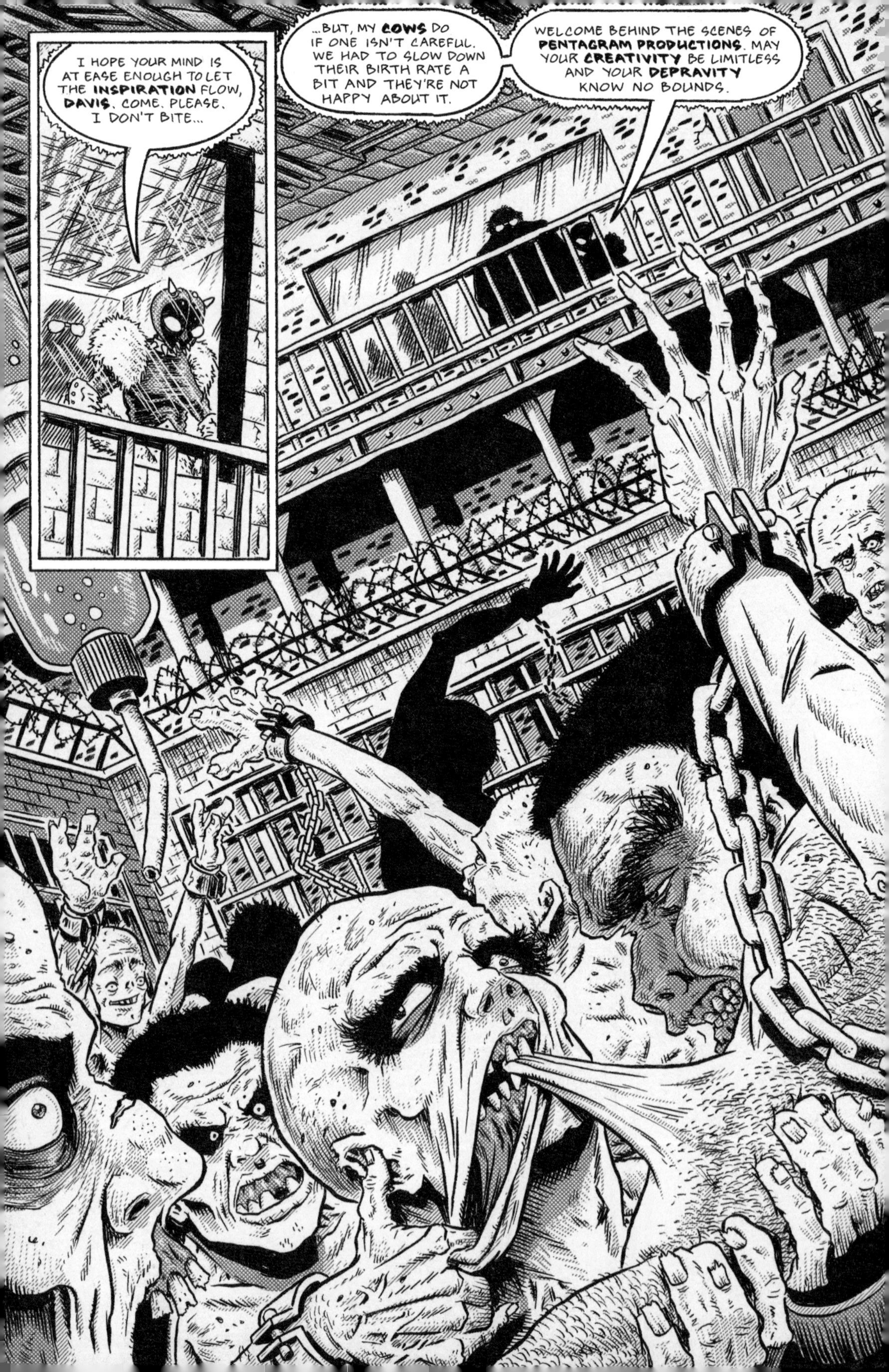
I HOPE YOUR MIND IS AT EASE ENOUGH TO LET THE INSPIRATION FLOW, DAVIS. COME. PLEASE. I DON'T BITE...
...BUT, MY COWS DO IF ONE ISN'T CAREFUL. WE HAD TO SLOW DOWN THEIR BIRTH RATE A BIT AND THEY'RE NOT HAPPY ABOUT IT.
WELCOME BEHIND THE SCENES OF PENTAGRAM PRODUCTIONS. MAY YOUR CREATIVITY BE LIMITLESS AND YOUR DEPRAVITY KNOW NO BOUNDS.

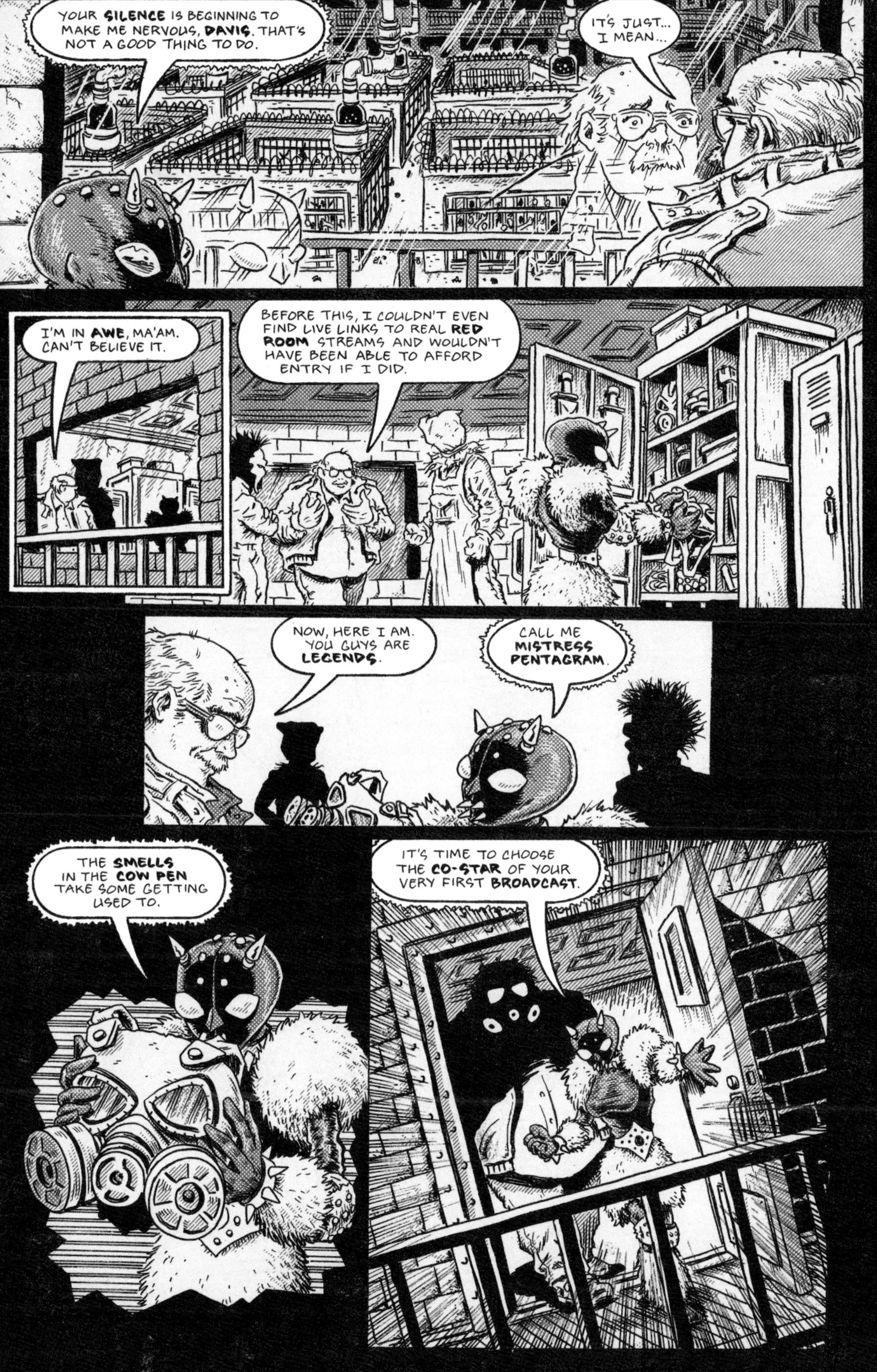
YOUR **SILENCE** IS BEGINNING TO MAKE ME NERVOUS, **DAVIS**. THAT'S NOT A GOOD THING TO DO.
IT'S JUST... I MEAN...
I'M IN **AWE**, MA'AM. CAN'T BELIEVE IT.
BEFORE THIS, I COULDN'T EVEN FIND LIVE LINKS TO REAL **RED ROOM** STREAMS AND WOULDN'T HAVE BEEN ABLE TO AFFORD ENTRY IF I DID.
NOW, HERE I AM. YOU GUYS ARE **LEGENDS**.
CALL ME **MISTRESS PENTAGRAM**.
THE **SMELLS** IN THE **COW PEN** TAKE SOME GETTING USED TO.
IT'S TIME TO CHOOSE THE **CO-STAR** OF YOUR VERY FIRST **BROADCAST**.

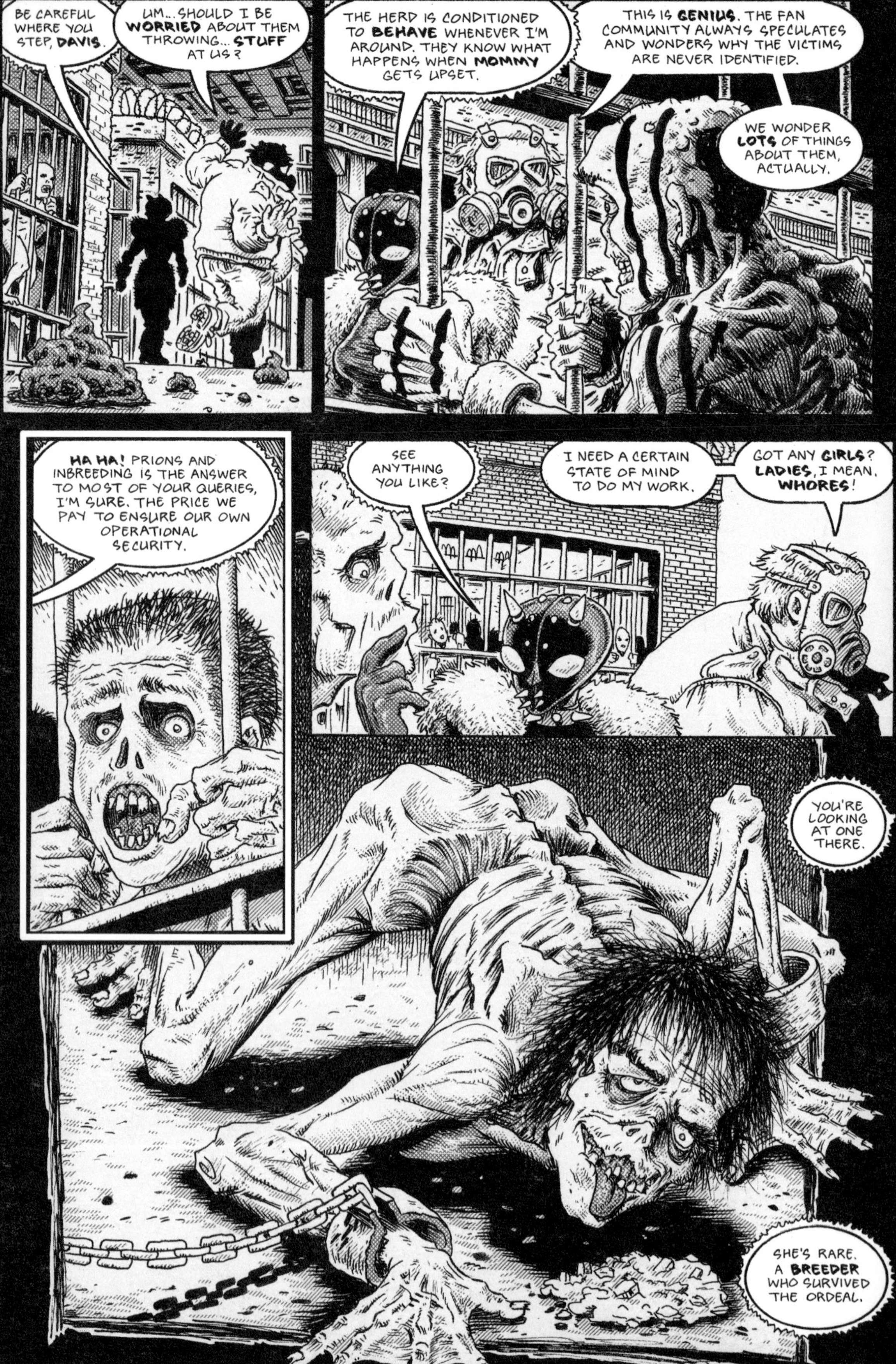
BE CAREFUL WHERE YOU STEP, DAVIS.
UM... SHOULD I BE WORRIED ABOUT THEM THROWING... STUFF AT US?
THE HERD IS CONDITIONED TO BEHAVE WHENEVER I'M AROUND. THEY KNOW WHAT HAPPENS WHEN MOMMY GETS UPSET.
THIS IS GENIUS. THE FAN COMMUNITY ALWAYS SPECULATES AND WONDERS WHY THE VICTIMS ARE NEVER IDENTIFIED.
WE WONDER LOTS OF THINGS ABOUT THEM, ACTUALLY.
HA HA! PRIONS AND INBREEDING IS THE ANSWER TO MOST OF YOUR QUERIES, I'M SURE. THE PRICE WE PAY TO ENSURE OUR OWN OPERATIONAL SECURITY.
SEE ANYTHING YOU LIKE?
I NEED A CERTAIN STATE OF MIND TO DO MY WORK.
GOT ANY GIRLS? LADIES, I MEAN. WHORES!
YOU'RE LOOKING AT ONE THERE.
SHE'S RARE. A BREEDER WHO SURVIVED THE ORDEAL.

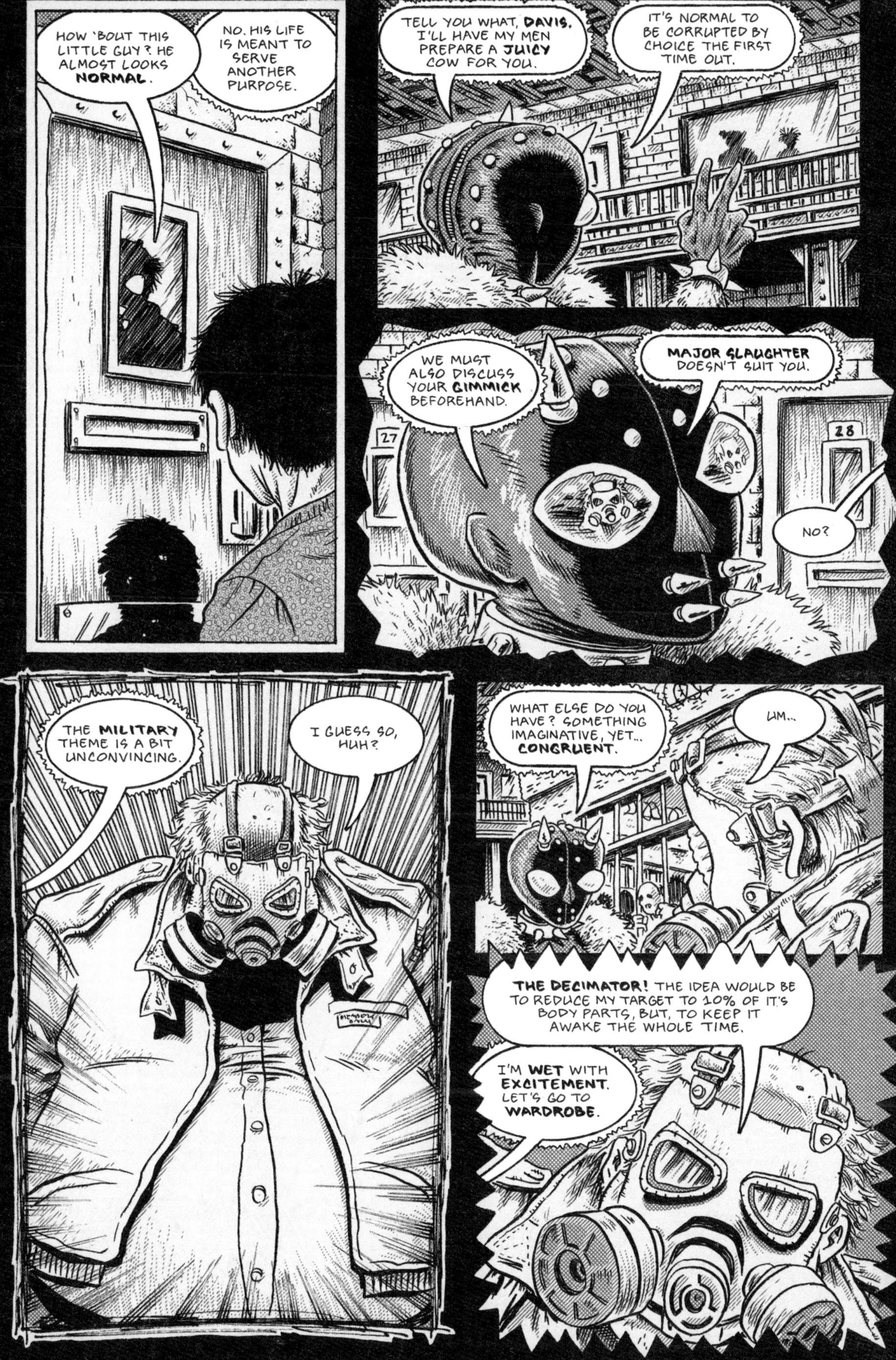
HOW 'BOUT THIS LITTLE GUY? HE ALMOST LOOKS NORMAL.
NO. HIS LIFE IS MEANT TO SERVE ANOTHER PURPOSE.
TELL YOU WHAT, DAVIS. I'LL HAVE MY MEN PREPARE A JUICY COW FOR YOU.
IT'S NORMAL TO BE CORRUPTED BY CHOICE THE FIRST TIME OUT.
WE MUST ALSO DISCUSS YOUR GIMMICK BEFOREHAND.
MAJOR SLAUGHTER DOESN'T SUIT YOU.
27
28
NO?
THE MILITARY THEME IS A BIT UNCONVINCING.
I GUESS SO, HUH?
WHAT ELSE DO YOU HAVE? SOMETHING IMAGINATIVE, YET... CONGRUENT.
UM...
THE DECIMATOR! THE IDEA WOULD BE TO REDUCE MY TARGET TO 10% OF IT'S BODY PARTS, BUT, TO KEEP IT AWAKE THE WHOLE TIME.
I'M WET WITH EXCITEMENT. LET'S GO TO WARDROBE.

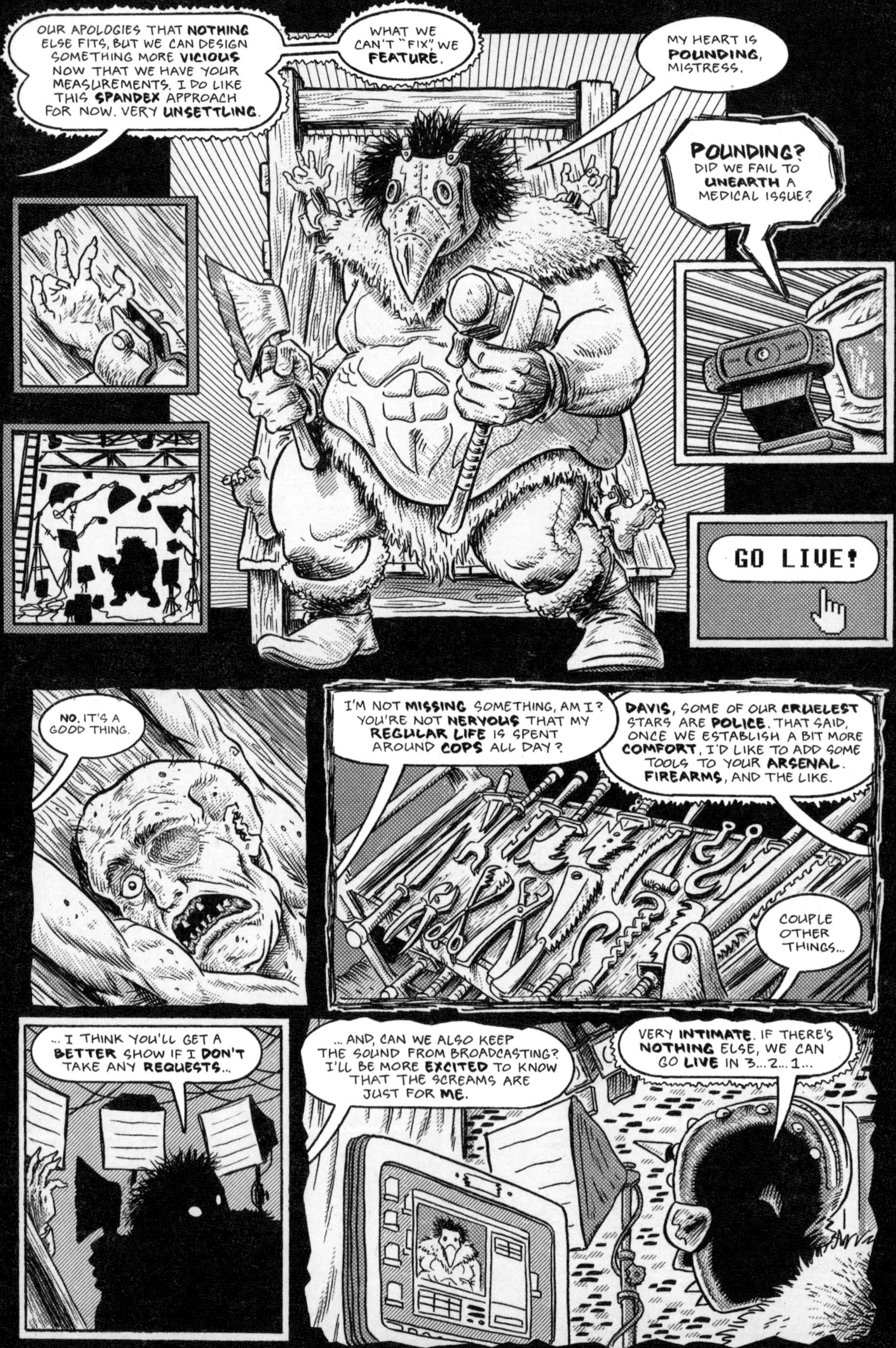

OUR APOLOGIES THAT NOTHING ELSE FITS, BUT WE CAN DESIGN SOMETHING MORE VICIOUS NOW THAT WE HAVE YOUR MEASUREMENTS. I DO LIKE THIS SPANDEX APPROACH FOR NOW. VERY UNSETTLING.
WHAT WE CAN'T "FIX," WE FEATURE.
MY HEART IS POUNDING, MISTRESS.
POUNDING? DID WE FAIL TO UNEARTH A MEDICAL ISSUE?
GO LIVE!
NO, IT'S A GOOD THING.
I'M NOT MISSING SOMETHING, AM I? YOU'RE NOT NERVOUS THAT MY REGULAR LIFE IS SPENT AROUND COPS ALL DAY?
DAVIS, SOME OF OUR CRUELEST STARS ARE POLICE. THAT SAID, ONCE WE ESTABLISH A BIT MORE COMFORT, I'D LIKE TO ADD SOME TOOLS TO YOUR ARSENAL. FIREARMS, AND THE LIKE.
COUPLE OTHER THINGS...
... I THINK YOU'LL GET A BETTER SHOW IF I DON'T TAKE ANY REQUESTS...
... AND, CAN WE ALSO KEEP THE SOUND FROM BROADCASTING? I'LL BE MORE EXCITED TO KNOW THAT THE SCREAMS ARE JUST FOR ME.
VERY INTIMATE. IF THERE'S NOTHING ELSE, WE CAN GO LIVE IN 3... 2... 1...

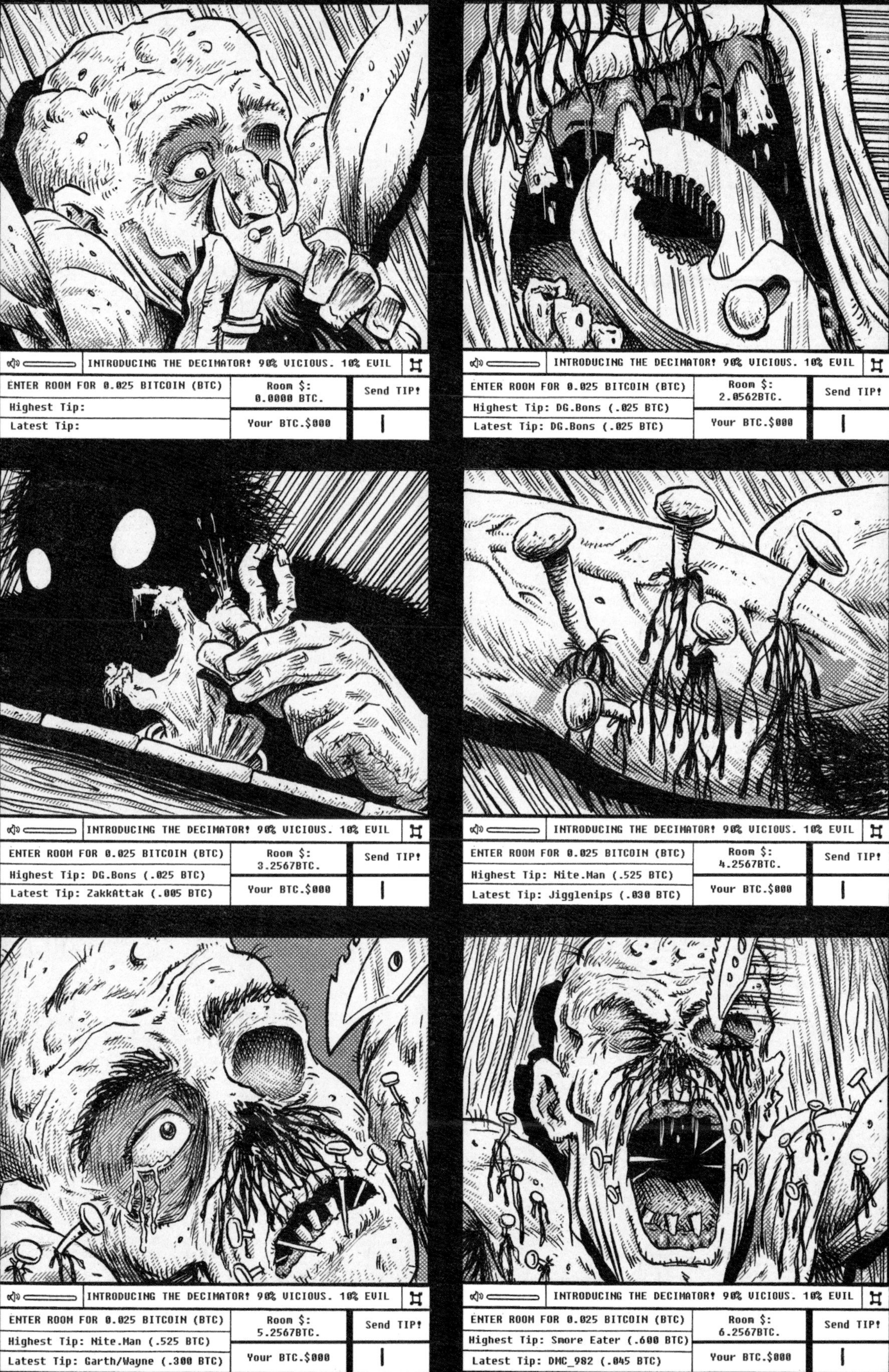
INTRODUCING THE DECIMATOR! 90% VICIOUS. 10% EVIL
ENTER ROOM FOR 0.025 BITCOIN (BTC)
Highest Tip:
Latest Tip:
Room $: 0.0000 BTC.
Your BTC.$000
Send TIP!
INTRODUCING THE DECIMATOR! 90% VICIOUS. 10% EVIL
ENTER ROOM FOR 0.025 BITCOIN (BTC)
Highest Tip: DG.Bons (.025 BTC)
Latest Tip: DG.Bons (.025 BTC)
Room $: 2.0562BTC.
Your BTC.$000
Send TIP!
INTRODUCING THE DECIMATOR! 90% VICIOUS. 10% EVIL
ENTER ROOM FOR 0.025 BITCOIN (BTC)
Highest Tip: DG.Bons (.025 BTC)
Latest Tip: ZakkAttak (.005 BTC)
Room $: 3.2567BTC.
Your BTC.$000
Send TIP!
INTRODUCING THE DECIMATOR! 90% VICIOUS. 10% EVIL
ENTER ROOM FOR 0.025 BITCOIN (BTC)
Highest Tip: Nite.Man (.525 BTC)
Latest Tip: Jigglenips (.030 BTC)
Room $: 4.2567BTC.
Your BTC.$000
Send TIP!
INTRODUCING THE DECIMATOR! 90% VICIOUS. 10% EVIL
ENTER ROOM FOR 0.025 BITCOIN (BTC)
Highest Tip: Nite.Man (.525 BTC)
Latest Tip: Garth/Wayne (.300 BTC)
Room $: 5.2567BTC.
Your BTC.$000
Send TIP!
INTRODUCING THE DECIMATOR! 90% VICIOUS. 10% EVIL
ENTER ROOM FOR 0.025 BITCOIN (BTC)
Highest Tip: Smore Eater (.600 BTC)
Latest Tip: DMC_982 (.045 BTC)
Room $: 6.2567BTC.
Your BTC.$000
Send TIP!

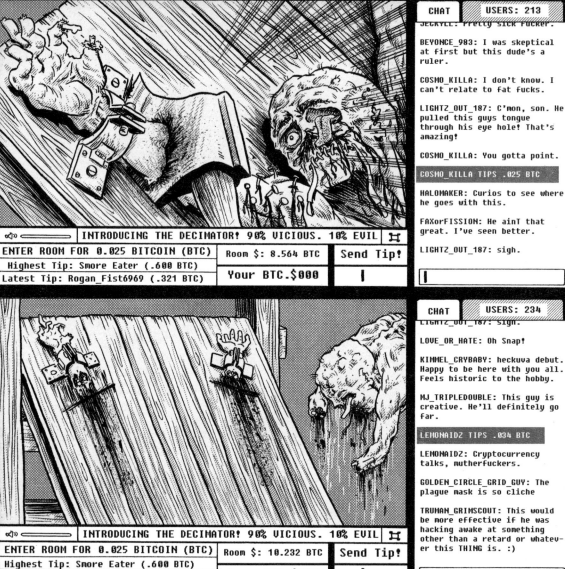

Panel 1

CHAT — USERS: 213

JECKYLL: Pretty sick fucker.

BEYONCE_983: I was skeptical at first but this dude's a ruler.

COSMO_KILLA: I don't know. I can't relate to fat fucks.

LIGHTZ_OUT_187: C'mon, son. He pulled this guys tongue through his eye hole! That's amazing!

COSMO_KILLA: You gotta point.

COSMO_KILLA TIPS .025 BTC

HALOMAKER: Curios to see where he goes with this.

FAXorFISSION: He ainT that great. I've seen better.

LIGHTZ_OUT_187: sigh.

INTRODUCING THE DECIMATOR! 90% VICIOUS. 10% EVIL

ENTER ROOM FOR 0.025 BITCOIN (BTC)
Highest Tip: Smore Eater (.600 BTC)
Latest Tip: Rogan_Fist6969 (.321 BTC)
Room $: 8.564 BTC
Your BTC.$000
Send Tip!

Panel 2

CHAT — USERS: 234

LIGHTZ_OUT_187: sigh.

LOVE_OR_HATE: Oh Snap!

KIMMEL_CRYBABY: heckuva debut. Happy to be here with you all. Feels historic to the hobby.

MJ_TRIPLEDOUBLE: This guy is creative. He'll definitely go far.

LEMONAIDZ TIPS .034 BTC

LEMONAIDZ: Cryptocurrency talks, mutherfuckers.

GOLDEN_CIRCLE_GRID_GUY: The plague mask is so cliche

TRUMAN_GRIMSCOUT: This would be more effective if he was hacking awake at something other than a retard or whatever this THING is. :)

INTRODUCING THE DECIMATOR! 90% VICIOUS. 10% EVIL

ENTER ROOM FOR 0.025 BITCOIN (BTC)
Highest Tip: Smore Eater (.600 BTC)
Latest Tip: LemonAIDZ (.034 BTC)
Room $: 10.232 BTC
Your BTC.$000
Send Tip!

Panel 3

CHAT — USERS: 279

er this THING is. :)

VAMPIRA_LIVES: Why do you have to say the ■R■ word, asshole.

RAW_SHARK_1986 TIPS .022 BTC

RAW_SHARK_1986: These multi-camera shots are so cinematic. Love Pentagram production values

NADSZACK: Regular folk would call this porn or gratuitious. Fucking soyboys.

GIRTY_GOODNESS: On one hand I'd like to get Red Rooms out of the shadows, but honestly would it be as fun if this shit was legal to watch?

DAMION_666_WAYNES: Ha! You're one of those legal, Death Row, Red Room advocates? Dream the fuck on!

INTRODUCING THE DECIMATOR! 90% VICIOUS. 10% EVIL

ENTER ROOM FOR 0.025 BITCOIN (BTC)
Highest Tip: Smore Eater (.600 BTC)
Latest Tip: Raw_Shark_1986 (.022 BTC)
Room $: 11.897 BTC
Your BTC.$000
Send Tip!

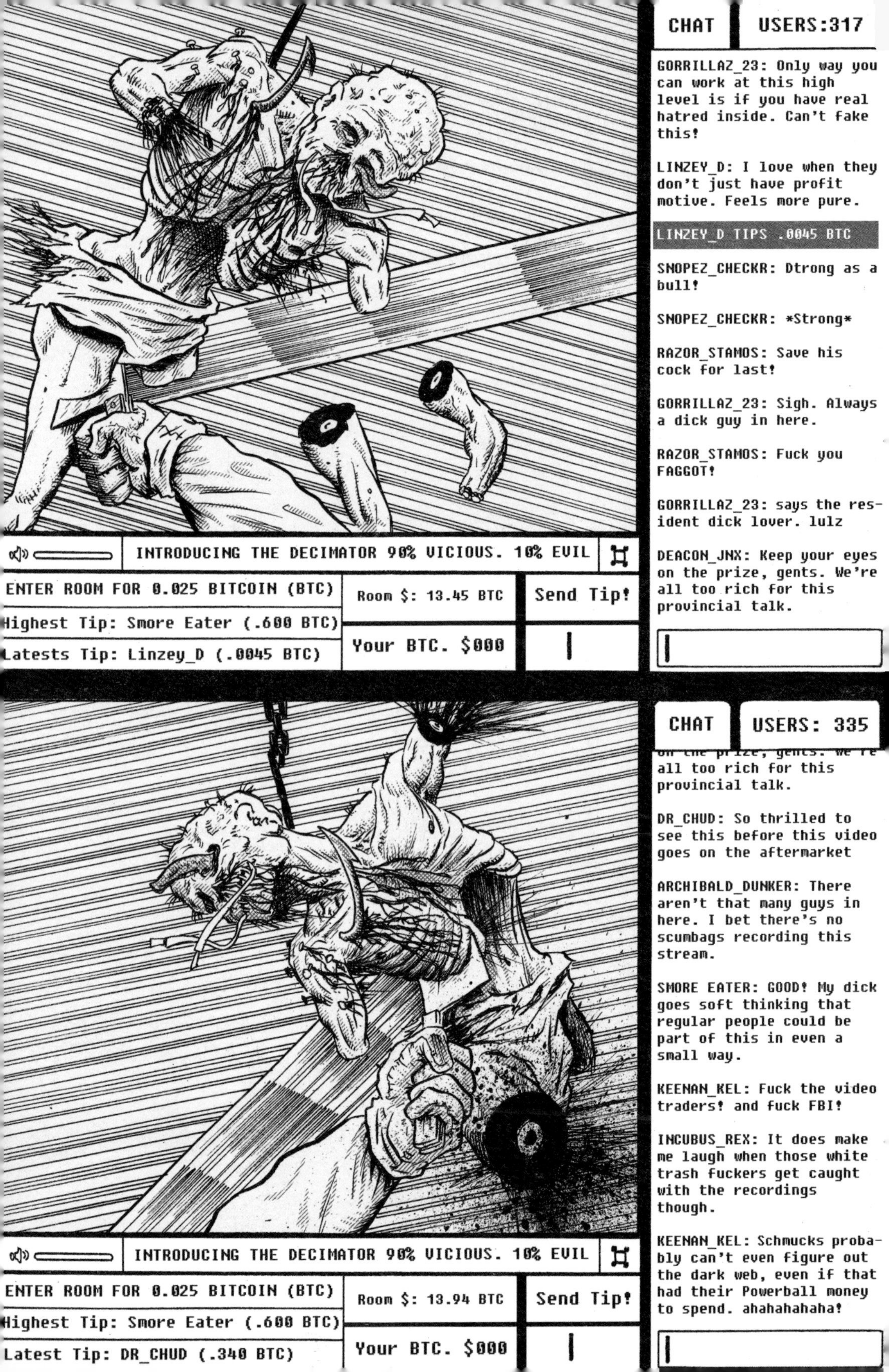
CHAT
USERS:317
GORRILLAZ_23: Only way you can work at this high level is if you have real hatred inside. Can't fake this!
LINZEY_D: I love when they don't just have profit motive. Feels more pure.
LINZEY_D TIPS .0045 BTC
SNOPEZ_CHECKR: Dtrong as a bull!
SNOPEZ_CHECKR: *Strong*
RAZOR_STAMOS: Save his cock for last!
GORRILLAZ_23: Sigh. Always a dick guy in here.
RAZOR_STAMOS: Fuck you FAGGOT!
GORRILLAZ_23: says the resident dick lover. lulz
DEACON_JNX: Keep your eyes on the prize, gents. We're all too rich for this provincial talk.
INTRODUCING THE DECIMATOR 90% VICIOUS. 10% EVIL
ENTER ROOM FOR 0.025 BITCOIN (BTC)
Room $: 13.45 BTC
Send Tip!
Highest Tip: Smore Eater (.600 BTC)
Your BTC. $000
Latests Tip: Linzey_D (.0045 BTC)
CHAT
USERS: 335
all too rich for this provincial talk.
DR_CHUD: So thrilled to see this before this video goes on the aftermarket
ARCHIBALD_DUNKER: There aren't that many guys in here. I bet there's no scumbags recording this stream.
SMORE EATER: GOOD! My dick goes soft thinking that regular people could be part of this in even a small way.
KEENAN_KEL: Fuck the video traders! and fuck FBI!
INCUBUS_REX: It does make me laugh when those white trash fuckers get caught with the recordings though.
KEENAN_KEL: Schmucks probably can't even figure out the dark web, even if that had their Powerball money to spend. ahahahahaha!
INTRODUCING THE DECIMATOR 90% VICIOUS. 10% EVIL
ENTER ROOM FOR 0.025 BITCOIN (BTC)
Room $: 13.94 BTC
Send Tip!
Highest Tip: Smore Eater (.600 BTC)
Your BTC. $000
Latest Tip: DR_CHUD (.340 BTC)

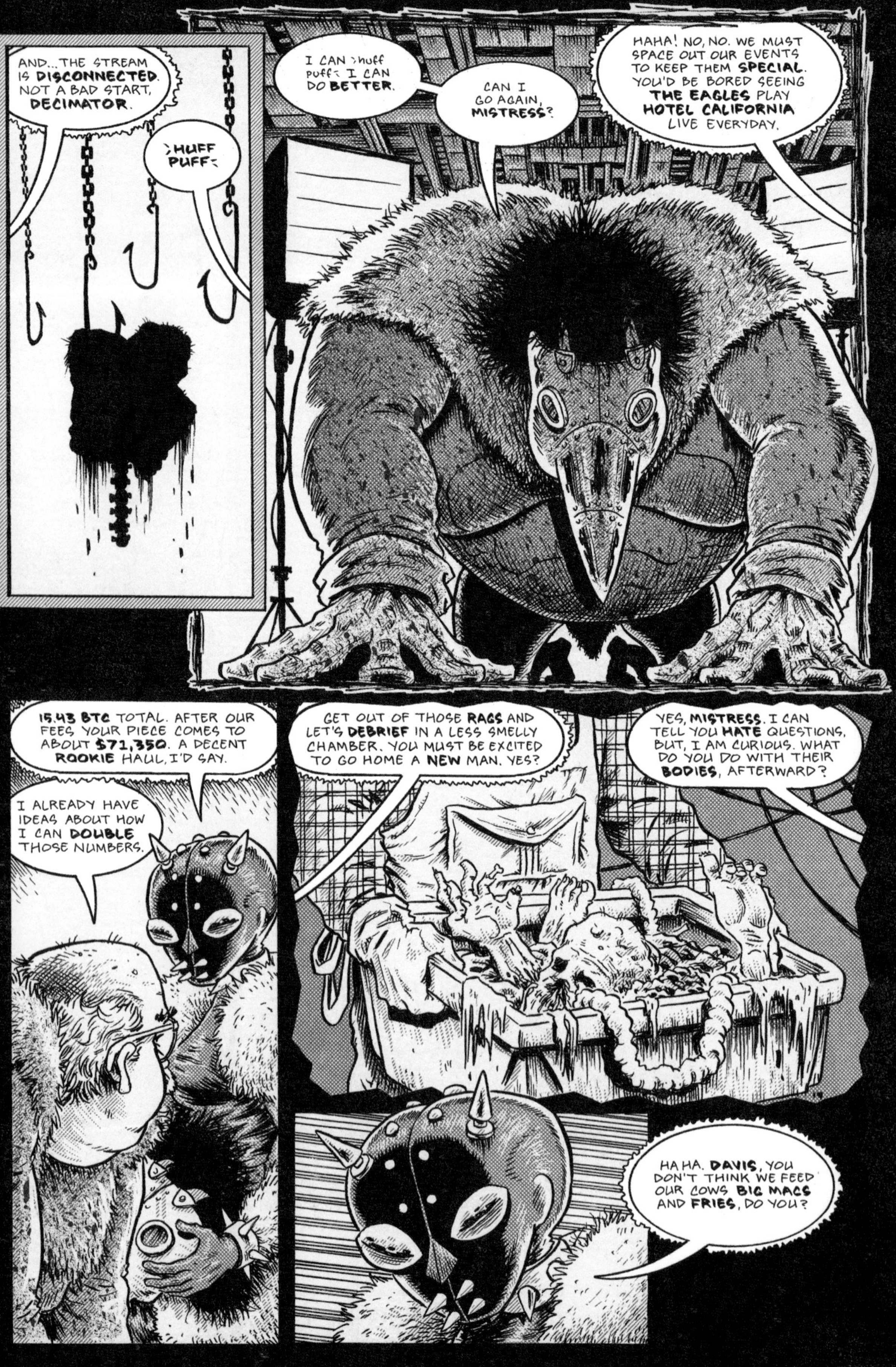
AND... THE STREAM IS DISCONNECTED. NOT A BAD START, DECIMATOR.
>HUFF PUFF<
I CAN >huff puff< I CAN DO BETTER.
CAN I GO AGAIN, MISTRESS?
HAHA! NO, NO. WE MUST SPACE OUT OUR EVENTS TO KEEP THEM SPECIAL. YOU'D BE BORED SEEING THE EAGLES PLAY HOTEL CALIFORNIA LIVE EVERYDAY.
15.43 BTC TOTAL. AFTER OUR FEES YOUR PIECE COMES TO ABOUT $71,350. A DECENT ROOKIE HAUL, I'D SAY.
I ALREADY HAVE IDEAS ABOUT HOW I CAN DOUBLE THOSE NUMBERS.
GET OUT OF THOSE RAGS AND LET'S DEBRIEF IN A LESS SMELLY CHAMBER. YOU MUST BE EXCITED TO GO HOME A NEW MAN, YES?
YES, MISTRESS. I CAN TELL YOU HATE QUESTIONS, BUT, I AM CURIOUS. WHAT DO YOU DO WITH THEIR BODIES, AFTERWARD?
HA HA. DAVIS, YOU DON'T THINK WE FEED OUR COWS BIG MACS AND FRIES, DO YOU?

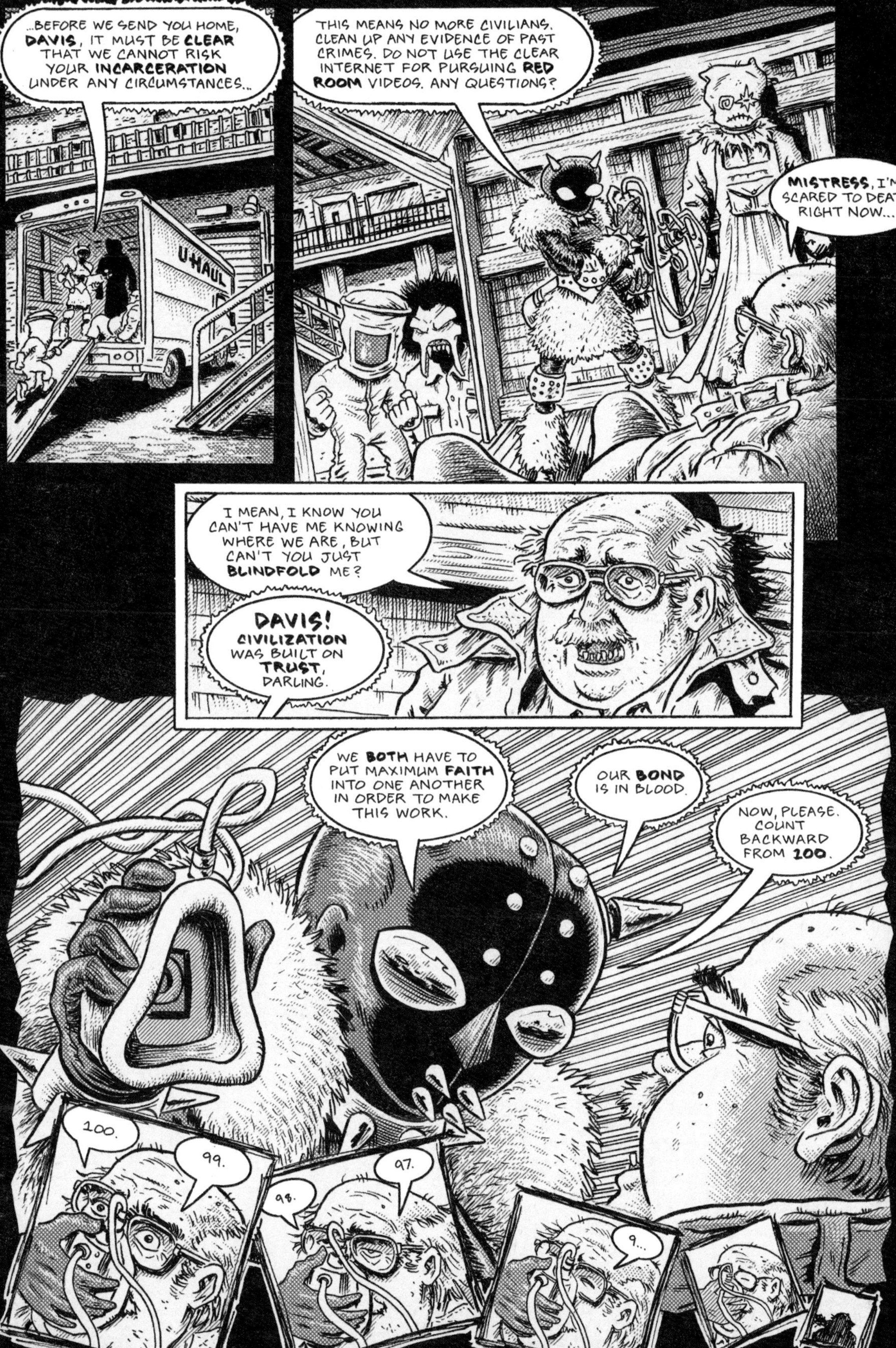
...BEFORE WE SEND YOU HOME, DAVIS, IT MUST BE CLEAR THAT WE CANNOT RISK YOUR INCARCERATION UNDER ANY CIRCUMSTANCES...
U-HAUL
THIS MEANS NO MORE CIVILIANS. CLEAN UP ANY EVIDENCE OF PAST CRIMES. DO NOT USE THE CLEAR INTERNET FOR PURSUING RED ROOM VIDEOS. ANY QUESTIONS?
MISTRESS, I'M SCARED TO DEATH RIGHT NOW...
I MEAN, I KNOW YOU CAN'T HAVE ME KNOWING WHERE WE ARE, BUT CAN'T YOU JUST BLINDFOLD ME?
DAVIS! CIVILIZATION WAS BUILT ON TRUST, DARLING.
WE BOTH HAVE TO PUT MAXIMUM FAITH INTO ONE ANOTHER IN ORDER TO MAKE THIS WORK.
OUR BOND IS IN BLOOD.
NOW, PLEASE. COUNT BACKWARD FROM 200.
100.
99.
98.
97.
9...

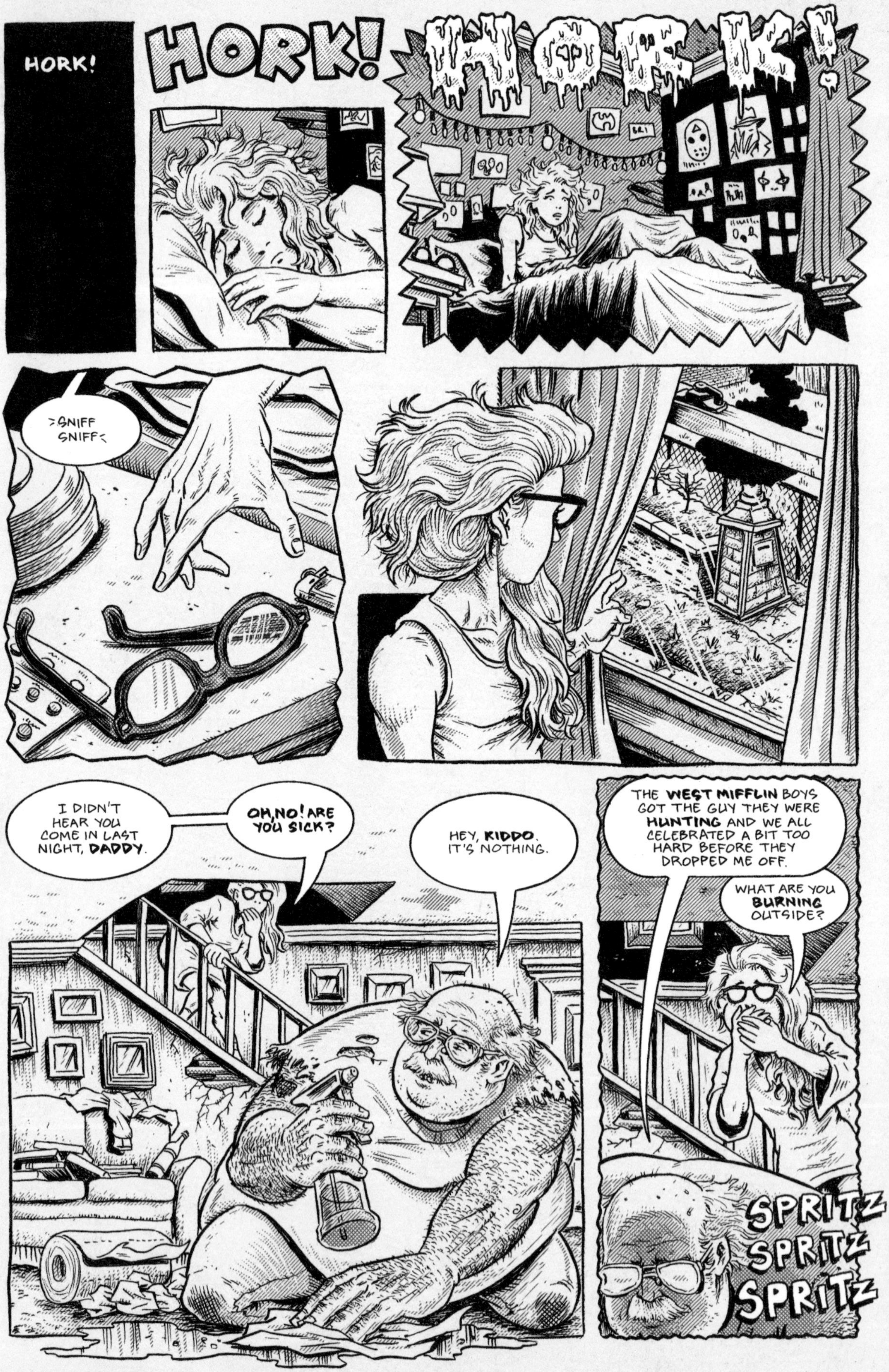
HORK!
HORK!
HORK!
>SNIFF SNIFF<
I DIDN'T HEAR YOU COME IN LAST NIGHT, DADDY.
OH, NO! ARE YOU SICK?
HEY, KIDDO. IT'S NOTHING.
THE WEST MIFFLIN BOYS GOT THE GUY THEY WERE HUNTING AND WE ALL CELEBRATED A BIT TOO HARD BEFORE THEY DROPPED ME OFF.
WHAT ARE YOU BURNING OUTSIDE?
SPRITZ SPRITZ SPRITZ

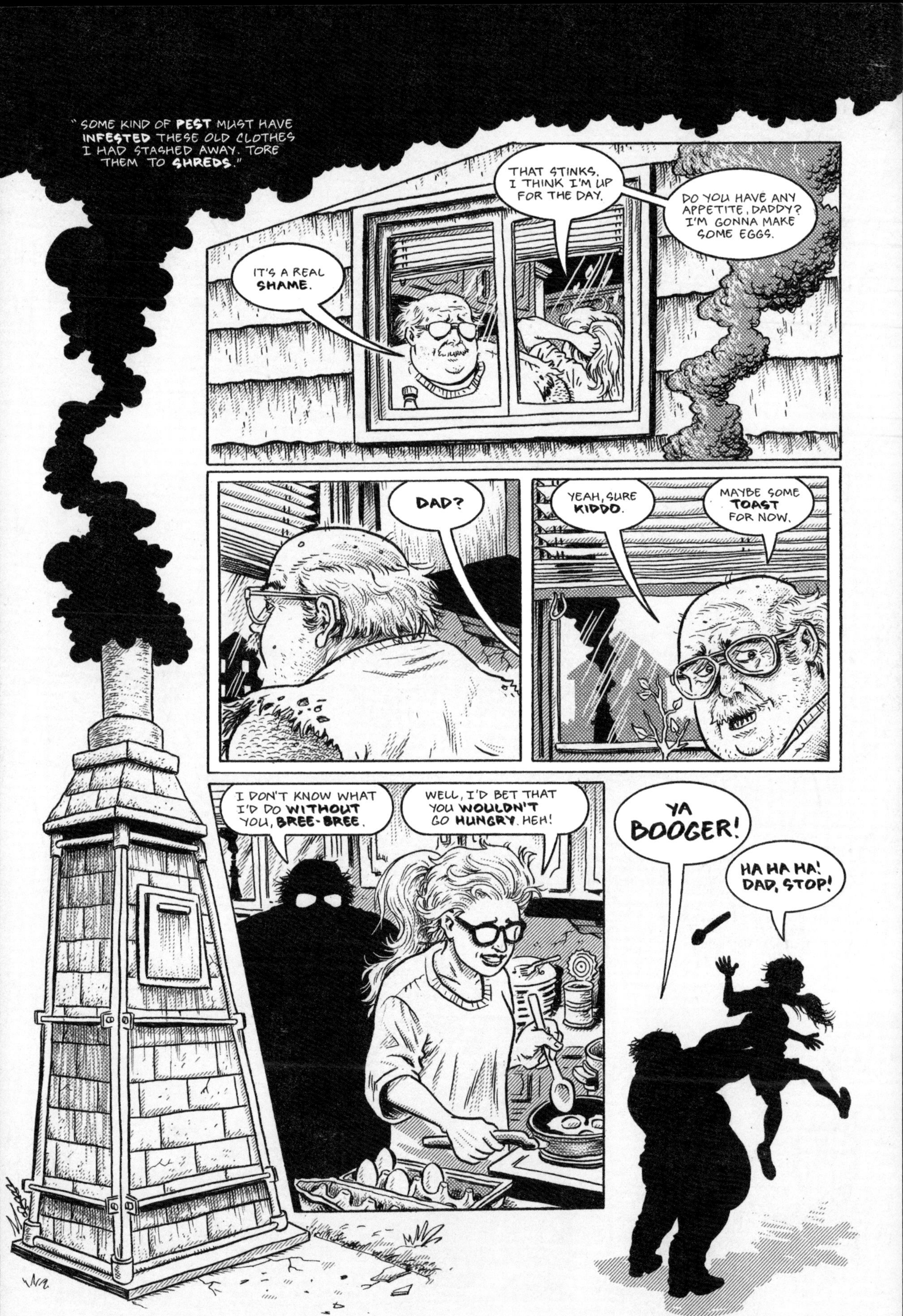
"SOME KIND OF PEST MUST HAVE INFESTED THESE OLD CLOTHES I HAD STASHED AWAY. TORE THEM TO SHREDS."
IT'S A REAL SHAME.
THAT STINKS. I THINK I'M UP FOR THE DAY.
DO YOU HAVE ANY APPETITE, DADDY? I'M GONNA MAKE SOME EGGS.
DAD?
YEAH, SURE KIDDO.
MAYBE SOME TOAST FOR NOW.
I DON'T KNOW WHAT I'D DO WITHOUT YOU, BREE-BREE.
WELL, I'D BET THAT YOU WOULDN'T GO HUNGRY. HEH!
YA BOOGER!
HA HA HA! DAD, STOP!

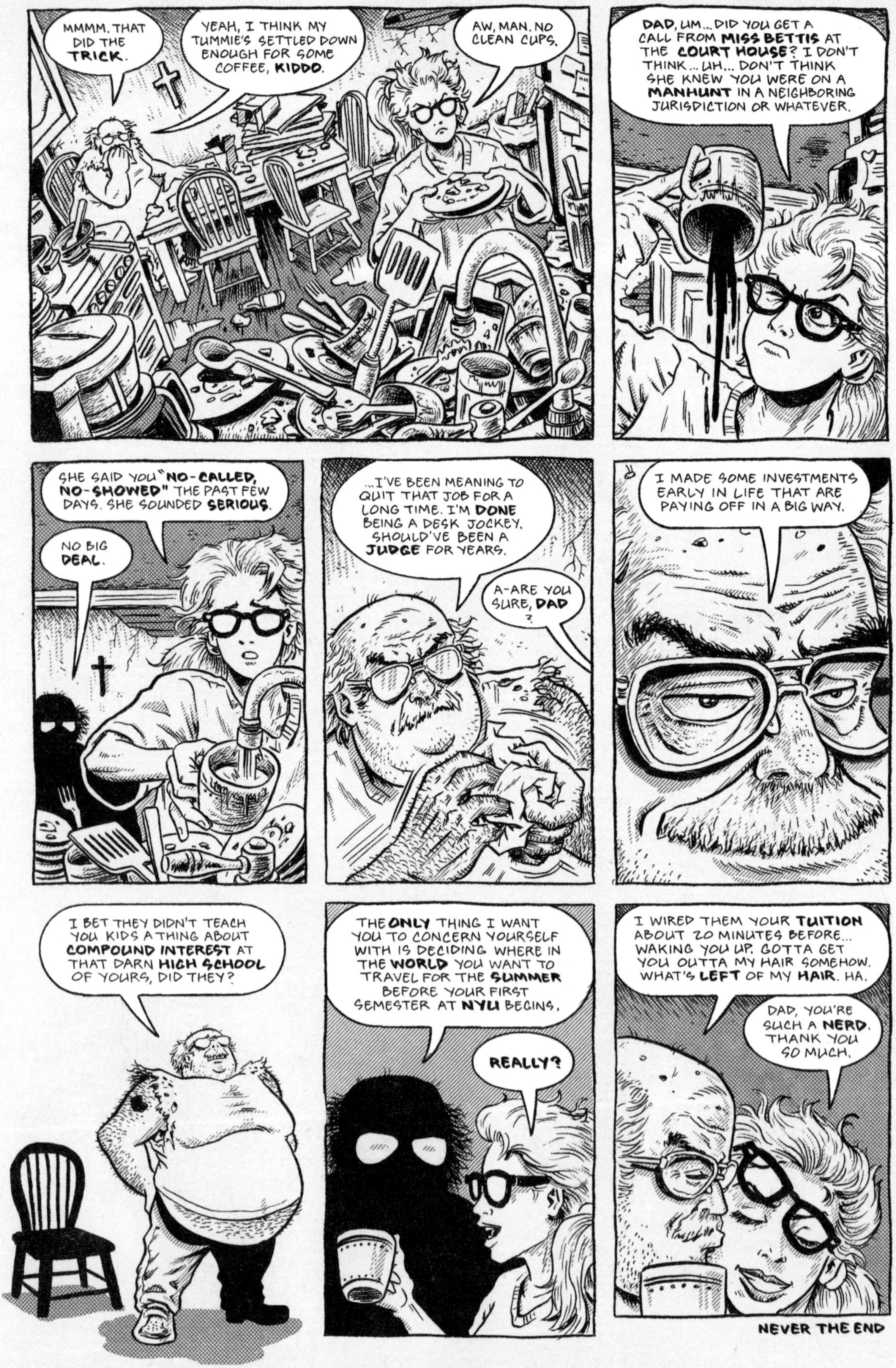
MMMM. THAT DID THE TRICK.
YEAH, I THINK MY TUMMIE'S SETTLED DOWN ENOUGH FOR SOME COFFEE, KIDDO.
AW, MAN. NO CLEAN CUPS.
DAD, UM... DID YOU GET A CALL FROM MISS BETTIS AT THE COURT HOUSE? I DON'T THINK... UH... DON'T THINK SHE KNEW YOU WERE ON A MANHUNT IN A NEIGHBORING JURISDICTION OR WHATEVER.
SHE SAID YOU "NO-CALLED, NO-SHOWED" THE PAST FEW DAYS. SHE SOUNDED SERIOUS.
NO BIG DEAL.
...I'VE BEEN MEANING TO QUIT THAT JOB FOR A LONG TIME. I'M DONE BEING A DESK JOCKEY. SHOULD'VE BEEN A JUDGE FOR YEARS.
A-ARE YOU SURE, DAD?
I MADE SOME INVESTMENTS EARLY IN LIFE THAT ARE PAYING OFF IN A BIG WAY.
I BET THEY DIDN'T TEACH YOU KIDS A THING ABOUT COMPOUND INTEREST AT THAT DARN HIGH SCHOOL OF YOURS, DID THEY?
THE ONLY THING I WANT YOU TO CONCERN YOURSELF WITH IS DECIDING WHERE IN THE WORLD YOU WANT TO TRAVEL FOR THE SUMMER BEFORE YOUR FIRST SEMESTER AT NYU BEGINS.
REALLY?
I WIRED THEM YOUR TUITION ABOUT 20 MINUTES BEFORE... WAKING YOU UP. GOTTA GET YOU OUTTA MY HAIR SOMEHOW. WHAT'S LEFT OF MY HAIR. HA.
DAD, YOU'RE SUCH A NERD. THANK YOU SO MUCH.
NEVER THE END

TWO

FRESH MEAT

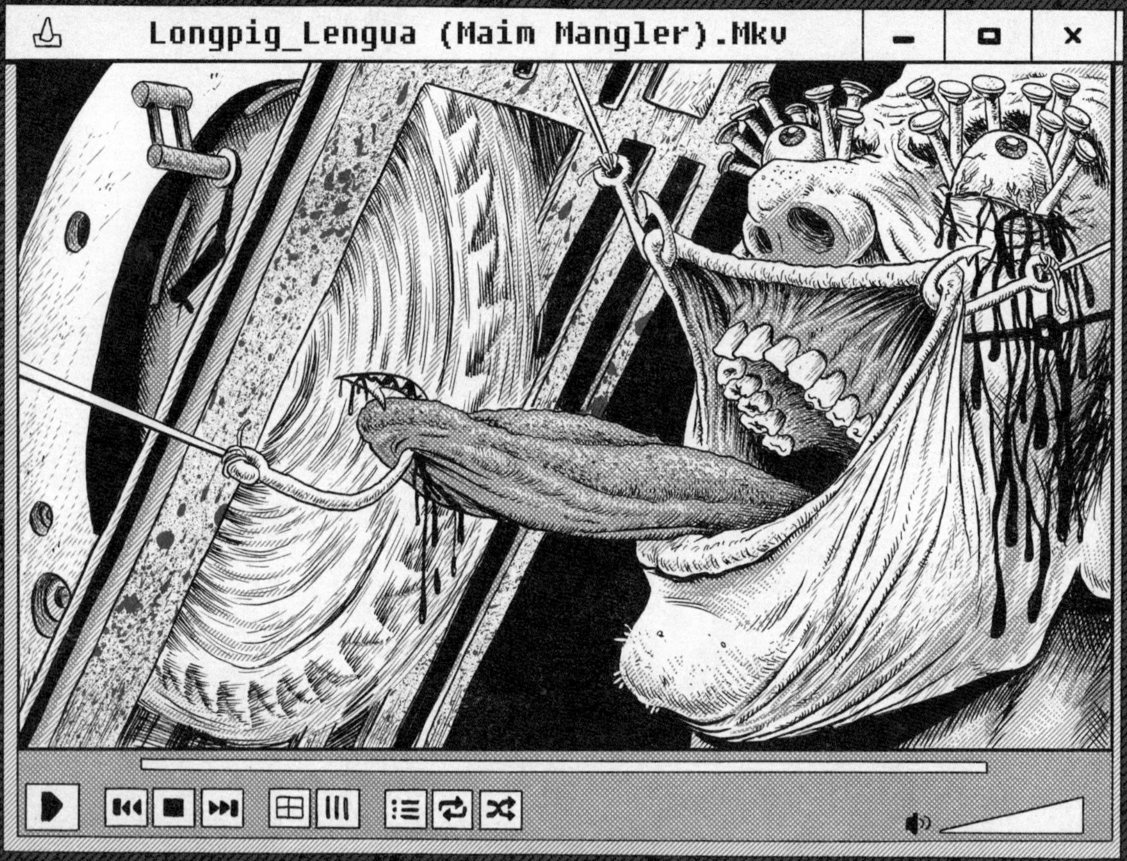
Longpig_Lengua (Maim Mangler).Mkv

The DARK WEB supplies ANONYMOUS INTERNET surfing, free from consequence. CRYPTOCURRENCY transactions lack a detectable paper trail, providing further obfuscation. These tools are being abused to grow a NEFARIOUS subculture and business of MURDER for ENTERTAINMENT in real time, via WEBCAM. WHO would participate in such a sick enterprise? WHO are the VICTIMS? WHO are the CUSTOMERS? WHO are the MURDERERS? Find out!

ED PISKOR PRESENTS: RED ROOM, THE ANTISOCIAL NETWORK

"THIS NEW **VIDEO** HIT THE **SPECTATORS OF CARNAGE** FORUM ON THE **DARK WEB** ABOUT AN HOUR AGO."

"ANOTHER **PENTAGRAM** RECORDING? IS IT THE **FAT MAN**, AGAIN?"

"**DECIMATOR.** YEP. >Sigh<"

"THEY MUST HAVE ABSORBED ALL OF OUR CLIENTELE BY NOW..."

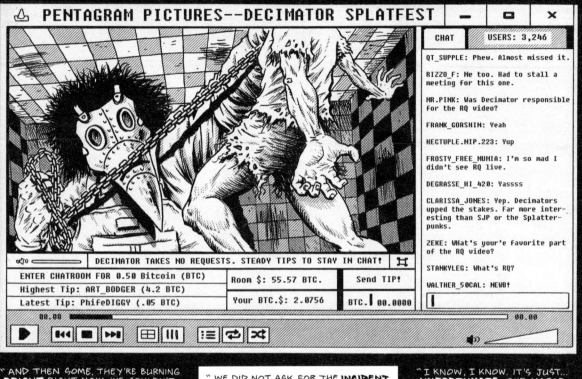

PENTAGRAM PICTURES--DECIMATOR SPLATFEST

CHAT | USERS: 3,246

QT_SUPPLE: Phew. Almost missed it.

RIZZO_F: Me too. Had to stall a meeting for this one.

MR.PINK: Was Decimator responsible for the RQ video?

FRANK_GORSHIN: Yeah

HECTUPLE.NIP.223: Yup

FROSTY_FREE_MUMIA: I'm so mad I didn't see RQ live.

DEGRASSE_HI_420: Yassss

CLARISSA_JONES: Yep. Decimators upped the stakes. Far more interesting than SJP or the Splatterpunks.

ZEKE: WHat's your'e favorite part of the RQ video?

STANKYLEG: What's RQ?

WALTHER_50CAL: NEWB!

DECIMATOR TAKES NO REQUESTS. STEADY TIPS TO STAY IN CHAT!

ENTER CHATROOM FOR 0.50 Bitcoin (BTC)
Highest Tip: ART_BODGER (4.2 BTC)
Latest Tip: PhifeDIGGY (.05 BTC)

Room $: 55.57 BTC.
Your BTC.$: 2.0756

Send TIP!
BTC. 00.0000

00.00   00.00

"AND THEN SOME. THEY'RE BURNING **BRIGHT** RIGHT NOW. WE COULDN'T HAVE CHOSEN A **WORSE** TIME TO GO ON **HIATUS.**"

"WE DID NOT ASK FOR THE **INCIDENT** AT **BRADDOCK PENITENTIARY.**"

"I KNOW, I KNOW. IT'S JUST... **UNFORTUNATE.** OUR MAJOR STRENGTH WAS OUR **RELIABLE** BROADCAST SCHEDULE."

PENTAGRAM PICTURES--DECIMATOR SPLATFEST

"WE BECAME **COMPLACENT**. WERE YOU **HAPPY** WITH OUR STANDING AMONGST OUR DISTINGUISHED COMPETITORS?"

"OF COURSE NOT, BUT WE WERE **UPWARDLY MOBILE** UNTIL IT ALL WENT AWAY. **SLOW** AND **STEADY** GROWTH."

"**PATHETIC!** BEING FORCED TO **REBOUND** IS SUCH A VALUABLE OPPORTUNITY TO FIX ALL OUR **DEFICIENCIES** AND **SHORTCOMINGS**."

PENTAGRAM PICTURES--DECIMATOR SPLATFEST

"WE WILL GAIN MORE **NOTORIETY**, MAKE MORE **MONEY**, AND WORK LESS HOURS ONCE WE IMPLEMENT THE GROUNDWORK OF OUR NEW **STRATEGY**.

"SPEAKING OF WHICH, HAVE YOU CHECKED IN ON THE **DOCTOR**? HE DIDN'T LOOK SO WELL YESTERDAY AFTER HIS WEEKLY VIDEO PAYMENT."

"YES. THERE'S NO CHANGE, BUT HE KNOWS THE **SCORE**."

"I HAVE EVERY CONFIDENCE THAT HE'LL HOLD UP HIS END OF THE DEAL FOR SOME TIME."

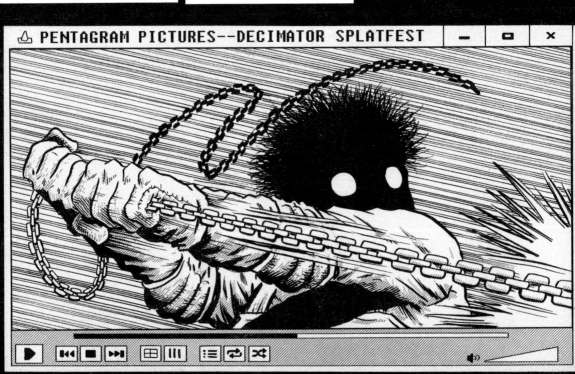

PENTAGRAM PICTURES--DECIMATOR SPLATFEST

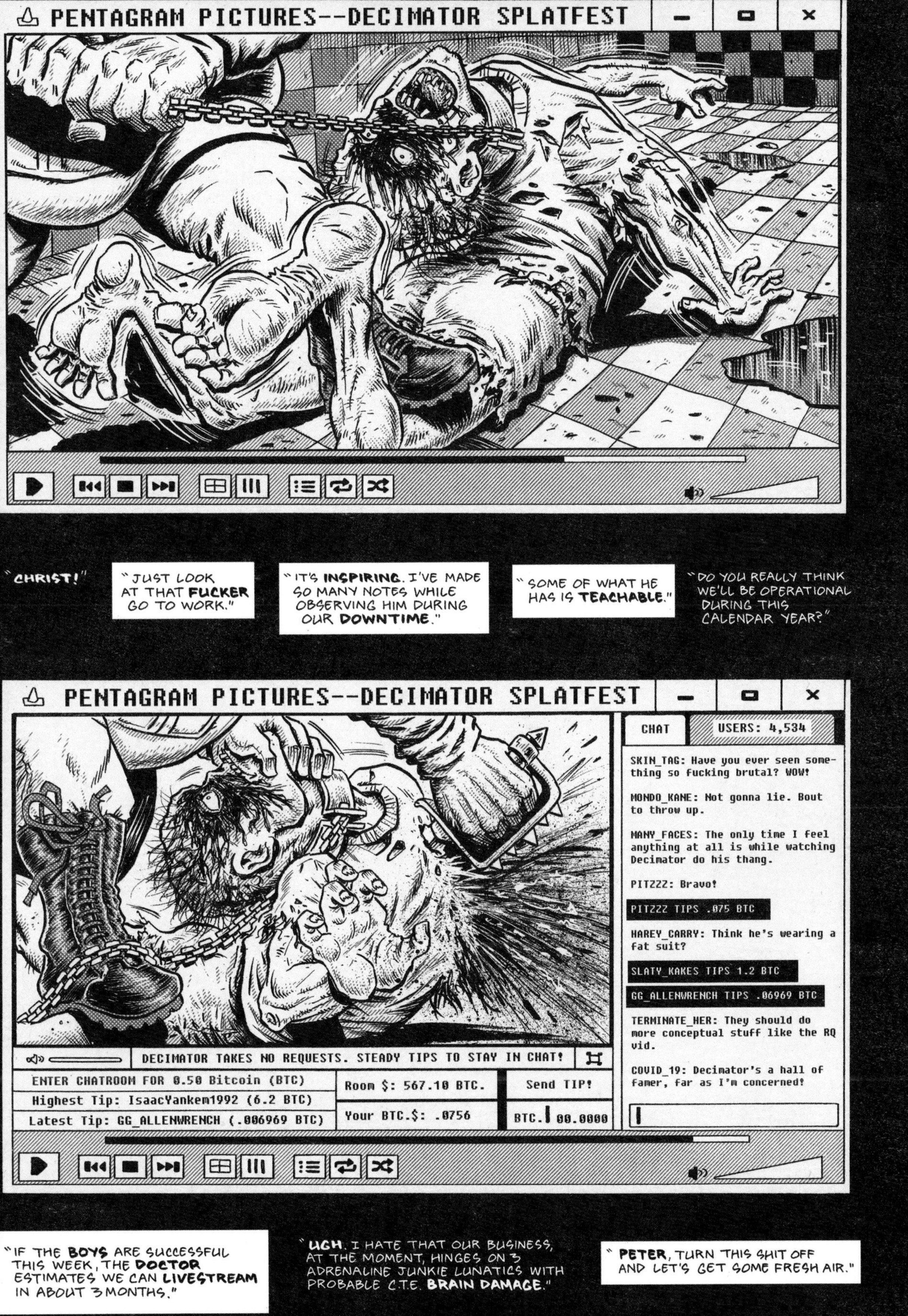
PENTAGRAM PICTURES--DECIMATOR SPLATFEST
"CHRIST!"
"JUST LOOK AT THAT FUCKER GO TO WORK."
"IT'S INSPIRING. I'VE MADE SO MANY NOTES WHILE OBSERVING HIM DURING OUR DOWNTIME."
"SOME OF WHAT HE HAS IS TEACHABLE."
"DO YOU REALLY THINK WE'LL BE OPERATIONAL DURING THIS CALENDAR YEAR?"
PENTAGRAM PICTURES--DECIMATOR SPLATFEST
CHAT
USERS: 4,534
SKIN_TAG: Have you ever seen something so fucking brutal? WOW!
MONDO_KANE: Not gonna lie. Bout to throw up.
MANY_FACES: The only time I feel anything at all is while watching Decimator do his thang.
PITZZZ: Bravo!
PITZZZ TIPS .075 BTC
HAREY_CARRY: Think he's wearing a fat suit?
SLATY_KAKES TIPS 1.2 BTC
GG_ALLENWRENCH TIPS .06969 BTC
TERMINATE_HER: They should do more conceptual stuff like the RQ vid.
COVID_19: Decimator's a hall of famer, far as I'm concerned!
DECIMATOR TAKES NO REQUESTS. STEADY TIPS TO STAY IN CHAT!
ENTER CHATROOM FOR 0.50 Bitcoin (BTC)
Highest Tip: IsaacYankem1992 (6.2 BTC)
Latest Tip: GG_ALLENWRENCH (.006969 BTC)
Room $: 567.10 BTC.
Your BTC.$: .0756
Send TIP!
BTC. 00.0000
"IF THE BOYS ARE SUCCESSFUL THIS WEEK, THE DOCTOR ESTIMATES WE CAN LIVESTREAM IN ABOUT 3 MONTHS."
"UGH. I HATE THAT OUR BUSINESS, AT THE MOMENT, HINGES ON 3 ADRENALINE JUNKIE LUNATICS WITH PROBABLE C.T.E. BRAIN DAMAGE."
"PETER, TURN THIS SHIT OFF AND LET'S GET SOME FRESH AIR."

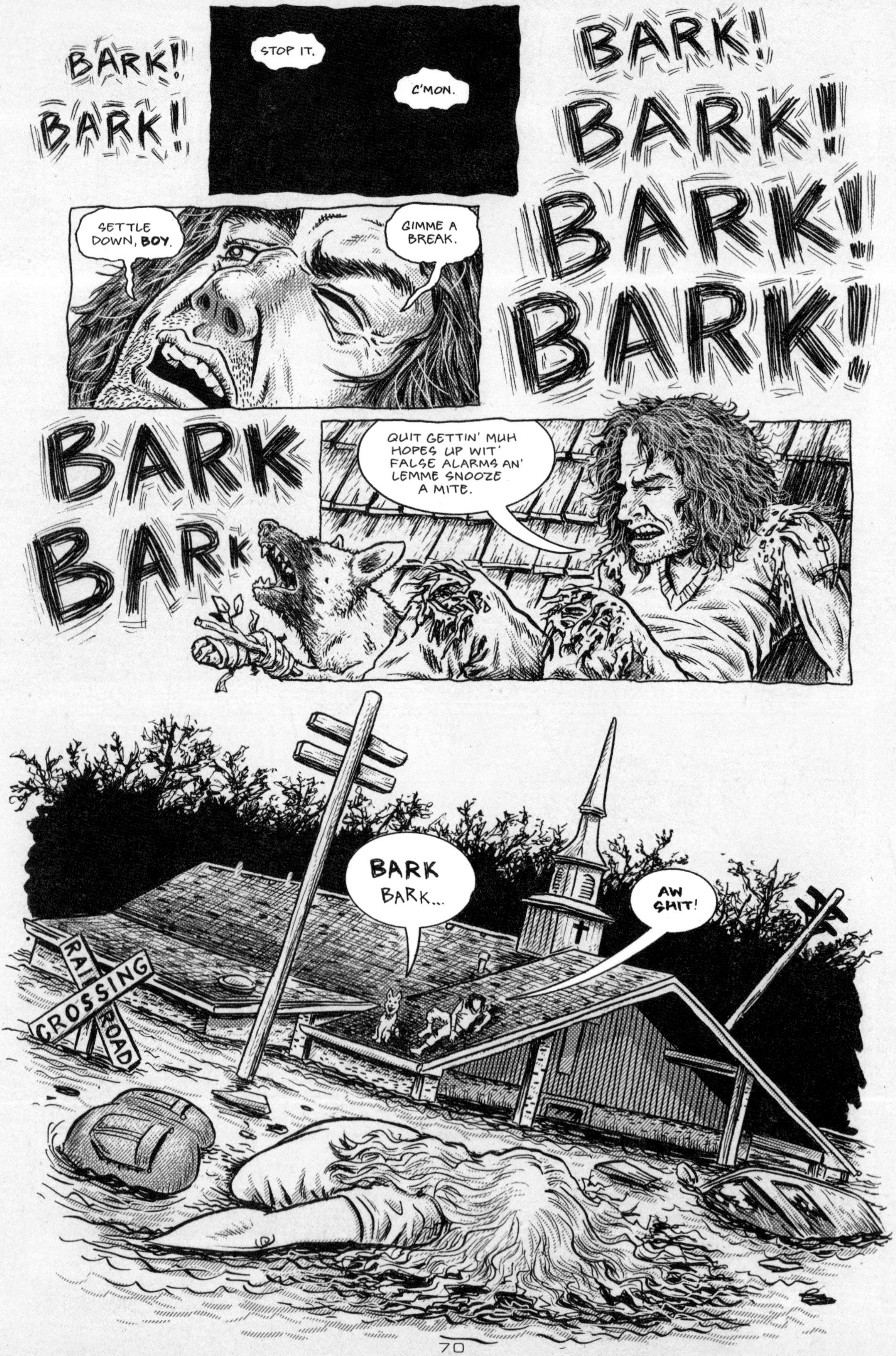
BARK!
BARK!
STOP IT.
C'MON.
BARK!
BARK!
BARK!
BARK!
SETTLE DOWN, **BOY**.
GIMME A BREAK.
BARK
BARK
QUIT GETTIN' MUH HOPES UP WIT' FALSE ALARMS AN' LEMME SNOOZE A MITE.
BARK
BARK...
AW SHIT!
RAILROAD
CROSSING

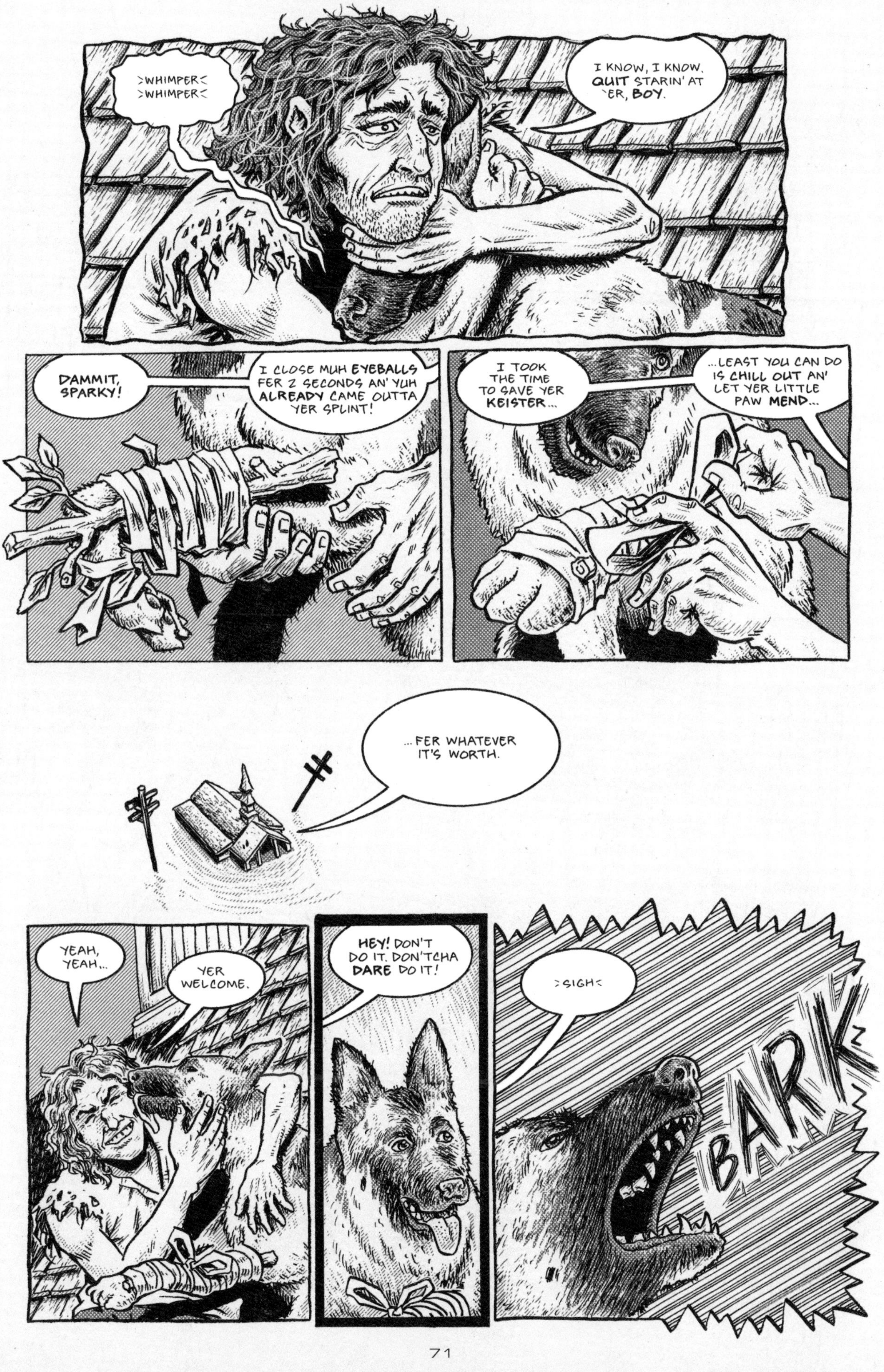
>WHIMPER<
>WHIMPER<
I KNOW, I KNOW. QUIT STARIN' AT 'ER, BOY.
DAMMIT, SPARKY!
I CLOSE MUH EYEBALLS FER 2 SECONDS AN' YUH ALREADY CAME OUTTA YER SPLINT!
I TOOK THE TIME TO SAVE YER KEISTER...
...LEAST YOU CAN DO IS CHILL OUT AN' LET YER LITTLE PAW MEND...
...FER WHATEVER IT'S WORTH.
YEAH, YEAH...
YER WELCOME.
HEY! DON'T DO IT. DON'TCHA DARE DO IT!
>SIGH<
BARK

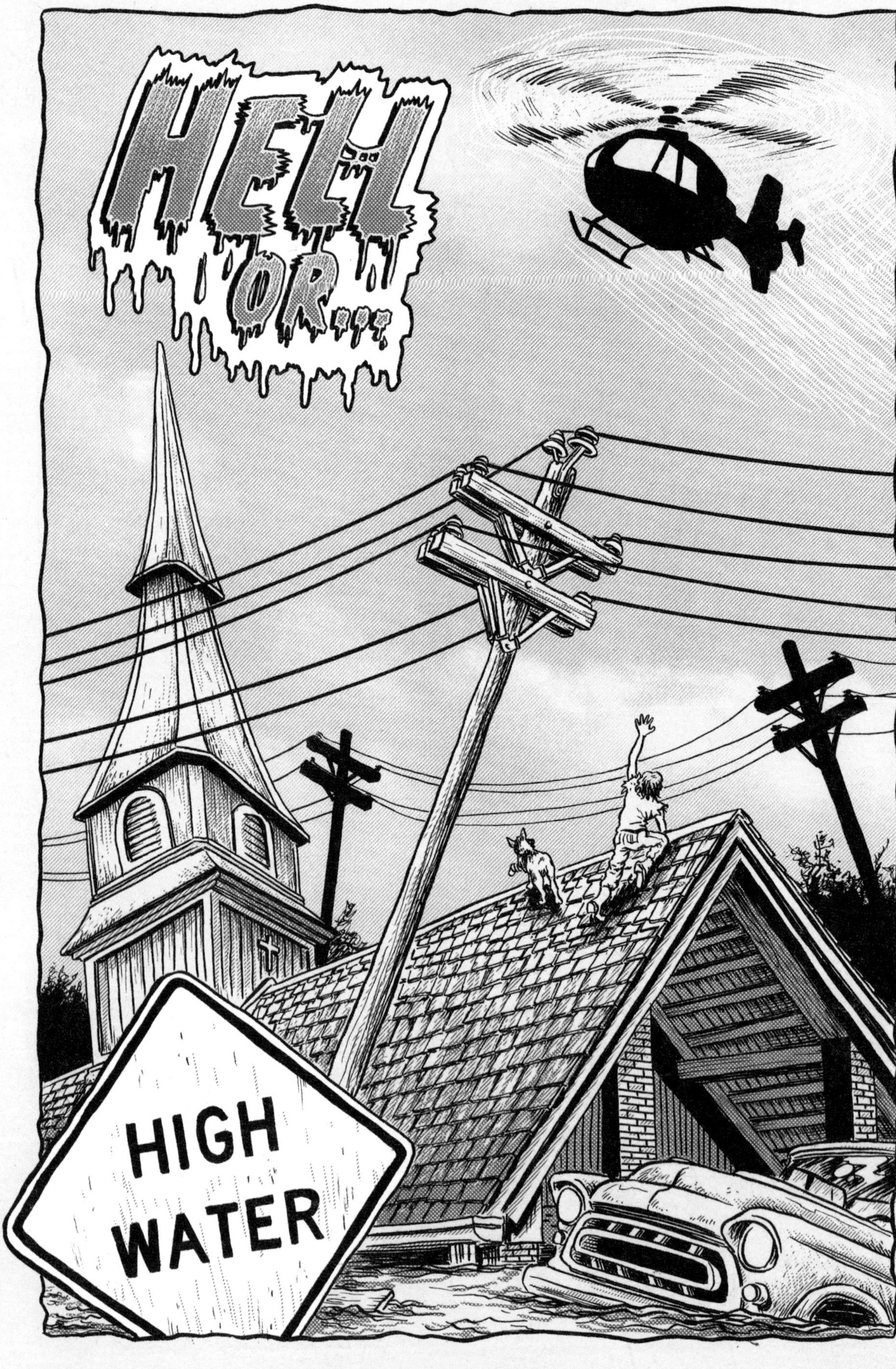
HELL OR...
HIGH WATER

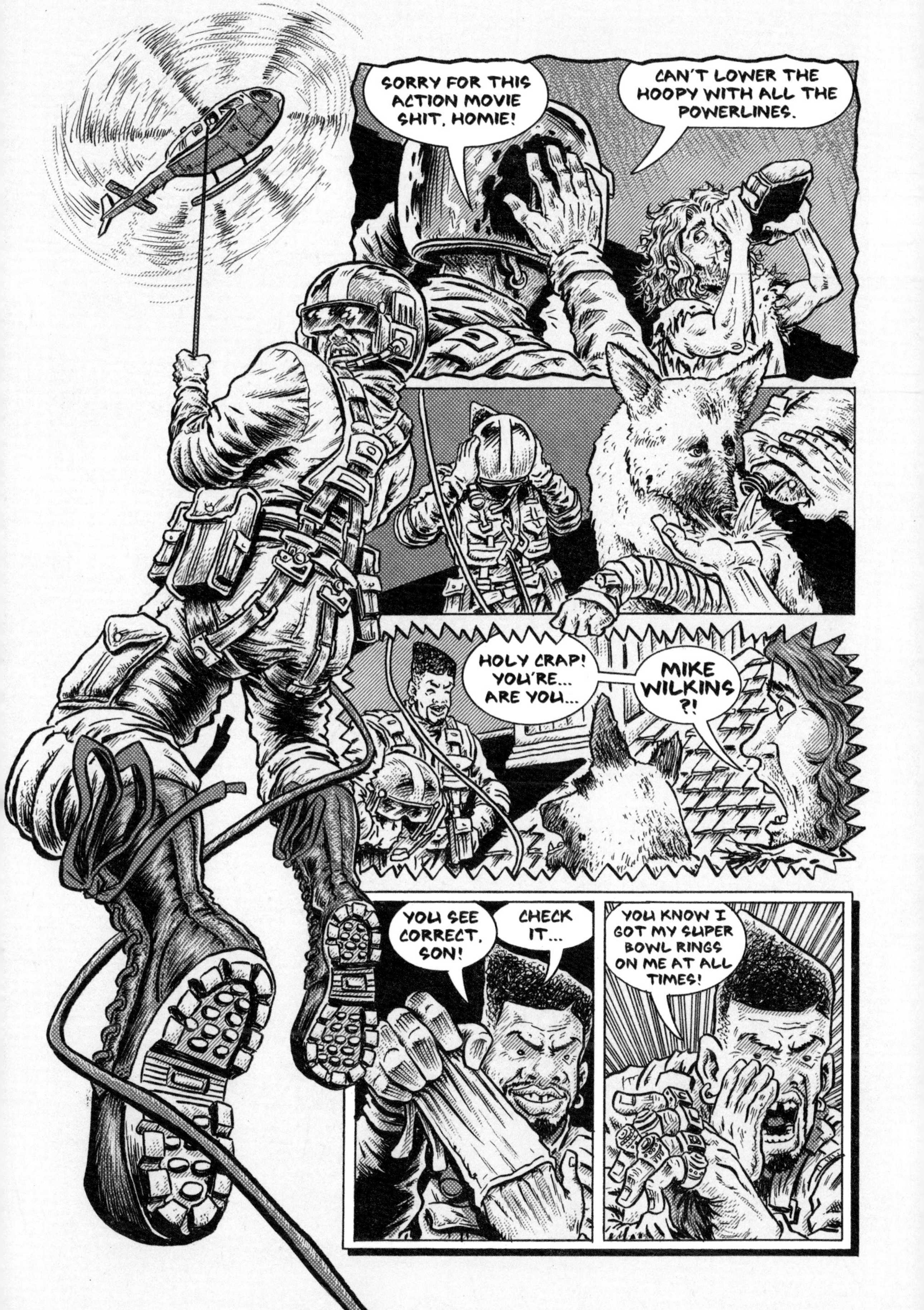

SORRY FOR THIS ACTION MOVIE SHIT, HOMIE!
CAN'T LOWER THE HOOPY WITH ALL THE POWERLINES.
HOLY CRAP! YOU'RE... ARE YOU...
MIKE WILKINS ?!
YOU SEE CORRECT, SON!
CHECK IT...
YOU KNOW I GOT MY SUPER BOWL RINGS ON ME AT ALL TIMES!

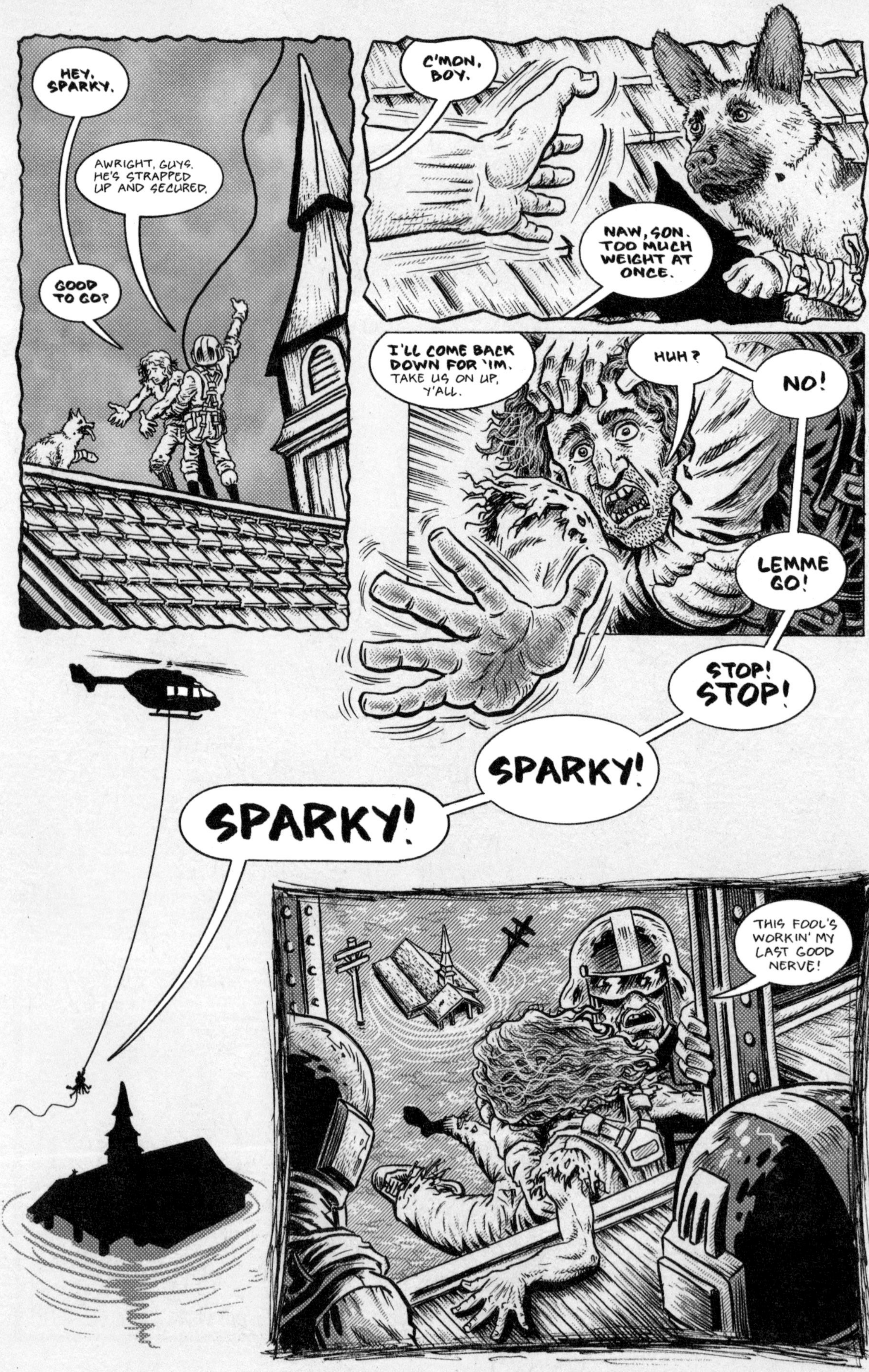
HEY, SPARKY.
AWRIGHT, GUYS. HE'S STRAPPED UP AND SECURED.
GOOD TO GO?
C'MON, BOY.
NAW, SON. TOO MUCH WEIGHT AT ONCE.
I'LL COME BACK DOWN FOR 'IM. TAKE US ON UP, Y'ALL.
HUH?
NO!
LEMME GO!
STOP! STOP!
SPARKY!
SPARKY!
THIS FOOL'S WORKIN' MY LAST GOOD NERVE!

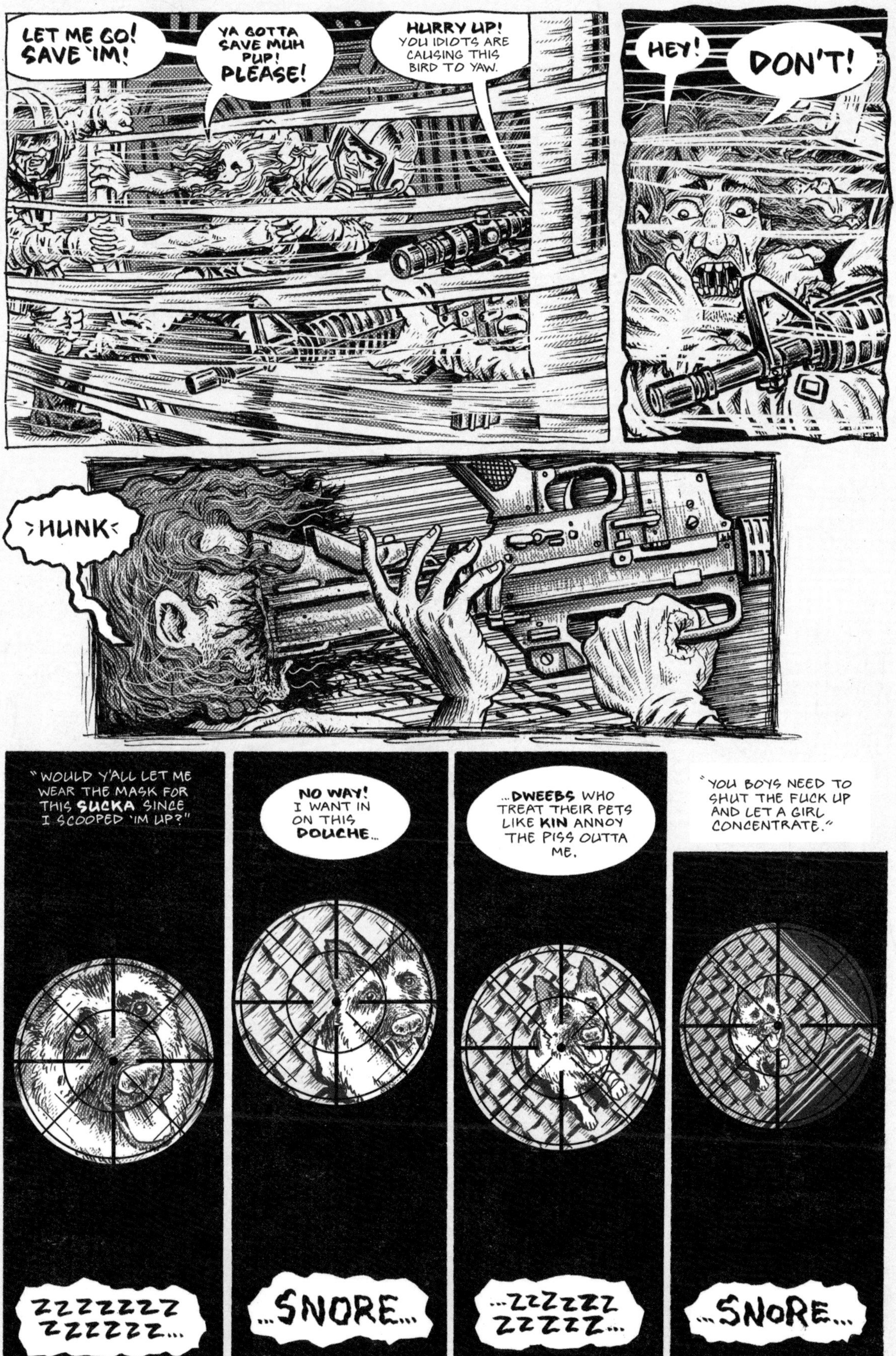
LET ME GO! SAVE 'IM!
YA GOTTA SAVE MUH PUP! PLEASE!
HURRY UP! YOU IDIOTS ARE CAUSING THIS BIRD TO YAW.
HEY!
DON'T!
>HUNK<
"WOULD Y'ALL LET ME WEAR THE MASK FOR THIS SUCKA SINCE I SCOOPED 'IM UP?"
ZZZZZZZ ZZZZZZ...
NO WAY! I WANT IN ON THIS DOUCHE...
...SNORE...
...DWEEBS WHO TREAT THEIR PETS LIKE KIN ANNOY THE PISS OUTTA ME.
...ZZZZZZ ZZZZZ...
"YOU BOYS NEED TO SHUT THE FUCK UP AND LET A GIRL CONCENTRATE."
...SNORE...

THE THREE DAYS WE GAVE YOU HAVE PASSED, DR. DANIELS.

DID YOU HIT YOUR DEADLINE? WE CONTINUE TO MAKE GOOD ON OUR END.

YOUR GRUNTS DIDN'T LEAVE ME MUCH TO WORK WITH, BUT, YES.

IT WILL TAKE ABOUT 4-6 WEEKS FOR HIS SWELLING TO COME DOWN FROM THE WHOLE ORDEAL.

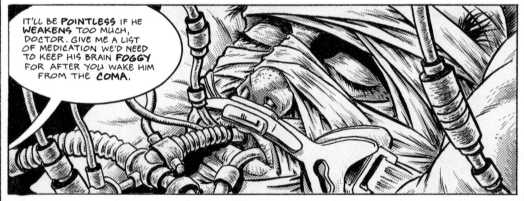

IT'LL BE POINTLESS IF HE WEAKENS TOO MUCH, DOCTOR. GIVE ME A LIST OF MEDICATION WE'D NEED TO KEEP HIS BRAIN FOGGY FOR AFTER YOU WAKE HIM FROM THE COMA.

IT... IT'S SUNDAY. CAN I SEE THEM?

PLEASE, LET ME SEE MY FAMILY.

LIKE CLOCKWORK, DR. DANIELS.

READY?

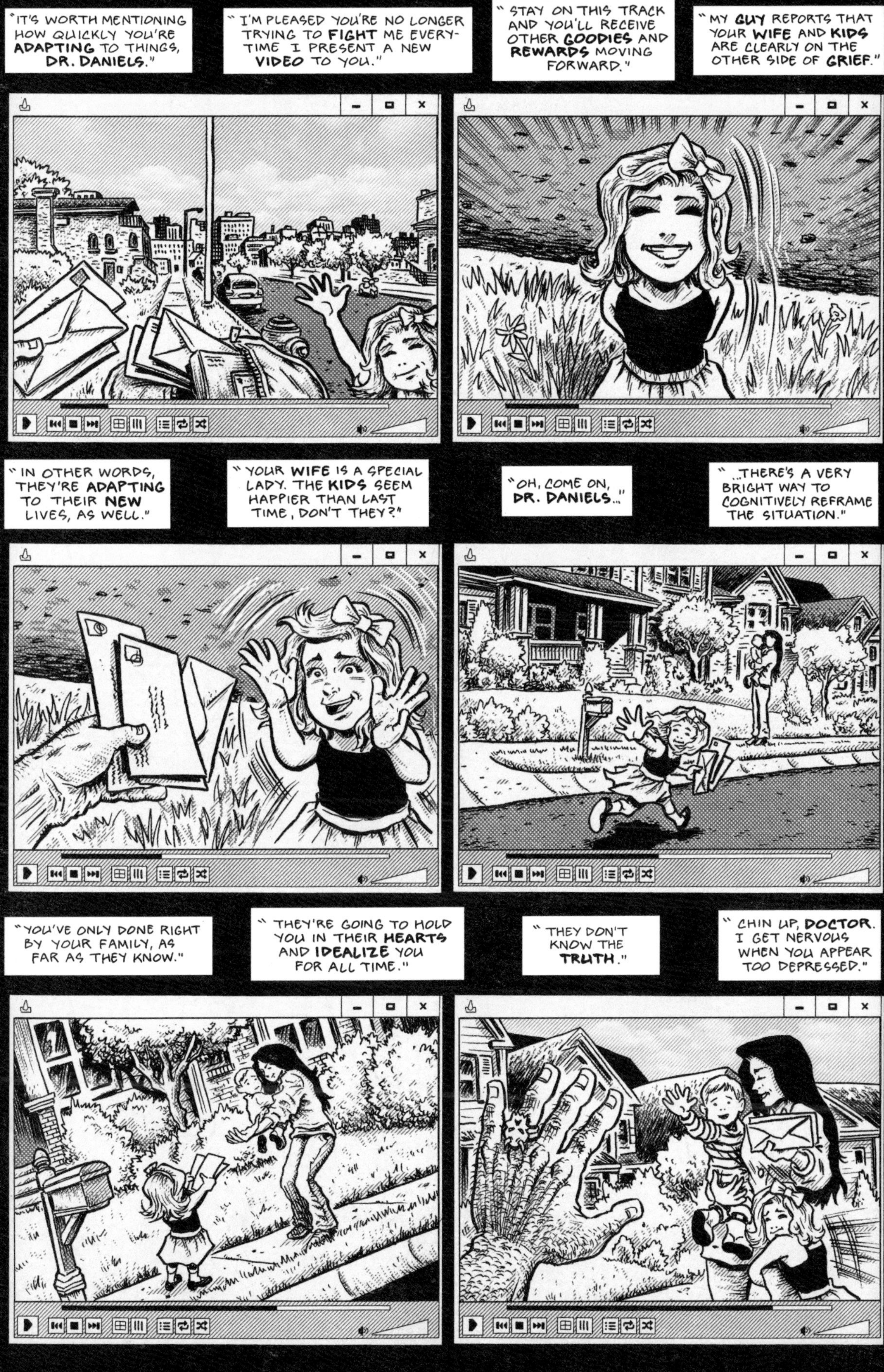
"IT'S WORTH MENTIONING HOW QUICKLY YOU'RE ADAPTING TO THINGS, DR. DANIELS."
"I'M PLEASED YOU'RE NO LONGER TRYING TO FIGHT ME EVERY-TIME I PRESENT A NEW VIDEO TO YOU."
"STAY ON THIS TRACK AND YOU'LL RECEIVE OTHER GOODIES AND REWARDS MOVING FORWARD."
"MY GUY REPORTS THAT YOUR WIFE AND KIDS ARE CLEARLY ON THE OTHER SIDE OF GRIEF."
"IN OTHER WORDS, THEY'RE ADAPTING TO THEIR NEW LIVES, AS WELL."
"YOUR WIFE IS A SPECIAL LADY. THE KIDS SEEM HAPPIER THAN LAST TIME, DON'T THEY?"
"OH, COME ON, DR. DANIELS..."
"...THERE'S A VERY BRIGHT WAY TO COGNITIVELY REFRAME THE SITUATION."
"YOU'VE ONLY DONE RIGHT BY YOUR FAMILY, AS FAR AS THEY KNOW."
"THEY'RE GOING TO HOLD YOU IN THEIR HEARTS AND IDEALIZE YOU FOR ALL TIME."
"THEY DON'T KNOW THE TRUTH."
"CHIN UP, DOCTOR. I GET NERVOUS WHEN YOU APPEAR TOO DEPRESSED."

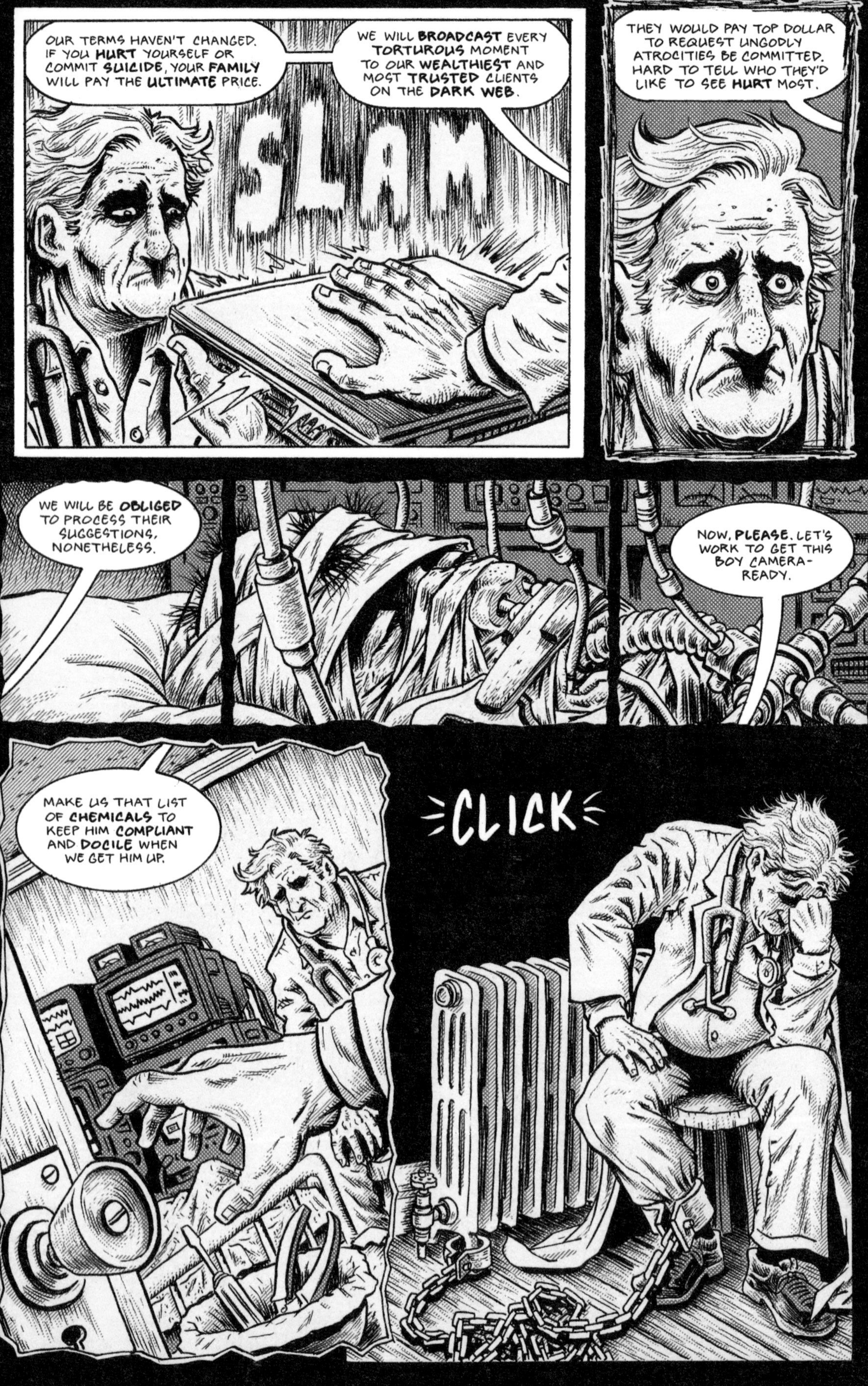
OUR TERMS HAVEN'T CHANGED. IF YOU HURT YOURSELF OR COMMIT SUICIDE, YOUR FAMILY WILL PAY THE ULTIMATE PRICE.
WE WILL BROADCAST EVERY TORTUROUS MOMENT TO OUR WEALTHIEST AND MOST TRUSTED CLIENTS ON THE DARK WEB.
SLAM
THEY WOULD PAY TOP DOLLAR TO REQUEST UNGODLY ATROCITIES BE COMMITTED. HARD TO TELL WHO THEY'D LIKE TO SEE HURT MOST.
WE WILL BE OBLIGED TO PROCESS THEIR SUGGESTIONS, NONETHELESS.
NOW, PLEASE. LET'S WORK TO GET THIS BOY CAMERA-READY.
MAKE US THAT LIST OF CHEMICALS TO KEEP HIM COMPLIANT AND DOCILE WHEN WE GET HIM UP.
CLICK

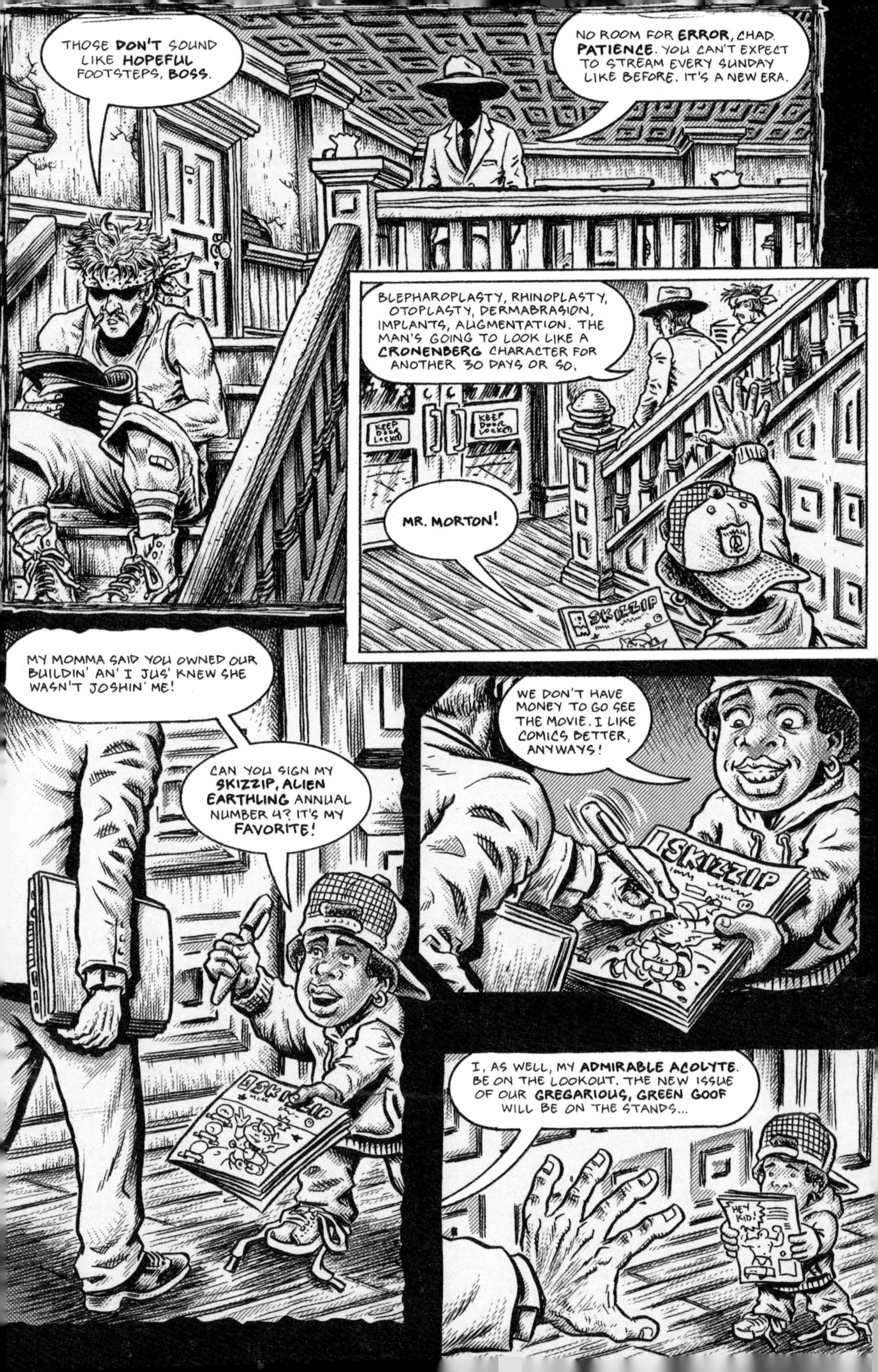

THOSE DON'T SOUND LIKE HOPEFUL FOOTSTEPS, BOSS.
NO ROOM FOR ERROR, CHAD. PATIENCE. YOU CAN'T EXPECT TO STREAM EVERY SUNDAY LIKE BEFORE. IT'S A NEW ERA.
BLEPHAROPLASTY, RHINOPLASTY, OTOPLASTY, DERMABRASION, IMPLANTS, AUGMENTATION. THE MAN'S GOING TO LOOK LIKE A CRONENBERG CHARACTER FOR ANOTHER 30 DAYS OR SO.
KEEP DOOR LOCKED
KEEP DOOR LOCKED
MR. MORTON!
SKIZZIP
MY MOMMA SAID YOU OWNED OUR BUILDIN' AN' I JUS' KNEW SHE WASN'T JOSHIN' ME!
CAN YOU SIGN MY SKIZZIP, ALIEN EARTHLING ANNUAL NUMBER 4? IT'S MY FAVORITE!
SKIZZIP
WE DON'T HAVE MONEY TO GO SEE THE MOVIE. I LIKE COMICS BETTER, ANYWAYS!
SKIZZIP
I, AS WELL, MY ADMIRABLE ACOLYTE. BE ON THE LOOKOUT. THE NEW ISSUE OF OUR GREGARIOUS, GREEN GOOF WILL BE ON THE STANDS...
HEY KID!

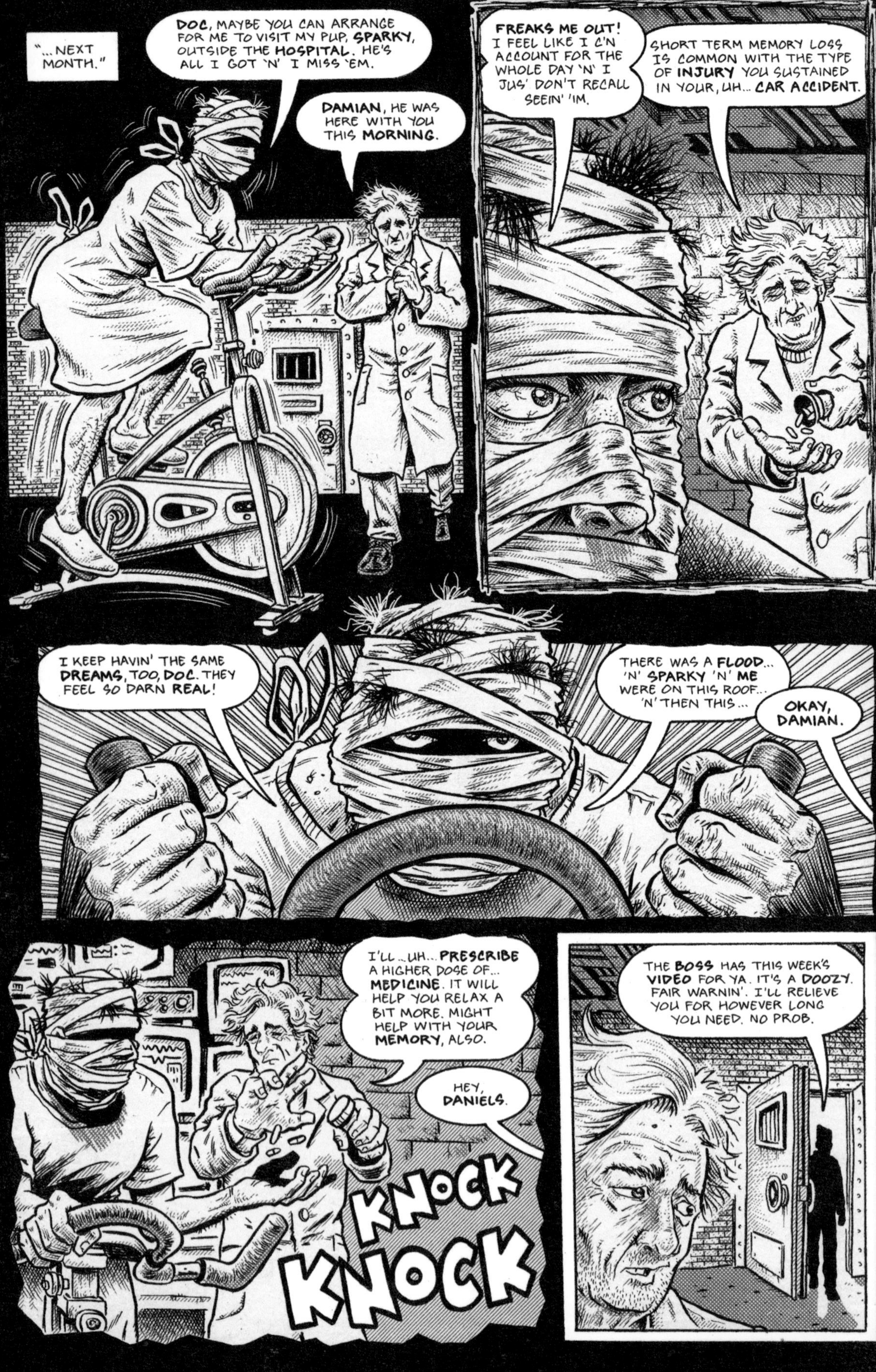
"...NEXT MONTH."
DOC, MAYBE YOU CAN ARRANGE FOR ME TO VISIT MY PUP, SPARKY, OUTSIDE THE HOSPITAL. HE'S ALL I GOT 'N' I MISS 'EM.
DAMIAN, HE WAS HERE WITH YOU THIS MORNING.
FREAKS ME OUT! I FEEL LIKE I C'N ACCOUNT FOR THE WHOLE DAY 'N' I JUS' DON'T RECALL SEEIN' 'IM.
SHORT TERM MEMORY LOSS IS COMMON WITH THE TYPE OF INJURY YOU SUSTAINED IN YOUR, UH... CAR ACCIDENT.
I KEEP HAVIN' THE SAME DREAMS, TOO, DOC. THEY FEEL SO DARN REAL!
THERE WAS A FLOOD... 'N' SPARKY 'N' ME WERE ON THIS ROOF... 'N' THEN THIS...
OKAY, DAMIAN.
I'LL...UH... PRESCRIBE A HIGHER DOSE OF... MEDICINE. IT WILL HELP YOU RELAX A BIT MORE. MIGHT HELP WITH YOUR MEMORY, ALSO.
HEY, DANIELS.
KNOCK KNOCK
THE BOSS HAS THIS WEEK'S VIDEO FOR YA. IT'S A DOOZY. FAIR WARNIN'. I'LL RELIEVE YOU FOR HOWEVER LONG YOU NEED. NO PROB.

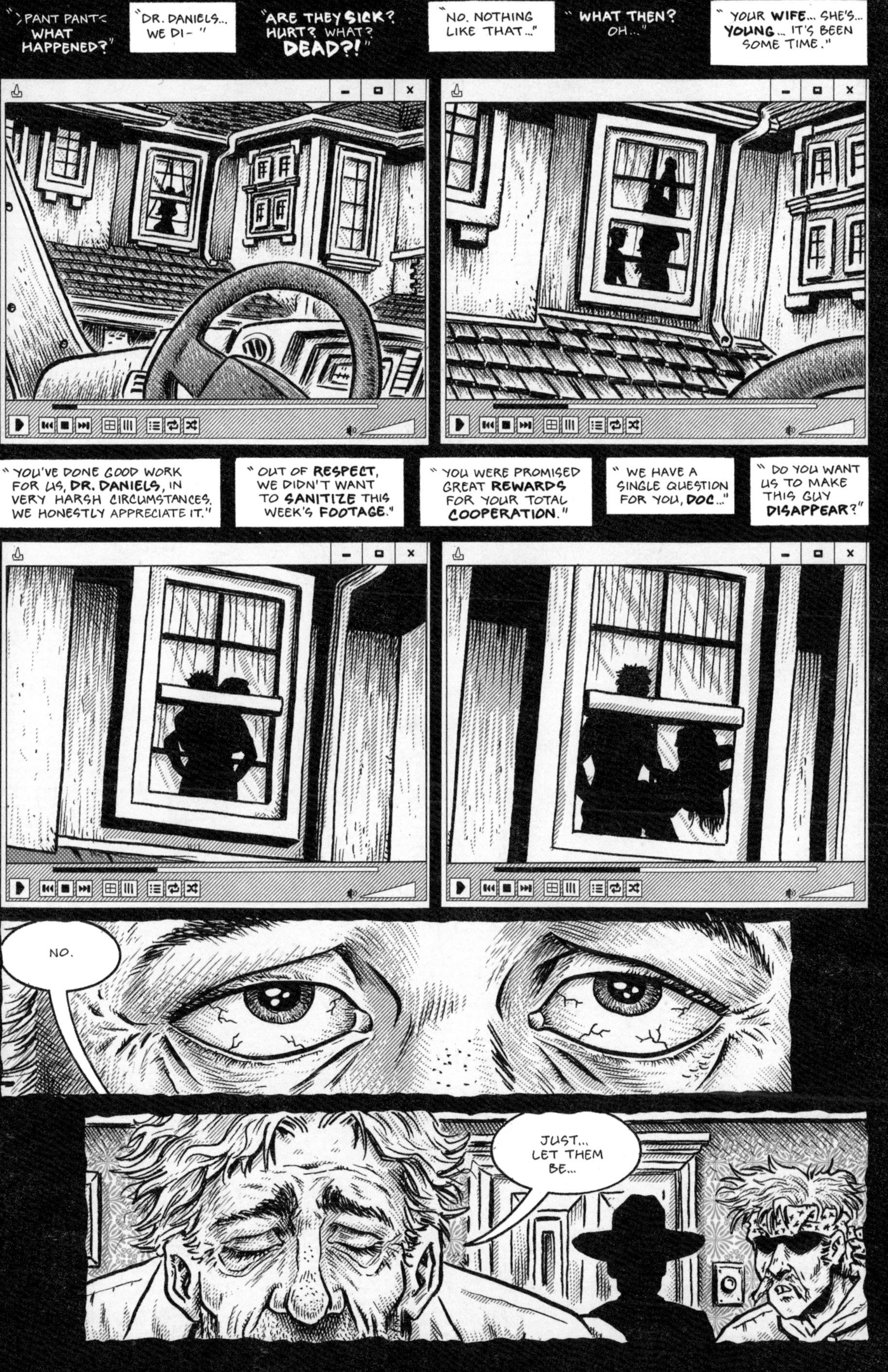
"PANT PANT= WHAT HAPPENED?"
"DR. DANIELS... WE DI- "
"ARE THEY SICK? HURT? WHAT? DEAD?!"
"NO. NOTHING LIKE THAT..."
"WHAT THEN? OH..."
"YOUR WIFE... SHE'S... YOUNG... IT'S BEEN SOME TIME."
"YOU'VE DONE GOOD WORK FOR US, DR. DANIELS, IN VERY HARSH CIRCUMSTANCES. WE HONESTLY APPRECIATE IT."
"OUT OF RESPECT, WE DIDN'T WANT TO SANITIZE THIS WEEK'S FOOTAGE."
"YOU WERE PROMISED GREAT REWARDS FOR YOUR TOTAL COOPERATION."
"WE HAVE A SINGLE QUESTION FOR YOU, DOC..."
"DO YOU WANT US TO MAKE THIS GUY DISAPPEAR?"
NO.
JUST... LET THEM BE...

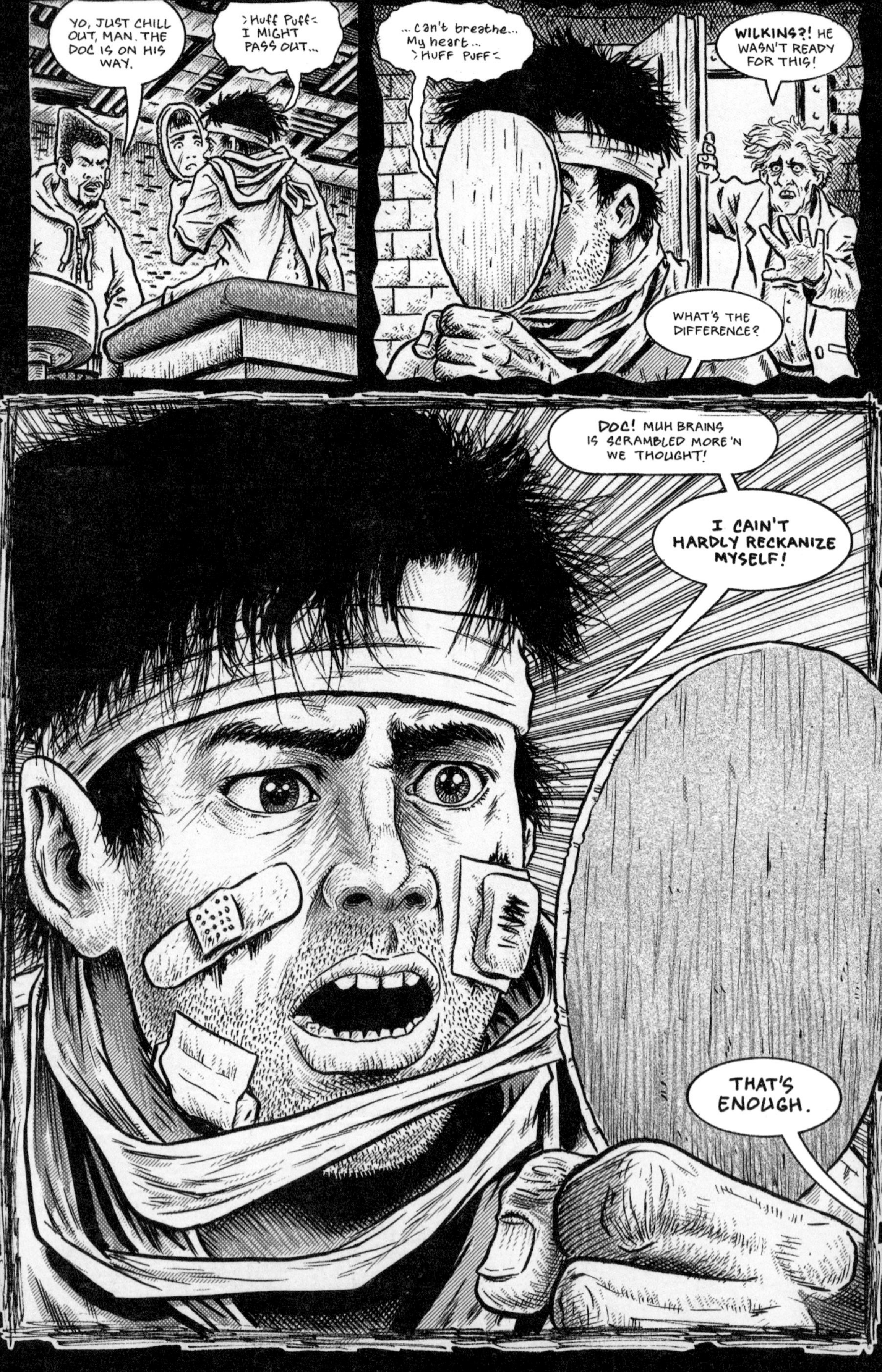
YO, JUST CHILL OUT, MAN. THE DOC IS ON HIS WAY.
>HUFF PUFF< I MIGHT PASS OUT...
...can't breathe... My heart... >HUFF PUFF<
WILKINS?! HE WASN'T READY FOR THIS!
WHAT'S THE DIFFERENCE?
DOC! MUH BRAINS IS SCRAMBLED MORE'N WE THOUGHT!
I CAIN'T HARDLY RECKANIZE MYSELF!
THAT'S ENOUGH.

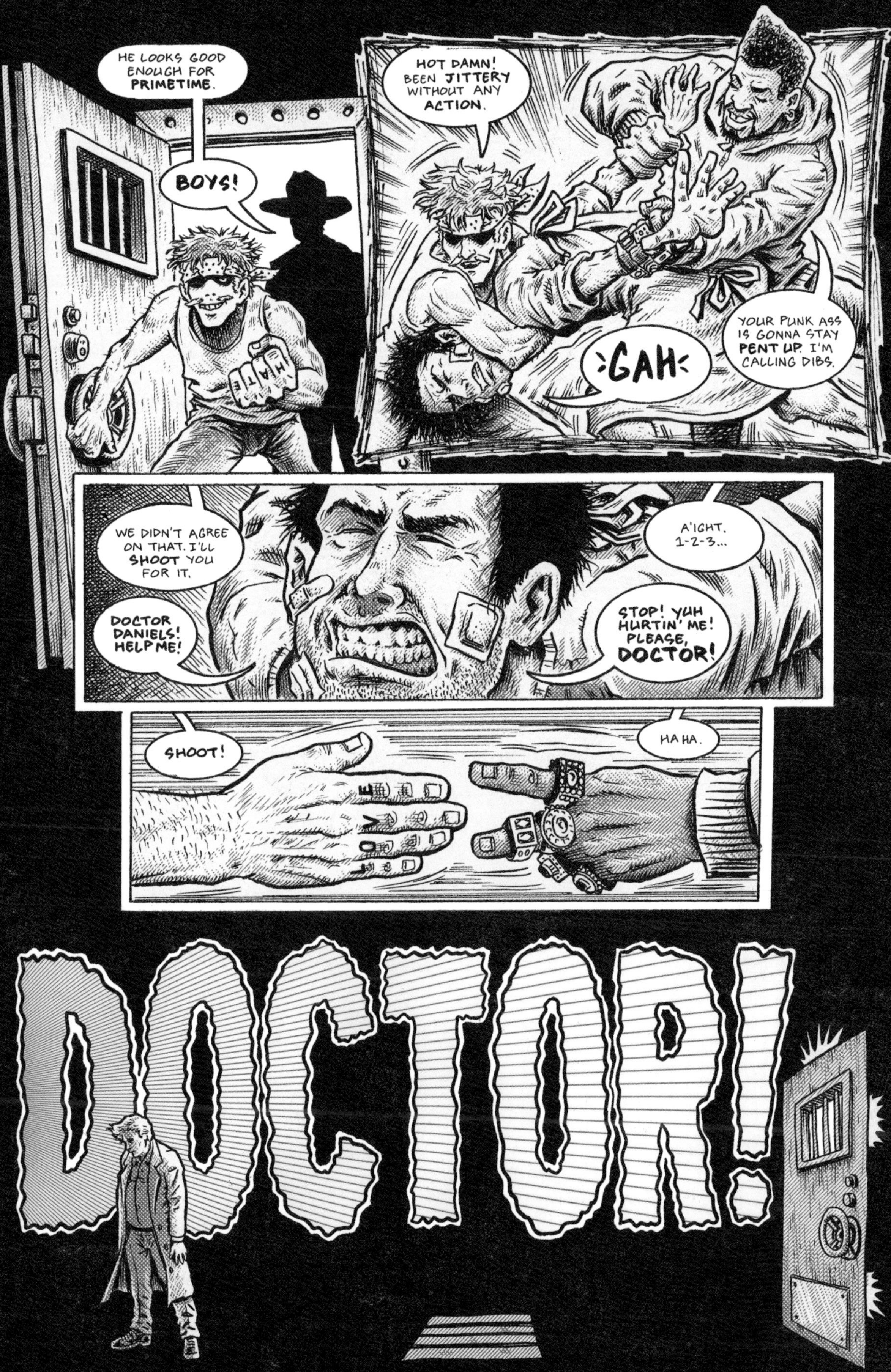
HE LOOKS GOOD ENOUGH FOR PRIMETIME.
BOYS!
HATE
HOT DAMN! BEEN JITTERY WITHOUT ANY ACTION.
GAH
YOUR PUNK ASS IS GONNA STAY PENT UP. I'M CALLING DIBS.
WE DIDN'T AGREE ON THAT. I'LL SHOOT YOU FOR IT.
DOCTOR DANIELS! HELP ME!
A'IGHT. 1-2-3...
STOP! YUH HURTIN' ME! PLEASE, DOCTOR!
SHOOT!
HA HA.
LOVE
DOCTOR!

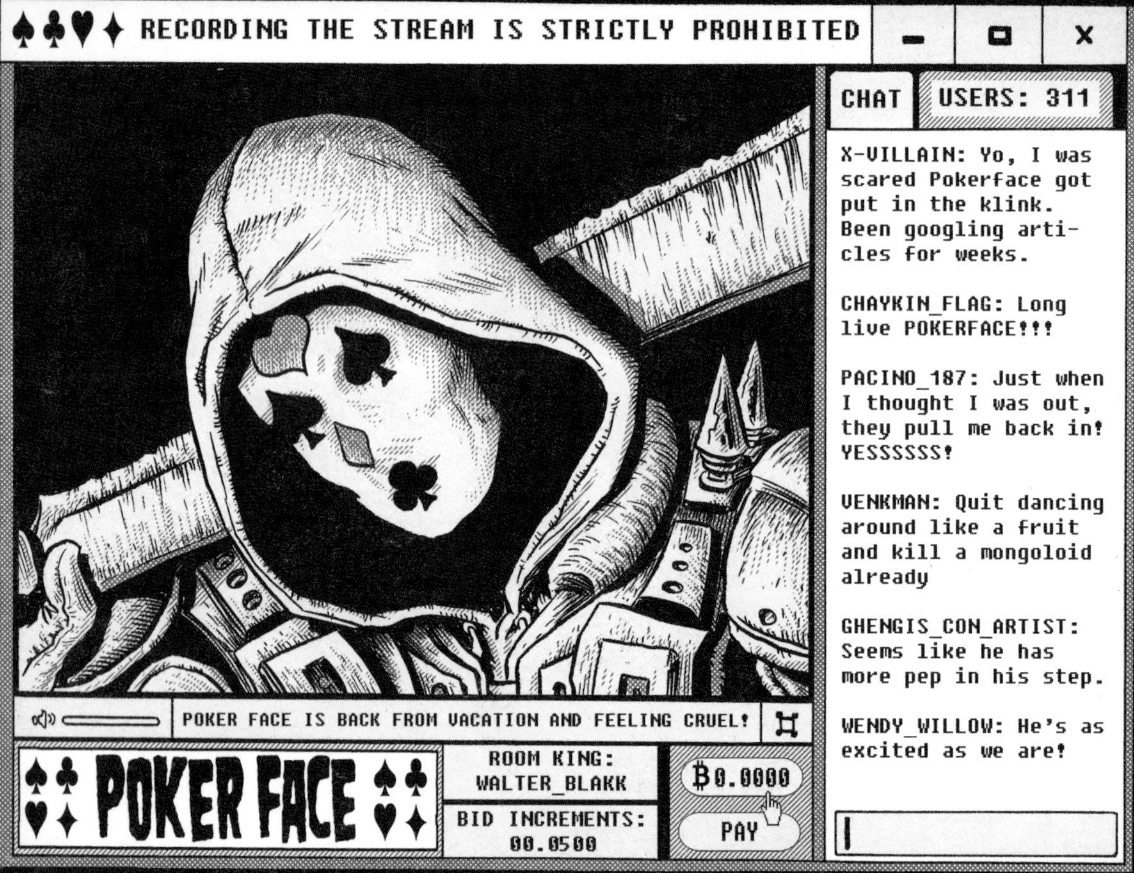
RECORDING THE STREAM IS STRICTLY PROHIBITED
CHAT
USERS: 311
X-VILLAIN: Yo, I was scared Pokerface got put in the klink. Been googling articles for weeks.
CHAYKIN_FLAG: Long live POKERFACE!!!
PACINO_187: Just when I thought I was out, they pull me back in! YESSSSSS!
VENKMAN: Quit dancing around like a fruit and kill a mongoloid already
GHENGIS_CON_ARTIST: Seems like he has more pep in his step.
WENDY_WILLOW: He's as excited as we are!
POKER FACE IS BACK FROM VACATION AND FEELING CRUEL!
POKER FACE
ROOM KING: WALTER_BLAKK
BID INCREMENTS: 00.0500
฿0.0000
PAY

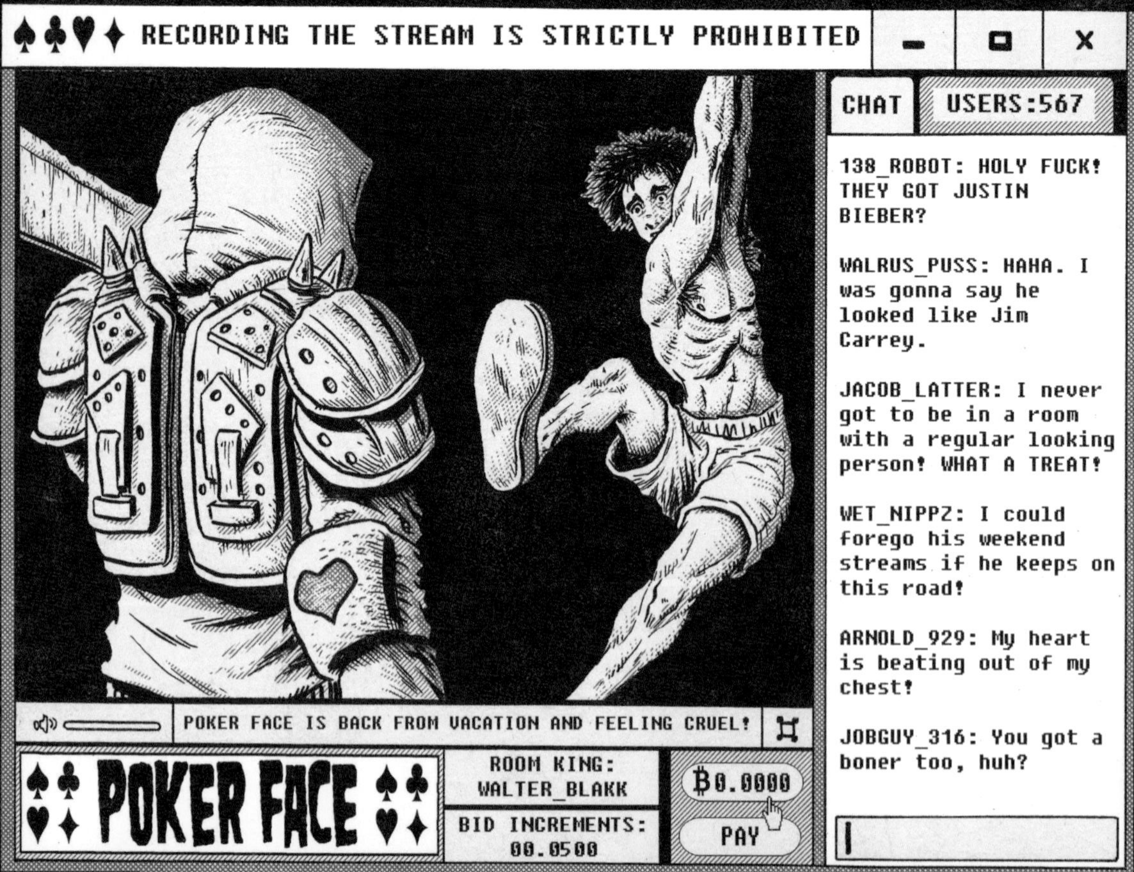
RECORDING THE STREAM IS STRICTLY PROHIBITED
CHAT
USERS:567
138_ROBOT: HOLY FUCK! THEY GOT JUSTIN BIEBER?
WALRUS_PUSS: HAHA. I was gonna say he looked like Jim Carrey.
JACOB_LATTER: I never got to be in a room with a regular looking person! WHAT A TREAT!
WET_NIPPZ: I could forego his weekend streams if he keeps on this road!
ARNOLD_929: My heart is beating out of my chest!
JOBGUY_316: You got a boner too, huh?
POKER FACE IS BACK FROM VACATION AND FEELING CRUEL!
POKER FACE
ROOM KING: WALTER_BLAKK
BID INCREMENTS: 00.0500
฿0.0000
PAY

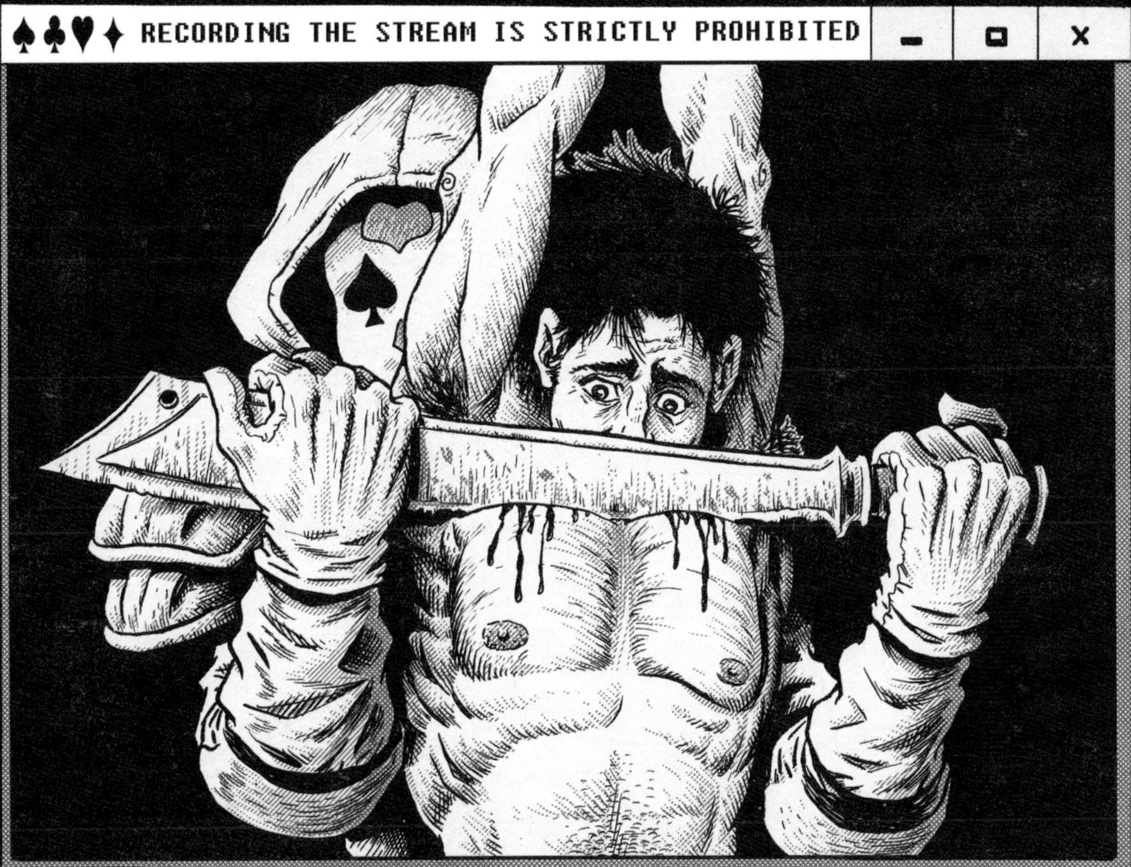
♠♣♥♦ RECORDING THE STREAM IS STRICTLY PROHIBITED
X

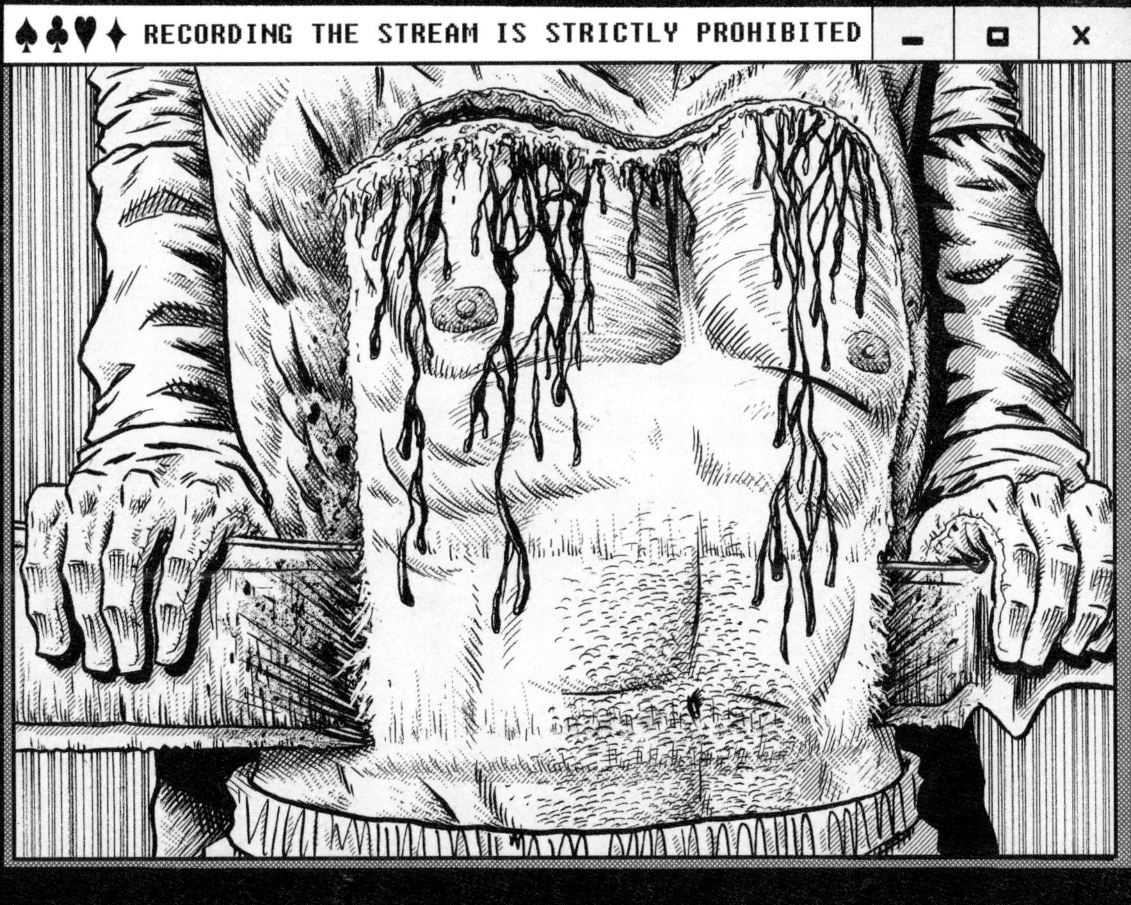
♠♣♥♦ RECORDING THE STREAM IS STRICTLY PROHIBITED
X

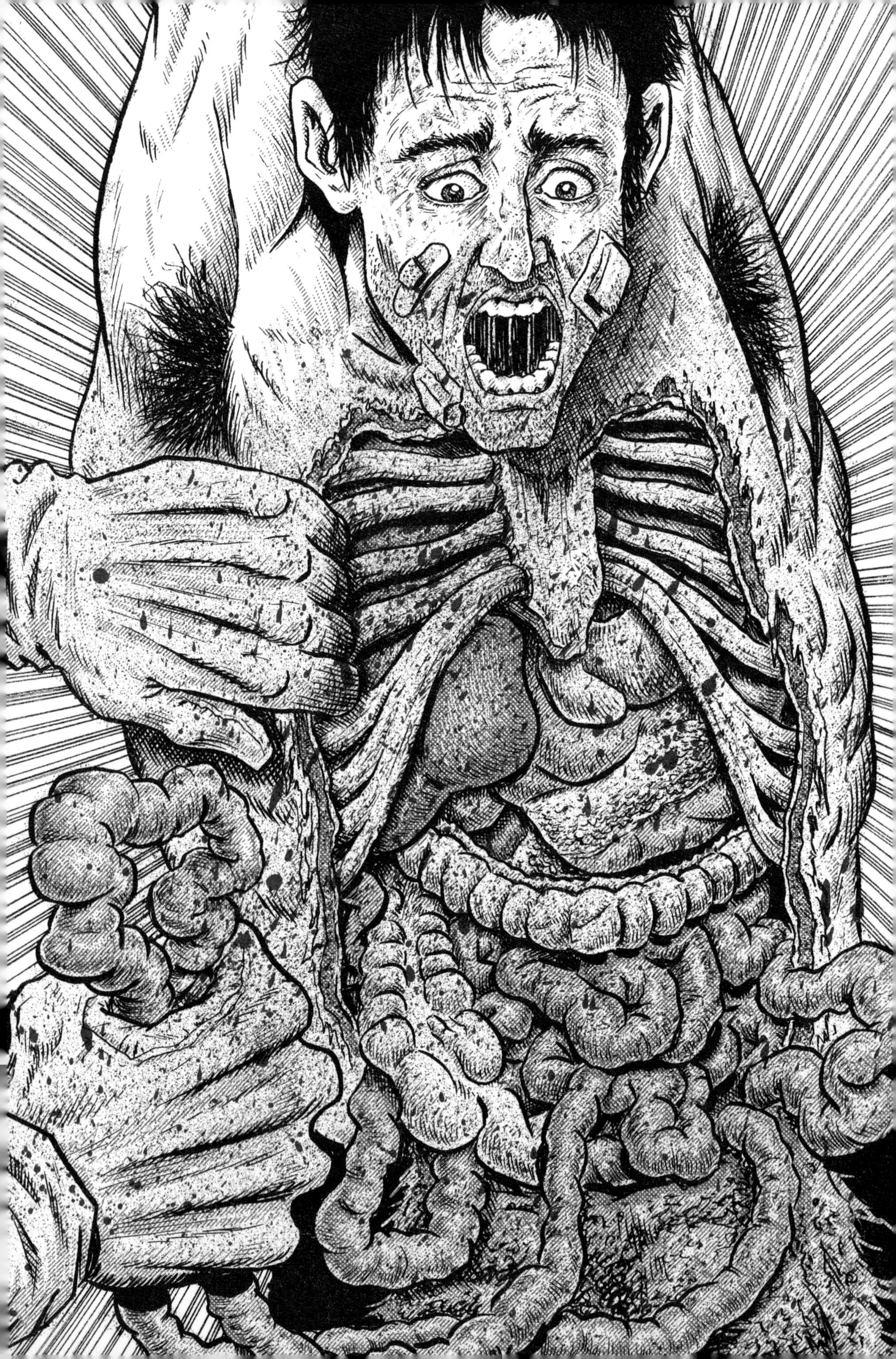

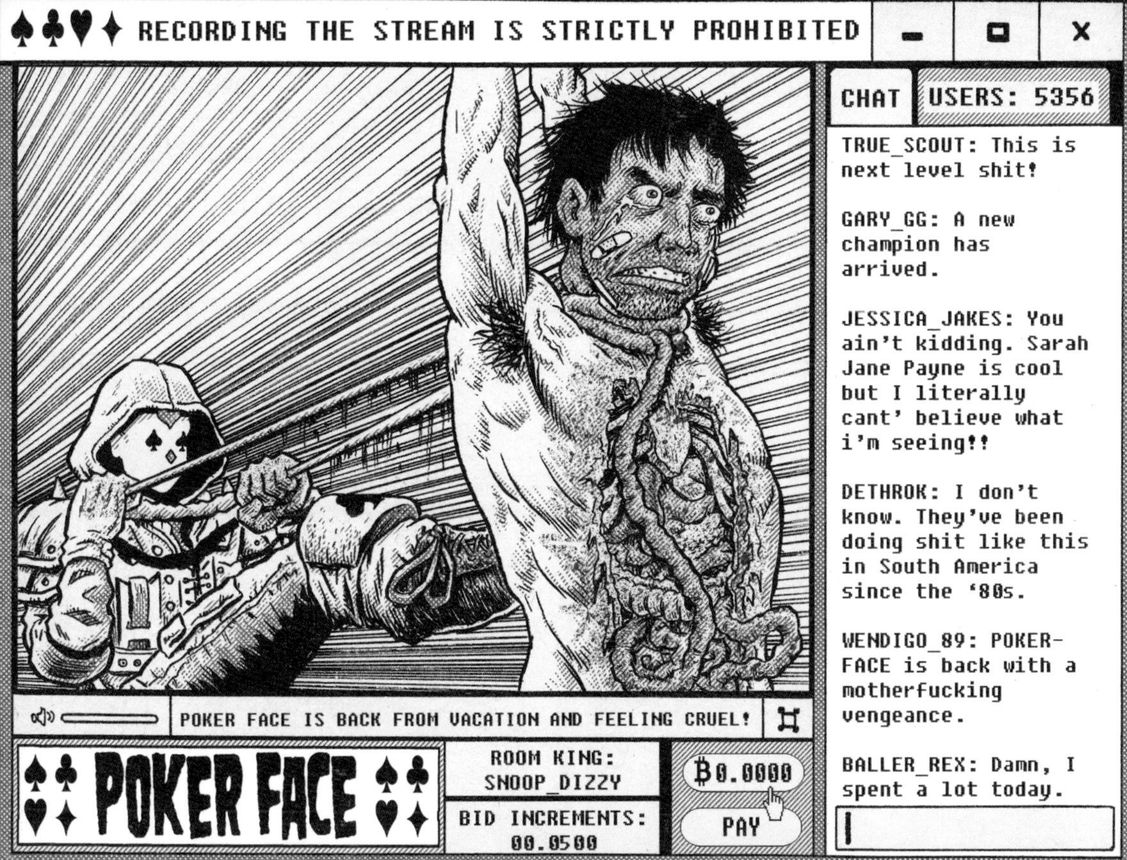
RECORDING THE STREAM IS STRICTLY PROHIBITED
CHAT
USERS: 5356
TRUE_SCOUT: This is next level shit!
GARY_GG: A new champion has arrived.
JESSICA_JAKES: You ain't kidding. Sarah Jane Payne is cool but I literally cant' believe what i'm seeing!!
DETHROK: I don't know. They've been doing shit like this in South America since the '80s.
WENDIGO_89: POKER-FACE is back with a motherfucking vengeance.
BALLER_REX: Damn, I spent a lot today.
POKER FACE IS BACK FROM VACATION AND FEELING CRUEL!
POKER FACE
ROOM KING: SNOOP_DIZZY
BID INCREMENTS: 00.0500
₿0.0000
PAY

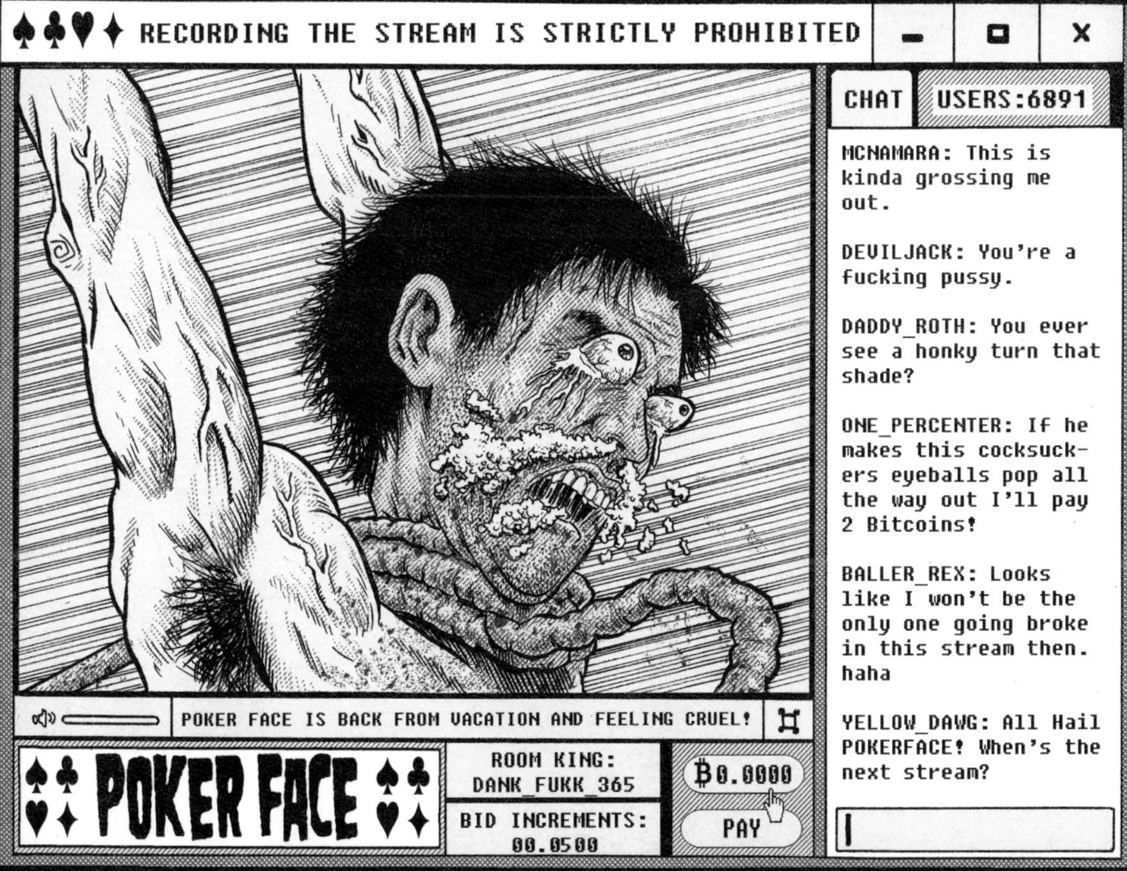
RECORDING THE STREAM IS STRICTLY PROHIBITED
CHAT
USERS:6891
MCNAMARA: This is kinda grossing me out.
DEVILJACK: You're a fucking pussy.
DADDY_ROTH: You ever see a honky turn that shade?
ONE_PERCENTER: If he makes this cocksuck-ers eyeballs pop all the way out I'll pay 2 Bitcoins!
BALLER_REX: Looks like I won't be the only one going broke in this stream then. haha
YELLOW_DAWG: All Hail POKERFACE! When's the next stream?
POKER FACE IS BACK FROM VACATION AND FEELING CRUEL!
POKER FACE
ROOM KING: DANK_FUKK_365
BID INCREMENTS: 00.0500
₿0.0000
PAY

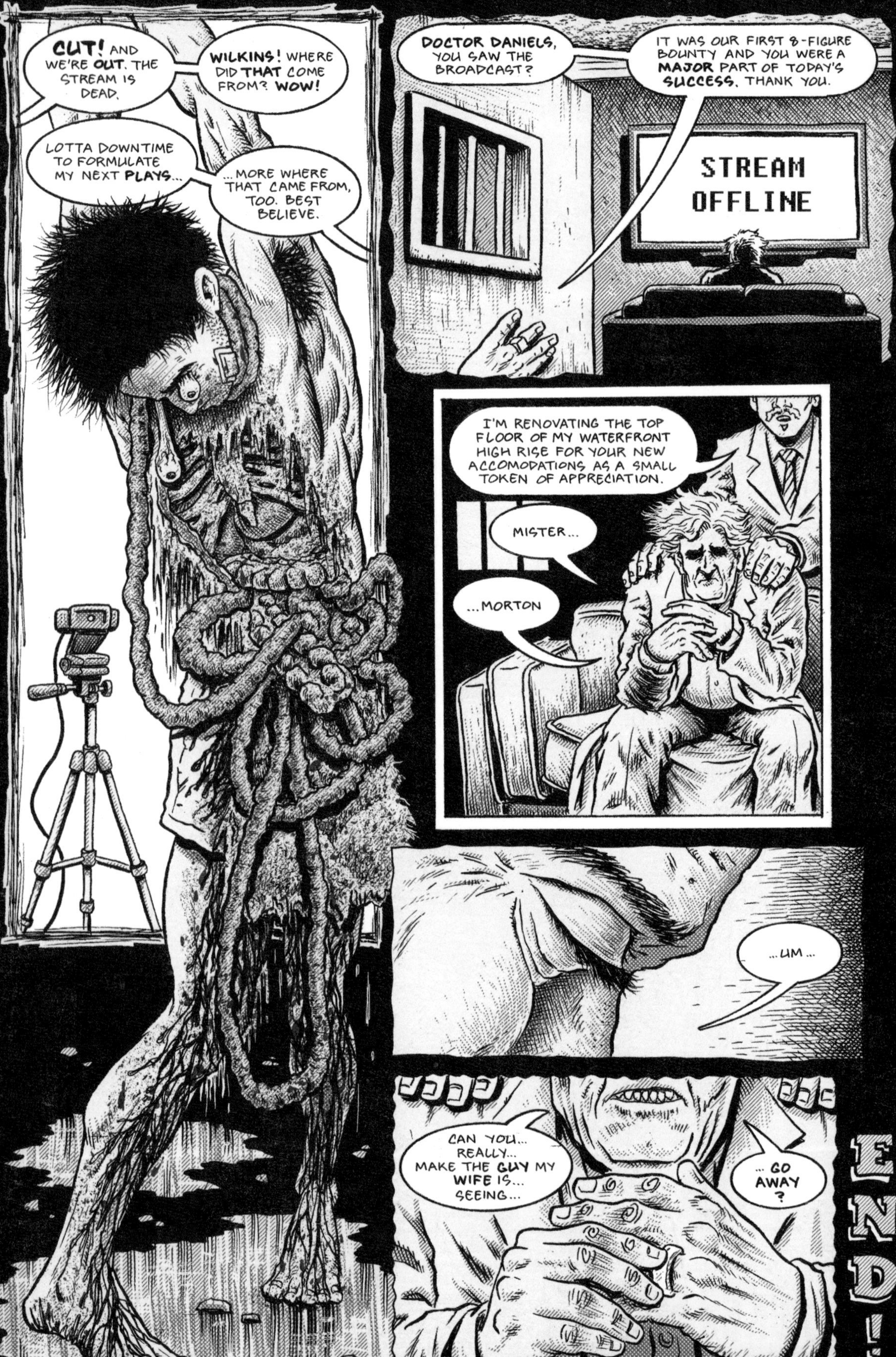
CUT! AND WE'RE OUT. THE STREAM IS DEAD.
WILKINS! WHERE DID THAT COME FROM? WOW!
LOTTA DOWNTIME TO FORMULATE MY NEXT PLAYS...
...MORE WHERE THAT CAME FROM, TOO. BEST BELIEVE.
DOCTOR DANIELS, YOU SAW THE BROADCAST?
IT WAS OUR FIRST 8-FIGURE BOUNTY AND YOU WERE A MAJOR PART OF TODAY'S SUCCESS. THANK YOU.
STREAM OFFLINE
I'M RENOVATING THE TOP FLOOR OF MY WATERFRONT HIGH RISE FOR YOUR NEW ACCOMODATIONS AS A SMALL TOKEN OF APPRECIATION.
MISTER...
...MORTON
...UM...
CAN YOU... REALLY... MAKE THE GUY MY WIFE IS... SEEING...
...GO AWAY?
END!

THREE

UNINTENDED CONSEQUENCES

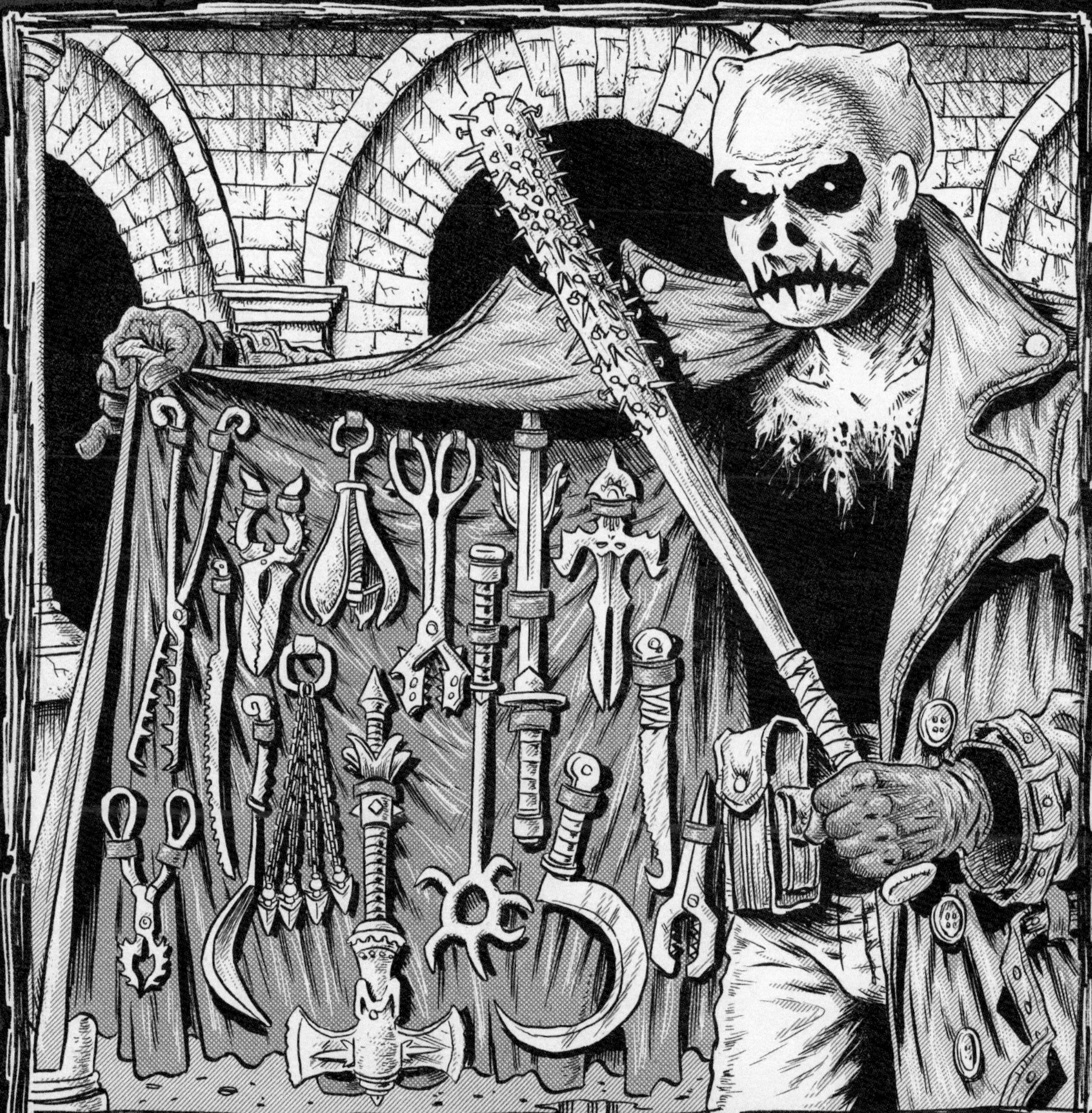

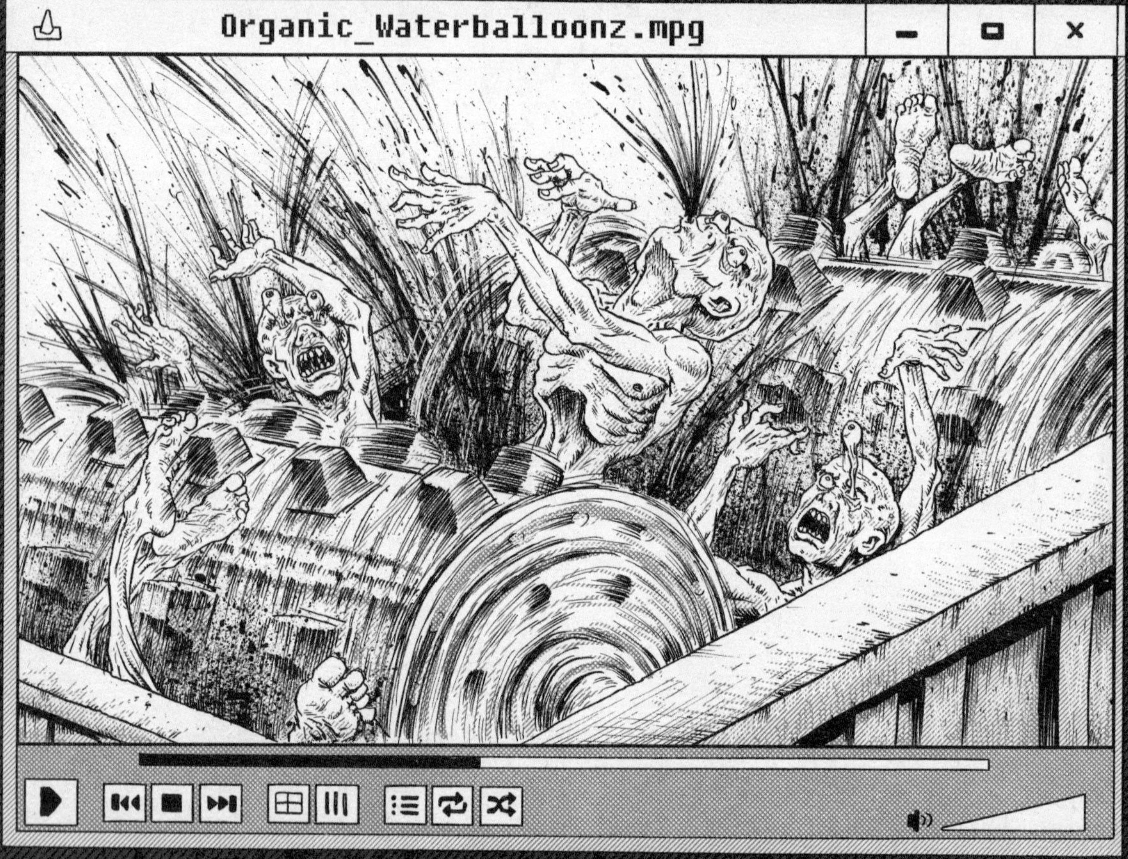
Organic_Waterballoonz.mpg

The DARK WEB provides means to use the internet ANONYMOUSLY, free from consequence. CRYPTOCURRENCY transactions lack a detectable paper trail, providing further obfuscation. These tools are being abused to create a NEFARIOUS subculture of MURDER for ENTERTAINMENT in real time via WEBCAM. WHO would participate in such a sick enterprise? WHO are the VICTIMS? WHO are the CUSTOMERS? WHO are the MURDERERS?

ED PISKOR PRESENTS: RED ROOM, THE ANTISOCIAL NETWORK

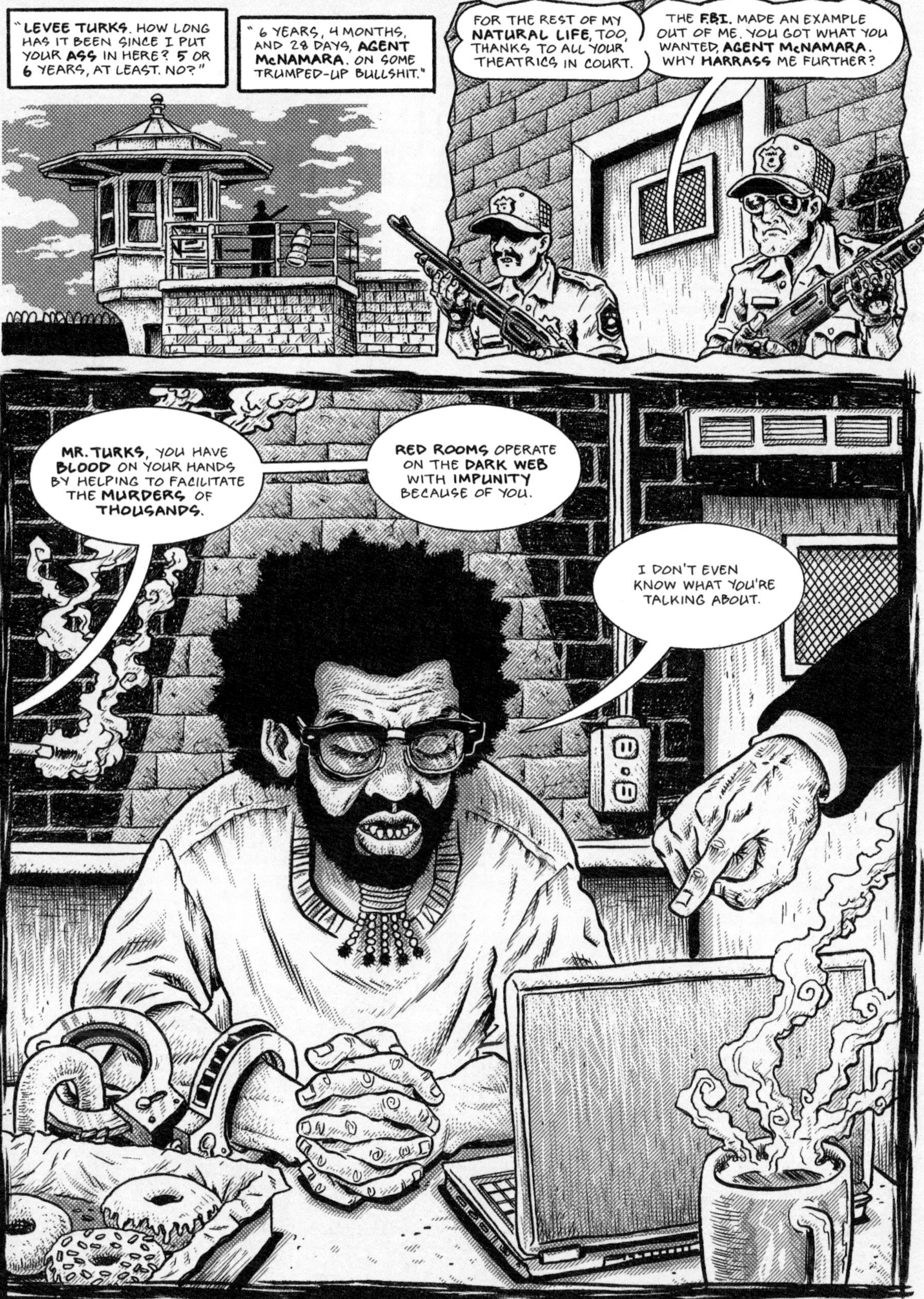
"LEVEE TURKS. HOW LONG HAS IT BEEN SINCE I PUT YOUR ASS IN HERE? 5 OR 6 YEARS, AT LEAST. NO?"
"6 YEARS, 4 MONTHS, AND 28 DAYS, AGENT McNAMARA. ON SOME TRUMPED-UP BULLSHIT."
FOR THE REST OF MY NATURAL LIFE, TOO, THANKS TO ALL YOUR THEATRICS IN COURT.
THE F.B.I. MADE AN EXAMPLE OUT OF ME. YOU GOT WHAT YOU WANTED, AGENT McNAMARA. WHY HARRASS ME FURTHER?
MR. TURKS, YOU HAVE BLOOD ON YOUR HANDS BY HELPING TO FACILITATE THE MURDERS OF THOUSANDS.
RED ROOMS OPERATE ON THE DARK WEB WITH IMPUNITY BECAUSE OF YOU.
I DON'T EVEN KNOW WHAT YOU'RE TALKING ABOUT.

" I WARNED YOU WHEN WE BUSTED YOUR **DARK WEB** DRUG EMPORIUM THAT IT WOULD HAVE A LASTING NEGATIVE EFFECT ON THE WORLD BEYOND YOUR MEAGER AND SHORT-SIGHTED **LIBERTARIAN** IDEALS."

"THE SUITE OF **ENCRYPTION** SOFTWARE YOU CREATED TO KEEP YOUR **BLACK MARKET** IN THE SHADOWS; THE **CHAT** CLIENT, THE **BITCOIN** TRADING APP, THE **ANONYMOUS** VIDEO STREAMING... IT'S ALL BEING USED IN THE SERVICE OF A MULTI-BILLION DOLLAR **SNUFF** INDUSTRY."

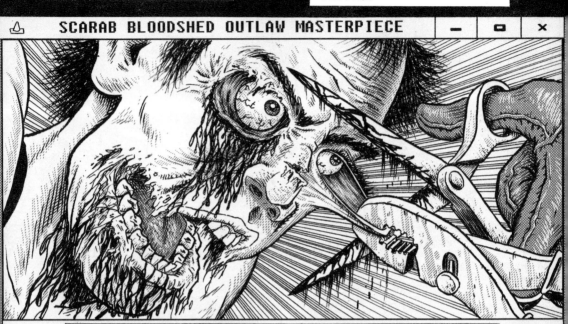

SCARAB BLOODSHED OUTLAW MASTERPIECE

" DID THOSE **CAM SLUT** CHATROOMS EXIST WHEN YOU WERE ON THE OUT-SIDE, **TURKS?** SEND THE GIRL SOME TIP MONEY, SHE PROCESSES PERVY REQUESTS. LIKE THAT..."

" **RED ROOMS** ARE THE **MURDER** AND **TORTURE** VERSION OF THE CONCEPT. YOUR SOFTWARE HAS BLOCKED EVERY ATTEMPT TO HOLD ALL **GUILTY** PARTIES **ACCOUNTABLE.**"

SCARAB BLOODSHED OUTLAW MASTERPIECE

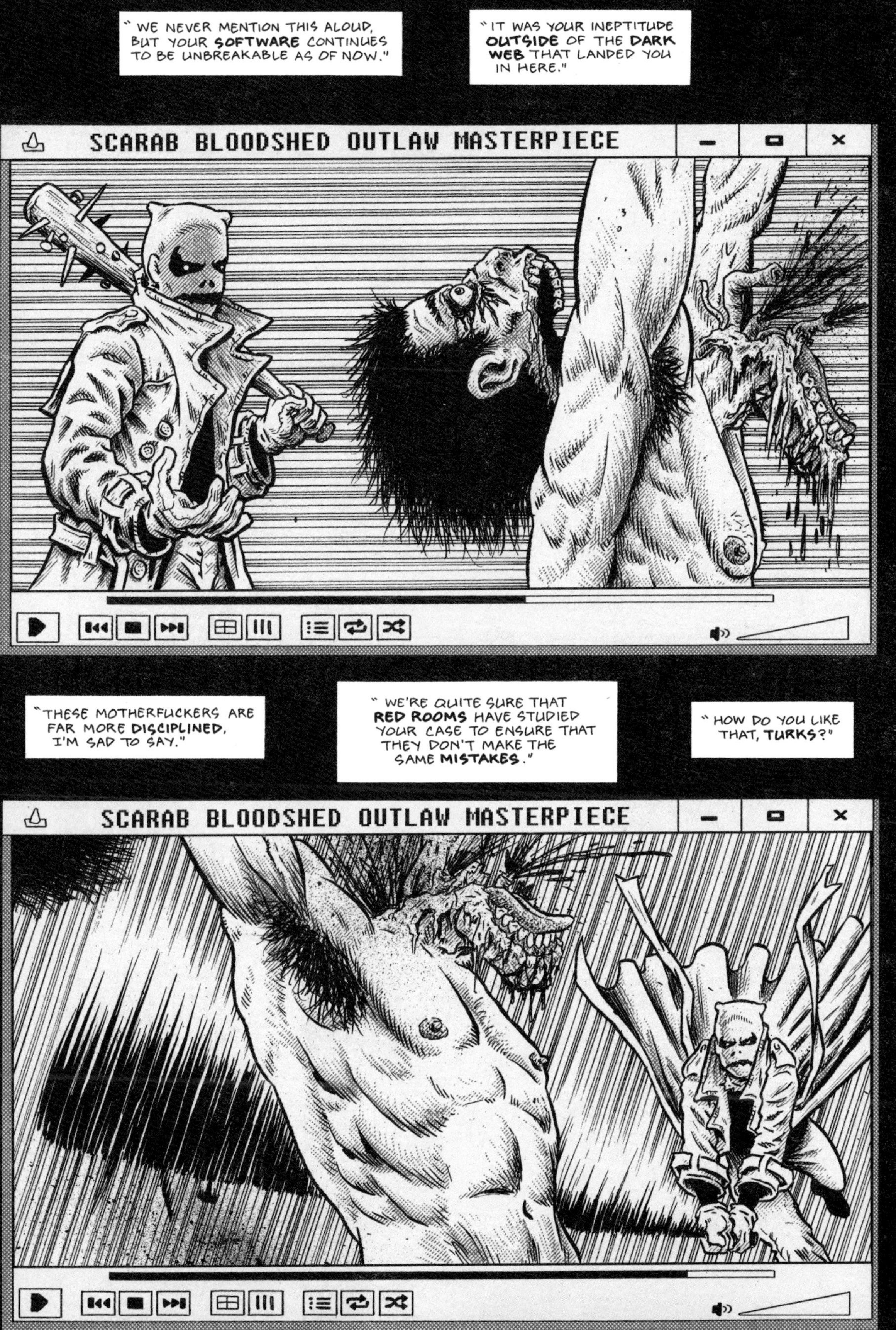

" WE NEVER MENTION THIS ALOUD, BUT YOUR **SOFTWARE** CONTINUES TO BE UNBREAKABLE AS OF NOW."
" IT WAS YOUR INEPTITUDE **OUTSIDE** OF THE **DARK WEB** THAT LANDED YOU IN HERE."
SCARAB BLOODSHED OUTLAW MASTERPIECE
"THESE MOTHERFUCKERS ARE FAR MORE **DISCIPLINED**, I'M SAD TO SAY."
" WE'RE QUITE SURE THAT **RED ROOMS** HAVE STUDIED YOUR CASE TO ENSURE THAT THEY DON'T MAKE THE SAME **MISTAKES**."
" HOW DO YOU LIKE THAT, **TURKS**?"
SCARAB BLOODSHED OUTLAW MASTERPIECE

SO, YOU **HERBS** GOTTA DO SOME REAL **POLICING** FOR A CHANGE, HUH?

"YOUR **WACK-ASS**, TAX PAYER FUNDED, SCRIPT-KITTY **HACKERS** AIN'T ABLE TO SUPERSEDE ALL THEIR COLLEGE BOOK-LEARNIN' ENOUGH TO GET THE JOB DONE..."

"...SO YA GOTTA MARCH YOUR **FUNKY ASSES** DOWN HERE TO WHAT? HOOK Y'ALL UP WITH A **BACK DOOR** TO MY **CODE** WHILE I **ROT** IN THIS **SHITHOLE?**"

AGENT McNAMARA, HOW DO I LIKE IT? MY **DICK** IS **LEGITIMATELY** HARD RIGHT NOW.

SCARAB BLOODSHED OUTLAW MASTERPIECE

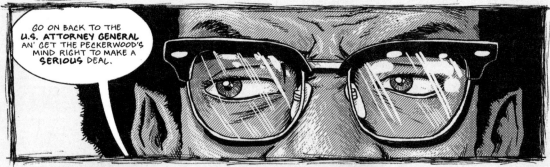

GO ON BACK TO THE **U.S. ATTORNEY GENERAL** AN' GET THE PECKERWOOD'S MIND RIGHT TO MAKE A **SERIOUS** DEAL.

Y'ALL MUST KNOW MY NEXT HEARING AIN'T THAT FAR AWAY.

MY **LAWYER** WILL BE IN TOUCH.

94

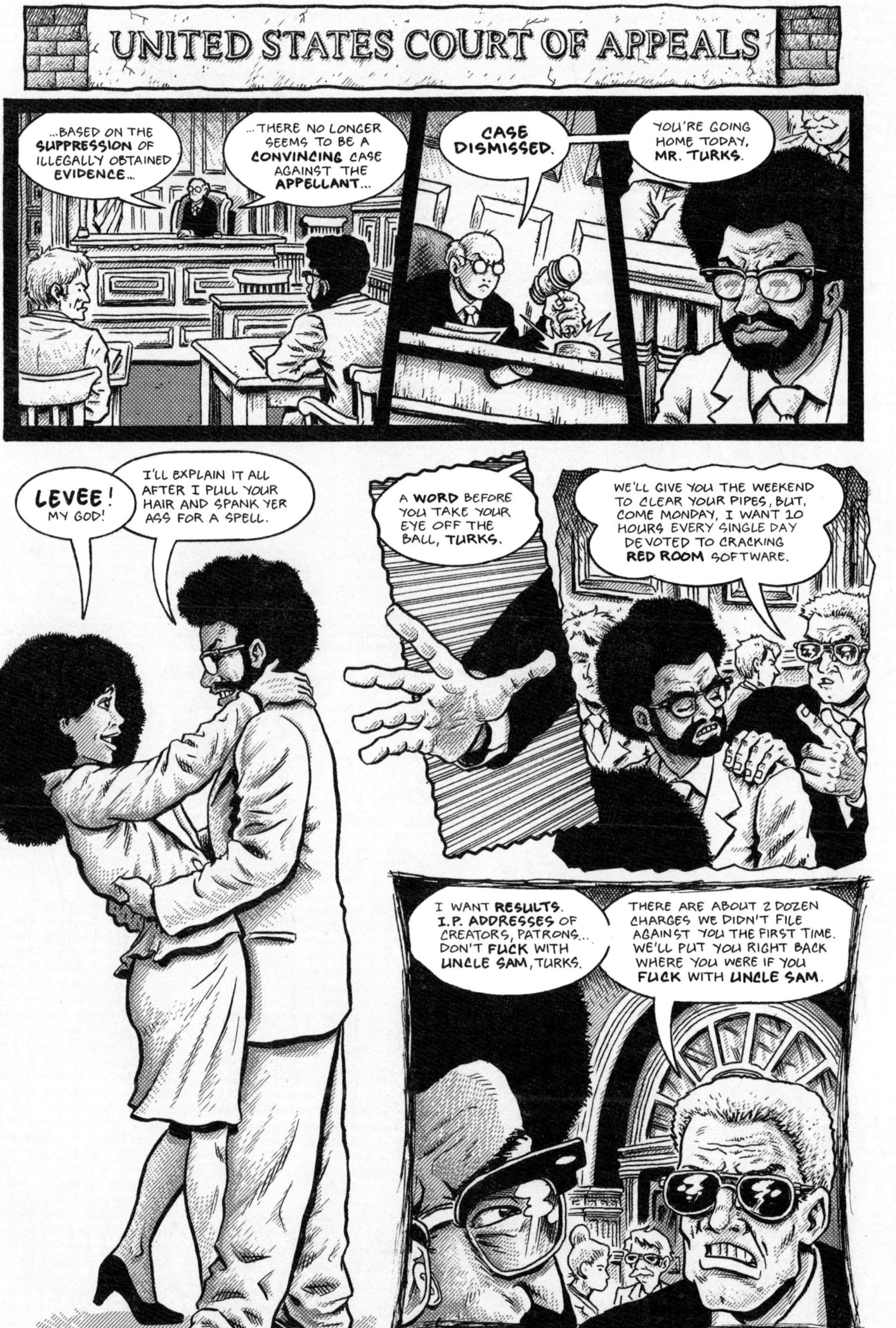
UNITED STATES COURT OF APPEALS
...BASED ON THE SUPPRESSION OF ILLEGALLY OBTAINED EVIDENCE...
...THERE NO LONGER SEEMS TO BE A CONVINCING CASE AGAINST THE APPELLANT...
CASE DISMISSED.
YOU'RE GOING HOME TODAY, MR. TURKS.
LEVEE! MY GOD!
I'LL EXPLAIN IT ALL AFTER I PULL YOUR HAIR AND SPANK YER ASS FOR A SPELL.
A WORD BEFORE YOU TAKE YOUR EYE OFF THE BALL, TURKS.
WE'LL GIVE YOU THE WEEKEND TO CLEAR YOUR PIPES, BUT, COME MONDAY, I WANT 10 HOURS EVERY SINGLE DAY DEVOTED TO CRACKING RED ROOM SOFTWARE.
I WANT RESULTS. I.P. ADDRESSES OF CREATORS, PATRONS... DON'T FUCK WITH UNCLE SAM, TURKS.
THERE ARE ABOUT 2 DOZEN CHARGES WE DIDN'T FILE AGAINST YOU THE FIRST TIME. WE'LL PUT YOU RIGHT BACK WHERE YOU WERE IF YOU FUCK WITH UNCLE SAM.

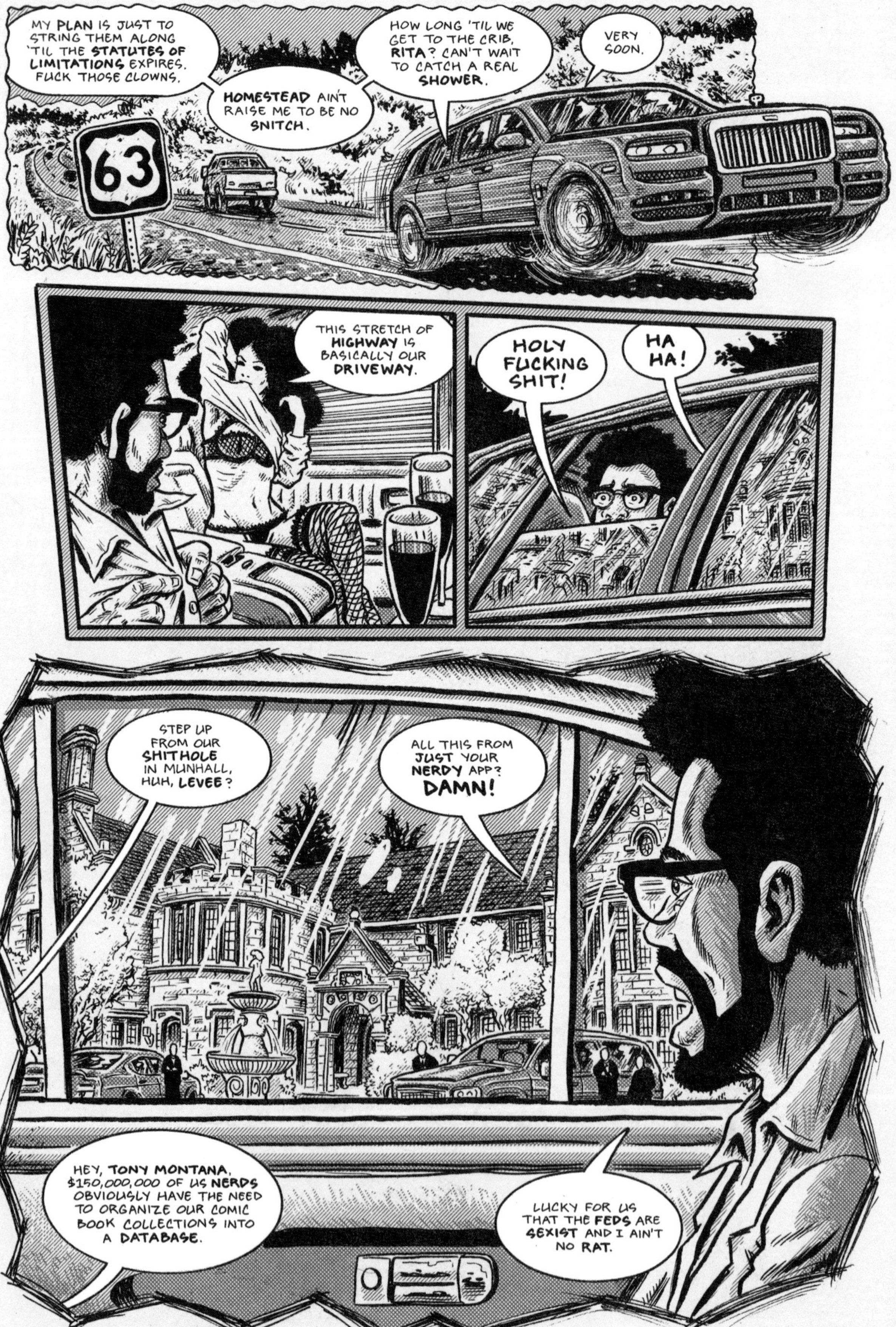
MY PLAN IS JUST TO STRING THEM ALONG 'TIL THE STATUTES OF LIMITATIONS EXPIRES. FUCK THOSE CLOWNS.
HOMESTEAD AIN'T RAISE ME TO BE NO SNITCH.
HOW LONG 'TIL WE GET TO THE CRIB, RITA? CAN'T WAIT TO CATCH A REAL SHOWER.
VERY SOON.
63
THIS STRETCH OF HIGHWAY IS BASICALLY OUR DRIVEWAY.
HOLY FUCKING SHIT!
HA HA!
STEP UP FROM OUR SHITHOLE IN MUNHALL, HUH, LEVEE?
ALL THIS FROM JUST YOUR NERDY APP? DAMN!
HEY, TONY MONTANA, $150,000,000 OF US NERDS OBVIOUSLY HAVE THE NEED TO ORGANIZE OUR COMIC BOOK COLLECTIONS INTO A DATABASE.
LUCKY FOR US THAT THE FEDS ARE SEXIST AND I AIN'T NO RAT.

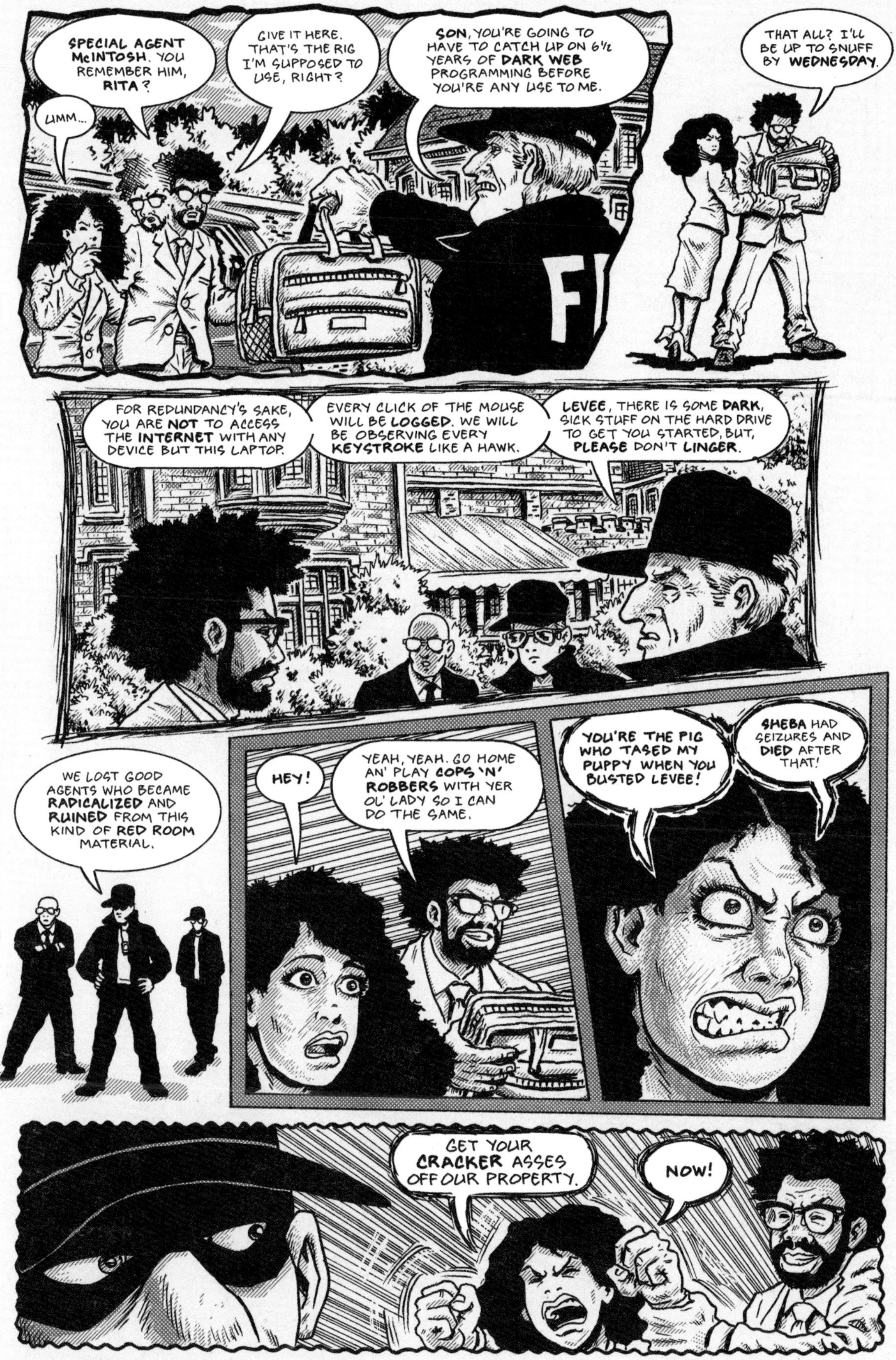
SPECIAL AGENT McINTOSH. YOU REMEMBER HIM, RITA?
UMM...
GIVE IT HERE. THAT'S THE RIG I'M SUPPOSED TO USE, RIGHT?
SON, YOU'RE GOING TO HAVE TO CATCH UP ON 6½ YEARS OF DARK WEB PROGRAMMING BEFORE YOU'RE ANY USE TO ME.
FI
THAT ALL? I'LL BE UP TO SNUFF BY WEDNESDAY.
FOR REDUNDANCY'S SAKE, YOU ARE NOT TO ACCESS THE INTERNET WITH ANY DEVICE BUT THIS LAPTOP.
EVERY CLICK OF THE MOUSE WILL BE LOGGED. WE WILL BE OBSERVING EVERY KEYSTROKE LIKE A HAWK.
LEVEE, THERE IS SOME DARK, SICK STUFF ON THE HARD DRIVE TO GET YOU STARTED, BUT, PLEASE DON'T LINGER.
WE LOST GOOD AGENTS WHO BECAME RADICALIZED AND RUINED FROM THIS KIND OF RED ROOM MATERIAL.
HEY!
YEAH, YEAH. GO HOME AN' PLAY COPS 'N' ROBBERS WITH YER OL' LADY SO I CAN DO THE SAME.
YOU'RE THE PIG WHO TASED MY PUPPY WHEN YOU BUSTED LEVEE!
SHEBA HAD SEIZURES AND DIED AFTER THAT!
GET YOUR CRACKER ASSES OFF OUR PROPERTY.
NOW!

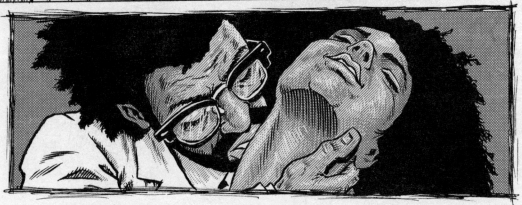

98

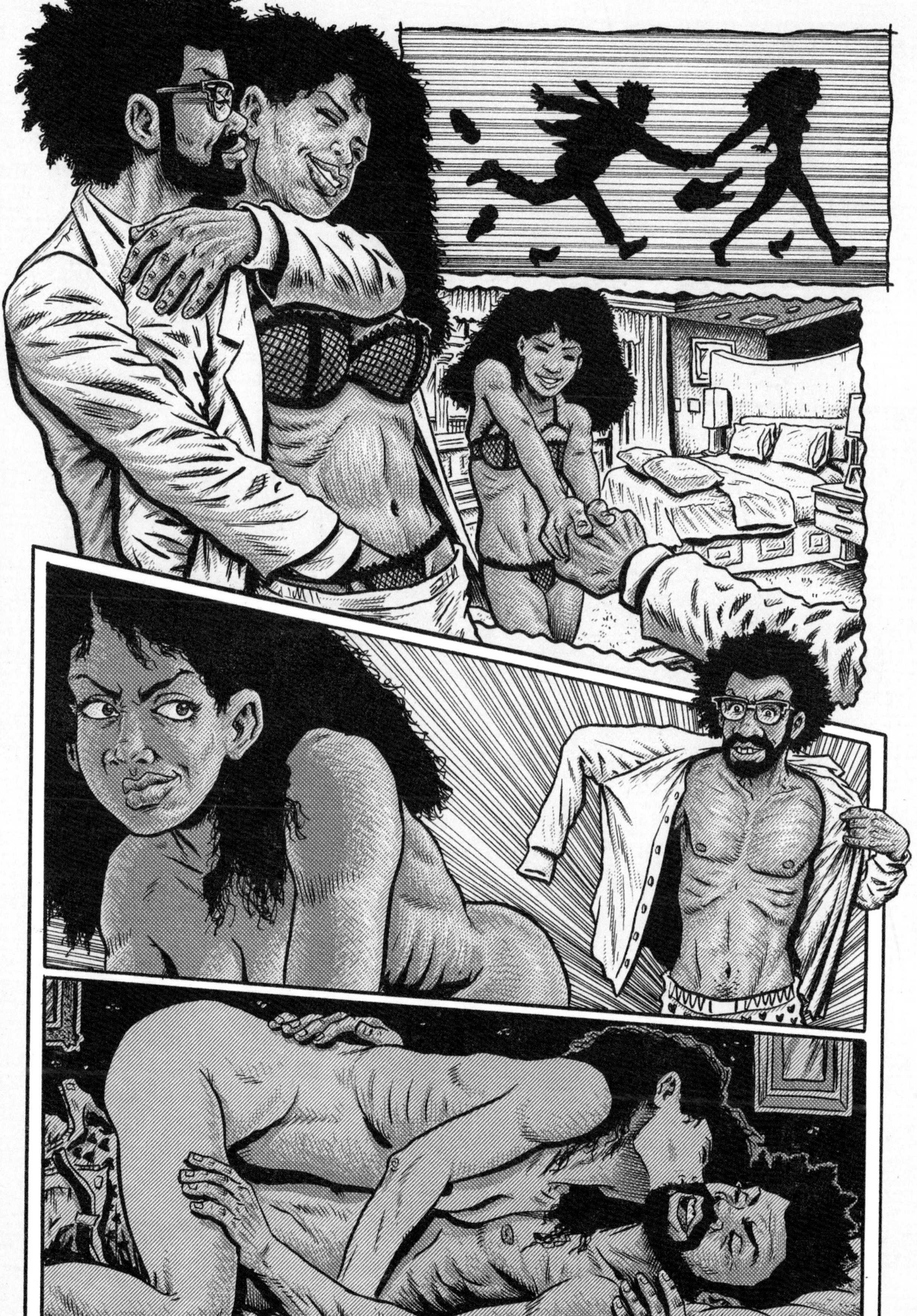

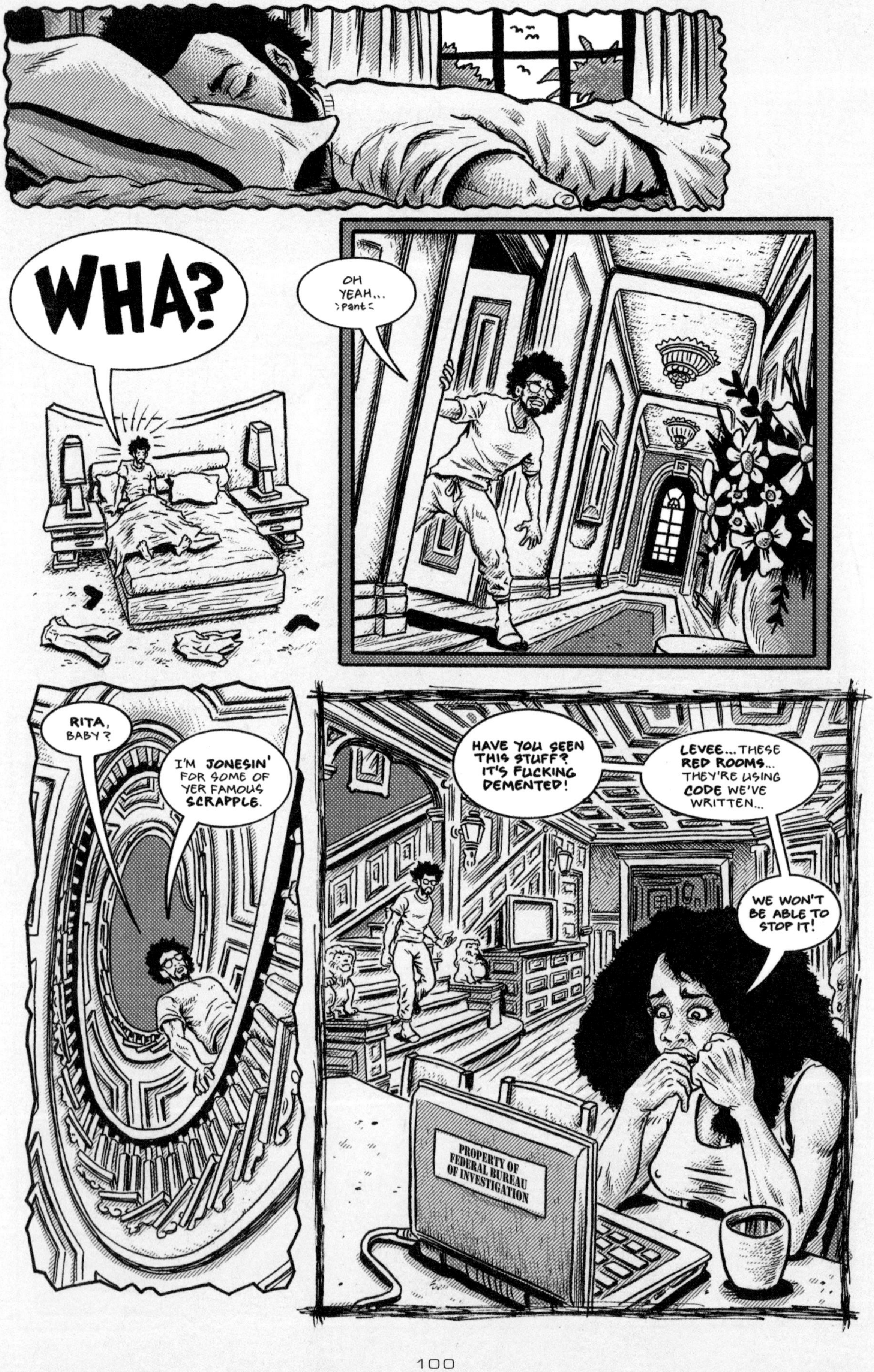
WHA?
OH YEAH... >pant<
RITA, BABY?
I'M JONESIN' FOR SOME OF YER FAMOUS SCRAPPLE.
HAVE YOU SEEN THIS STUFF? IT'S FUCKING DEMENTED!
LEVEE... THESE RED ROOMS... THEY'RE USING CODE WE'VE WRITTEN...
WE WON'T BE ABLE TO STOP IT!
PROPERTY OF FEDERAL BUREAU OF INVESTIGATION

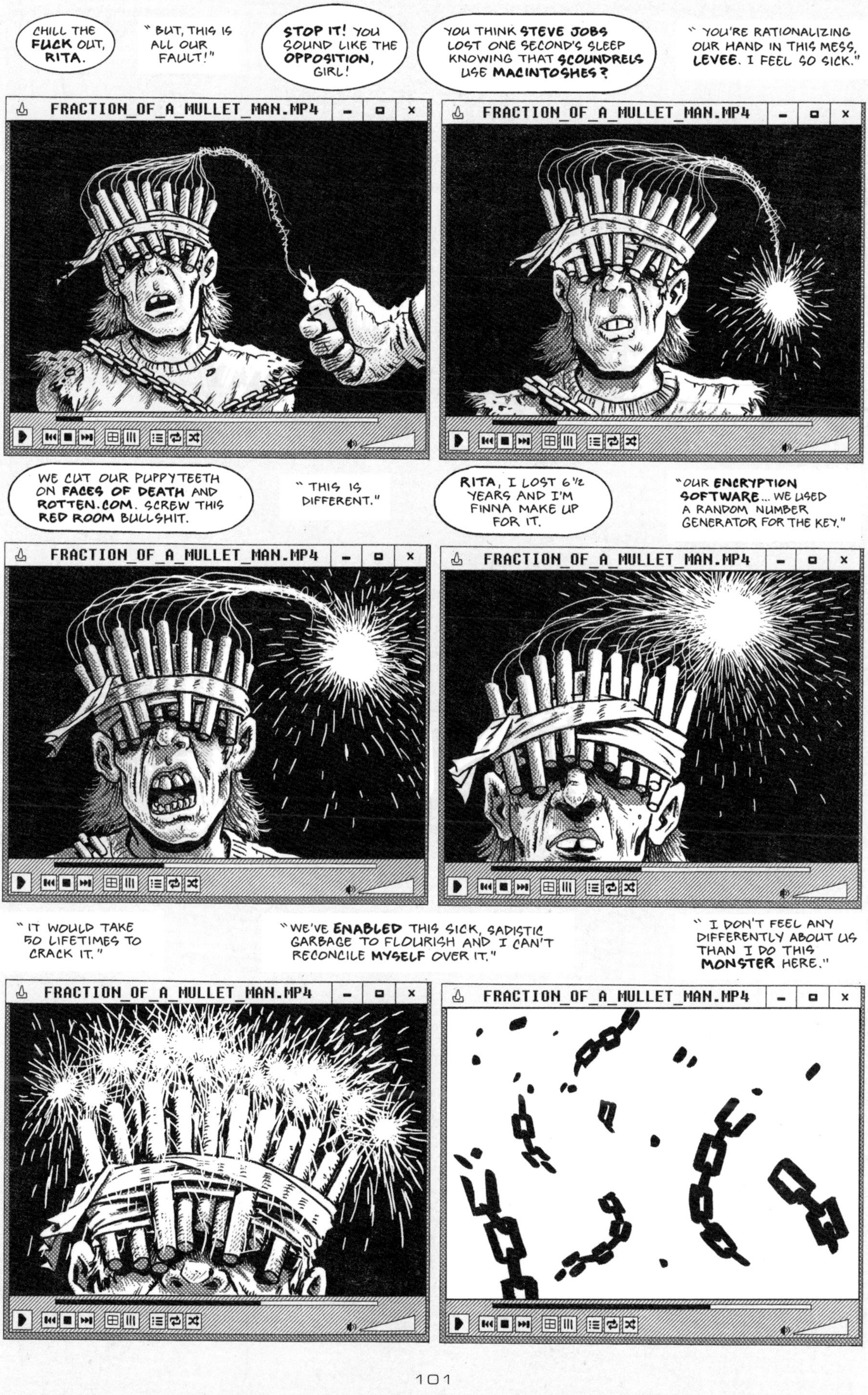
CHILL THE FUCK OUT, RITA.
" BUT, THIS IS ALL OUR FAULT!"
STOP IT! YOU SOUND LIKE THE OPPOSITION, GIRL!
YOU THINK STEVE JOBS LOST ONE SECOND'S SLEEP KNOWING THAT SCOUNDRELS USE MACINTOSHES?
" YOU'RE RATIONALIZING OUR HAND IN THIS MESS, LEVEE. I FEEL SO SICK."
FRACTION_OF_A_MULLET_MAN.MP4
FRACTION_OF_A_MULLET_MAN.MP4
WE CUT OUR PUPPYTEETH ON FACES OF DEATH AND ROTTEN.COM. SCREW THIS RED ROOM BULLSHIT.
" THIS IS DIFFERENT."
RITA, I LOST 6½ YEARS AND I'M FINNA MAKE UP FOR IT.
"OUR ENCRYPTION SOFTWARE... WE USED A RANDOM NUMBER GENERATOR FOR THE KEY."
FRACTION_OF_A_MULLET_MAN.MP4
FRACTION_OF_A_MULLET_MAN.MP4
" IT WOULD TAKE 50 LIFETIMES TO CRACK IT."
"WE'VE ENABLED THIS SICK, SADISTIC GARBAGE TO FLOURISH AND I CAN'T RECONCILE MYSELF OVER IT."
" I DON'T FEEL ANY DIFFERENTLY ABOUT US THAN I DO THIS MONSTER HERE."
FRACTION_OF_A_MULLET_MAN.MP4
FRACTION_OF_A_MULLET_MAN.MP4

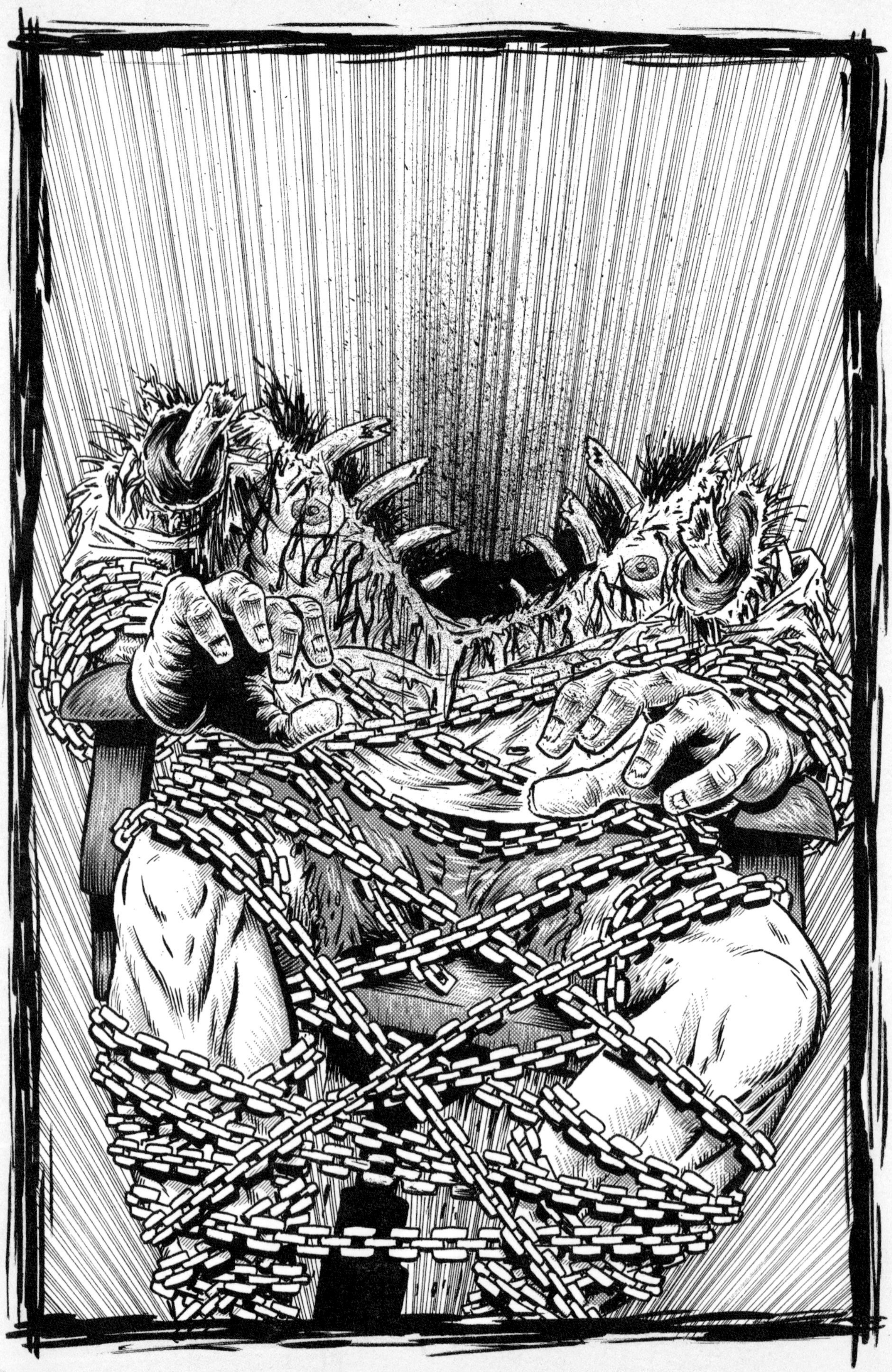

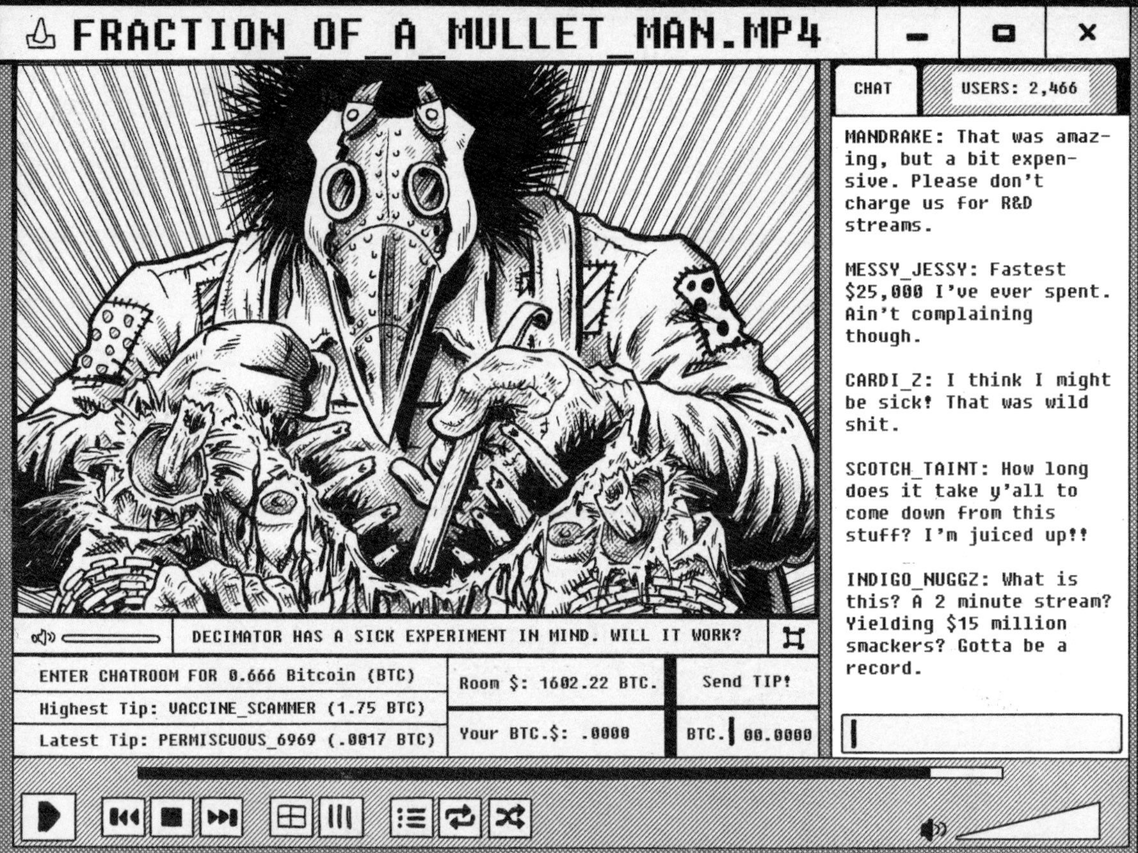
FRACTION_OF_A_MULLET_MAN.MP4
CHAT
USERS: 2,466
MANDRAKE: That was amazing, but a bit expensive. Please don't charge us for R&D streams.
MESSY_JESSY: Fastest $25,000 I've ever spent. Ain't complaining though.
CARDI_Z: I think I might be sick! That was wild shit.
SCOTCH_TAINT: How long does it take y'all to come down from this stuff? I'm juiced up!!
INDIGO_NUGGZ: What is this? A 2 minute stream? Yielding $15 million smackers? Gotta be a record.
DECIMATOR HAS A SICK EXPERIMENT IN MIND. WILL IT WORK?
ENTER CHATROOM FOR 0.666 Bitcoin (BTC)
Highest Tip: VACCINE_SCAMMER (1.75 BTC)
Latest Tip: PERMISCUOUS_6969 (.0017 BTC)
Room $: 1602.22 BTC.
Your BTC.$: .0000
Send TIP!
BTC. 00.0000

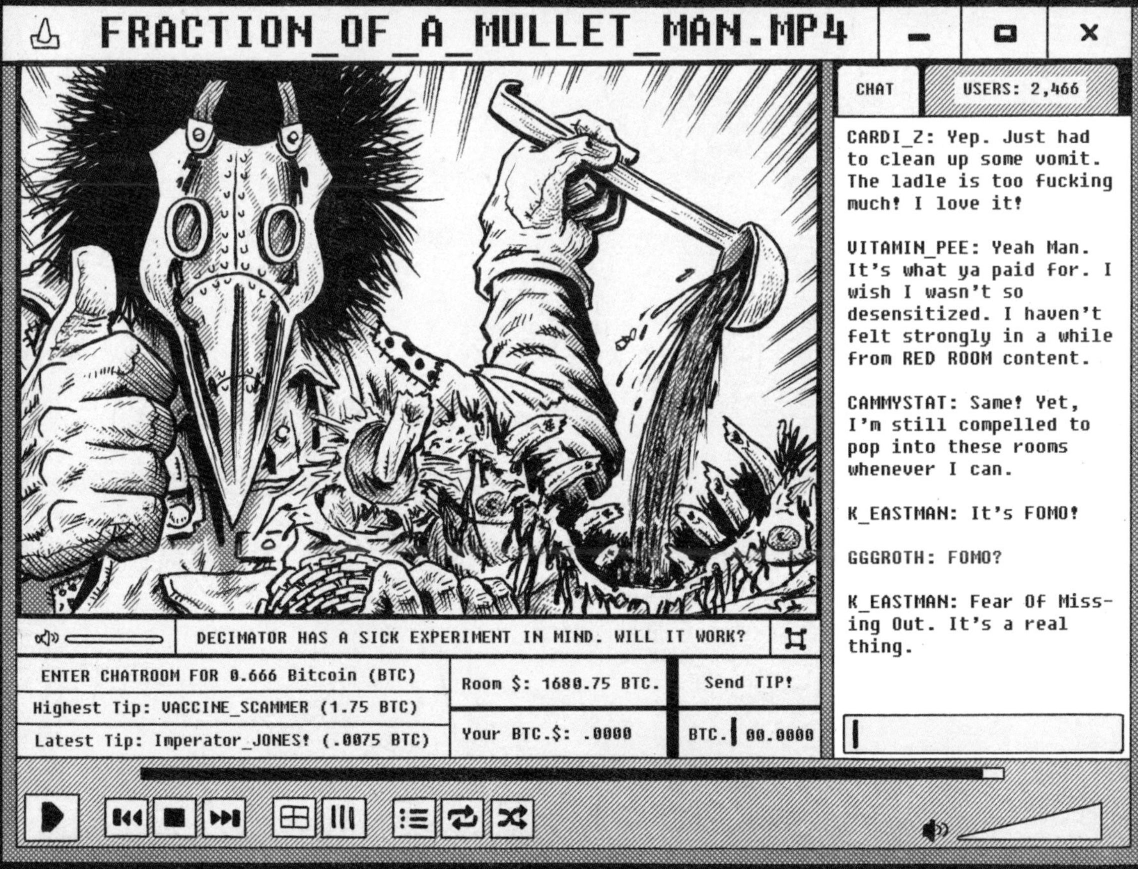
FRACTION_OF_A_MULLET_MAN.MP4
CHAT
USERS: 2,466
CARDI_Z: Yep. Just had to clean up some vomit. The ladle is too fucking much! I love it!
VITAMIN_PEE: Yeah Man. It's what ya paid for. I wish I wasn't so desensitized. I haven't felt strongly in a while from RED ROOM content.
CAMMYSTAT: Same! Yet, I'm still compelled to pop into these rooms whenever I can.
K_EASTMAN: It's FOMO!
GGGROTH: FOMO?
K_EASTMAN: Fear Of Missing Out. It's a real thing.
DECIMATOR HAS A SICK EXPERIMENT IN MIND. WILL IT WORK?
ENTER CHATROOM FOR 0.666 Bitcoin (BTC)
Highest Tip: VACCINE_SCAMMER (1.75 BTC)
Latest Tip: Imperator_JONES! (.0075 BTC)
Room $: 1680.75 BTC.
Your BTC.$: .0000
Send TIP!
BTC. 00.0000

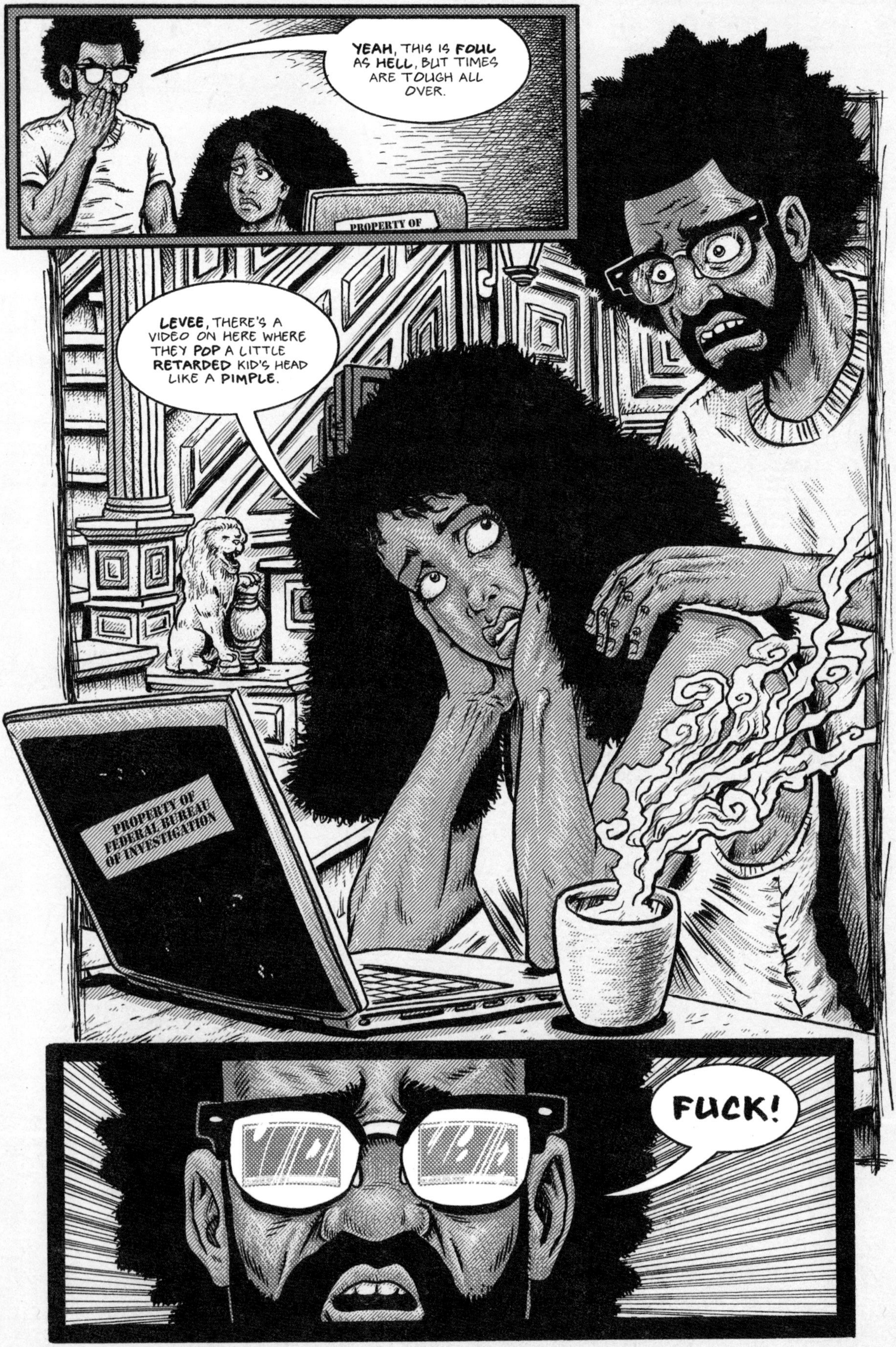
YEAH, THIS IS FOUL AS HELL, BUT TIMES ARE TOUGH ALL OVER.
PROPERTY OF
LEVEE, THERE'S A VIDEO ON HERE WHERE THEY POP A LITTLE RETARDED KID'S HEAD LIKE A PIMPLE.
PROPERTY OF FEDERAL BUREAU OF INVESTIGATION
FUCK!

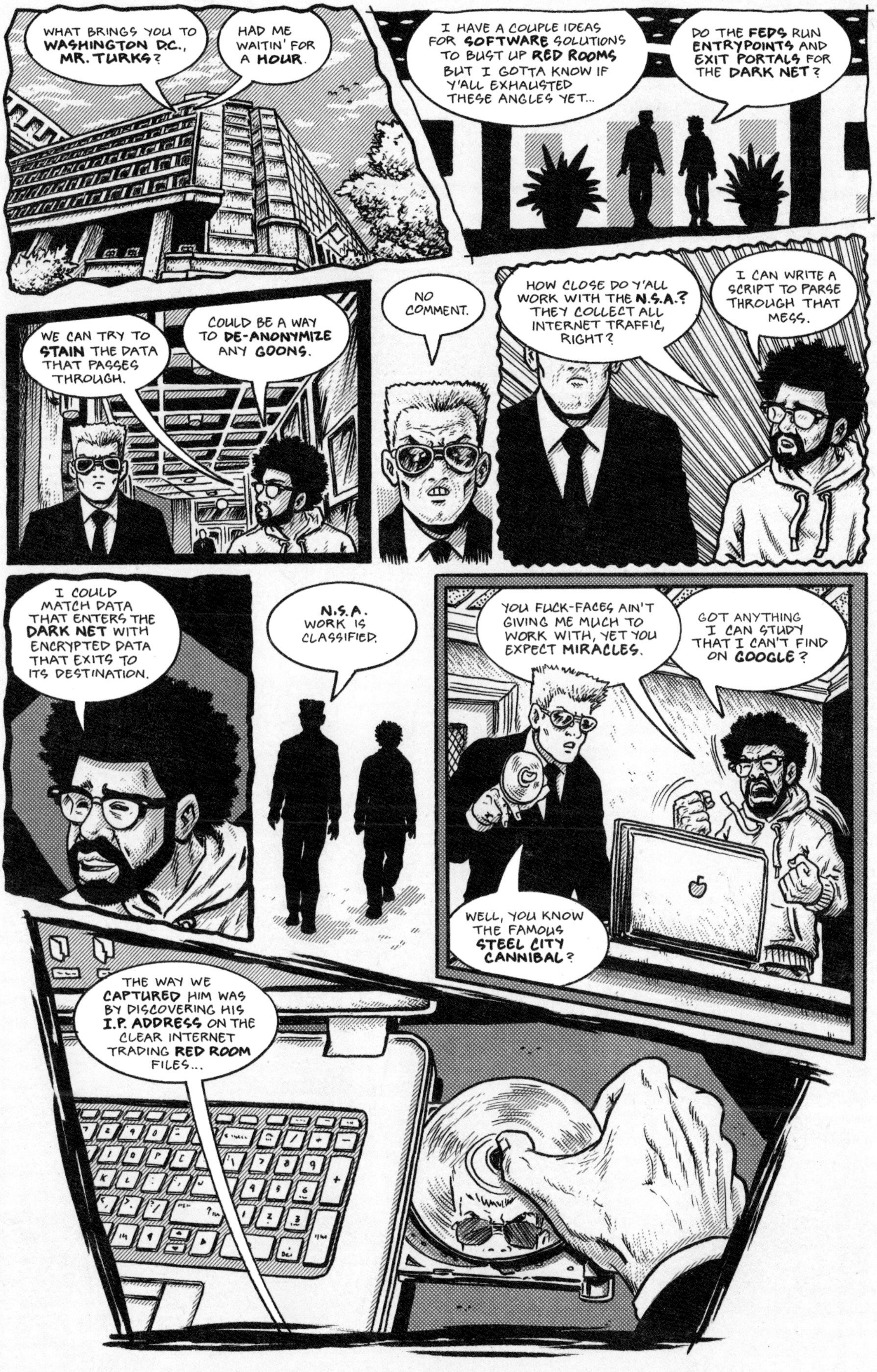
WHAT BRINGS YOU TO WASHINGTON D.C., MR. TURKS?
HAD ME WAITIN' FOR A HOUR.
I HAVE A COUPLE IDEAS FOR SOFTWARE SOLUTIONS TO BUST UP RED ROOMS BUT I GOTTA KNOW IF Y'ALL EXHAUSTED THESE ANGLES YET...
DO THE FEDS RUN ENTRYPOINTS AND EXIT PORTALS FOR THE DARK NET?
WE CAN TRY TO STAIN THE DATA THAT PASSES THROUGH.
COULD BE A WAY TO DE-ANONYMIZE ANY GOONS.
NO COMMENT.
HOW CLOSE DO Y'ALL WORK WITH THE N.S.A.? THEY COLLECT ALL INTERNET TRAFFIC, RIGHT?
I CAN WRITE A SCRIPT TO PARSE THROUGH THAT MESS.
I COULD MATCH DATA THAT ENTERS THE DARK NET WITH ENCRYPTED DATA THAT EXITS TO ITS DESTINATION.
N.S.A. WORK IS CLASSIFIED.
YOU FUCK-FACES AIN'T GIVING ME MUCH TO WORK WITH, YET YOU EXPECT MIRACLES.
GOT ANYTHING I CAN STUDY THAT I CAN'T FIND ON GOOGLE?
WELL, YOU KNOW THE FAMOUS STEEL CITY CANNIBAL?
THE WAY WE CAPTURED HIM WAS BY DISCOVERING HIS I.P. ADDRESS ON THE CLEAR INTERNET TRADING RED ROOM FILES...

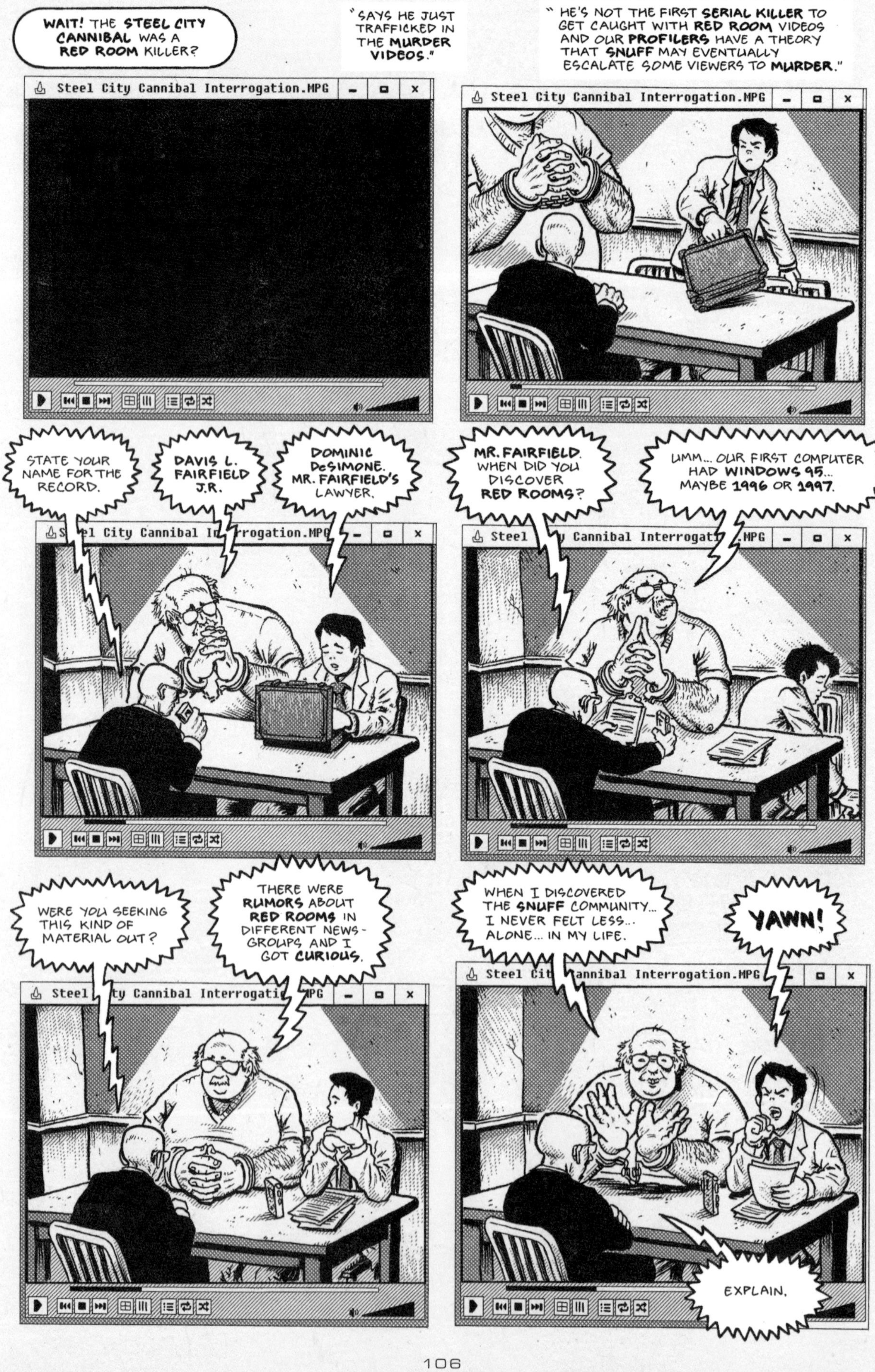
WAIT! THE STEEL CITY CANNIBAL WAS A RED ROOM KILLER?
"SAYS HE JUST TRAFFICKED IN THE MURDER VIDEOS."
"HE'S NOT THE FIRST SERIAL KILLER TO GET CAUGHT WITH RED ROOM VIDEOS AND OUR PROFILERS HAVE A THEORY THAT SNUFF MAY EVENTUALLY ESCALATE SOME VIEWERS TO MURDER."
Steel City Cannibal Interrogation.MPG
Steel City Cannibal Interrogation.MPG
STATE YOUR NAME FOR THE RECORD.
DAVIS L. FAIRFIELD J.R.
DOMINIC DeSIMONE. MR. FAIRFIELD'S LAWYER.
MR. FAIRFIELD. WHEN DID YOU DISCOVER RED ROOMS?
UMM... OUR FIRST COMPUTER HAD WINDOWS 95... MAYBE 1996 OR 1997.
WERE YOU SEEKING THIS KIND OF MATERIAL OUT?
THERE WERE RUMORS ABOUT RED ROOMS IN DIFFERENT NEWS-GROUPS AND I GOT CURIOUS.
WHEN I DISCOVERED THE SNUFF COMMUNITY... I NEVER FELT LESS... ALONE... IN MY LIFE.
YAWN!
Steel City Cannibal Interrogation.MPG
EXPLAIN.

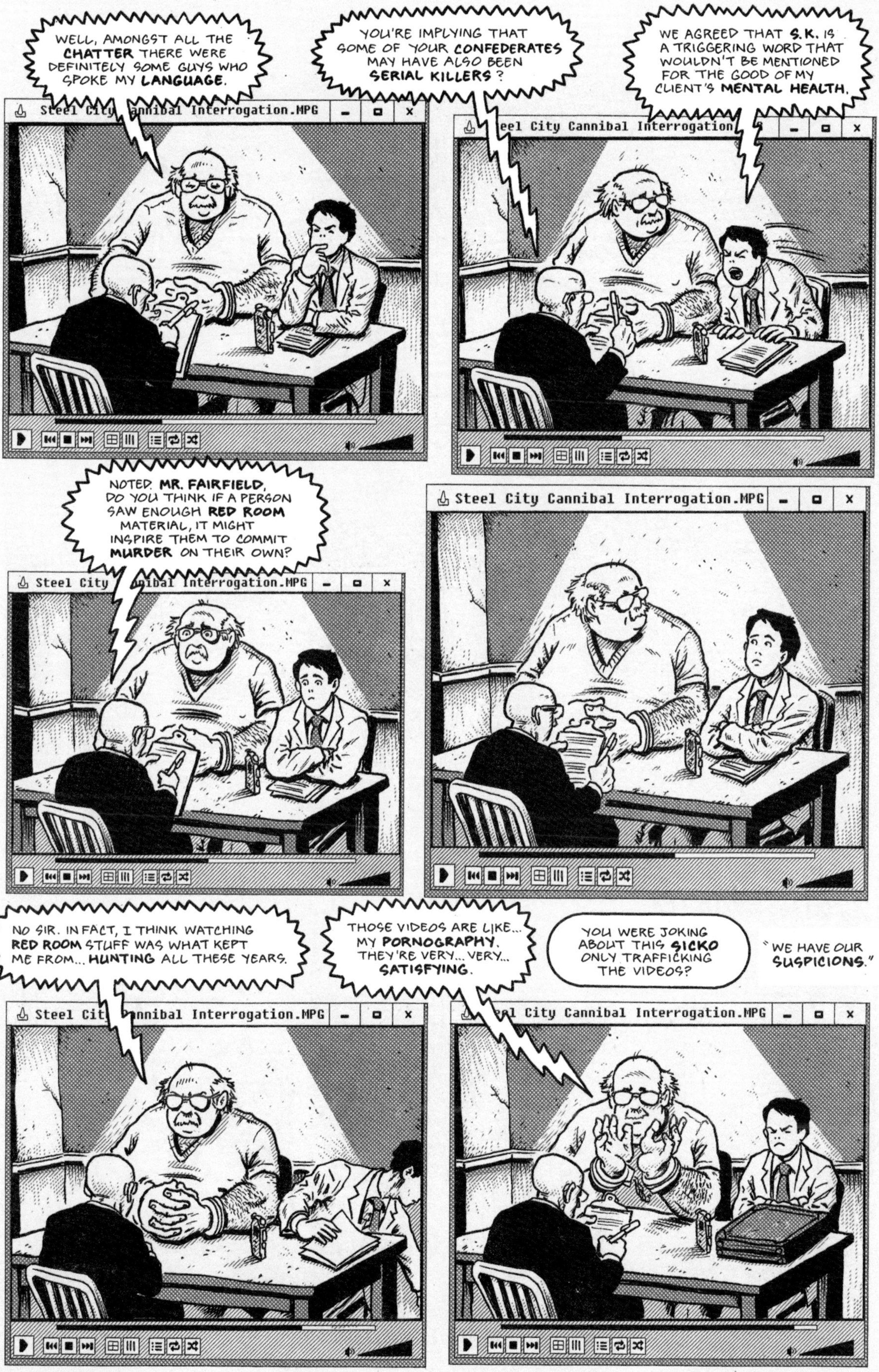
WELL, AMONGST ALL THE CHATTER THERE WERE DEFINITELY SOME GUYS WHO SPOKE MY LANGUAGE.
Steel City Cannibal Interrogation.MPG
YOU'RE IMPLYING THAT SOME OF YOUR CONFEDERATES MAY HAVE ALSO BEEN SERIAL KILLERS?
WE AGREED THAT S.K. IS A TRIGGERING WORD THAT WOULDN'T BE MENTIONED FOR THE GOOD OF MY CLIENT'S MENTAL HEALTH.
Steel City Cannibal Interrogation
NOTED. MR. FAIRFIELD, DO YOU THINK IF A PERSON SAW ENOUGH RED ROOM MATERIAL, IT MIGHT INSPIRE THEM TO COMMIT MURDER ON THEIR OWN?
Steel City Cannibal Interrogation.MPG
Steel City Cannibal Interrogation.MPG
NO SIR. IN FACT, I THINK WATCHING RED ROOM STUFF WAS WHAT KEPT ME FROM... HUNTING ALL THESE YEARS.
Steel City Cannibal Interrogation.MPG
THOSE VIDEOS ARE LIKE... MY PORNOGRAPHY. THEY'RE VERY... VERY... SATISFYING.
YOU WERE JOKING ABOUT THIS SICKO ONLY TRAFFICKING THE VIDEOS?
"WE HAVE OUR SUSPICIONS."
Steel City Cannibal Interrogation.MPG

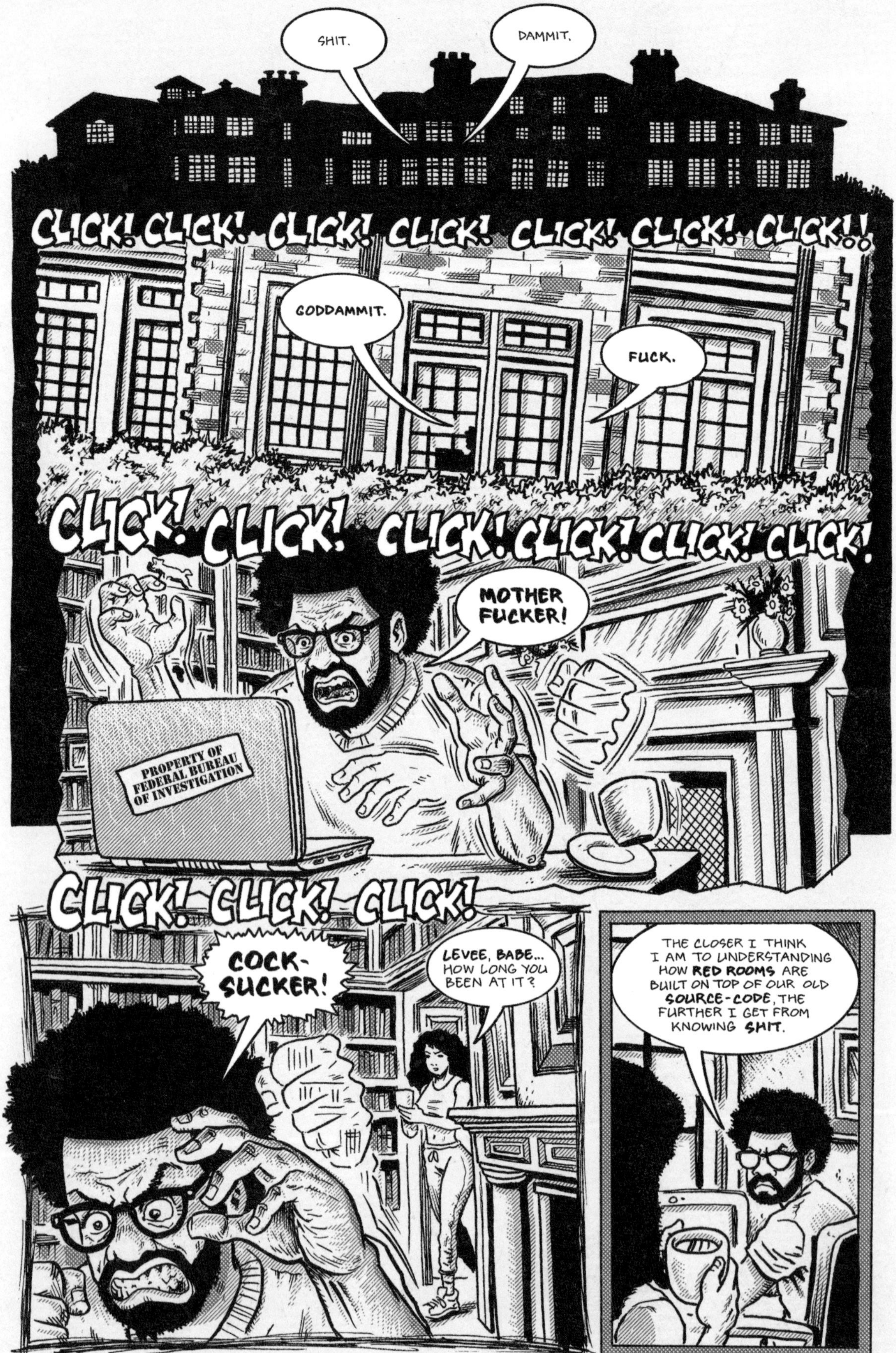
SHIT.
DAMMIT.
CLICK! CLICK! CLICK! CLICK! CLICK! CLICK! CLICK!
GODDAMMIT.
FUCK.
CLICK! CLICK! CLICK! CLICK! CLICK! CLICK!
MOTHER FUCKER!
PROPERTY OF FEDERAL BUREAU OF INVESTIGATION
CLICK! CLICK! CLICK!
COCK-SUCKER!
LEVEE, BABE... HOW LONG YOU BEEN AT IT?
THE CLOSER I THINK I AM TO UNDERSTANDING HOW RED ROOMS ARE BUILT ON TOP OF OUR OLD SOURCE-CODE, THE FURTHER I GET FROM KNOWING SHIT.

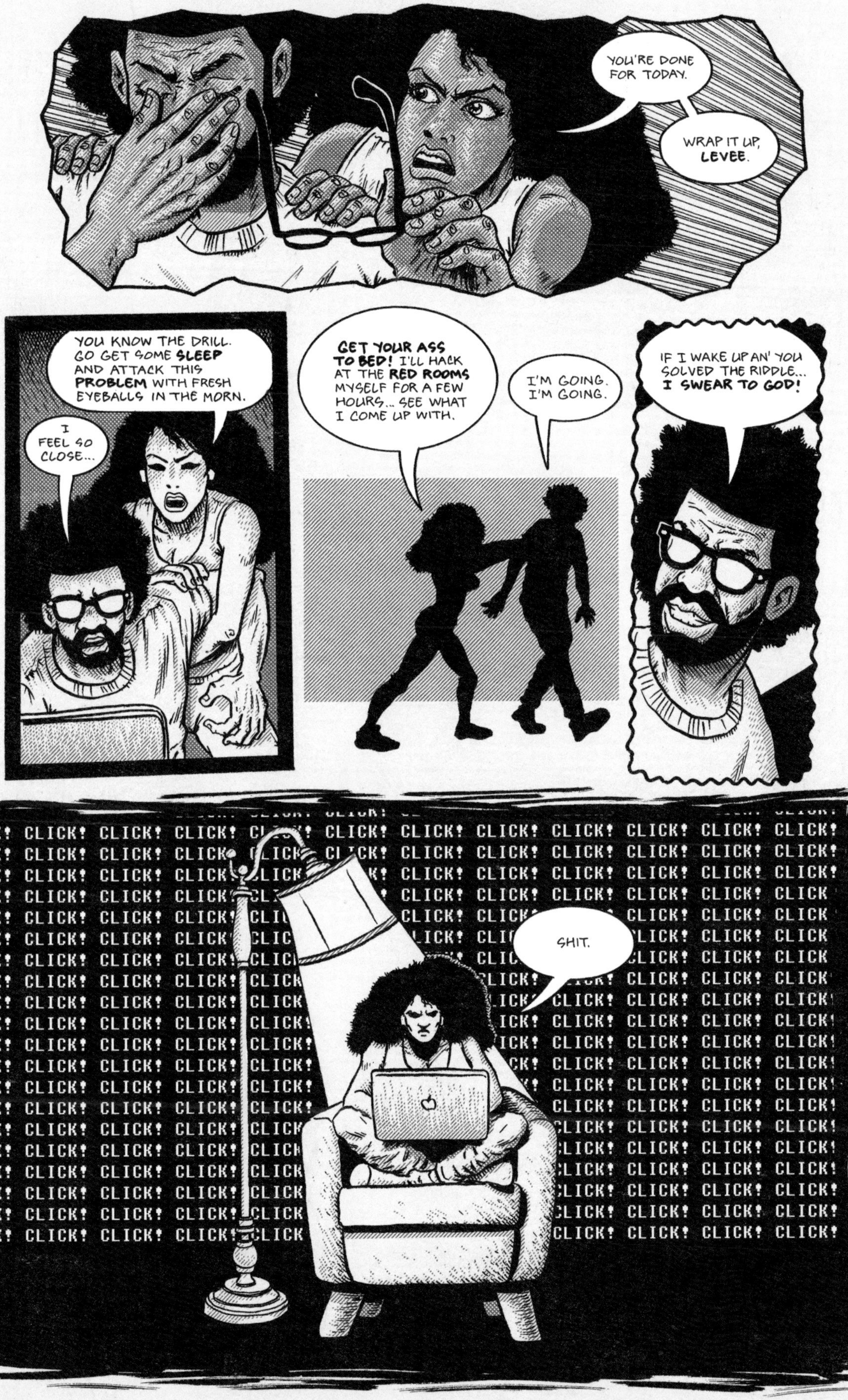
YOU'RE DONE FOR TODAY.
WRAP IT UP, LEVEE.
YOU KNOW THE DRILL. GO GET SOME SLEEP AND ATTACK THIS PROBLEM WITH FRESH EYEBALLS IN THE MORN.
I FEEL SO CLOSE...
GET YOUR ASS TO BED! I'LL HACK AT THE RED ROOMS MYSELF FOR A FEW HOURS... SEE WHAT I COME UP WITH.
I'M GOING. I'M GOING.
IF I WAKE UP AN' YOU SOLVED THE RIDDLE... I SWEAR TO GOD!
CLICK! CLICK! CLICK! CLICK! CLICK! CLICK! CLICK! CLICK! CLICK! CLICK! CLICK!
SHIT.

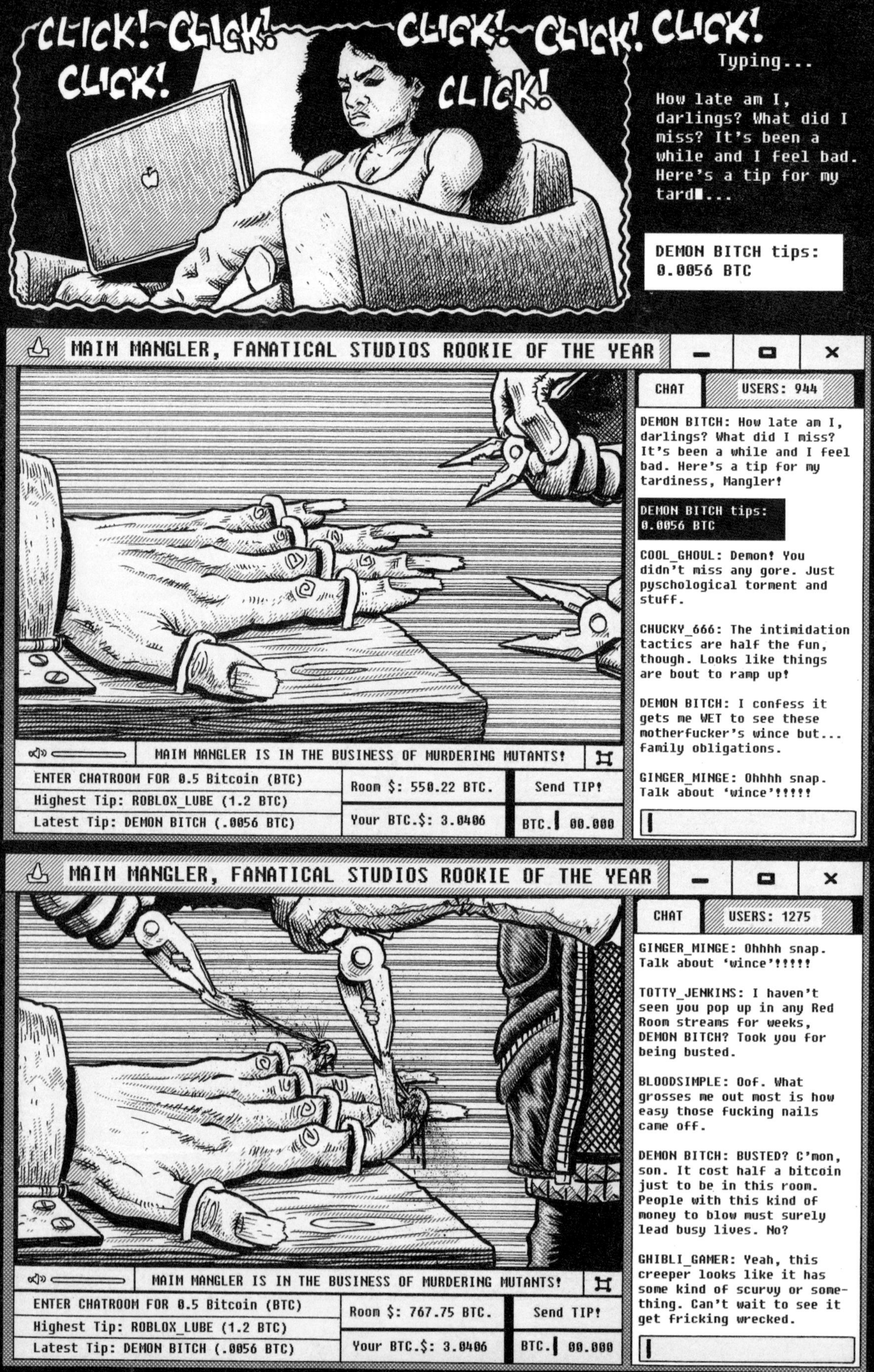
CLICK! CLICK! CLICK!
CLICK! CLICK! CLICK! CLICK!
Typing...
How late am I, darlings? What did I miss? It's been a while and I feel bad. Here's a tip for my tard█...
DEMON BITCH tips: 0.0056 BTC
MAIM MANGLER, FANATICAL STUDIOS ROOKIE OF THE YEAR
CHAT
USERS: 944
DEMON BITCH: How late am I, darlings? What did I miss? It's been a while and I feel bad. Here's a tip for my tardiness, Mangler!
DEMON BITCH tips: 0.0056 BTC
COOL_GHOUL: Demon! You didn't miss any gore. Just pyschological torment and stuff.
CHUCKY_666: The intimidation tactics are half the fun, though. Looks like things are bout to ramp up!
DEMON BITCH: I confess it gets me WET to see these motherfucker's wince but... family obligations.
GINGER_MINGE: Ohhhh snap. Talk about 'wince'!!!!!
MAIM MANGLER IS IN THE BUSINESS OF MURDERING MUTANTS!
ENTER CHATROOM FOR 0.5 Bitcoin (BTC)
Highest Tip: ROBLOX_LUBE (1.2 BTC)
Latest Tip: DEMON BITCH (.0056 BTC)
Room $: 550.22 BTC.
Your BTC.$: 3.0406
Send TIP!
BTC. 00.000
MAIM MANGLER, FANATICAL STUDIOS ROOKIE OF THE YEAR
CHAT
USERS: 1275
GINGER_MINGE: Ohhhh snap. Talk about 'wince'!!!!!
TOTTY_JENKINS: I haven't seen you pop up in any Red Room streams for weeks, DEMON BITCH? Took you for being busted.
BLOODSIMPLE: Oof. What grosses me out most is how easy those fucking nails came off.
DEMON BITCH: BUSTED? C'mon, son. It cost half a bitcoin just to be in this room. People with this kind of money to blow must surely lead busy lives. No?
GHIBLI_GAMER: Yeah, this creeper looks like it has some kind of scurvy or something. Can't wait to see it get fricking wrecked.
MAIM MANGLER IS IN THE BUSINESS OF MURDERING MUTANTS!
ENTER CHATROOM FOR 0.5 Bitcoin (BTC)
Highest Tip: ROBLOX_LUBE (1.2 BTC)
Latest Tip: DEMON BITCH (.0056 BTC)
Room $: 767.75 BTC.
Your BTC.$: 3.0406
Send TIP!
BTC. 00.000

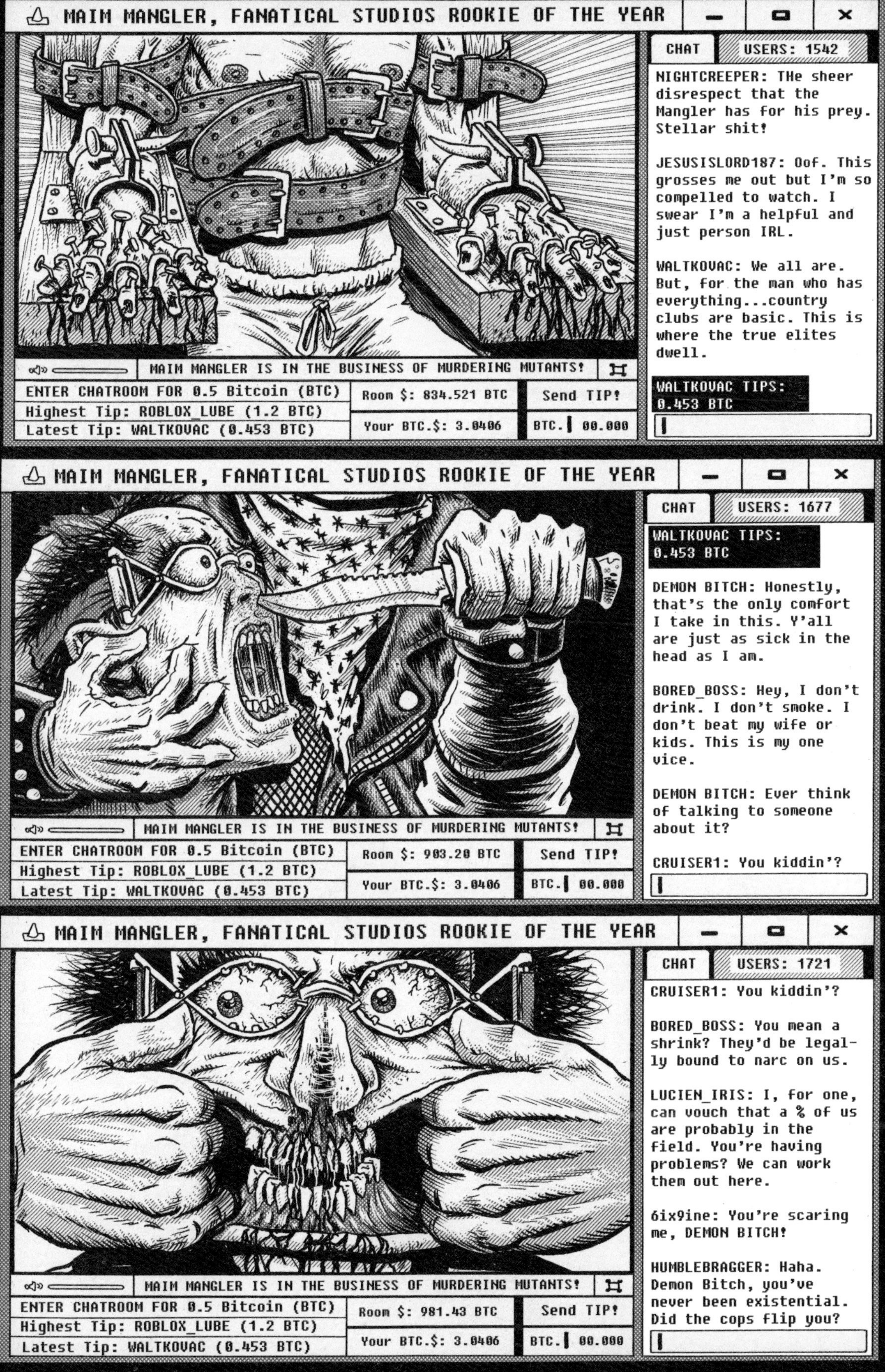
MAIM MANGLER, FANATICAL STUDIOS ROOKIE OF THE YEAR
CHAT
USERS: 1542
NIGHTCREEPER: THe sheer disrespect that the Mangler has for his prey. Stellar shit!
JESUSISLORD187: Oof. This grosses me out but I'm so compelled to watch. I swear I'm a helpful and just person IRL.
WALTKOVAC: We all are. But, for the man who has everything...country clubs are basic. This is where the true elites dwell.
WALTKOVAC TIPS: 0.453 BTC
MAIM MANGLER IS IN THE BUSINESS OF MURDERING MUTANTS!
ENTER CHATROOM FOR 0.5 Bitcoin (BTC)
Highest Tip: ROBLOX_LUBE (1.2 BTC)
Latest Tip: WALTKOVAC (0.453 BTC)
Room $: 834.521 BTC
Your BTC.$: 3.0406
Send TIP!
BTC. 00.000
MAIM MANGLER, FANATICAL STUDIOS ROOKIE OF THE YEAR
CHAT
USERS: 1677
WALTKOVAC TIPS: 0.453 BTC
DEMON BITCH: Honestly, that's the only comfort I take in this. Y'all are just as sick in the head as I am.
BORED_BOSS: Hey, I don't drink. I don't smoke. I don't beat my wife or kids. This is my one vice.
DEMON BITCH: Ever think of talking to someone about it?
CRUISER1: You kiddin'?
MAIM MANGLER IS IN THE BUSINESS OF MURDERING MUTANTS!
ENTER CHATROOM FOR 0.5 Bitcoin (BTC)
Highest Tip: ROBLOX_LUBE (1.2 BTC)
Latest Tip: WALTKOVAC (0.453 BTC)
Room $: 903.20 BTC
Your BTC.$: 3.0406
Send TIP!
BTC. 00.000
MAIM MANGLER, FANATICAL STUDIOS ROOKIE OF THE YEAR
CHAT
USERS: 1721
CRUISER1: You kiddin'?
BORED_BOSS: You mean a shrink? They'd be legally bound to narc on us.
LUCIEN_IRIS: I, for one, can vouch that a % of us are probably in the field. You're having problems? We can work them out here.
6ix9ine: You're scaring me, DEMON BITCH!
HUMBLEBRAGGER: Haha. Demon Bitch, you've never been existential. Did the cops flip you?
MAIM MANGLER IS IN THE BUSINESS OF MURDERING MUTANTS!
ENTER CHATROOM FOR 0.5 Bitcoin (BTC)
Highest Tip: ROBLOX_LUBE (1.2 BTC)
Latest Tip: WALTKOVAC (0.453 BTC)
Room $: 981.43 BTC
Your BTC.$: 3.0406
Send TIP!
BTC. 00.000

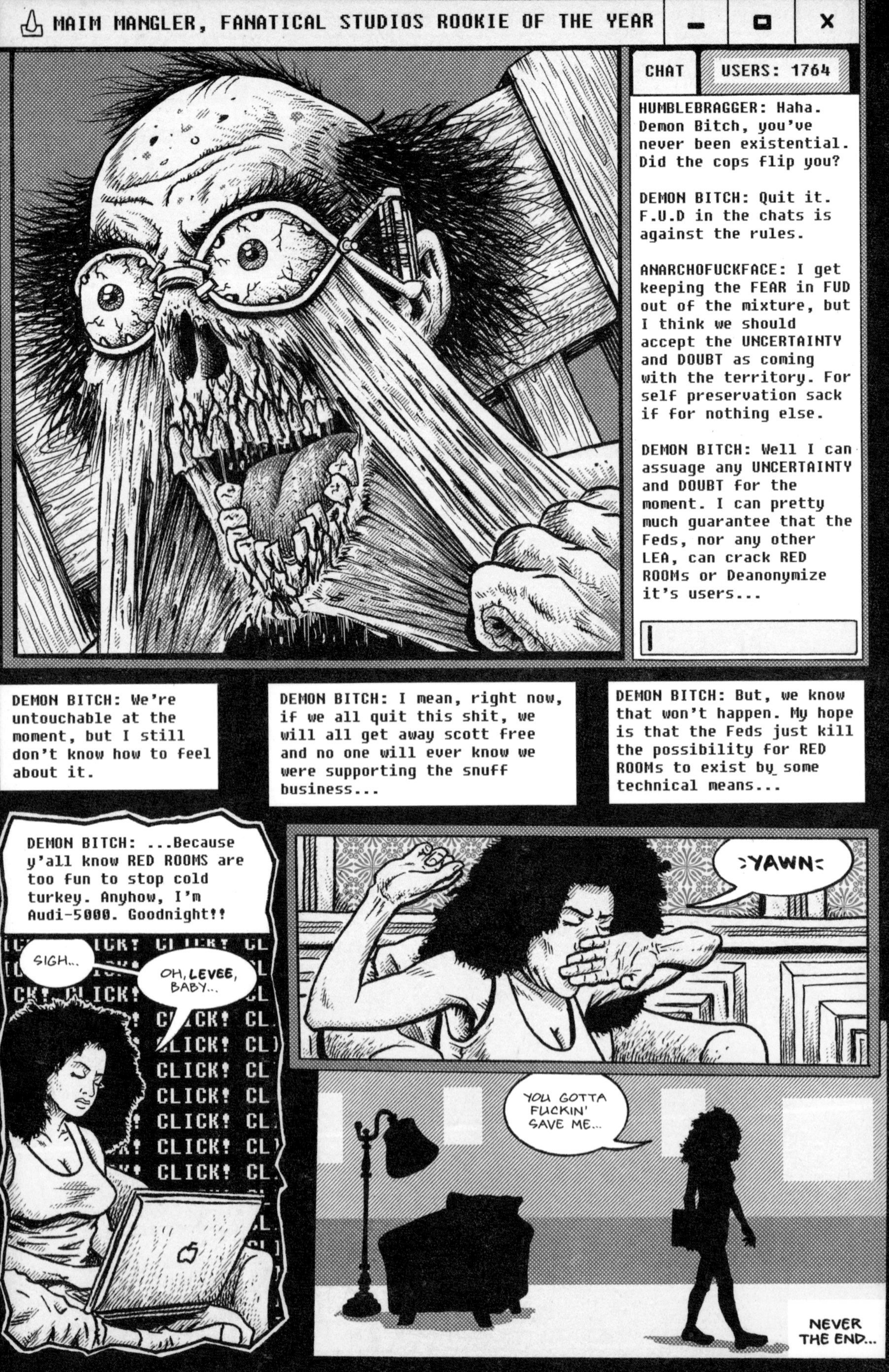

MAIM MANGLER, FANATICAL STUDIOS ROOKIE OF THE YEAR
CHAT
USERS: 1764
HUMBLEBRAGGER: Haha. Demon Bitch, you've never been existential. Did the cops flip you?
DEMON BITCH: Quit it. F.U.D in the chats is against the rules.
ANARCHOFUCKFACE: I get keeping the FEAR in FUD out of the mixture, but I think we should accept the UNCERTAINTY and DOUBT as coming with the territory. For self preservation sack if for nothing else.
DEMON BITCH: Well I can assuage any UNCERTAINTY and DOUBT for the moment. I can pretty much guarantee that the Feds, nor any other LEA, can crack RED ROOMs or Deanonymize it's users...
DEMON BITCH: We're untouchable at the moment, but I still don't know how to feel about it.
DEMON BITCH: I mean, right now, if we all quit this shit, we will all get away scott free and no one will ever know we were supporting the snuff business...
DEMON BITCH: But, we know that won't happen. My hope is that the Feds just kill the possibility for RED ROOMs to exist by some technical means...
DEMON BITCH: ...Because y'all know RED ROOMS are too fun to stop cold turkey. Anyhow, I'm Audi-5000. Goodnight!!
SIGH...
OH, LEVEE, BABY...
CLICK! CLICK! CLICK! CLICK! CLICK! CLICK! CLICK!
YAWN
YOU GOTTA FUCKIN' SAVE ME...
NEVER THE END...

FOUR

DONNA BUTCHER

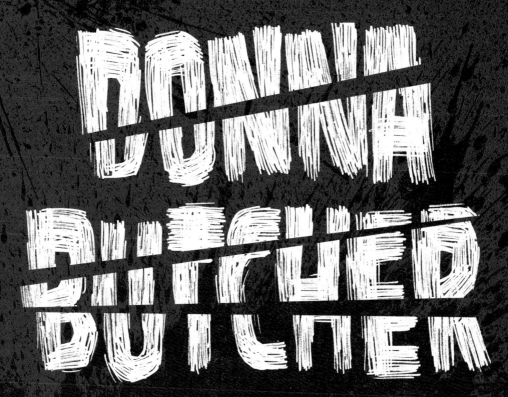

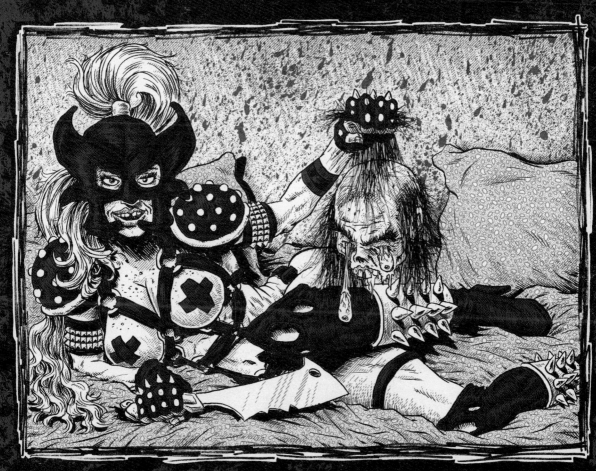

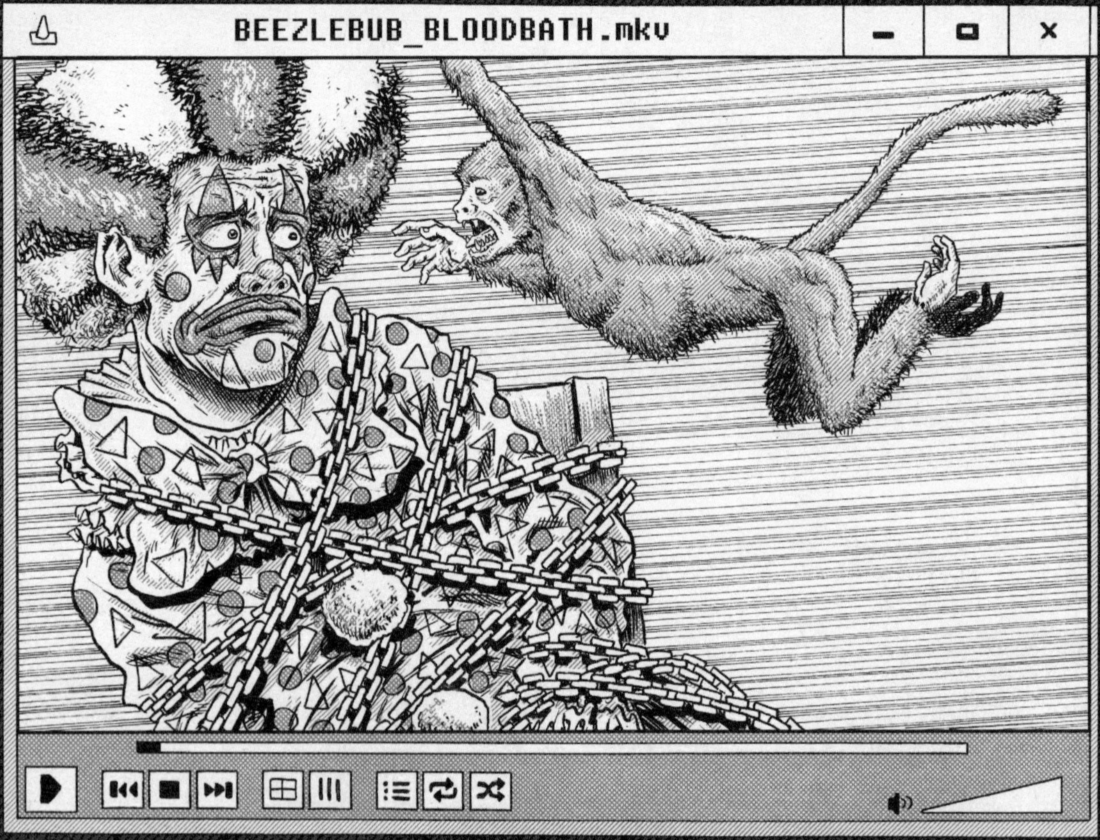
BEEZLEBUB_BLOODBATH.mkv

The DARK WEB provides means to use the internet ANONYMOUSLY, free from consequence. CRYPTOCURRENCY transactions lack a detectable paper trail, providing further obfuscation. These tools are being abused to create a NEFARIOUS subculture of MURDER for ENTERTAINMENT in real time via WEBCAM. WHO would participate in such a sick enterprise? WHO are the VICTIMS? WHO are the CUSTOMERS? WHO are the MURDERERS?

ED PISKOR PRESENTS: **RED ROOM**, *THE ANTISOCIAL NETWORK*

HEE-HEE-HEE... WELCOME BACK TO THIS DARK ALLEY OF THE ***INTERWEBS***, MY SALACIOUS ***SIMPS*** AND ***THOTS***. I SEE YOU'RE CRAVING MORE ***GORY*** GOODNESS FROM THE VAULTS OF YOUR FAVORITE ***INFLUENCER*** OF ***ILL REPUTE***, THE ONE AND ONLY ***CRYPTO-CURRENCY KEEPER!*** DID YOU KNOW THAT ***RED ROOMS*** EXISTED BEFORE ***AL GORE*** INVENTED THE ***INTERNET?*** YES, THERE WERE PLENTY OF ***SNUFF VIDEOS*** CREATED ON COMMISSION FOR FUN AND PROFIT, THOUGH, AS YOU CAN GUESS, THE ***CAMCORDER CONFEDERATES*** INVOLVED DIDN'T HAVE THE ***CLOAK OF ANONYMITY*** LIKE THEY DO NOW, WHICH BRINGS US TO TODAY'S EPISODE FROM THE ***VHS/BETAMAX*** ERA OF ***TORTURE PORN***. THIS LITTLE ***DITTY*** FOR YOUR ***TITTIES*** IS CALLED...

CYCLICAL TERROR!

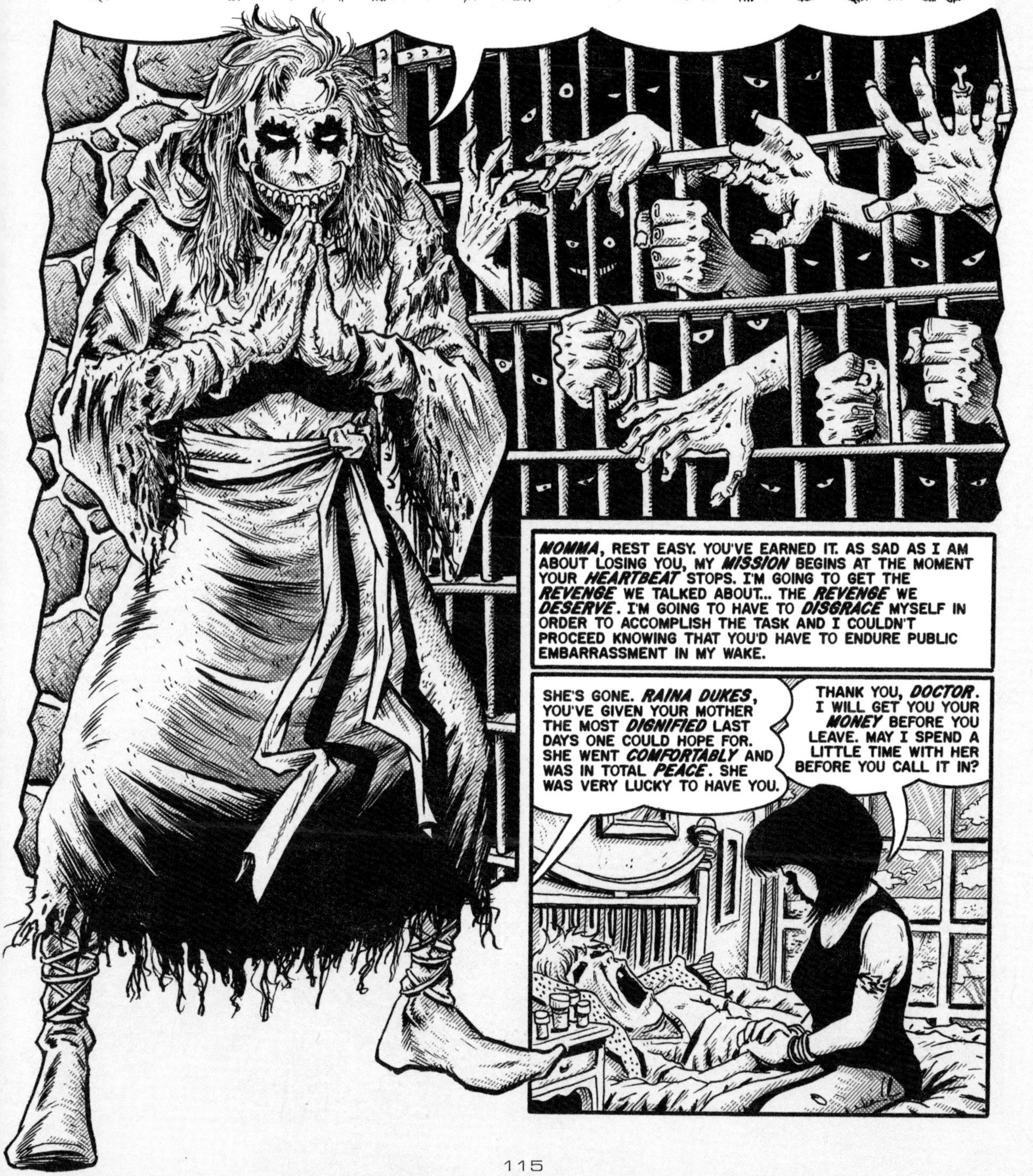
MOMMA, REST EASY. YOU'VE EARNED IT. AS SAD AS I AM ABOUT LOSING YOU, MY MISSION BEGINS AT THE MOMENT YOUR HEARTBEAT STOPS. I'M GOING TO GET THE REVENGE WE TALKED ABOUT... THE REVENGE WE DESERVE. I'M GOING TO HAVE TO DISGRACE MYSELF IN ORDER TO ACCOMPLISH THE TASK AND I COULDN'T PROCEED KNOWING THAT YOU'D HAVE TO ENDURE PUBLIC EMBARRASSMENT IN MY WAKE.
SHE'S GONE. RAINA DUKES, YOU'VE GIVEN YOUR MOTHER THE MOST DIGNIFIED LAST DAYS ONE COULD HOPE FOR. SHE WENT COMFORTABLY AND WAS IN TOTAL PEACE. SHE WAS VERY LUCKY TO HAVE YOU.
THANK YOU, DOCTOR. I WILL GET YOU YOUR MONEY BEFORE YOU LEAVE. MAY I SPEND A LITTLE TIME WITH HER BEFORE YOU CALL IT IN?

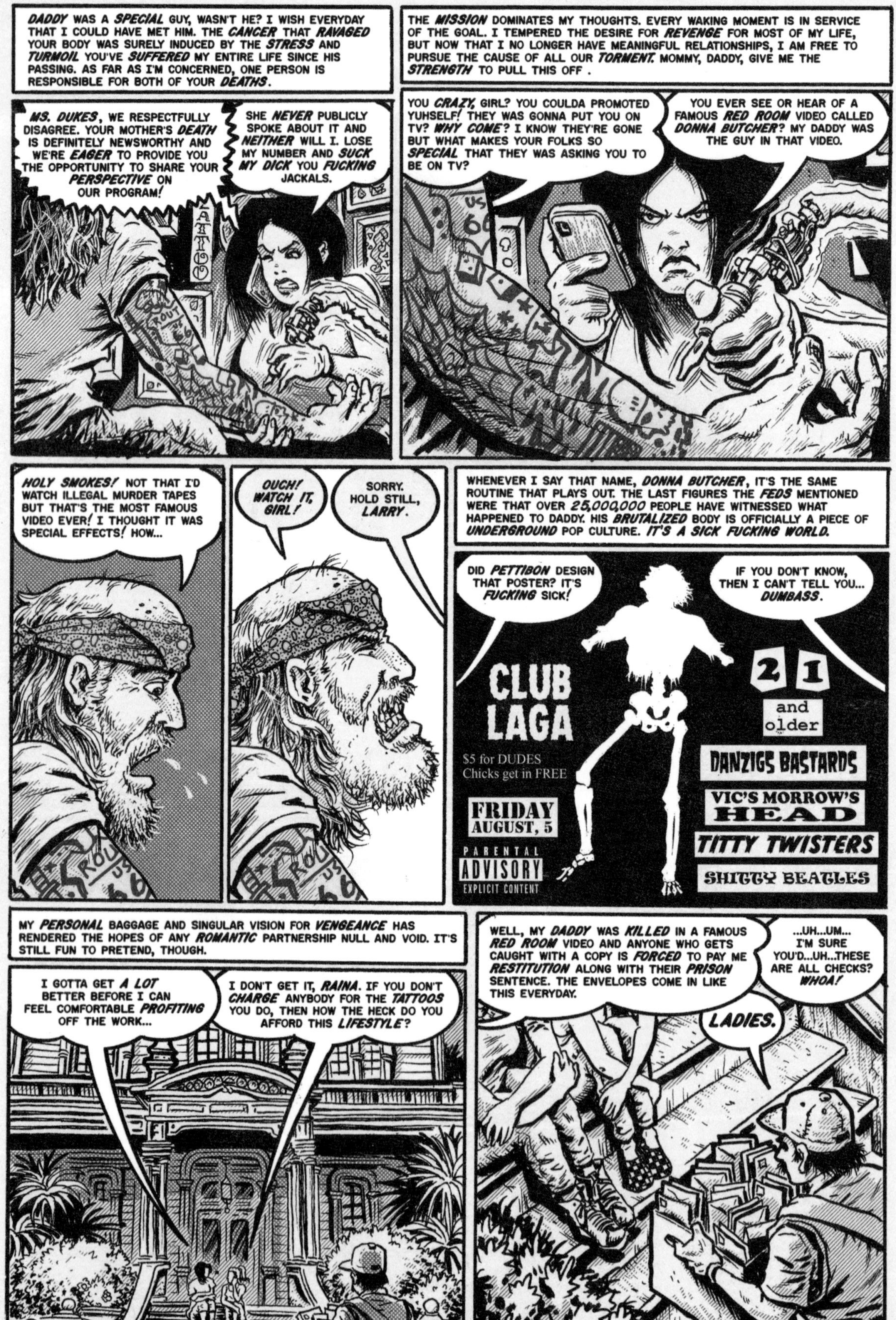
DADDY WAS A SPECIAL GUY, WASN'T HE? I WISH EVERYDAY THAT I COULD HAVE MET HIM. THE CANCER THAT RAVAGED YOUR BODY WAS SURELY INDUCED BY THE STRESS AND TURMOIL YOU'VE SUFFERED MY ENTIRE LIFE SINCE HIS PASSING. AS FAR AS I'M CONCERNED, ONE PERSON IS RESPONSIBLE FOR BOTH OF YOUR DEATHS.
THE MISSION DOMINATES MY THOUGHTS. EVERY WAKING MOMENT IS IN SERVICE OF THE GOAL. I TEMPERED THE DESIRE FOR REVENGE FOR MOST OF MY LIFE, BUT NOW THAT I NO LONGER HAVE MEANINGFUL RELATIONSHIPS, I AM FREE TO PURSUE THE CAUSE OF ALL OUR TORMENT. MOMMY, DADDY, GIVE ME THE STRENGTH TO PULL THIS OFF .
MS. DUKES, WE RESPECTFULLY DISAGREE. YOUR MOTHER'S DEATH IS DEFINITELY NEWSWORTHY AND WE'RE EAGER TO PROVIDE YOU THE OPPORTUNITY TO SHARE YOUR PERSPECTIVE ON OUR PROGRAM!
SHE NEVER PUBLICLY SPOKE ABOUT IT AND NEITHER WILL I. LOSE MY NUMBER AND SUCK MY DICK YOU FUCKING JACKALS.
TATTOO
YOU CRAZY, GIRL? YOU COULDA PROMOTED YUHSELF! THEY WAS GONNA PUT YOU ON TV? WHY COME? I KNOW THEY'RE GONE BUT WHAT MAKES YOUR FOLKS SO SPECIAL THAT THEY WAS ASKING YOU TO BE ON TV?
YOU EVER SEE OR HEAR OF A FAMOUS RED ROOM VIDEO CALLED DONNA BUTCHER? MY DADDY WAS THE GUY IN THAT VIDEO.
HOLY SMOKES! NOT THAT I'D WATCH ILLEGAL MURDER TAPES BUT THAT'S THE MOST FAMOUS VIDEO EVER! I THOUGHT IT WAS SPECIAL EFFECTS! HOW...
OUCH! WATCH IT, GIRL!
SORRY. HOLD STILL, LARRY.
WHENEVER I SAY THAT NAME, DONNA BUTCHER, IT'S THE SAME ROUTINE THAT PLAYS OUT. THE LAST FIGURES THE FEDS MENTIONED WERE THAT OVER 25,000,000 PEOPLE HAVE WITNESSED WHAT HAPPENED TO DADDY. HIS BRUTALIZED BODY IS OFFICIALLY A PIECE OF UNDERGROUND POP CULTURE. IT'S A SICK FUCKING WORLD.
DID PETTIBON DESIGN THAT POSTER? IT'S FUCKING SICK!
IF YOU DON'T KNOW, THEN I CAN'T TELL YOU... DUMBASS.
CLUB LAGA
$5 for DUDES
Chicks get in FREE
FRIDAY AUGUST, 5
PARENTAL ADVISORY EXPLICIT CONTENT
21 and older
DANZIGS BASTARDS
VIC'S MORROW'S HEAD
TITTY TWISTERS
SHITTY BEATLES
MY PERSONAL BAGGAGE AND SINGULAR VISION FOR VENGEANCE HAS RENDERED THE HOPES OF ANY ROMANTIC PARTNERSHIP NULL AND VOID. IT'S STILL FUN TO PRETEND, THOUGH.
I GOTTA GET A LOT BETTER BEFORE I CAN FEEL COMFORTABLE PROFITING OFF THE WORK...
I DON'T GET IT, RAINA. IF YOU DON'T CHARGE ANYBODY FOR THE TATTOOS YOU DO, THEN HOW THE HECK DO YOU AFFORD THIS LIFESTYLE?
WELL, MY DADDY WAS KILLED IN A FAMOUS RED ROOM VIDEO AND ANYONE WHO GETS CAUGHT WITH A COPY IS FORCED TO PAY ME RESTITUTION ALONG WITH THEIR PRISON SENTENCE. THE ENVELOPES COME IN LIKE THIS EVERYDAY.
...UH...UM... I'M SURE YOU'D...UH...THESE ARE ALL CHECKS? WHOA!
LADIES.

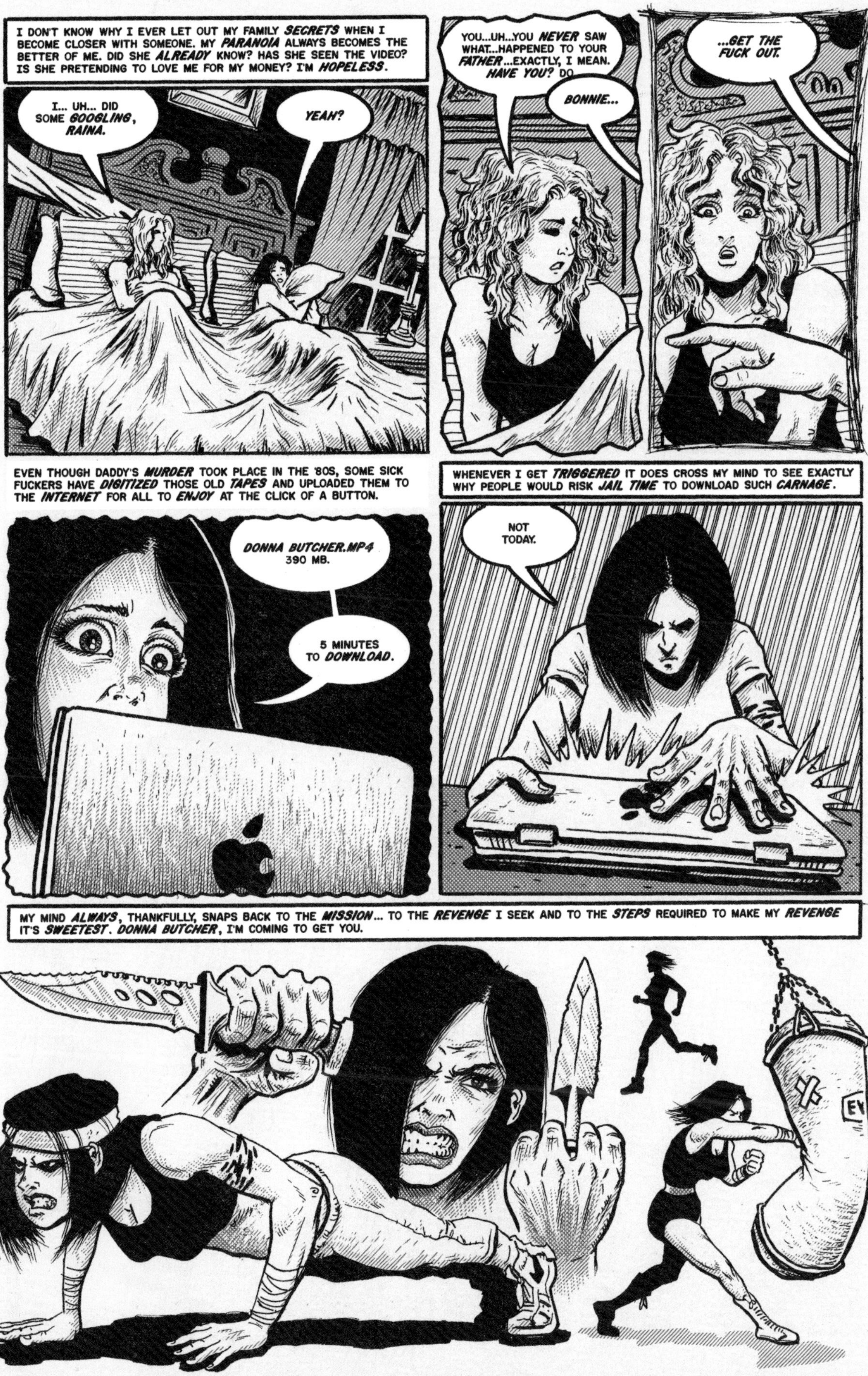

I DON'T KNOW WHY I EVER LET OUT MY FAMILY SECRETS WHEN I BECOME CLOSER WITH SOMEONE. MY PARANOIA ALWAYS BECOMES THE BETTER OF ME. DID SHE ALREADY KNOW? HAS SHE SEEN THE VIDEO? IS SHE PRETENDING TO LOVE ME FOR MY MONEY? I'M HOPELESS.
I... UH... DID SOME GOOGLING, RAINA.
YEAH?
YOU...UH...YOU NEVER SAW WHAT...HAPPENED TO YOUR FATHER...EXACTLY, I MEAN. HAVE YOU? DO
BONNIE...
...GET THE FUCK OUT.
EVEN THOUGH DADDY'S MURDER TOOK PLACE IN THE '80S, SOME SICK FUCKERS HAVE DIGITIZED THOSE OLD TAPES AND UPLOADED THEM TO THE INTERNET FOR ALL TO ENJOY AT THE CLICK OF A BUTTON.
WHENEVER I GET TRIGGERED IT DOES CROSS MY MIND TO SEE EXACTLY WHY PEOPLE WOULD RISK JAIL TIME TO DOWNLOAD SUCH CARNAGE.
DONNA BUTCHER.MP4 390 MB.
5 MINUTES TO DOWNLOAD.
NOT TODAY.
MY MIND ALWAYS, THANKFULLY, SNAPS BACK TO THE MISSION... TO THE REVENGE I SEEK AND TO THE STEPS REQUIRED TO MAKE MY REVENGE IT'S SWEETEST. DONNA BUTCHER, I'M COMING TO GET YOU.

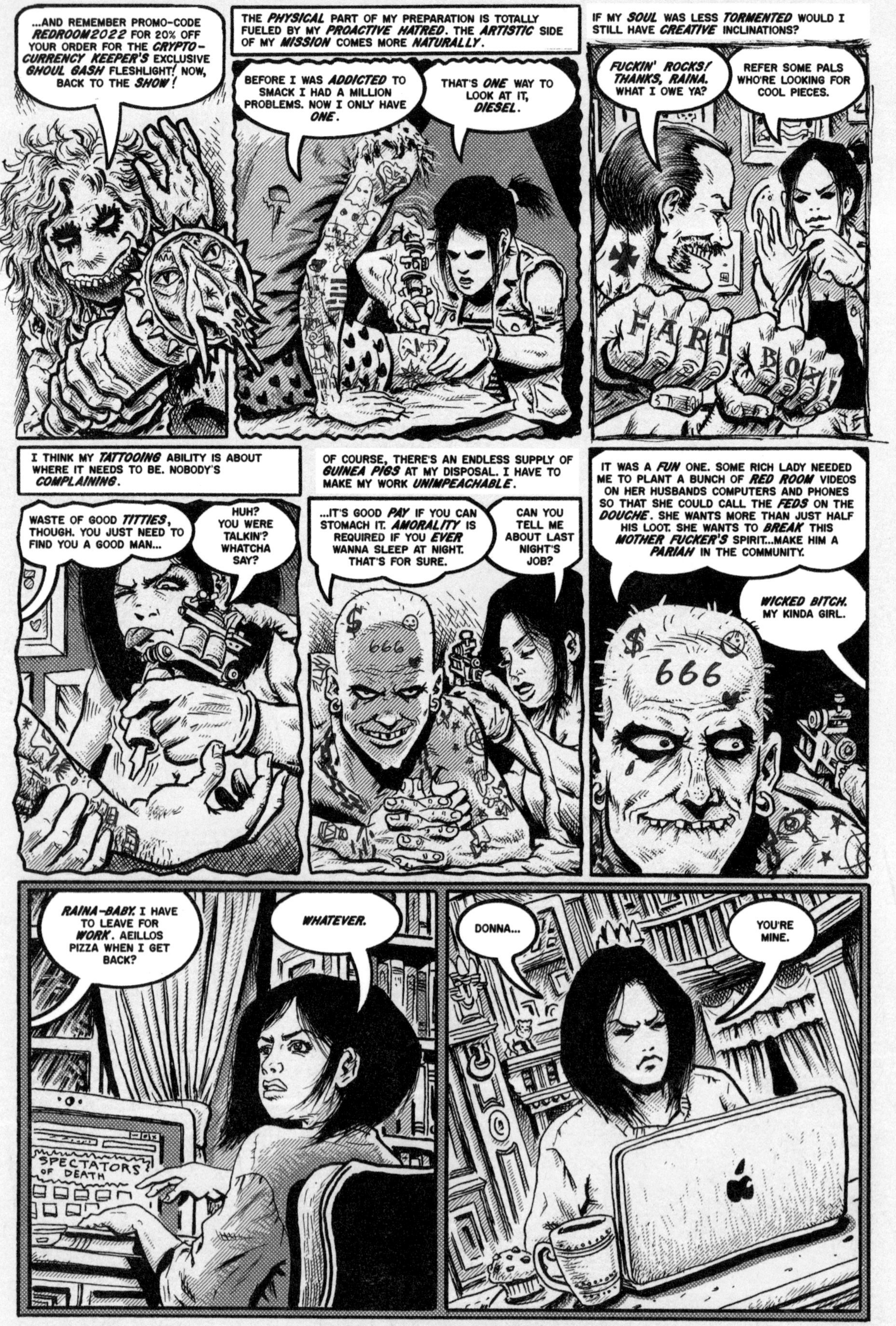
...AND REMEMBER PROMO-CODE REDROOM2022 FOR 20% OFF YOUR ORDER FOR THE CRYPTO-CURRENCY KEEPER'S EXCLUSIVE GHOUL GASH FLESHLIGHT! NOW, BACK TO THE SHOW!
THE PHYSICAL PART OF MY PREPARATION IS TOTALLY FUELED BY MY PROACTIVE HATRED. THE ARTISTIC SIDE OF MY MISSION COMES MORE NATURALLY.
BEFORE I WAS ADDICTED TO SMACK I HAD A MILLION PROBLEMS. NOW I ONLY HAVE ONE.
THAT'S ONE WAY TO LOOK AT IT, DIESEL.
IF MY SOUL WAS LESS TORMENTED WOULD I STILL HAVE CREATIVE INCLINATIONS?
FUCKIN' ROCKS! THANKS, RAINA. WHAT I OWE YA?
REFER SOME PALS WHO'RE LOOKING FOR COOL PIECES.
FART BOX!
I THINK MY TATTOOING ABILITY IS ABOUT WHERE IT NEEDS TO BE. NOBODY'S COMPLAINING.
WASTE OF GOOD TITTIES, THOUGH. YOU JUST NEED TO FIND YOU A GOOD MAN...
HUH? YOU WERE TALKIN'? WHATCHA SAY?
OF COURSE, THERE'S AN ENDLESS SUPPLY OF GUINEA PIGS AT MY DISPOSAL. I HAVE TO MAKE MY WORK UNIMPEACHABLE.
...IT'S GOOD PAY IF YOU CAN STOMACH IT. AMORALITY IS REQUIRED IF YOU EVER WANNA SLEEP AT NIGHT. THAT'S FOR SURE.
CAN YOU TELL ME ABOUT LAST NIGHT'S JOB?
666
IT WAS A FUN ONE. SOME RICH LADY NEEDED ME TO PLANT A BUNCH OF RED ROOM VIDEOS ON HER HUSBANDS COMPUTERS AND PHONES SO THAT SHE COULD CALL THE FEDS ON THE DOUCHE. SHE WANTS MORE THAN JUST HALF HIS LOOT. SHE WANTS TO BREAK THIS MOTHER FUCKER'S SPIRIT...MAKE HIM A PARIAH IN THE COMMUNITY.
WICKED BITCH. MY KINDA GIRL.
666
RAINA-BABY. I HAVE TO LEAVE FOR WORK. AEILLOS PIZZA WHEN I GET BACK?
WHATEVER.
SPECTATORS OF DEATH
DONNA...
YOU'RE MINE.

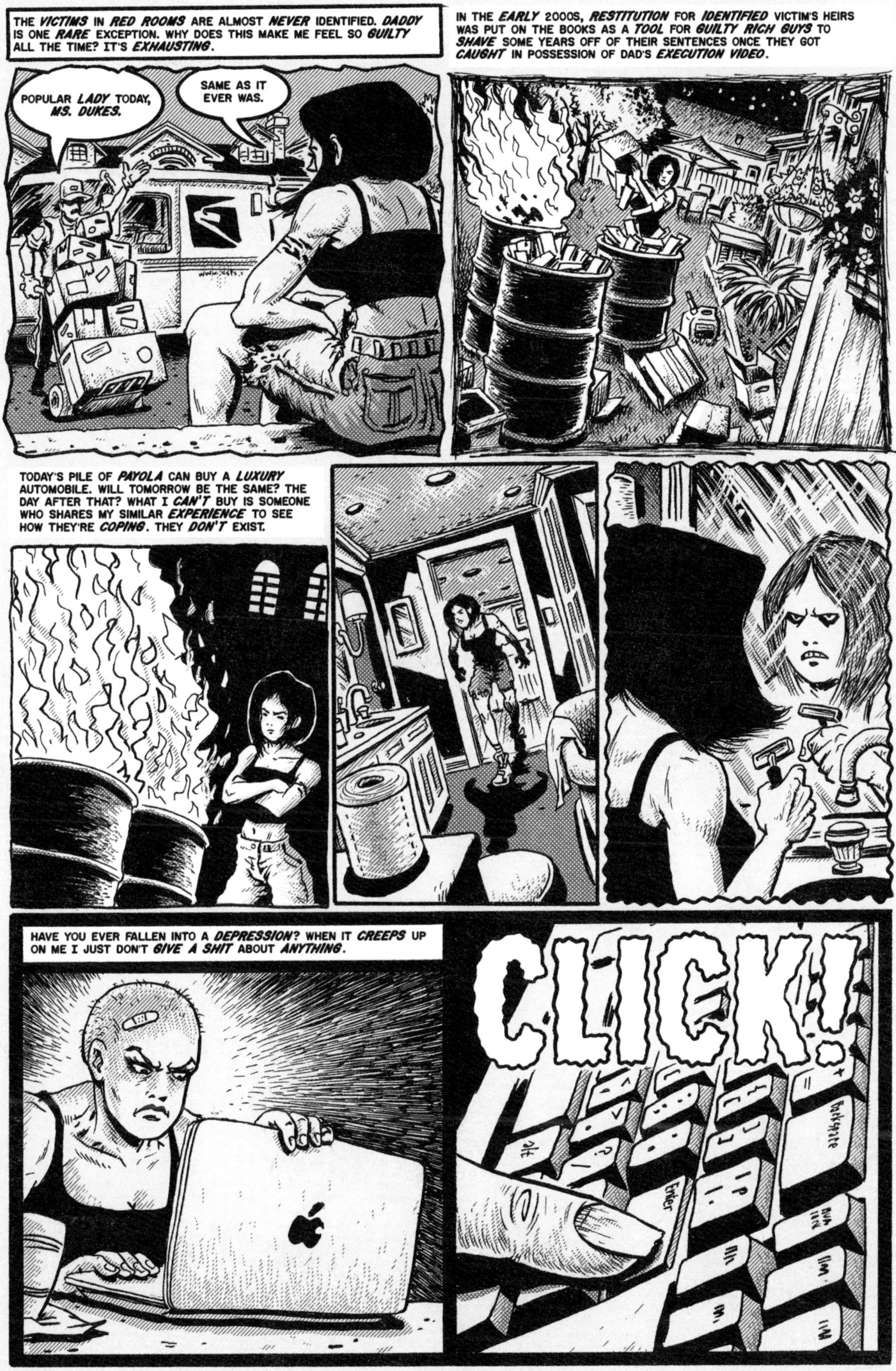
THE VICTIMS IN RED ROOMS ARE ALMOST NEVER IDENTIFIED. DADDY IS ONE RARE EXCEPTION. WHY DOES THIS MAKE ME FEEL SO GUILTY ALL THE TIME? IT'S EXHAUSTING.
POPULAR LADY TODAY, MS. DUKES.
SAME AS IT EVER WAS.
IN THE EARLY 2000S, RESTITUTION FOR IDENTIFIED VICTIM'S HEIRS WAS PUT ON THE BOOKS AS A TOOL FOR GUILTY RICH GUYS TO SHAVE SOME YEARS OFF OF THEIR SENTENCES ONCE THEY GOT CAUGHT IN POSSESSION OF DAD'S EXECUTION VIDEO.
TODAY'S PILE OF PAYOLA CAN BUY A LUXURY AUTOMOBILE. WILL TOMORROW BE THE SAME? THE DAY AFTER THAT? WHAT I CAN'T BUY IS SOMEONE WHO SHARES MY SIMILAR EXPERIENCE TO SEE HOW THEY'RE COPING. THEY DON'T EXIST.
HAVE YOU EVER FALLEN INTO A DEPRESSION? WHEN IT CREEPS UP ON ME I JUST DON'T GIVE A SHIT ABOUT ANYTHING.
CLICK!

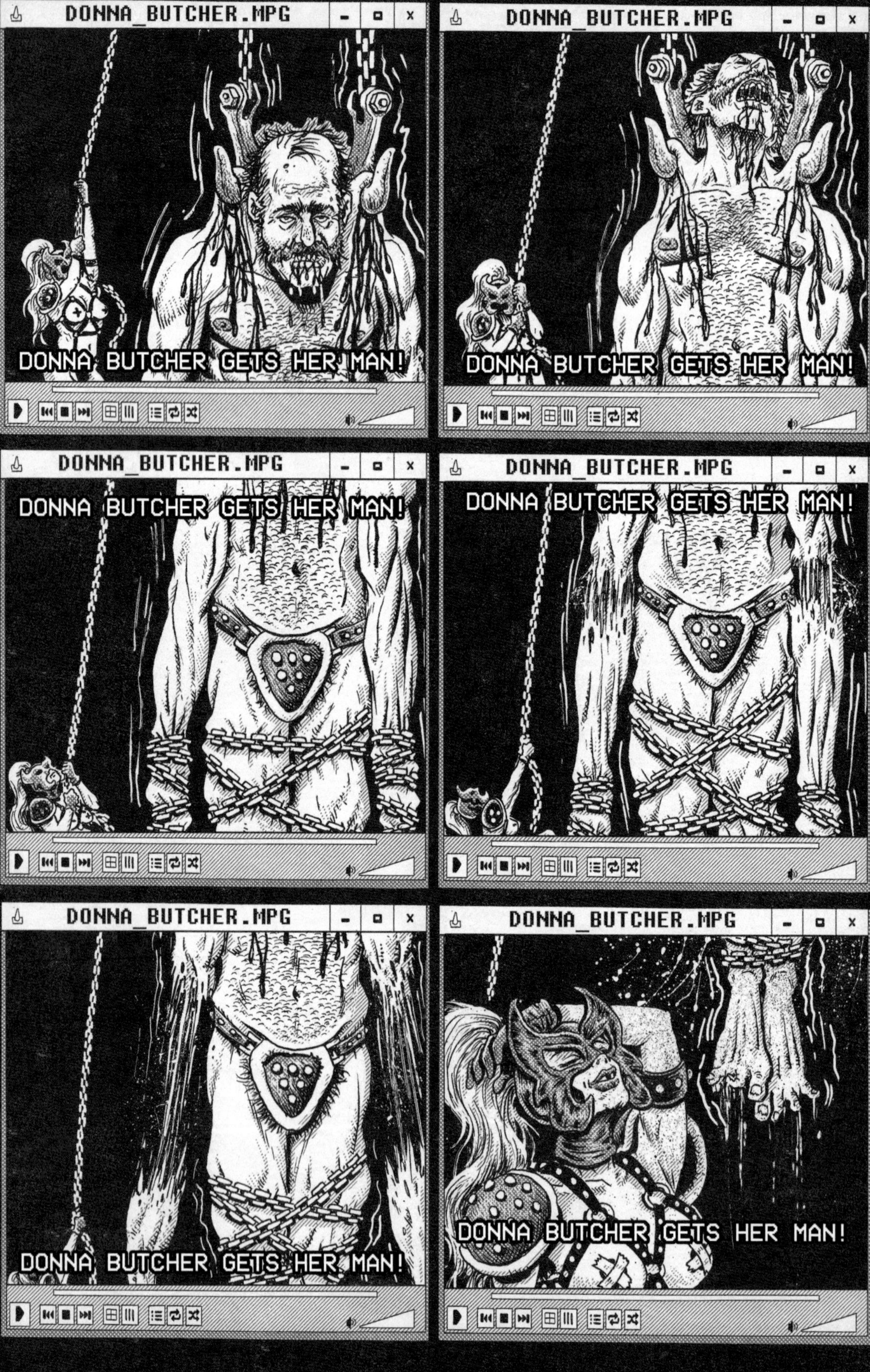
DONNA_BUTCHER.MPG
DONNA BUTCHER GETS HER MAN!
DONNA_BUTCHER.MPG
DONNA BUTCHER GETS HER MAN!
DONNA_BUTCHER.MPG
DONNA BUTCHER GETS HER MAN!
DONNA_BUTCHER.MPG
DONNA BUTCHER GETS HER MAN!
DONNA_BUTCHER.MPG
DONNA BUTCHER GETS HER MAN!
DONNA_BUTCHER.MPG
DONNA BUTCHER GETS HER MAN!

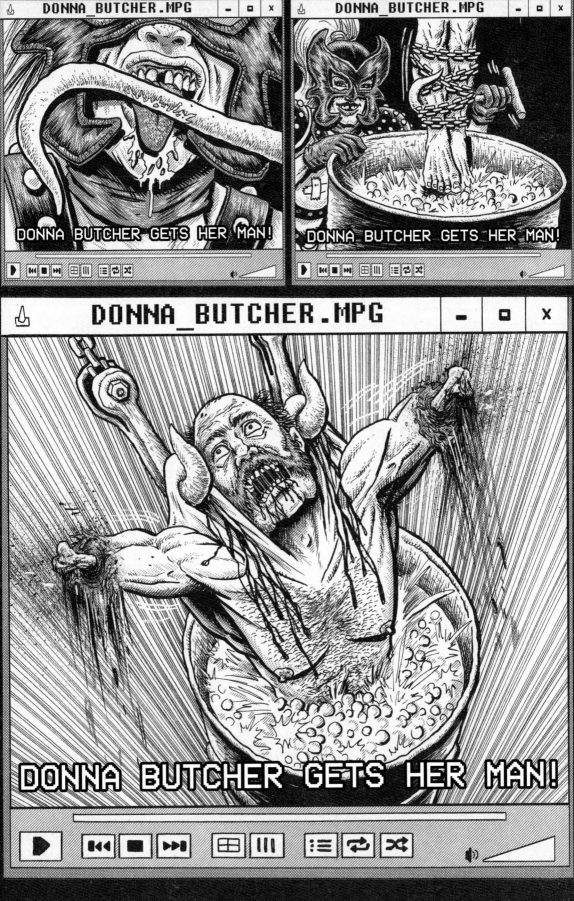

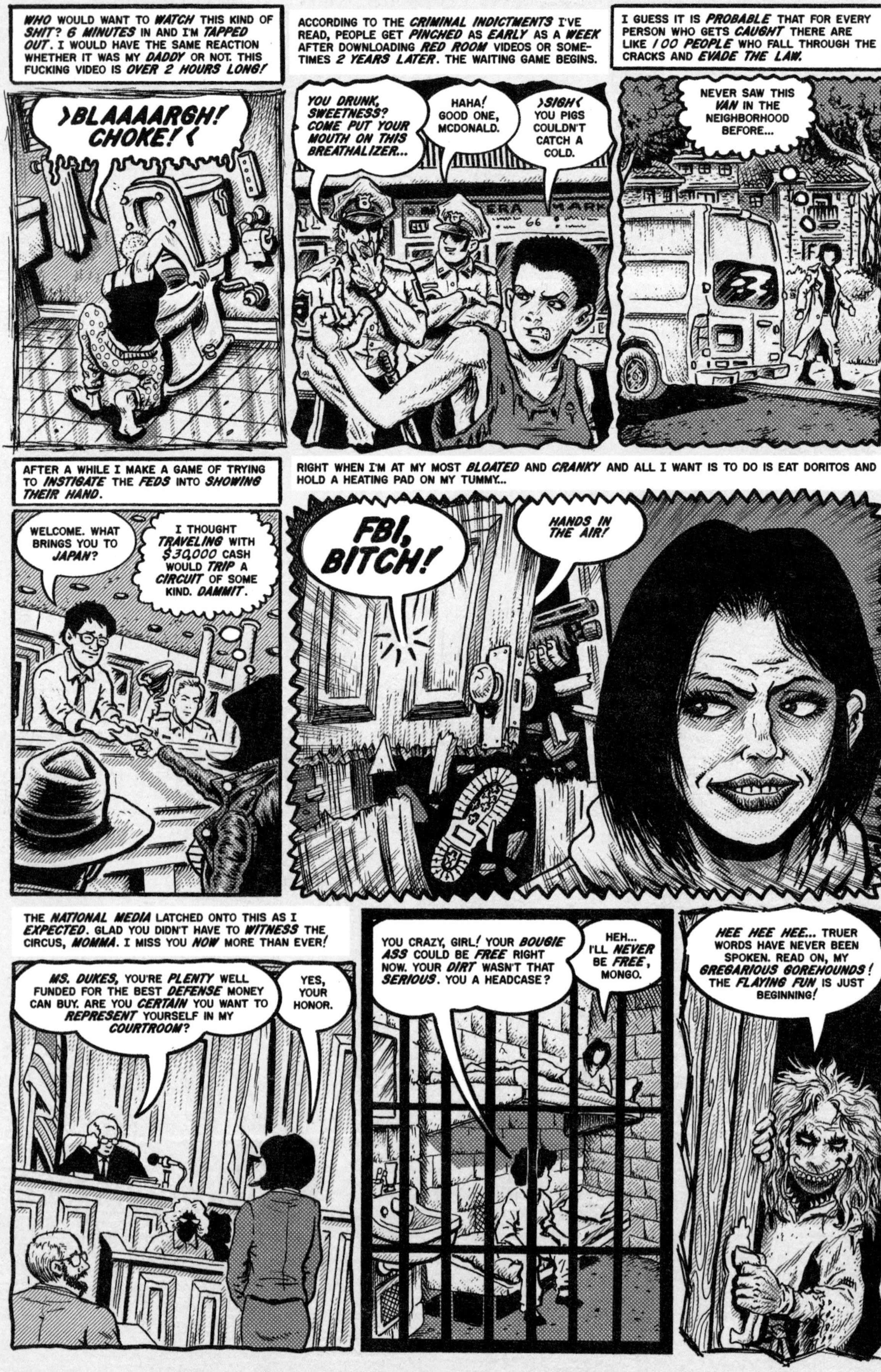
WHO WOULD WANT TO WATCH THIS KIND OF SHIT? 6 MINUTES IN AND I'M TAPPED OUT. I WOULD HAVE THE SAME REACTION WHETHER IT WAS MY DADDY OR NOT. THIS FUCKING VIDEO IS OVER 2 HOURS LONG!
›BLAAAARGH! CHOKE!‹
ACCORDING TO THE CRIMINAL INDICTMENTS I'VE READ, PEOPLE GET PINCHED AS EARLY AS A WEEK AFTER DOWNLOADING RED ROOM VIDEOS OR SOMETIMES 2 YEARS LATER. THE WAITING GAME BEGINS.
YOU DRUNK, SWEETNESS? COME PUT YOUR MOUTH ON THIS BREATHALIZER...
HAHA! GOOD ONE, MCDONALD.
›SIGH‹ YOU PIGS COULDN'T CATCH A COLD.
I GUESS IT IS PROBABLE THAT FOR EVERY PERSON WHO GETS CAUGHT THERE ARE LIKE 100 PEOPLE WHO FALL THROUGH THE CRACKS AND EVADE THE LAW.
NEVER SAW THIS VAN IN THE NEIGHBORHOOD BEFORE...
AFTER A WHILE I MAKE A GAME OF TRYING TO INSTIGATE THE FEDS INTO SHOWING THEIR HAND.
WELCOME. WHAT BRINGS YOU TO JAPAN?
I THOUGHT TRAVELING WITH $30,000 CASH WOULD TRIP A CIRCUIT OF SOME KIND. DAMMIT.
RIGHT WHEN I'M AT MY MOST BLOATED AND CRANKY AND ALL I WANT IS TO DO IS EAT DORITOS AND HOLD A HEATING PAD ON MY TUMMY...
FBI, BITCH!
HANDS IN THE AIR!
THE NATIONAL MEDIA LATCHED ONTO THIS AS I EXPECTED. GLAD YOU DIDN'T HAVE TO WITNESS THE CIRCUS, MOMMA. I MISS YOU NOW MORE THAN EVER!
MS. DUKES, YOU'RE PLENTY WELL FUNDED FOR THE BEST DEFENSE MONEY CAN BUY. ARE YOU CERTAIN YOU WANT TO REPRESENT YOURSELF IN MY COURTROOM?
YES, YOUR HONOR.
YOU CRAZY, GIRL! YOUR BOUGIE ASS COULD BE FREE RIGHT NOW. YOUR DIRT WASN'T THAT SERIOUS. YOU A HEADCASE?
HEH... I'LL NEVER BE FREE, MONGO.
HEE HEE HEE... TRUER WORDS HAVE NEVER BEEN SPOKEN. READ ON, MY GREGARIOUS GOREHOUNDS! THE FLAYING FUN IS JUST BEGINNING!

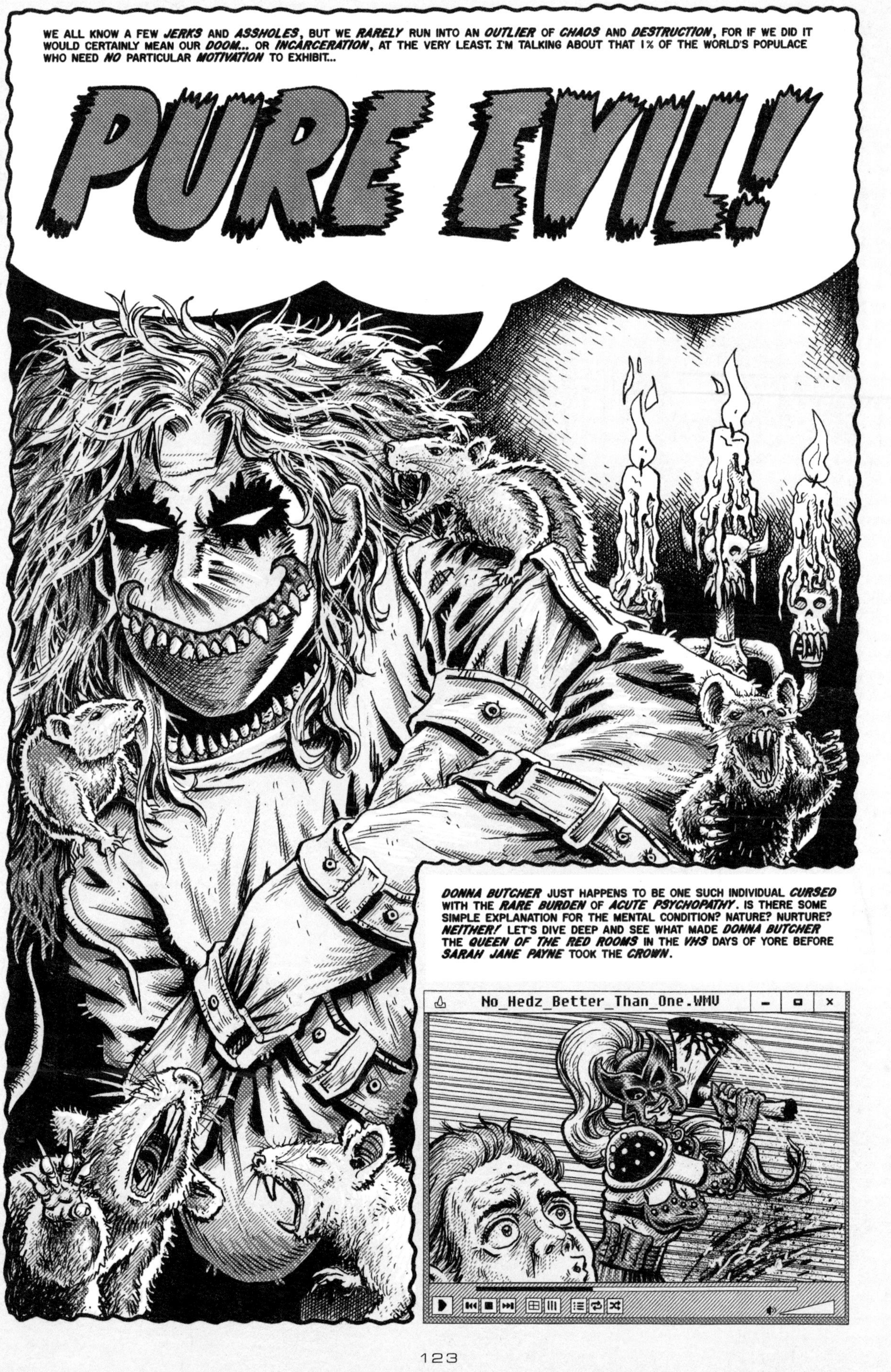

WE ALL KNOW A FEW JERKS AND ASSHOLES, BUT WE RARELY RUN INTO AN OUTLIER OF CHAOS AND DESTRUCTION, FOR IF WE DID IT WOULD CERTAINLY MEAN OUR DOOM... OR INCARCERATION, AT THE VERY LEAST. I'M TALKING ABOUT THAT 1% OF THE WORLD'S POPULACE WHO NEED NO PARTICULAR MOTIVATION TO EXHIBIT...
PURE EVIL!
DONNA BUTCHER JUST HAPPENS TO BE ONE SUCH INDIVIDUAL CURSED WITH THE RARE BURDEN OF ACUTE PSYCHOPATHY. IS THERE SOME SIMPLE EXPLANATION FOR THE MENTAL CONDITION? NATURE? NURTURE? NEITHER! LET'S DIVE DEEP AND SEE WHAT MADE DONNA BUTCHER THE QUEEN OF THE RED ROOMS IN THE VHS DAYS OF YORE BEFORE SARAH JANE PAYNE TOOK THE CROWN.
No_Hedz_Better_Than_One.WMV

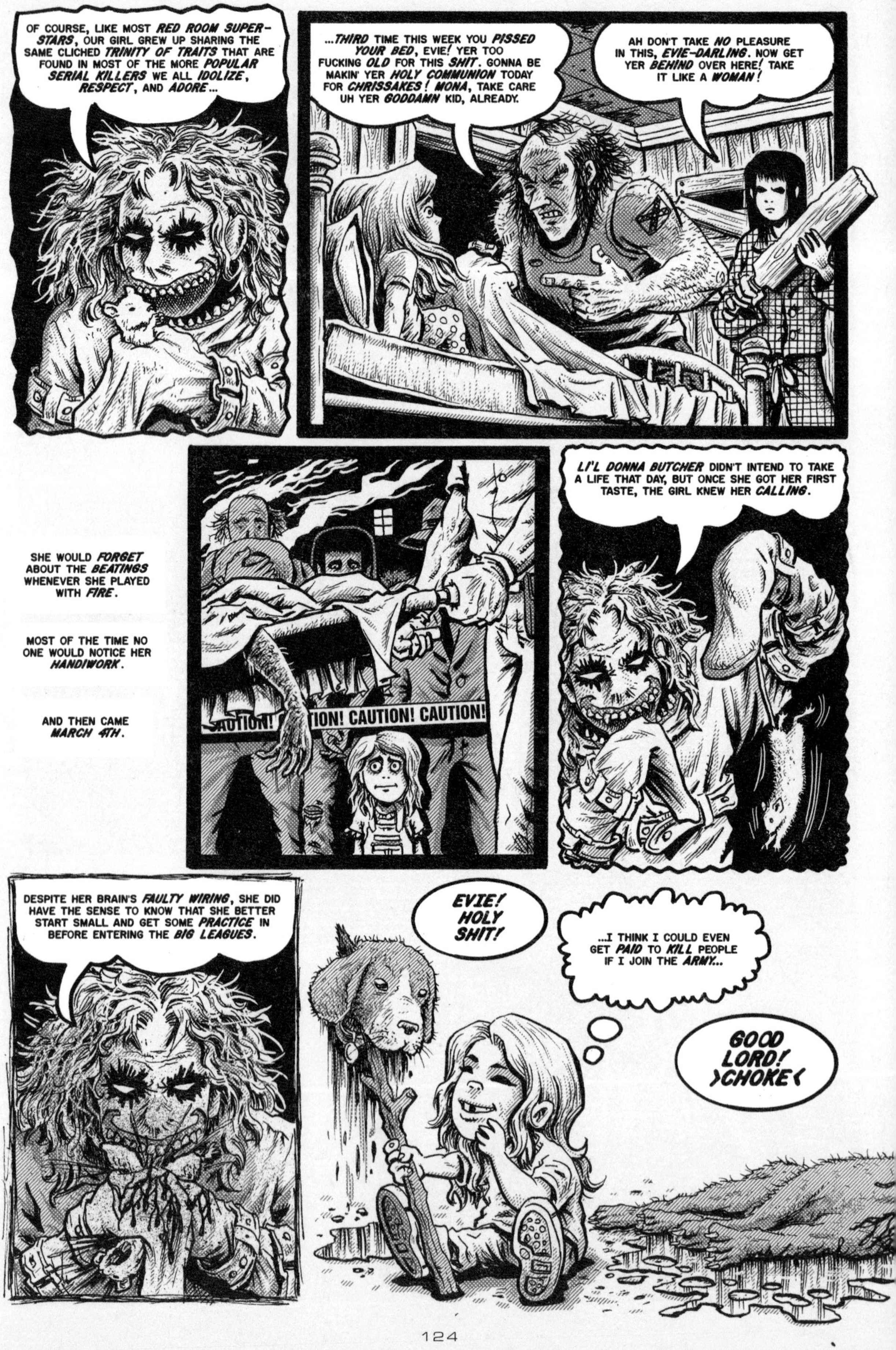
OF COURSE, LIKE MOST RED ROOM SUPER-STARS, OUR GIRL GREW UP SHARING THE SAME CLICHED TRINITY OF TRAITS THAT ARE FOUND IN MOST OF THE MORE POPULAR SERIAL KILLERS WE ALL IDOLIZE, RESPECT, AND ADORE...
...THIRD TIME THIS WEEK YOU PISSED YOUR BED, EVIE! YER TOO FUCKING OLD FOR THIS SHIT. GONNA BE MAKIN' YER HOLY COMMUNION TODAY FOR CHRISSAKES! MONA, TAKE CARE UH YER GODDAMN KID, ALREADY.
AH DON'T TAKE NO PLEASURE IN THIS, EVIE-DARLING. NOW GET YER BEHIND OVER HERE! TAKE IT LIKE A WOMAN!
SHE WOULD FORGET ABOUT THE BEATINGS WHENEVER SHE PLAYED WITH FIRE.
MOST OF THE TIME NO ONE WOULD NOTICE HER HANDIWORK.
AND THEN CAME MARCH 4TH.
CAUTION! CAUTION! CAUTION!
LI'L DONNA BUTCHER DIDN'T INTEND TO TAKE A LIFE THAT DAY, BUT ONCE SHE GOT HER FIRST TASTE, THE GIRL KNEW HER CALLING.
DESPITE HER BRAIN'S FAULTY WIRING, SHE DID HAVE THE SENSE TO KNOW THAT SHE BETTER START SMALL AND GET SOME PRACTICE IN BEFORE ENTERING THE BIG LEAGUES.
EVIE! HOLY SHIT!
...I THINK I COULD EVEN GET PAID TO KILL PEOPLE IF I JOIN THE ARMY...
GOOD LORD! >CHOKE<

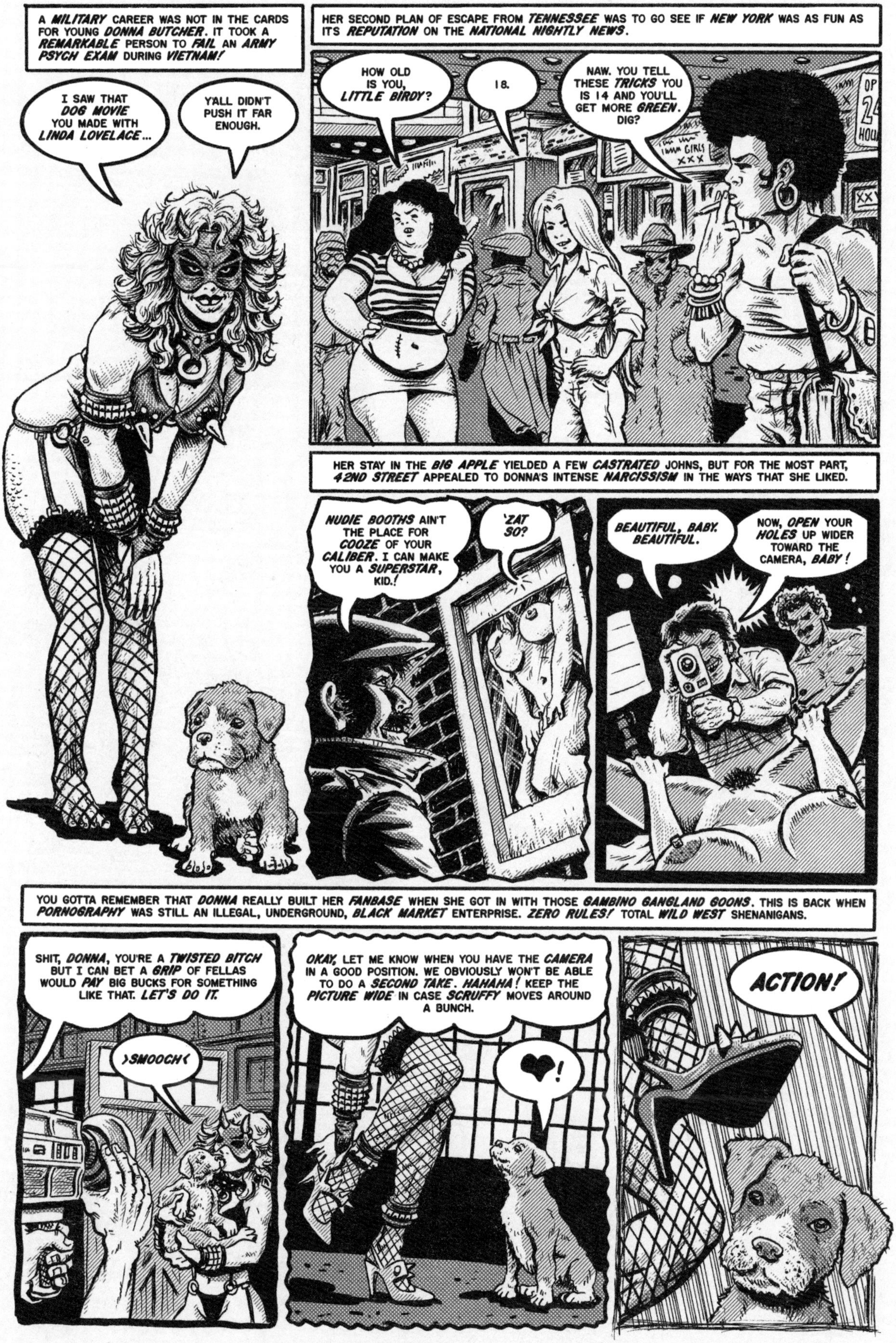
A MILITARY CAREER WAS NOT IN THE CARDS FOR YOUNG DONNA BUTCHER. IT TOOK A REMARKABLE PERSON TO FAIL AN ARMY PSYCH EXAM DURING VIETNAM!
I SAW THAT DOG MOVIE YOU MADE WITH LINDA LOVELACE...
Y'ALL DIDN'T PUSH IT FAR ENOUGH.
HER SECOND PLAN OF ESCAPE FROM TENNESSEE WAS TO GO SEE IF NEW YORK WAS AS FUN AS ITS REPUTATION ON THE NATIONAL NIGHTLY NEWS.
HOW OLD IS YOU, LITTLE BIRDY?
18.
NAW. YOU TELL THESE TRICKS YOU IS 14 AND YOU'LL GET MORE GREEN. DIG?
HER STAY IN THE BIG APPLE YIELDED A FEW CASTRATED JOHNS, BUT FOR THE MOST PART, 42ND STREET APPEALED TO DONNA'S INTENSE NARCISSISM IN THE WAYS THAT SHE LIKED.
NUDIE BOOTHS AIN'T THE PLACE FOR COOZE OF YOUR CALIBER. I CAN MAKE YOU A SUPERSTAR, KID.!
'ZAT SO?
BEAUTIFUL, BABY. BEAUTIFUL.
NOW, OPEN YOUR HOLES UP WIDER TOWARD THE CAMERA, BABY!
YOU GOTTA REMEMBER THAT DONNA REALLY BUILT HER FANBASE WHEN SHE GOT IN WITH THOSE GAMBINO GANGLAND GOONS. THIS IS BACK WHEN PORNOGRAPHY WAS STILL AN ILLEGAL, UNDERGROUND, BLACK MARKET ENTERPRISE. ZERO RULES! TOTAL WILD WEST SHENANIGANS.
SHIT, DONNA, YOU'RE A TWISTED BITCH BUT I CAN BET A GRIP OF FELLAS WOULD PAY BIG BUCKS FOR SOMETHING LIKE THAT. LET'S DO IT.
›SMOOCH‹
OKAY, LET ME KNOW WHEN YOU HAVE THE CAMERA IN A GOOD POSITION. WE OBVIOUSLY WON'T BE ABLE TO DO A SECOND TAKE. HAHAHA! KEEP THE PICTURE WIDE IN CASE SCRUFFY MOVES AROUND A BUNCH.
!
ACTION!

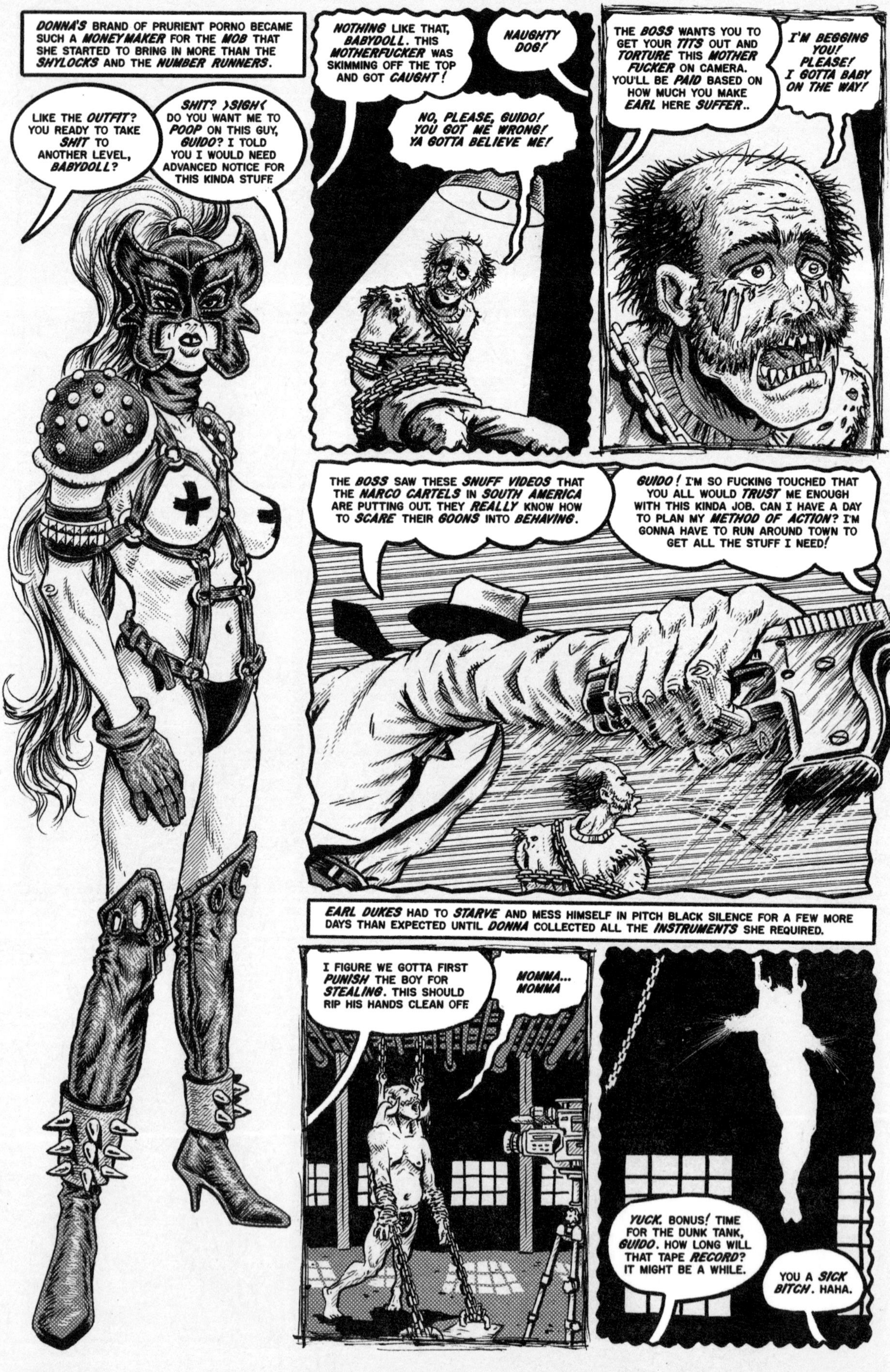

DONNA'S BRAND OF PRURIENT PORNO BECAME SUCH A MONEYMAKER FOR THE MOB THAT SHE STARTED TO BRING IN MORE THAN THE SHYLOCKS AND THE NUMBER RUNNERS.
LIKE THE OUTFIT? YOU READY TO TAKE SHIT TO ANOTHER LEVEL, BABYDOLL?
SHIT? >SIGH< DO YOU WANT ME TO POOP ON THIS GUY, GUIDO? I TOLD YOU I WOULD NEED ADVANCED NOTICE FOR THIS KINDA STUFF.
NOTHING LIKE THAT, BABYDOLL. THIS MOTHERFUCKER WAS SKIMMING OFF THE TOP AND GOT CAUGHT!
NAUGHTY DOG!
NO, PLEASE, GUIDO! YOU GOT ME WRONG! YA GOTTA BELIEVE ME!
THE BOSS WANTS YOU TO GET YOUR TITS OUT AND TORTURE THIS MOTHER FUCKER ON CAMERA. YOU'LL BE PAID BASED ON HOW MUCH YOU MAKE EARL HERE SUFFER..
I'M BEGGING YOU! PLEASE! I GOTTA BABY ON THE WAY!
THE BOSS SAW THESE SNUFF VIDEOS THAT THE NARCO CARTELS IN SOUTH AMERICA ARE PUTTING OUT. THEY REALLY KNOW HOW TO SCARE THEIR GOONS INTO BEHAVING.
GUIDO! I'M SO FUCKING TOUCHED THAT YOU ALL WOULD TRUST ME ENOUGH WITH THIS KINDA JOB. CAN I HAVE A DAY TO PLAN MY METHOD OF ACTION? I'M GONNA HAVE TO RUN AROUND TOWN TO GET ALL THE STUFF I NEED!
EARL DUKES HAD TO STARVE AND MESS HIMSELF IN PITCH BLACK SILENCE FOR A FEW MORE DAYS THAN EXPECTED UNTIL DONNA COLLECTED ALL THE INSTRUMENTS SHE REQUIRED.
I FIGURE WE GOTTA FIRST PUNISH THE BOY FOR STEALING. THIS SHOULD RIP HIS HANDS CLEAN OFF.
MOMMA... MOMMA
YUCK. BONUS! TIME FOR THE DUNK TANK, GUIDO. HOW LONG WILL THAT TAPE RECORD? IT MIGHT BE A WHILE.
YOU A SICK BITCH. HAHA.

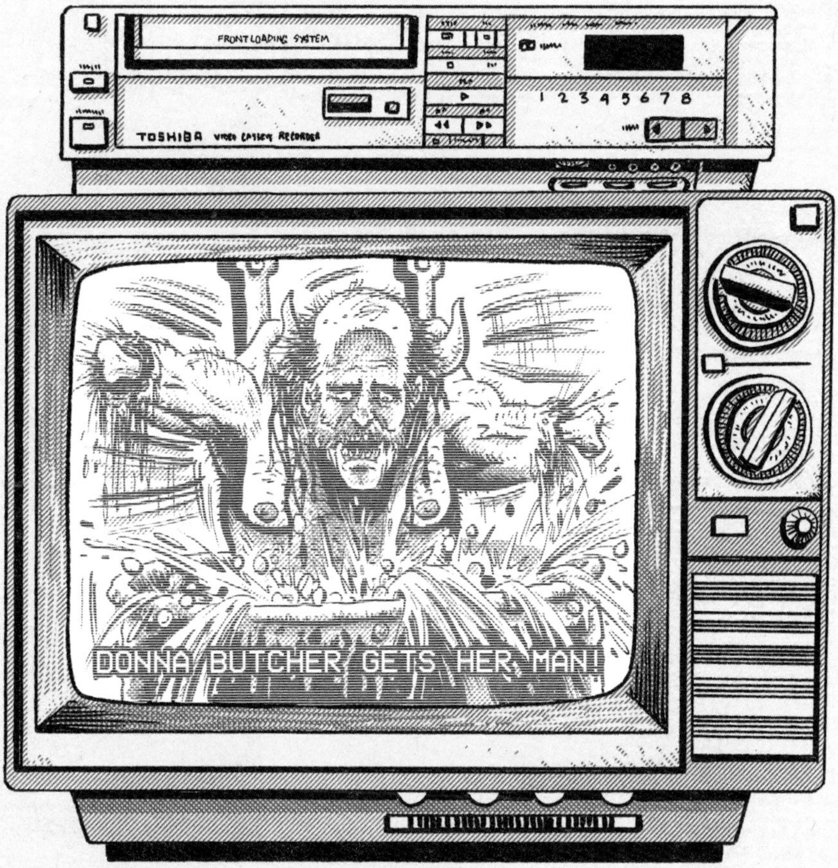
BABYDOLL, ARE YOUR EARS RINGING FROM THEM SCREAMS? WHERE YOU COME UP WITH THAT SHIT?
FRONTLOADING SYSTEM
TOSHIBA VIDEO CASSETTE RECORDER
1 2 3 4 5 6 7 8
I WANTED TO GIVE THE BOSS A LITTLE TASTE OF BRAZIL SINCE THOSE GUYS INSPIRED HIM TO GIVE ME A SHOT AT EARNING.
WHAT'S HE GONNA DO WITH THIS TAPE, GUIDO?
I THINK THIS IS GONNA BE A TRAINING VIDEO FOR THE OTHER TRUCK DRIVERS OR SOME SHIT.
DONNA BUTCHER GETS HER, MAN!
STEAL A PACKAGE AND THIS WILL HAPPEN. LIKE THAT.

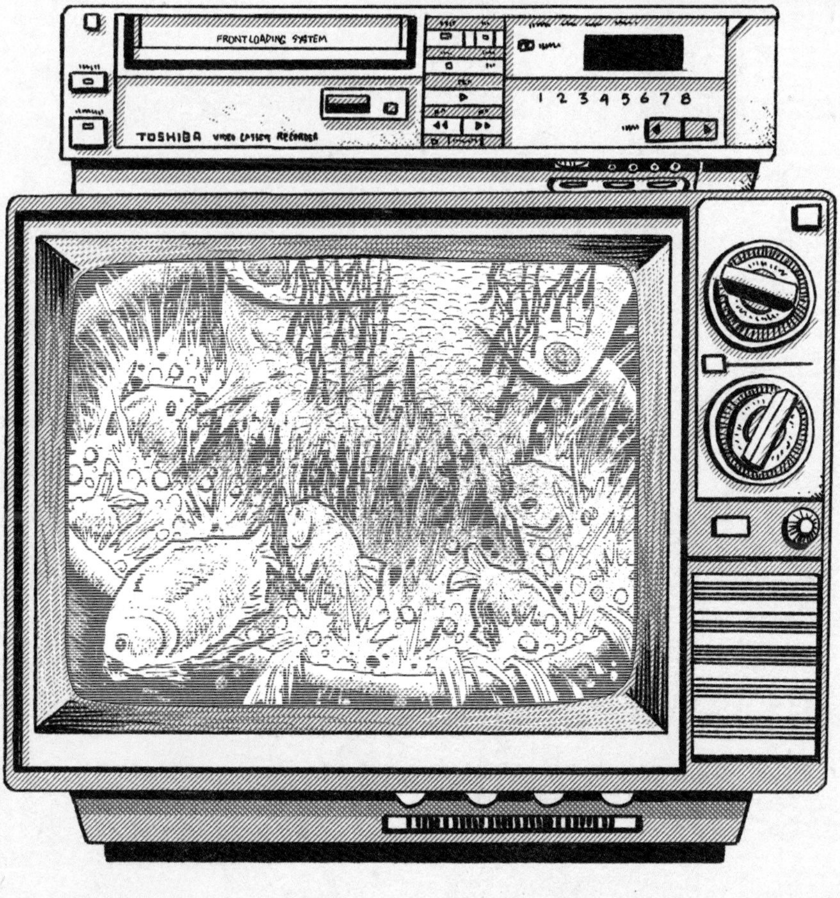
FRONTLOADING SYSTEM
TOSHIBA VIDEO CASSETTE RECORDER
1 2 3 4 5 6 7 8
OH MAN. I HOPE HE LIKES IT. I'M KINDA JAZZED TO DO MORE WORK LIKE THIS. THINK HE'LL LIKE IT?
I THINK HE'LL APPRECIATE YOUR ENTHUSIASM, BABYDOLL.
I'VE BEEN MEANING TO SAY SOMETHING, GUIDO. I DON'T LIKE WHEN YOU CALL ME "BABYDOLL".
HUH, WHAT ARE YOU DOING?
BABYDOLL, PUT THAT HAMMER DOWN!
AAAAAAAARGH!

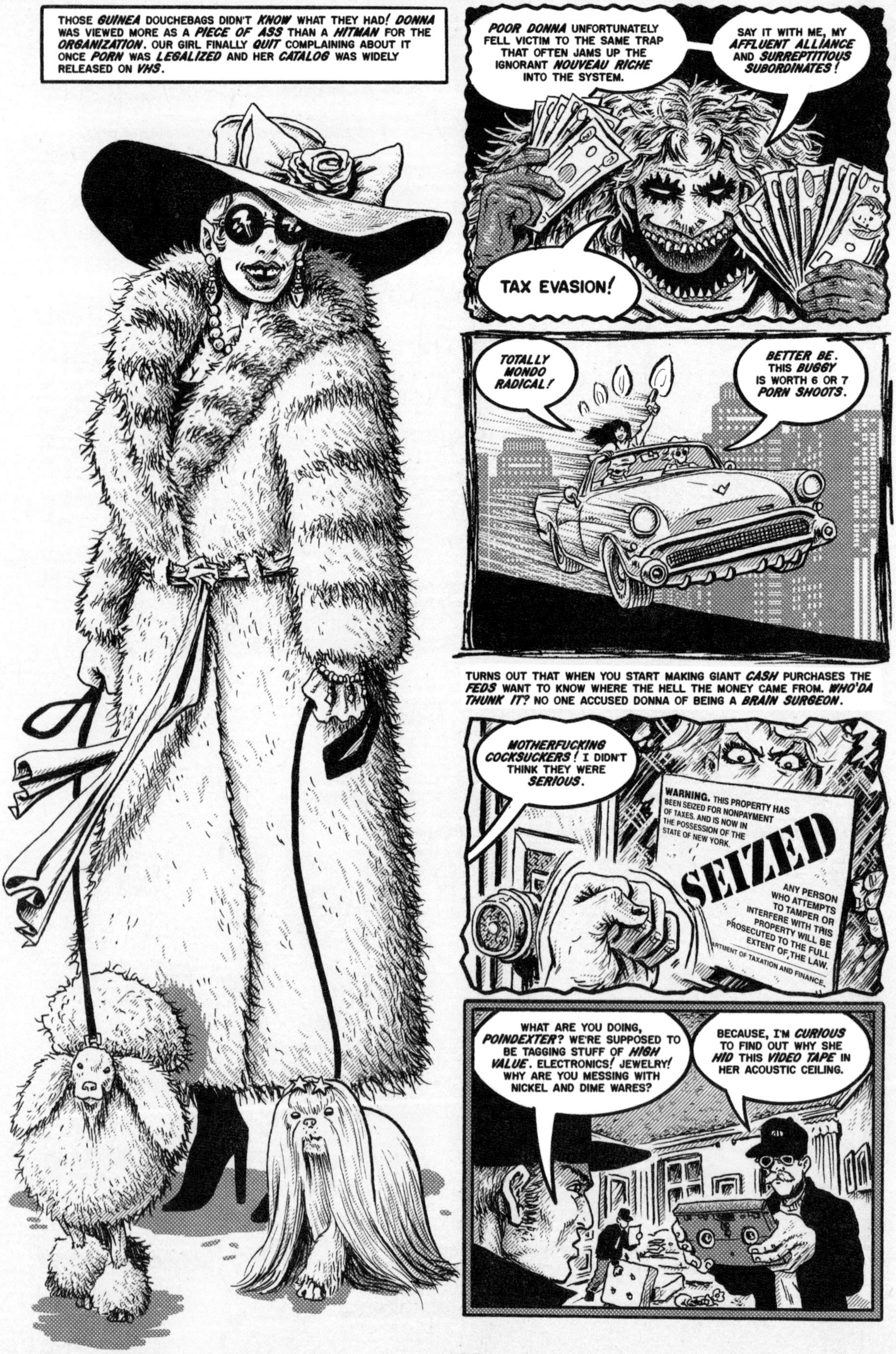
THOSE GUINEA DOUCHEBAGS DIDN'T KNOW WHAT THEY HAD! DONNA WAS VIEWED MORE AS A PIECE OF ASS THAN A HITMAN FOR THE ORGANIZATION. OUR GIRL FINALLY QUIT COMPLAINING ABOUT IT ONCE PORN WAS LEGALIZED AND HER CATALOG WAS WIDELY RELEASED ON VHS.
POOR DONNA UNFORTUNATELY FELL VICTIM TO THE SAME TRAP THAT OFTEN JAMS UP THE IGNORANT NOUVEAU RICHE INTO THE SYSTEM.
SAY IT WITH ME, MY AFFLUENT ALLIANCE AND SURREPTITIOUS SUBORDINATES!
TAX EVASION!
TOTALLY MONDO RADICAL!
BETTER BE. THIS BUGGY IS WORTH 6 OR 7 PORN SHOOTS.
TURNS OUT THAT WHEN YOU START MAKING GIANT CASH PURCHASES THE FEDS WANT TO KNOW WHERE THE HELL THE MONEY CAME FROM. WHO'DA THUNK IT? NO ONE ACCUSED DONNA OF BEING A BRAIN SURGEON.
MOTHERFUCKING COCKSUCKERS! I DIDN'T THINK THEY WERE SERIOUS.
WARNING. THIS PROPERTY HAS BEEN SEIZED FOR NONPAYMENT OF TAXES. AND IS NOW IN THE POSSESSION OF THE STATE OF NEW YORK.
SEIZED
ANY PERSON WHO ATTEMPTS TO TAMPER OR INTERFERE WITH THIS PROPERTY WILL BE PROSECUTED TO THE FULL EXTENT OF THE LAW.
ARTMENT OF TAXATION AND FINANCE.
WHAT ARE YOU DOING, POINDEXTER? WE'RE SUPPOSED TO BE TAGGING STUFF OF HIGH VALUE. ELECTRONICS! JEWELRY! WHY ARE YOU MESSING WITH NICKEL AND DIME WARES?
BECAUSE, I'M CURIOUS TO FIND OUT WHY SHE HID THIS VIDEO TAPE IN HER ACOUSTIC CEILING.

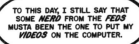

TO THIS DAY, I STILL SAY THAT SOME *NERD* FROM THE *FEDS* MUSTA BEEN THE ONE TO PUT MY *VIDEOS* ON THE COMPUTER.

MY...*ASSOCIATES* HAD JUST AS MUCH INCENTIVE FOR MY *WORK* TO REMAIN *PRIVATE* AS I HAD. THEY EVEN BOUGHT ME THE BEST *DEFENSE* POSSIBLE IN THE SITUATION. THAT'S WHY MY *FAT FANNY* AIN'T *EVER* GETTIN' *COOKED* OVER THERE IN BUILDING "C".

SHIT, MY *BOSSES* AIN'T EVEN KNOW ABOUT THE *PRIVATE TAPES* I MADE JUST FOR ME. I HEARD THOSE ONES ARE *SUPER POPULAR* ON THE *COMPUTER*, TOO.

Donna's_triple_double.mp4

HAPPY BIRTHDAY TO ME

THERE WAS NO MORE *DEFENSE* ONCE THE *JURY* SAW THE *KIN* OF MY *PREY* IDENTIFY THEIR PEOPLE IN EACH *VIDEO*. I SHOULDA *MASKED* ALL THOSE *FAGGOTS* UP BEFORE *RECORDING*.

>SIGH<

THE REST OF THE TRIAL WAS A TOTAL *WASTE* OF EVERYONE'S TIME. *FORMAL BULLSHIT*.

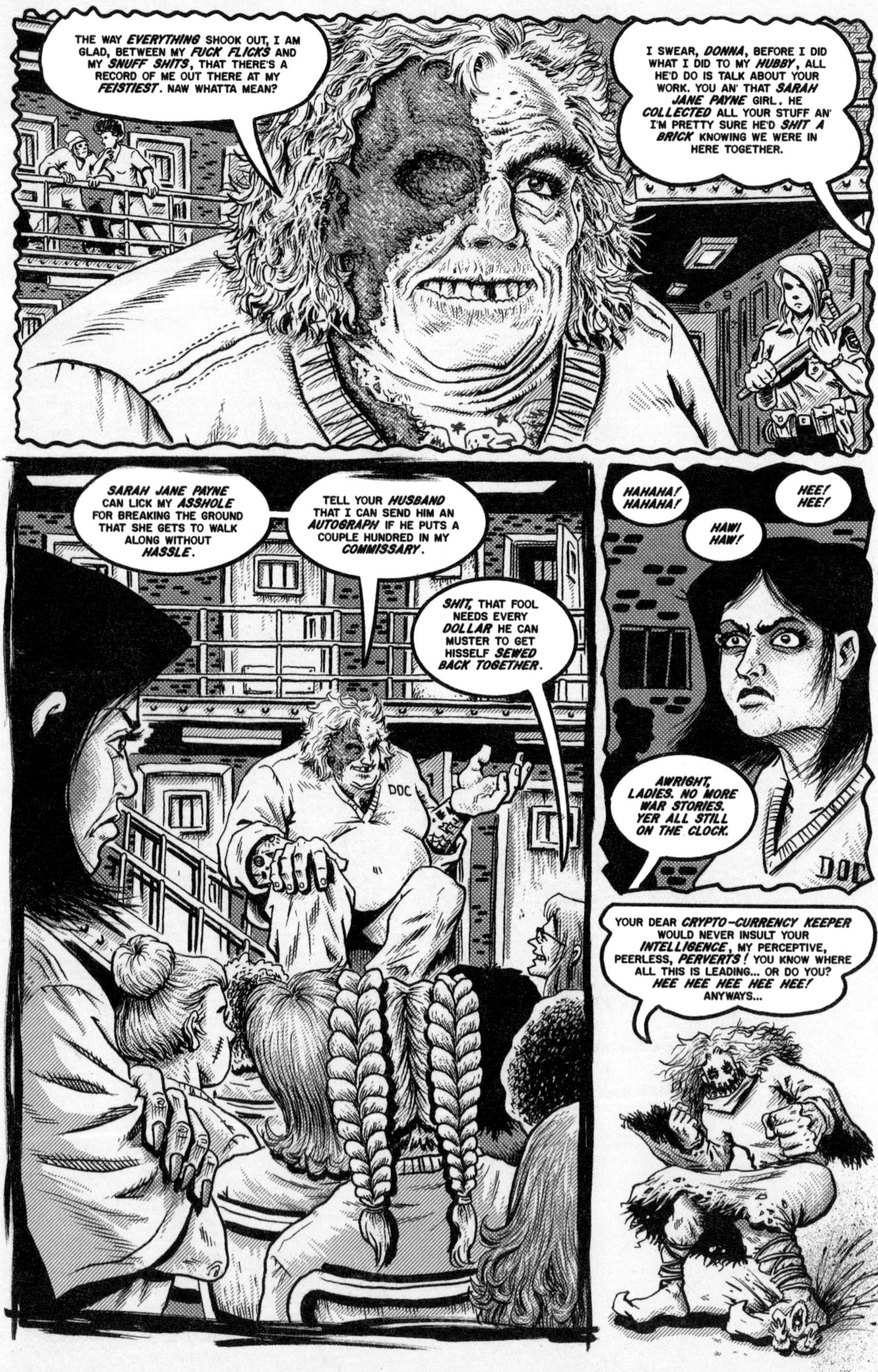
THE WAY EVERYTHING SHOOK OUT, I AM GLAD, BETWEEN MY FUCK FLICKS AND MY SNUFF SHITS, THAT THERE'S A RECORD OF ME OUT THERE AT MY FEISTIEST. NAW WHATTA MEAN?
I SWEAR, DONNA, BEFORE I DID WHAT I DID TO MY HUBBY, ALL HE'D DO IS TALK ABOUT YOUR WORK. YOU AN' THAT SARAH JANE PAYNE GIRL. HE COLLECTED ALL YOUR STUFF AN' I'M PRETTY SURE HE'D SHIT A BRICK KNOWING WE WERE IN HERE TOGETHER.
SARAH JANE PAYNE CAN LICK MY ASSHOLE FOR BREAKING THE GROUND THAT SHE GETS TO WALK ALONG WITHOUT HASSLE.
TELL YOUR HUSBAND THAT I CAN SEND HIM AN AUTOGRAPH IF HE PUTS A COUPLE HUNDRED IN MY COMMISSARY.
SHIT, THAT FOOL NEEDS EVERY DOLLAR HE CAN MUSTER TO GET HISSELF SEWED BACK TOGETHER.
DOC
HAHAHA! HAHAHA!
HAW! HAW!
HEE! HEE!
AWRIGHT, LADIES. NO MORE WAR STORIES. YER ALL STILL ON THE CLOCK.
DOC
YOUR DEAR CRYPTO-CURRENCY KEEPER WOULD NEVER INSULT YOUR INTELLIGENCE, MY PERCEPTIVE, PEERLESS, PERVERTS! YOU KNOW WHERE ALL THIS IS LEADING... OR DO YOU? HEE HEE HEE HEE HEE! ANYWAYS...

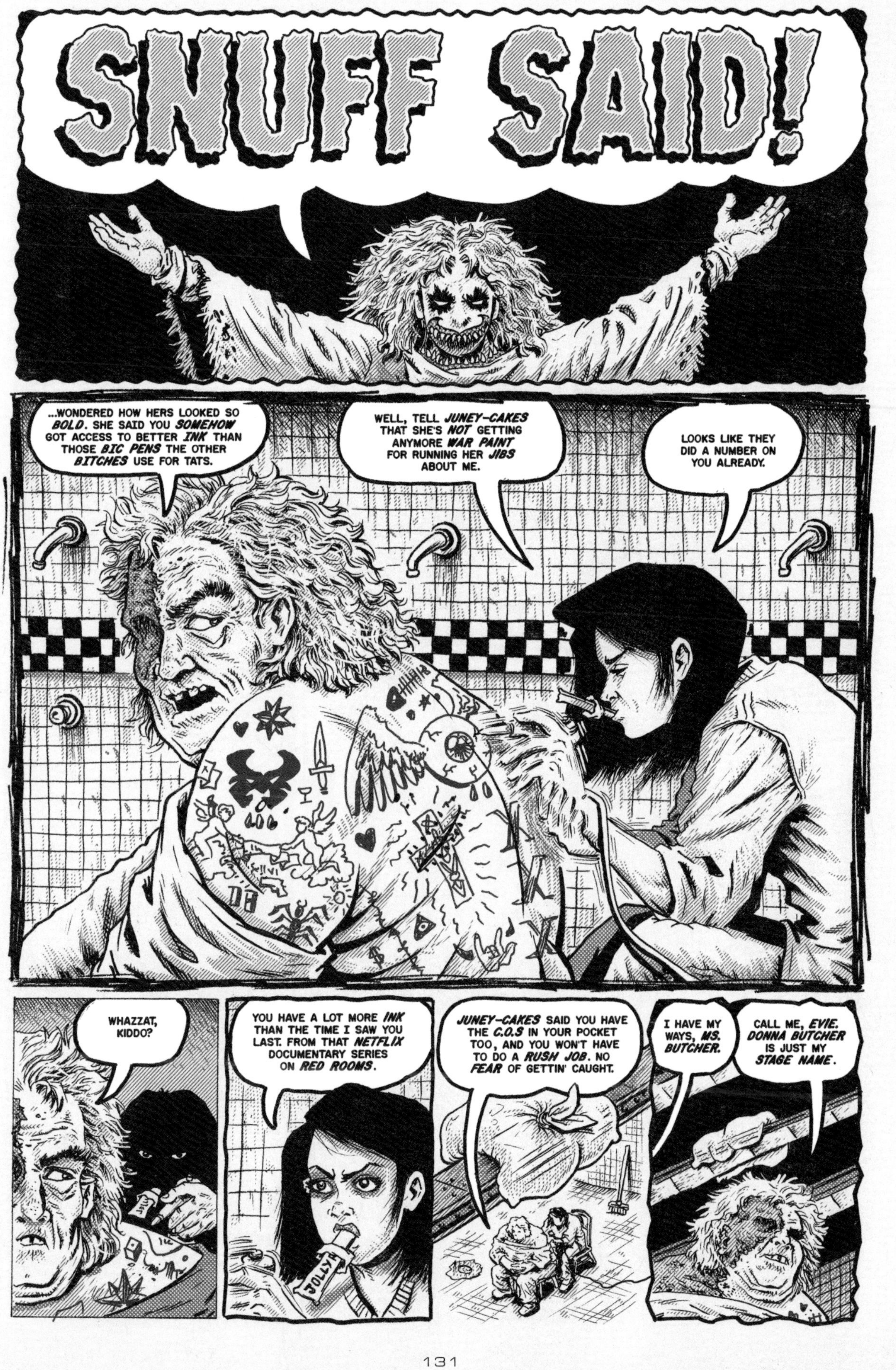
SNUFF SAID!
...WONDERED HOW HERS LOOKED SO BOLD. SHE SAID YOU SOMEHOW GOT ACCESS TO BETTER INK THAN THOSE BIC PENS THE OTHER BITCHES USE FOR TATS.
WELL, TELL JUNEY-CAKES THAT SHE'S NOT GETTING ANYMORE WAR PAINT FOR RUNNING HER JIBS ABOUT ME.
LOOKS LIKE THEY DID A NUMBER ON YOU ALREADY.
WHAZZAT, KIDDO?
YOU HAVE A LOT MORE INK THAN THE TIME I SAW YOU LAST. FROM THAT NETFLIX DOCUMENTARY SERIES ON RED ROOMS.
JUNEY-CAKES SAID YOU HAVE THE C.O.S IN YOUR POCKET TOO, AND YOU WON'T HAVE TO DO A RUSH JOB. NO FEAR OF GETTIN' CAUGHT.
I HAVE MY WAYS, MS. BUTCHER.
CALL ME, EVIE. DONNA BUTCHER IS JUST MY STAGE NAME.

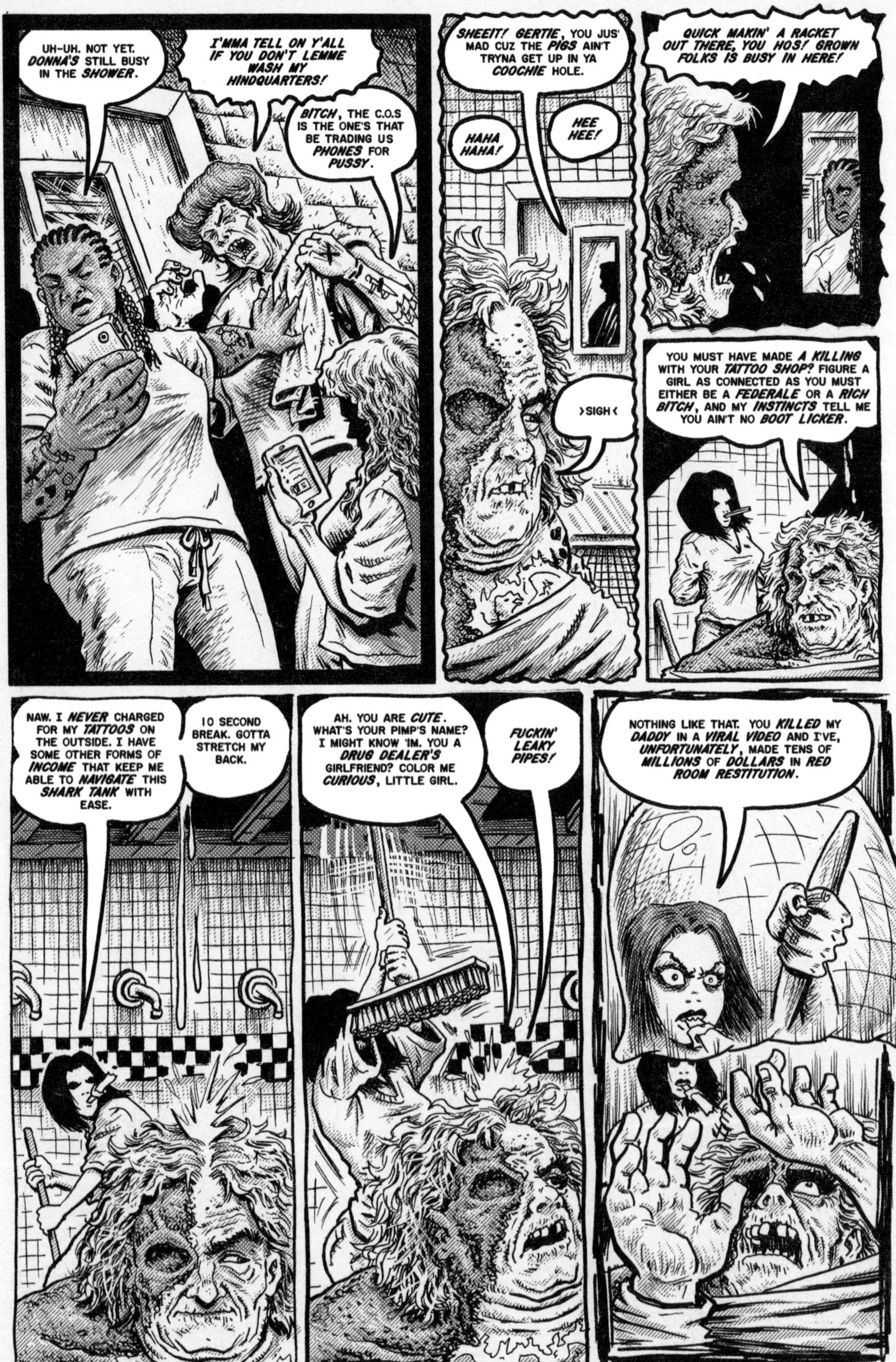
UH-UH. NOT YET. DONNA'S STILL BUSY IN THE SHOWER.
I'MMA TELL ON Y'ALL IF YOU DON'T LEMME WASH MY HINDQUARTERS!
BITCH, THE C.O.S IS THE ONE'S THAT BE TRADING US PHONES FOR PUSSY.
SHEEIT! GERTIE, YOU JUS' MAD CUZ THE PIGS AIN'T TRYNA GET UP IN YA COOCHIE HOLE.
HAHA HAHA!
HEE HEE!
›SIGH‹
QUICK MAKIN' A RACKET OUT THERE, YOU HOS! GROWN FOLKS IS BUSY IN HERE!
YOU MUST HAVE MADE A KILLING WITH YOUR TATTOO SHOP? FIGURE A GIRL AS CONNECTED AS YOU MUST EITHER BE A FEDERALE OR A RICH BITCH, AND MY INSTINCTS TELL ME YOU AIN'T NO BOOT LICKER.
NAW. I NEVER CHARGED FOR MY TATTOOS ON THE OUTSIDE. I HAVE SOME OTHER FORMS OF INCOME THAT KEEP ME ABLE TO NAVIGATE THIS SHARK TANK WITH EASE.
10 SECOND BREAK. GOTTA STRETCH MY BACK.
AH. YOU ARE CUTE. WHAT'S YOUR PIMP'S NAME? I MIGHT KNOW 'IM. YOU A DRUG DEALER'S GIRLFRIEND? COLOR ME CURIOUS, LITTLE GIRL.
FUCKIN' LEAKY PIPES!
NOTHING LIKE THAT. YOU KILLED MY DADDY IN A VIRAL VIDEO AND I'VE, UNFORTUNATELY, MADE TENS OF MILLIONS OF DOLLARS IN RED ROOM RESTITUTION.

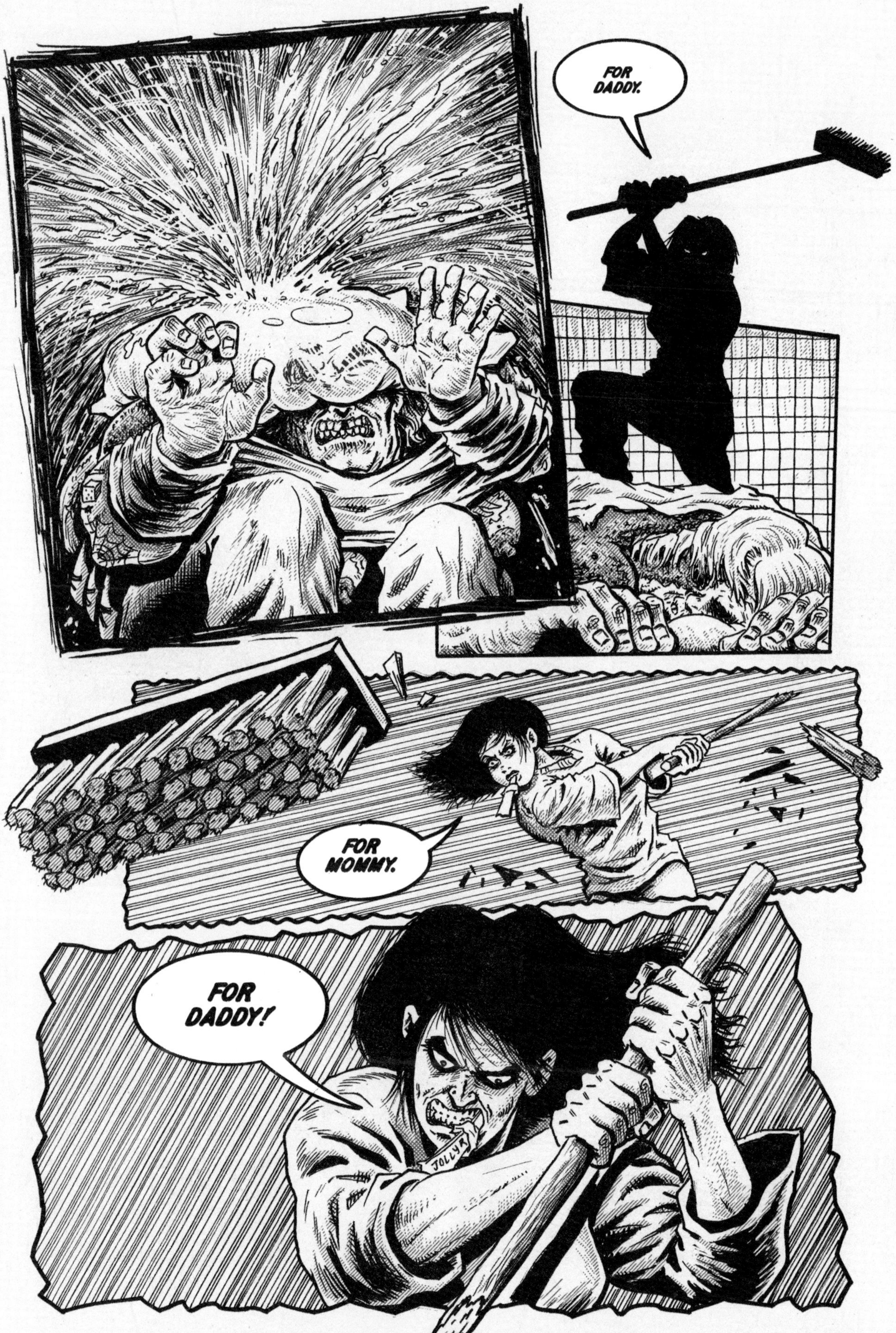
FOR DADDY.
FOR MOMMY.
FOR DADDY!
JOLLY

FOR DADDY! FOR MOMMY! FOR DADDY! MOMMY! FOR MOMMY! DADDY! FOR DADDY! MOMMY! FOR DADDY! MOMMY! FOR DADDY! FOR MOMMY! FOR MOMMY! DADDY! FOR DADDY! FOR MOMMY! FOR DADDY! FOR MOMMY! FOR DADDY! FOR MOMMY! FOR DADDY! FOR MOMMY! FOR DADDY! FOR MOMMY! FOR DADDY! MOMMY! FOR DADDY! FOR MOMMY! FOR DADDY! FOR MOMMY! FOR MOMMY!

FOR MOMMY!

FOR DADDY!

WHAT? YOU *SICK FUCKERS* THOUGHT YOU WERE GOING TO SEE EVERY *POKE RAINA* MADE INTO THAT *OL' HEIFER?* GIMME A BREAK! THERE'S A MORE *INTERESTING ENDING* TO THE STORY... BUT, I WILL GIVE YOU *ONE* MORE *GORY* DETAIL....

SHOULD WE STEP IN, ALREADY?

SHIT. BITCH IS *POSSESSED.* YOU GONNA STOP HER?

EWWWW!

THIS IS GOIN' ON WORLDSTAR!

DONNA_BUTCHER_EXECUTION_REVENGE.mp4 — □ X

WORLDSTAR!

WORLDSTAR!

HUH?

OH FUCK!

DONNA_BUTCHER_EXECUTION_REVENGE.mp4 — □ X

EEEEEE!

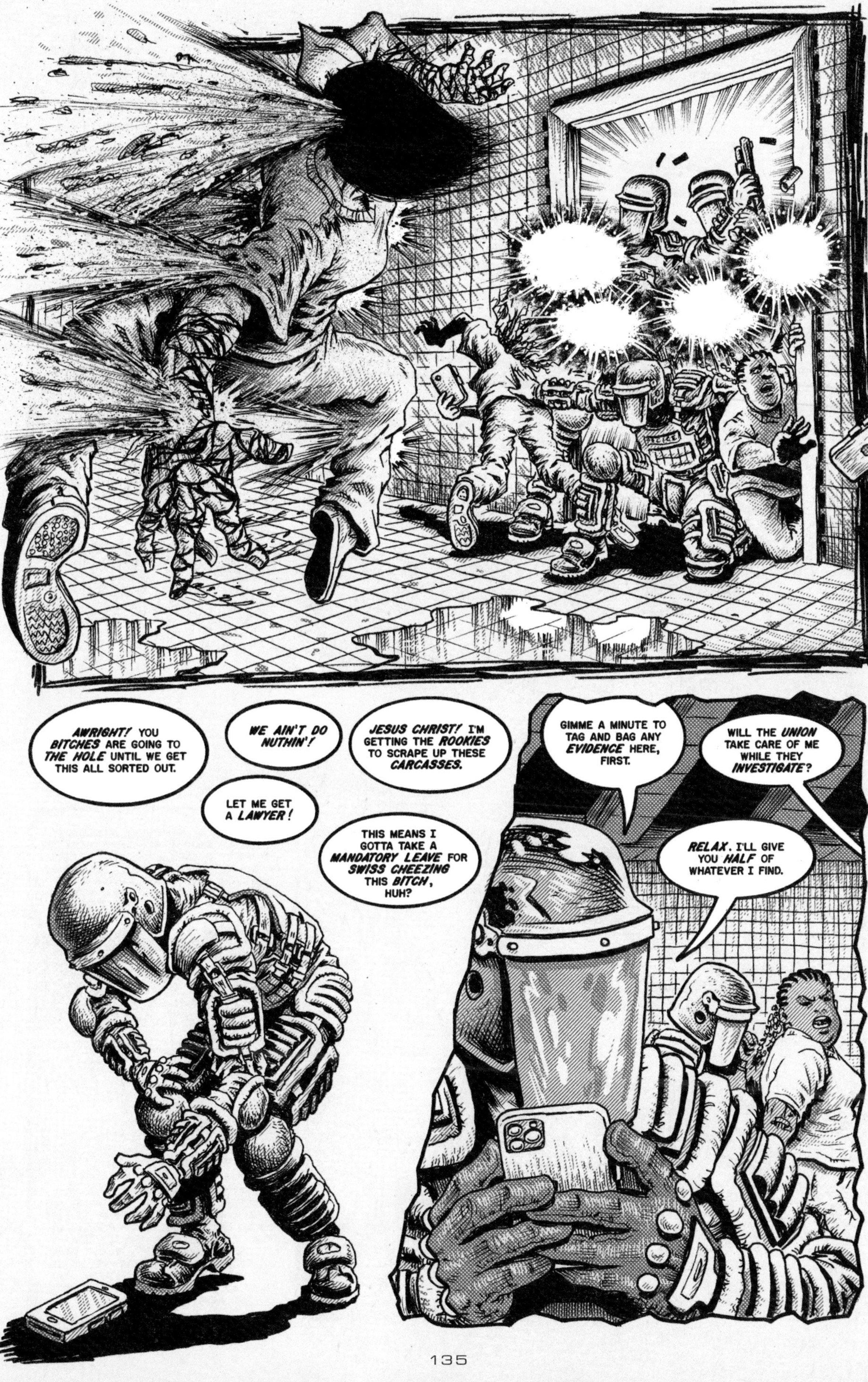
AWRIGHT! YOU BITCHES ARE GOING TO THE HOLE UNTIL WE GET THIS ALL SORTED OUT.
WE AIN'T DO NUTHIN'!
JESUS CHRIST! I'M GETTING THE ROOKIES TO SCRAPE UP THESE CARCASSES.
LET ME GET A LAWYER!
THIS MEANS I GOTTA TAKE A MANDATORY LEAVE FOR SWISS CHEEZING THIS BITCH, HUH?
GIMME A MINUTE TO TAG AND BAG ANY EVIDENCE HERE, FIRST.
WILL THE UNION TAKE CARE OF ME WHILE THEY INVESTIGATE?
RELAX. I'LL GIVE YOU HALF OF WHATEVER I FIND.

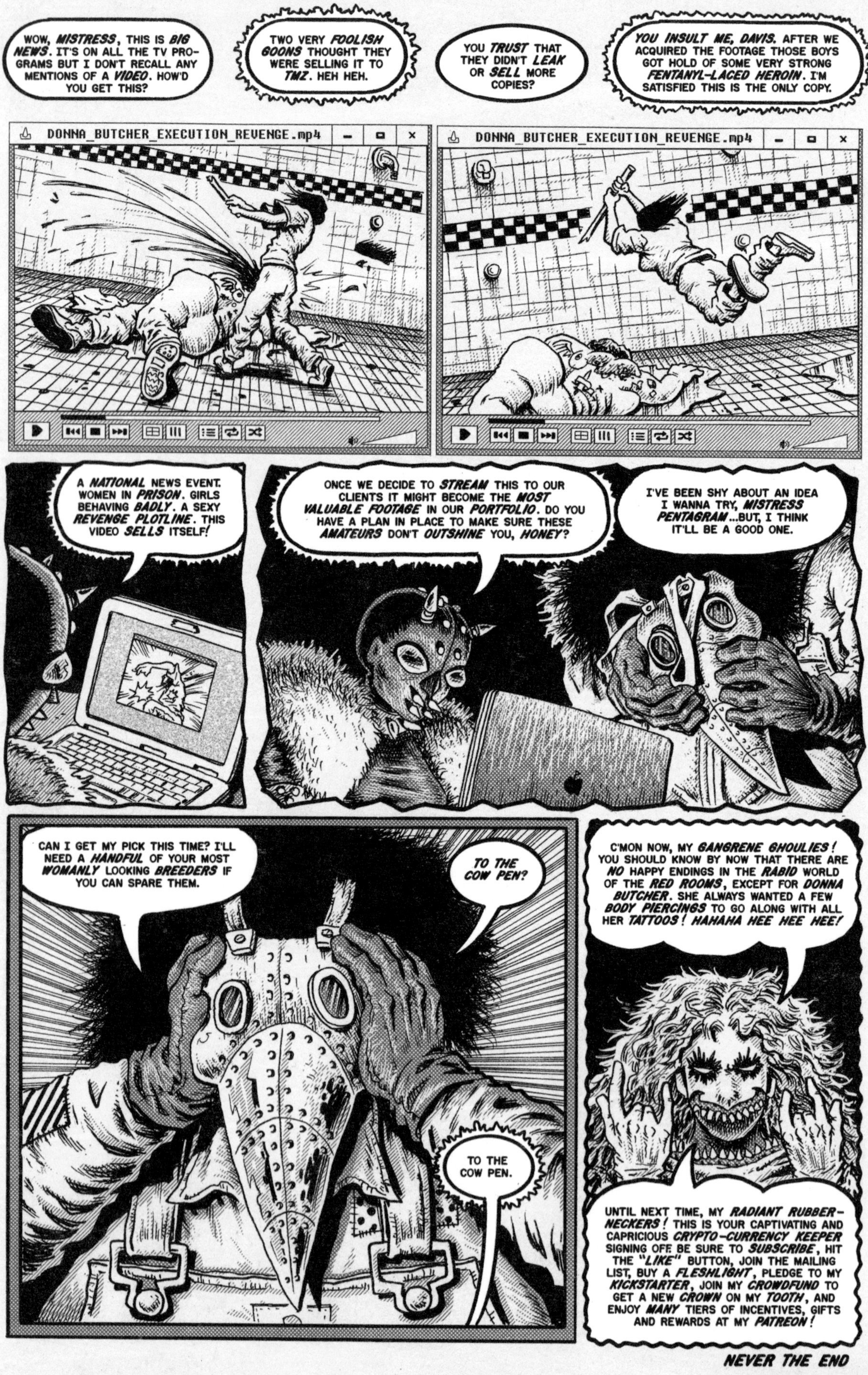
WOW, MISTRESS, THIS IS BIG NEWS. IT'S ON ALL THE TV PROGRAMS BUT I DON'T RECALL ANY MENTIONS OF A VIDEO. HOW'D YOU GET THIS?
TWO VERY FOOLISH GOONS THOUGHT THEY WERE SELLING IT TO TMZ. HEH HEH.
YOU TRUST THAT THEY DIDN'T LEAK OR SELL MORE COPIES?
YOU INSULT ME, DAVIS. AFTER WE ACQUIRED THE FOOTAGE THOSE BOYS GOT HOLD OF SOME VERY STRONG FENTANYL-LACED HEROIN. I'M SATISFIED THIS IS THE ONLY COPY.
DONNA_BUTCHER_EXECUTION_REVENGE.mp4
DONNA_BUTCHER_EXECUTION_REVENGE.mp4
A NATIONAL NEWS EVENT. WOMEN IN PRISON. GIRLS BEHAVING BADLY. A SEXY REVENGE PLOTLINE. THIS VIDEO SELLS ITSELF!
ONCE WE DECIDE TO STREAM THIS TO OUR CLIENTS IT MIGHT BECOME THE MOST VALUABLE FOOTAGE IN OUR PORTFOLIO. DO YOU HAVE A PLAN IN PLACE TO MAKE SURE THESE AMATEURS DON'T OUTSHINE YOU, HONEY?
I'VE BEEN SHY ABOUT AN IDEA I WANNA TRY, MISTRESS PENTAGRAM...BUT, I THINK IT'LL BE A GOOD ONE.
CAN I GET MY PICK THIS TIME? I'LL NEED A HANDFUL OF YOUR MOST WOMANLY LOOKING BREEDERS IF YOU CAN SPARE THEM.
TO THE COW PEN?
TO THE COW PEN.
C'MON NOW, MY GANGRENE GHOULIES! YOU SHOULD KNOW BY NOW THAT THERE ARE NO HAPPY ENDINGS IN THE RABID WORLD OF THE RED ROOMS, EXCEPT FOR DONNA BUTCHER. SHE ALWAYS WANTED A FEW BODY PIERCINGS TO GO ALONG WITH ALL HER TATTOOS! HAHAHA HEE HEE HEE!
UNTIL NEXT TIME, MY RADIANT RUBBER-NECKERS! THIS IS YOUR CAPTIVATING AND CAPRICIOUS CRYPTO-CURRENCY KEEPER SIGNING OFF. BE SURE TO SUBSCRIBE, HIT THE "LIKE" BUTTON, JOIN THE MAILING LIST, BUY A FLESHLIGHT, PLEDGE TO MY KICKSTARTER, JOIN MY CROWDFUND TO GET A NEW CROWN ON MY TOOTH, AND ENJOY MANY TIERS OF INCENTIVES, GIFTS AND REWARDS AT MY PATREON!

NEVER THE END

DECIMATOR PRESENTS: THE RAT QUEENS!

— □ ✕

CHAT | USERS: 3,012

TONY_ALTO: We had chickens when I was little. If one of those little bastards got wounded and bled all the others would go into a frenzzy and cannibalize that sucker!

DARWIN_DOLPHIN: Yeah, we are definitely seeing some basic instincts at play right here.

WILSON9322: That's probably all these retards are capable of. They look like they can form opinions to you?

LEVAY_FOLLOWER: Barely advanced primates.

BEARD_FANOOK: You guys are gonna call me crazy and I guess there's no way to prove it, but if you cleaned one of these bitches up, I would totally fuck it.

BARKER_KETCHUM: Yer SICK!

PENTAGRAM PICTURES | DO NOT RECORD! | ฿ 06.5237
BE GLAD YOU'RE NOT THEM! TIP YOUR HOST LIBERALLY!

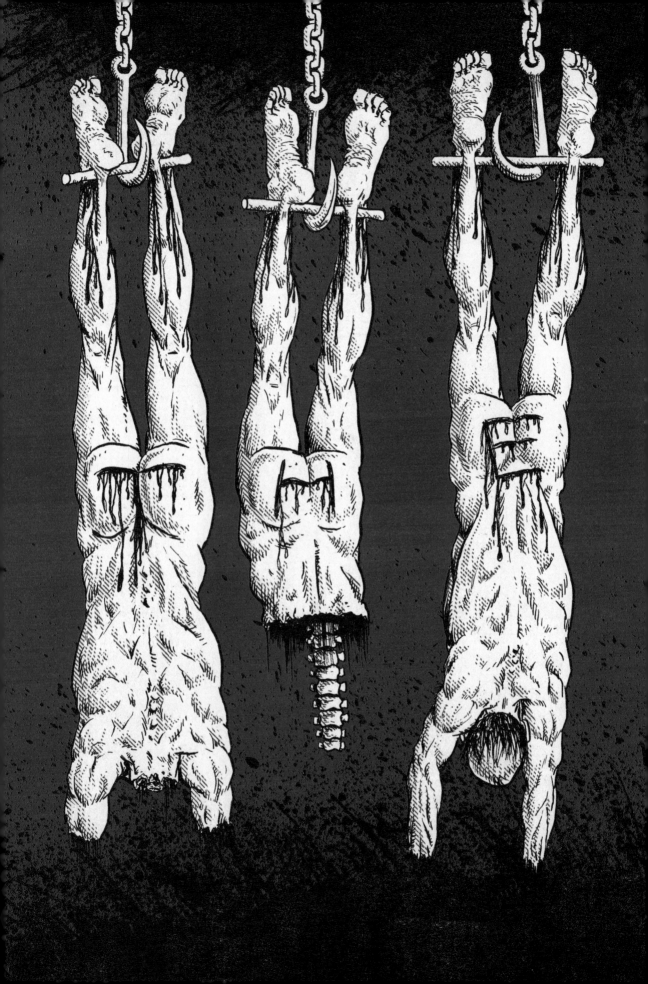

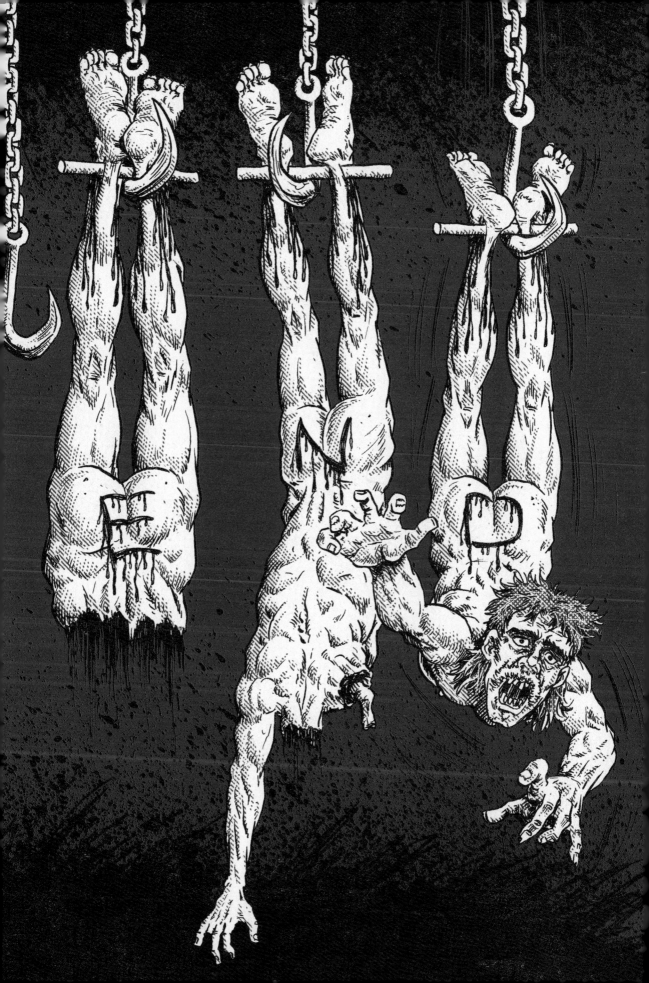

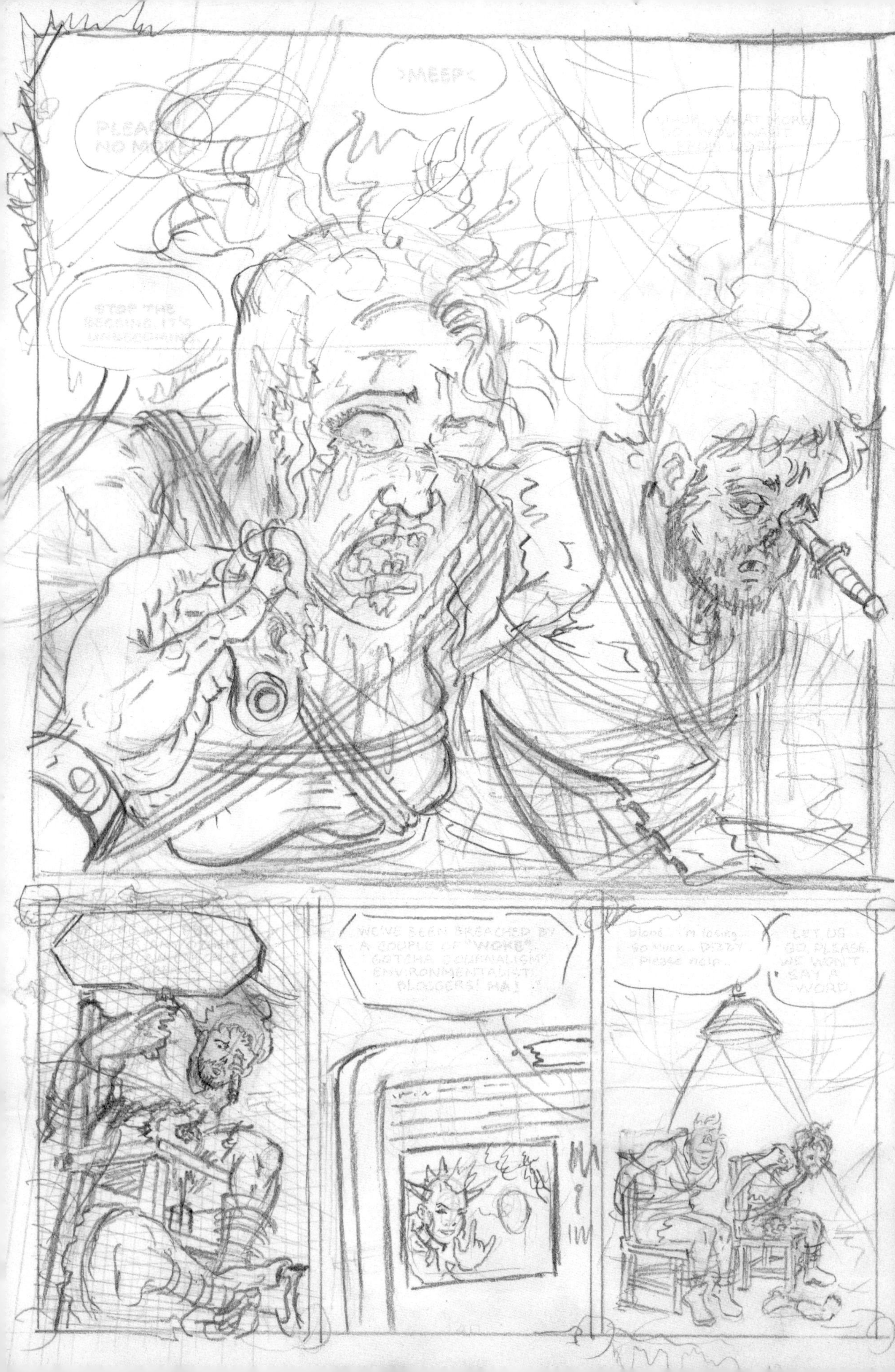
>MEEP<
WE'VE BEEN BREACHED BY A COUPLE OF "WOKE" GOTCHA JOURNALISM ENVIRONMENTALIST BLOGGERS! HA!
LET US GO, PLEASE. WE WON'T SAY A WORD.

SKETCHBOOK

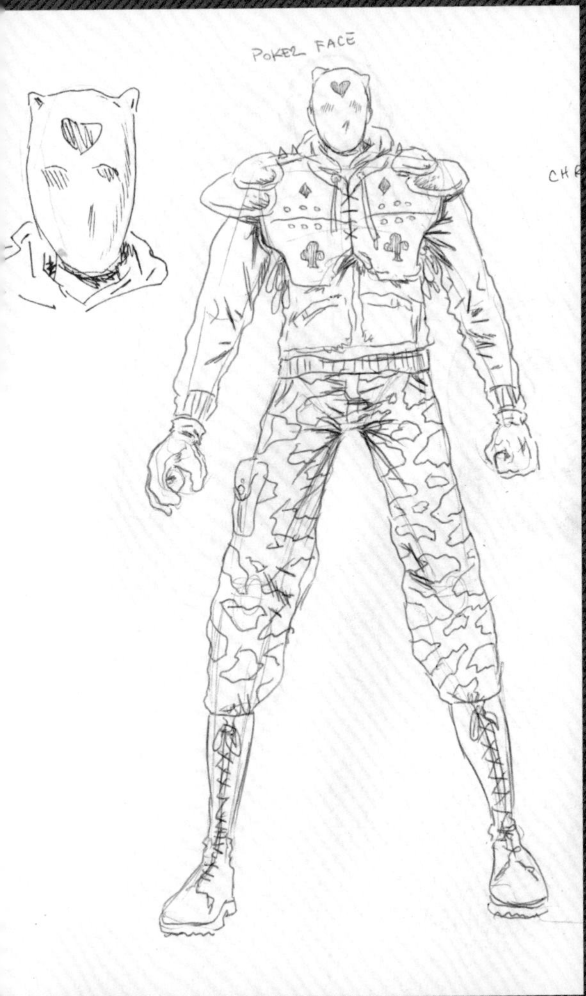
POKER FACE

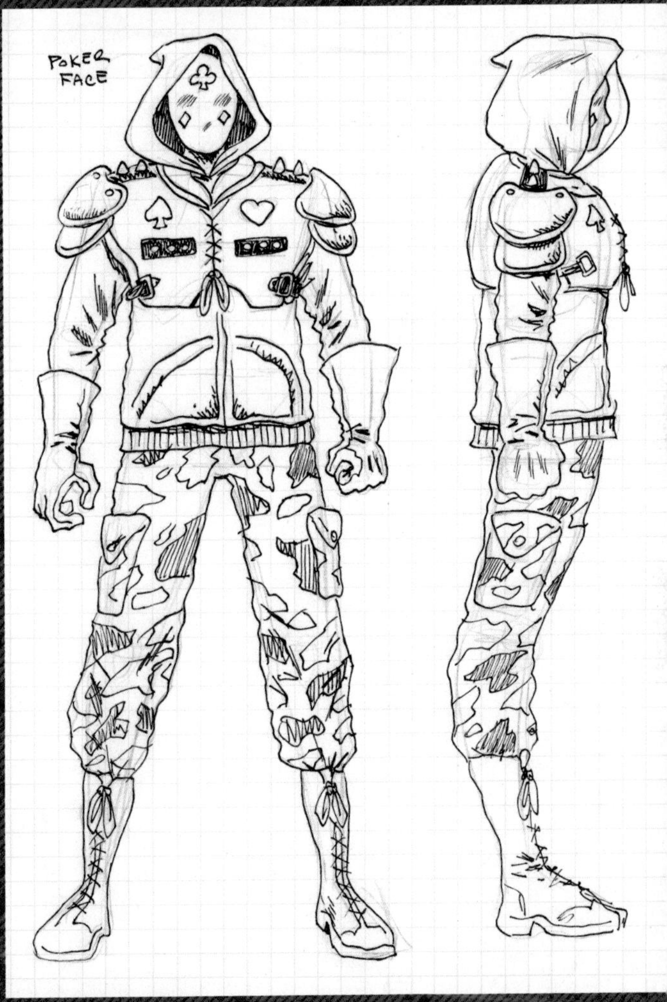
POKER FACE

ABOVE: **I wanted all the *Red Room* uniforms to be easy to cosplay, but also, I wanted them to be creepy and memorable. Pokerface took a few tries.**

OPPOSITE: **The pencils for the first issue were all done this quickly because I wanted to loosen up and do most of the drawing in ink. Almost no backgrounds were pencilled except for a perspective grid.**

Red Room wasn't going to look aesthetically the same as my *Hip Hop* comics but it kind of started out there. I knew I wanted some cool, grey values and was toying with halftoning pencil shading for that effect. Maybe I still will for a future issue?

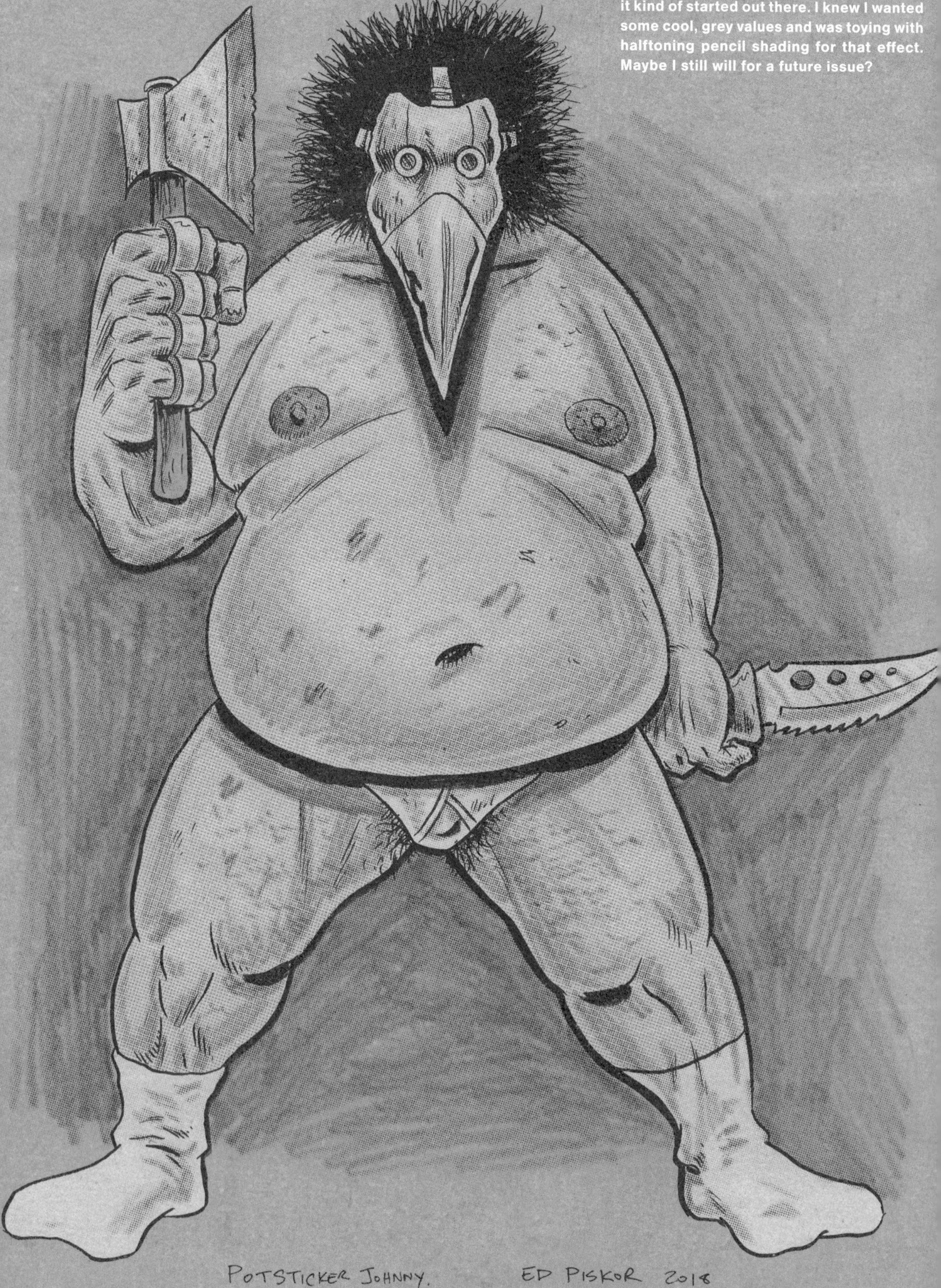

POTSTICKER JOHNNY.   ED PISKOR 2018

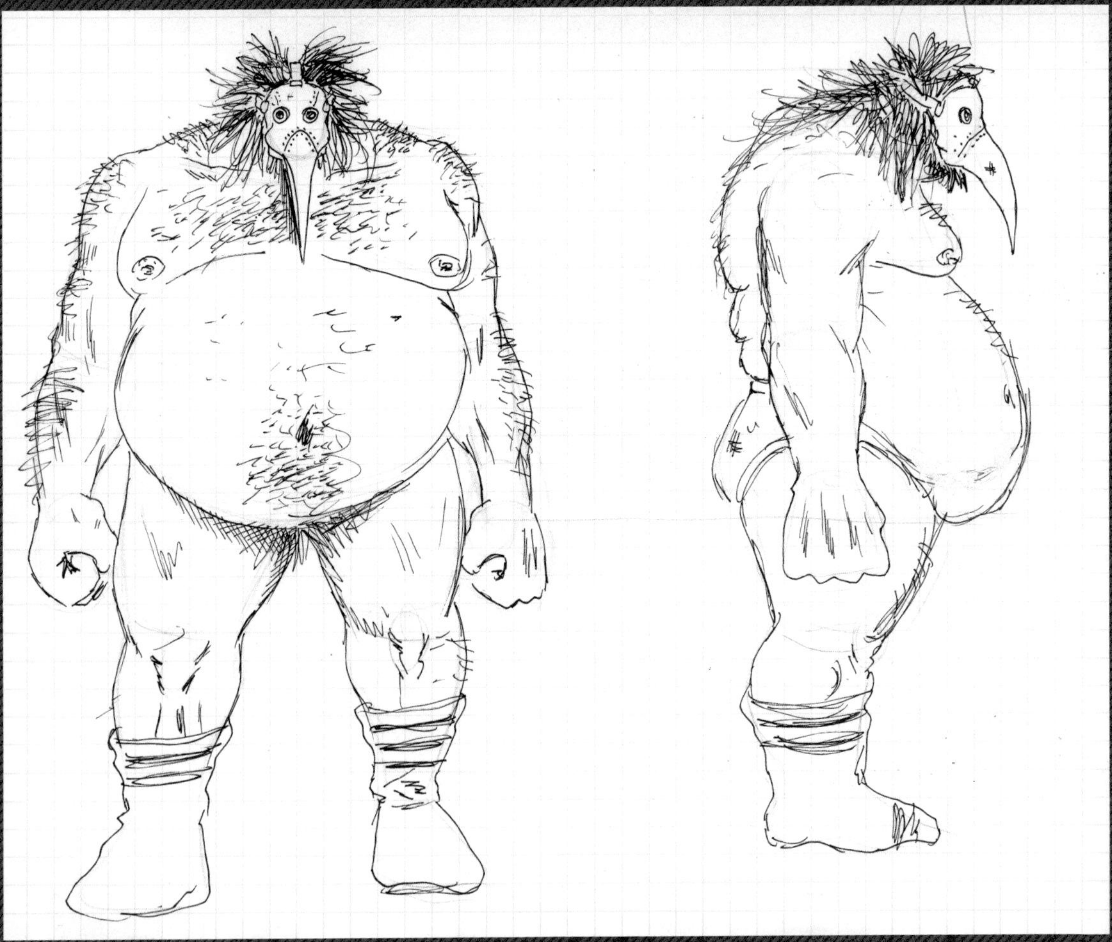

The proportions of the drawing style weren't in stone at the beginning either and I was thinking of elongating all the characters in a Peter Chung fashion to add more unease to the material.

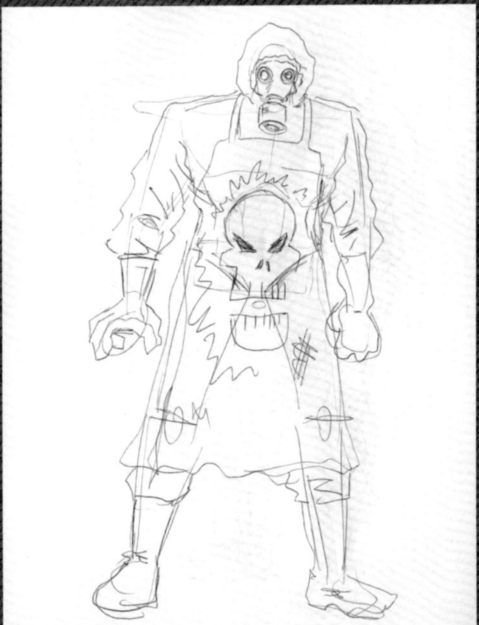

Lots of trial and error when designing the Red Roomers. I want killer icons!

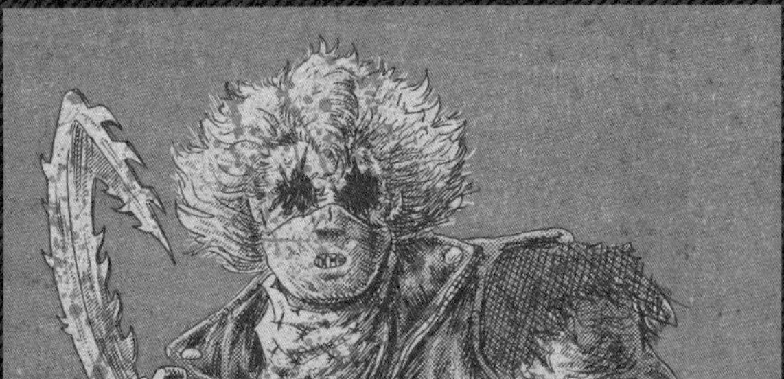

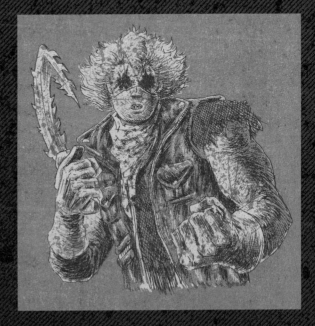

The Maim Mangler. So far I haven't told you his (her?) story. The looseness of this drawing was inspired by looking at Vince Locke and was a potential road to go down for the aesthetics of the series.

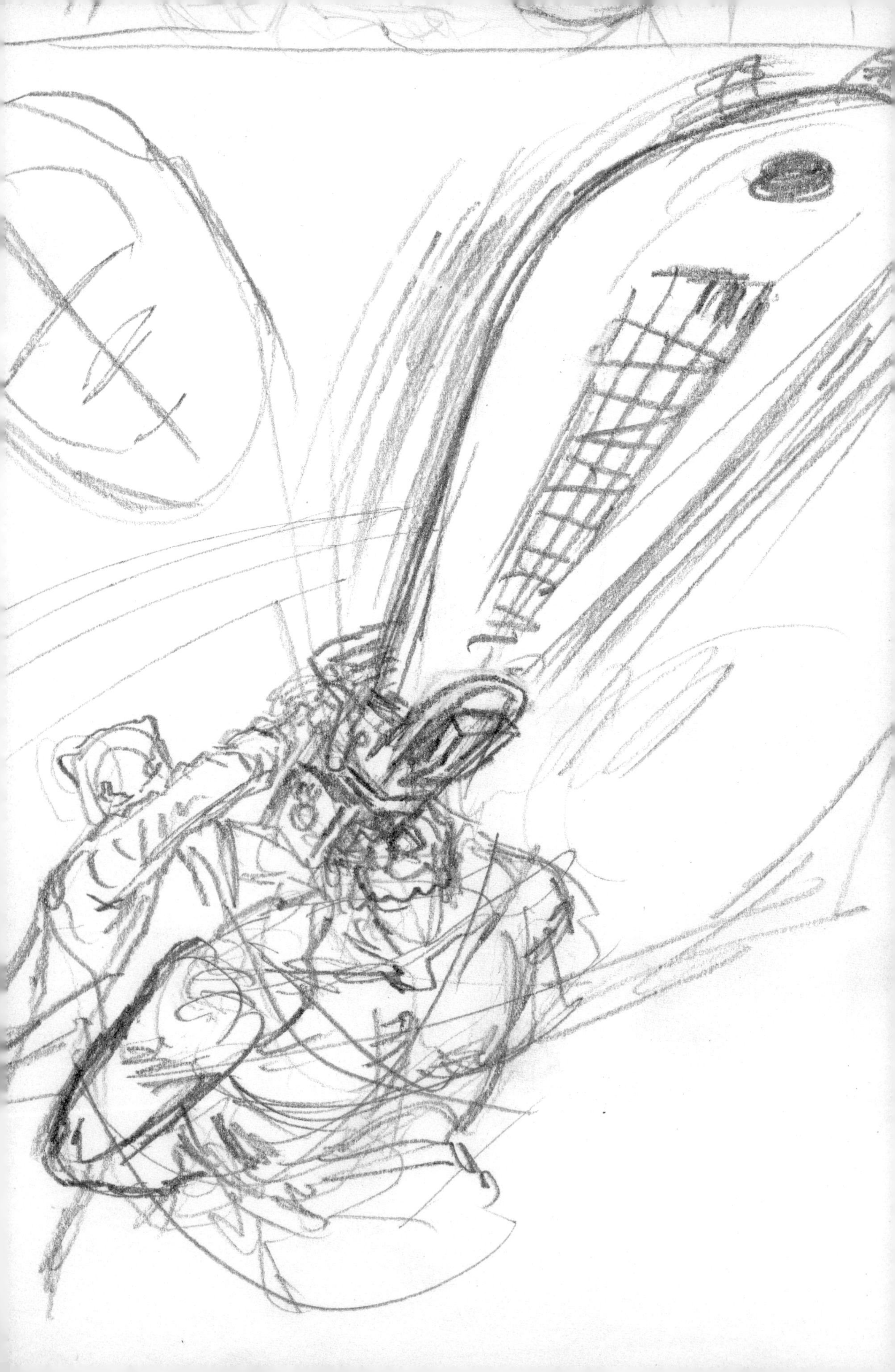

ONE OF THREE

I bought myself a little free time in between other projects when I decided to get more serious about my *Red Room* idea. It was a good thing, too, because I didn't know exactly what this comic should be so I made a quick and dirty first draft on typing paper. There are three 32-page segments to this draft and we'll be serializing them across the next two collections as well. As you can see, things in this "Mach 1" version have changed a lot compared to what you've just read in this book, but it might be fun to compare and contrast. I'm a process junkie and I know some of you are, too.

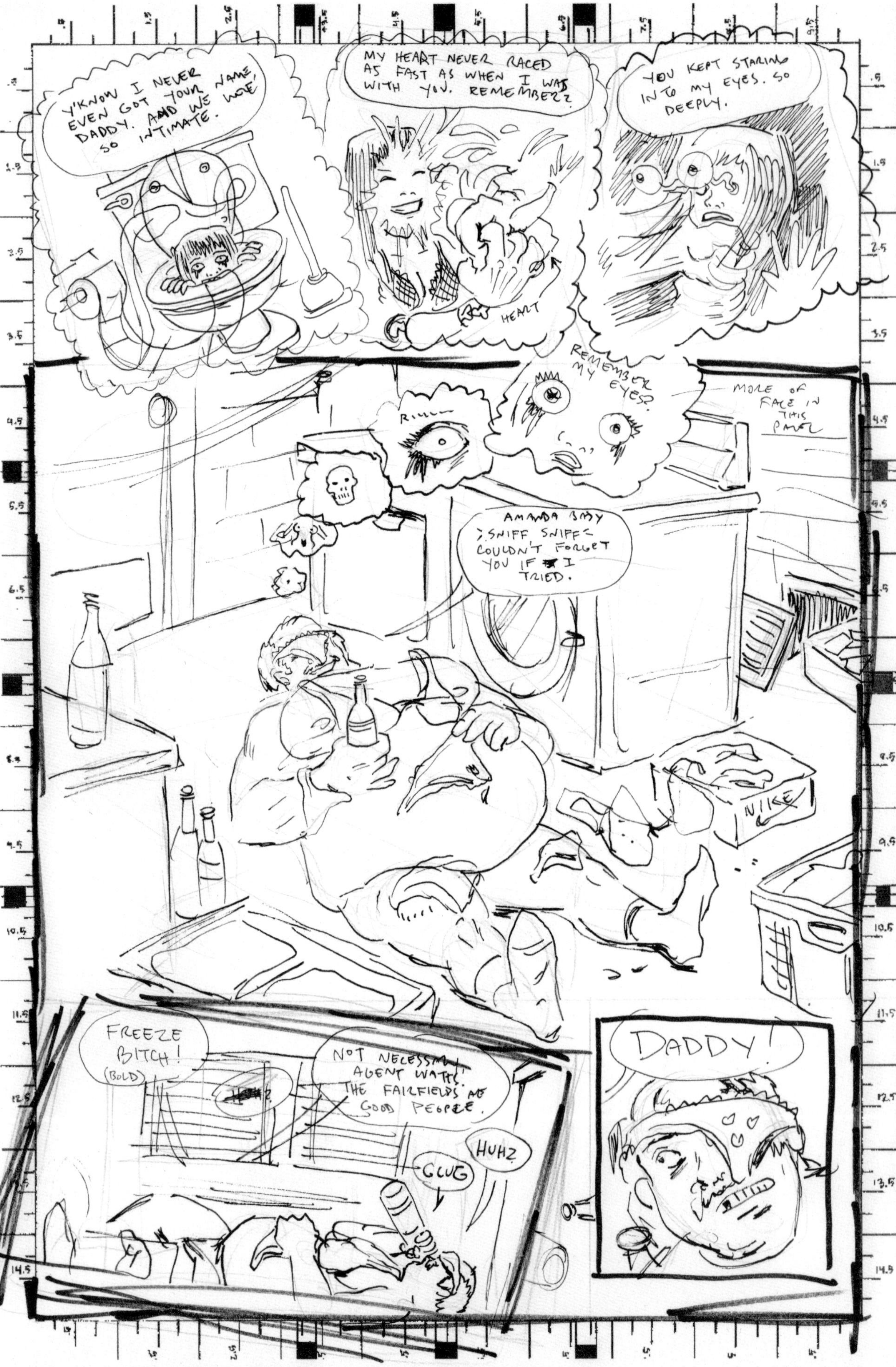
Y'KNOW I NEVER EVEN GOT YOUR NAME DADDY. AND WE WERE SO INTIMATE.
MY HEART NEVER RACED AS FAST AS WHEN I WAS WITH YOU. REMEMBER?
HEART
YOU KEPT STARING INTO MY EYES. SO DEEPLY.
REMEMBER MY EYES?
MORE OF FACE IN THIS PANEL
AMANDA BABY >SNIFF SNIFF< COULDN'T FORGET YOU IF I TRIED.
FREEZE BITCH! (BOLD)
NOT NECESSARY AGENT WATTS! THE FAIRFIELDS ARE GOOD PEOPLE.
HUH?
GLUG
DADDY!

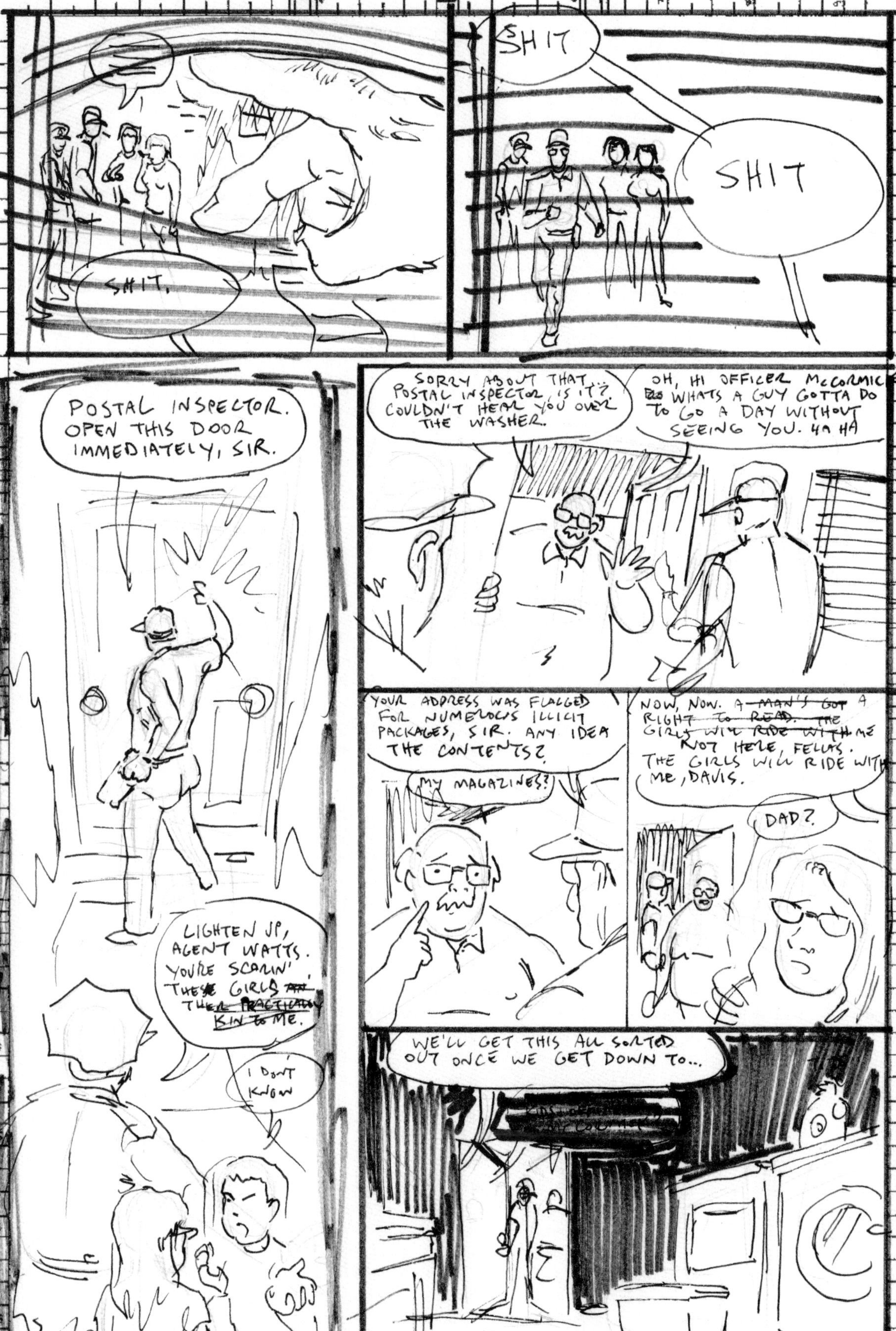
SHIT.
SHIT
SHIT
POSTAL INSPECTOR. OPEN THIS DOOR IMMEDIATELY, SIR.
SORRY ABOUT THAT... POSTAL INSPECTOR, IS IT? COULDN'T HEAR YOU OVER THE WASHER.
OH, HI OFFICER McCORMIC WHATS A GUY GOTTA DO TO GO A DAY WITHOUT SEEING YOU. HA HA
LIGHTEN UP, AGENT WATTS. YOU'RE SCARIN' THESE GIRLS PRACTICALLY KIN TO ME.
I DON'T KNOW
YOUR ADDRESS WAS FLAGGED FOR NUMEROUS ILLICIT PACKAGES, SIR. ANY IDEA THE CONTENTS?
MY MAGAZINES?
NOW, NOW. A MAN'S GOT A RIGHT TO READ. THE GIRLS WILL RIDE WITH ME NOT HERE, FELLAS. THE GIRLS WILL RIDE WITH ME, DAVIS.
DAD?
WE'LL GET THIS ALL SORTED OUT ONCE WE GET DOWN TO...

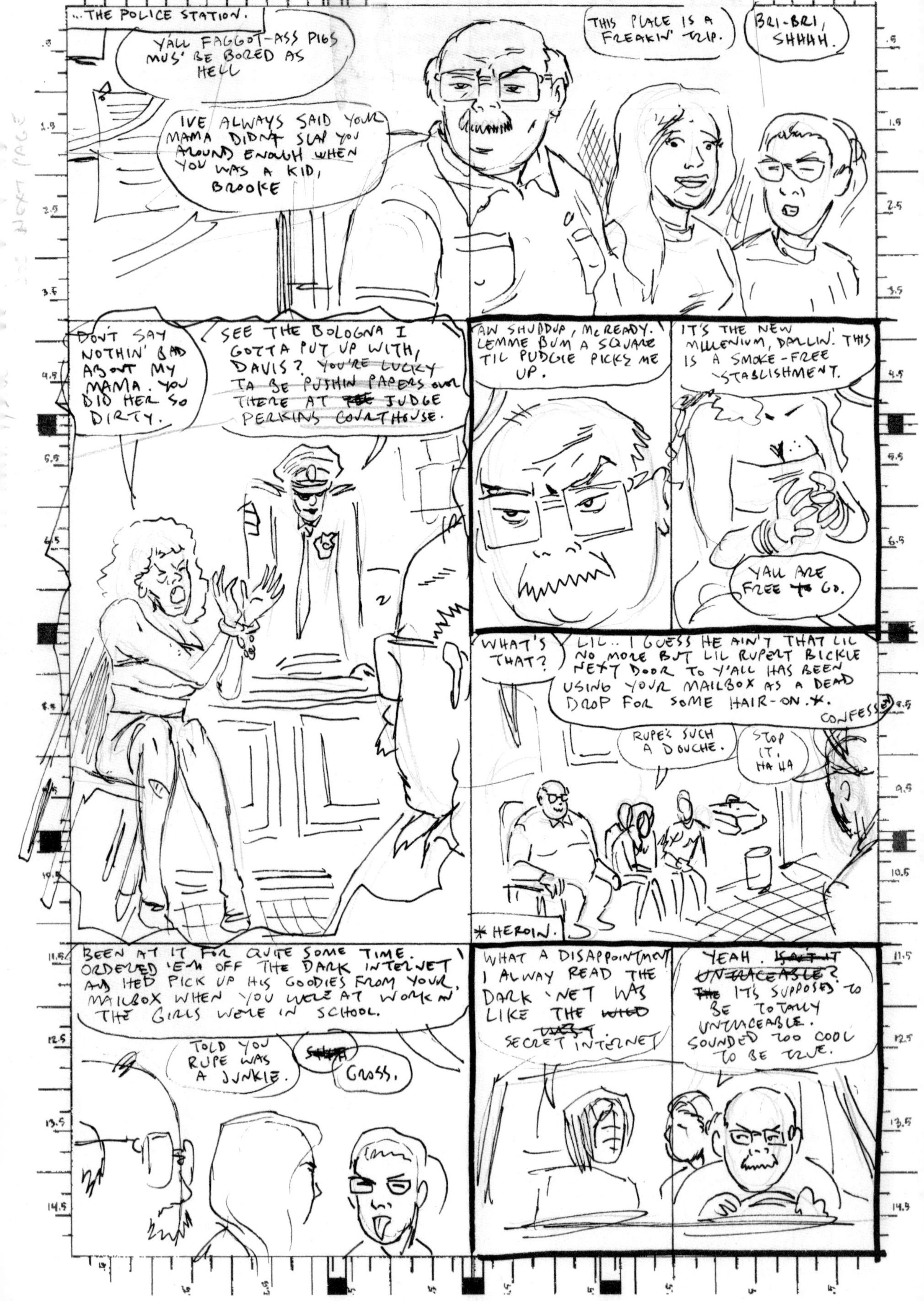
...THE POLICE STATION.
Y'ALL FAGGOT-ASS PIGS MUS' BE BORED AS HELL
IVE ALWAYS SAID YOUR MAMA DIDN'T SLAP YOU AROUND ENOUGH WHEN YOU WAS A KID, BROOKE
THIS PLACE IS A FREAKIN' TRIP.
BRI-BRI, SHHHH.
DON'T SAY NOTHIN' BAD ABOUT MY MAMA. YOU DID HER SO DIRTY.
SEE THE BOLOGNA I GOTTA PUT UP WITH, DAVIS? YOU'RE LUCKY TA BE PUSHIN PAPERS OVER THERE AT JUDGE PERKINS COURTHOUSE.
AW SHUDDUP, McREADY. LEMME BUM A SQUARE TIL PUDGIE PICKS ME UP.
IT'S THE NEW MILLENIUM, DARLIN'. THIS IS A SMOKE-FREE 'STABLISHMENT.
Y'ALL ARE FREE GO.
WHAT'S THAT?
LIL.. I GUESS HE AIN'T THAT LIL NO MORE BUT LIL RUPERT BICKLE NEXT DOOR TO Y'ALL HAS BEEN USING YOUR MAILBOX AS A DEAD DROP FOR SOME HAIR-ON.* CONFESSED
RUPE'S SUCH A DOUCHE.
STOP IT. HA HA
* HEROIN.
BEEN AT IT FOR QUITE SOME TIME. ORDERED 'EM OFF THE DARK INTERNET AND HE'D PICK UP HIS GOODIES FROM YOUR MAILBOX WHEN YOU WERE AT WORK AN' THE GIRLS WERE IN SCHOOL.
TOLD YOU RUPE WAS A JUNKIE.
GROSS.
WHAT A DISAPPOINTMENT. I ALWAY READ THE DARK 'NET WAS LIKE THE SECRET INTERNET
YEAH. IT'S SUPPOSED TO BE TOTALLY UNTRACEABLE. SOUNDED TOO COOL TO BE TRUE.

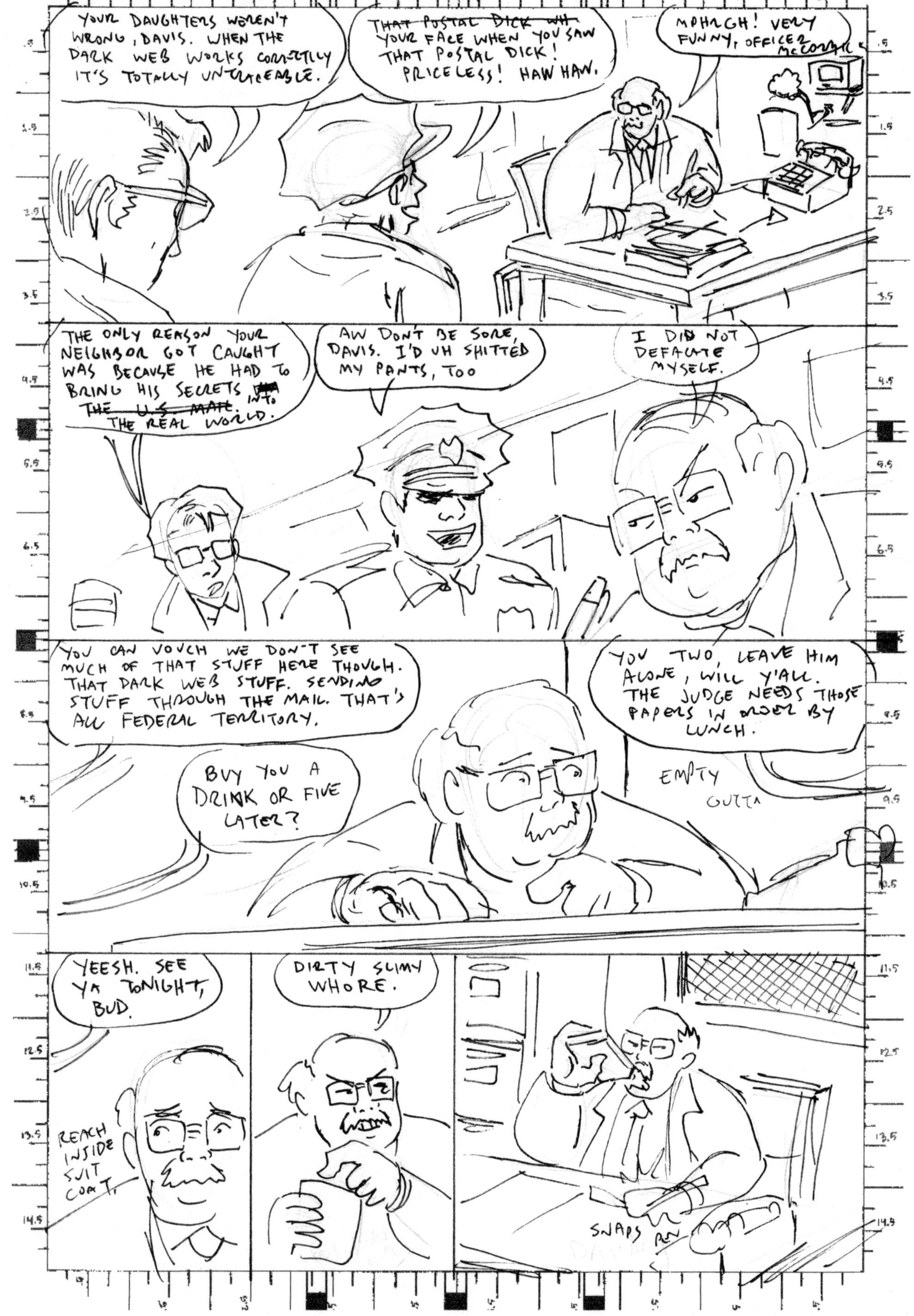
YOUR DAUGHTERS WEREN'T WRONG, DAVIS. WHEN THE DARK WEB WORKS CORRECTLY IT'S TOTALLY UNTRACEABLE.
THAT POSTAL DICK WH YOUR FACE WHEN YOU SAW THAT POSTAL DICK! PRICELESS! HAW HAW.
MPHRGH! VERY FUNNY, OFFICER McCORMIC
THE ONLY REASON YOUR NEIGHBOR GOT CAUGHT WAS BECAUSE HE HAD TO BRING HIS SECRETS THE U.S. MAIL INTO THE REAL WORLD.
AW DON'T BE SORE, DAVIS. I'D UH SHITTED MY PANTS, TOO
I DID NOT DEFACATE MYSELF.
YOU CAN VOUCH WE DON'T SEE MUCH OF THAT STUFF HERE THOUGH. THAT DARK WEB STUFF. SENDING STUFF THROUGH THE MAIL. THAT'S ALL FEDERAL TERRITORY.
YOU TWO, LEAVE HIM ALONE, WILL Y'ALL. THE JUDGE NEEDS THOSE PAPERS IN ORDER BY LUNCH.
BUY YOU A DRINK OR FIVE LATER?
EMPTY GUTTA
YEESH. SEE YA TONIGHT, BUD.
REACH INSIDE SUIT COAT.
DIRTY SLIMY WHORE.
SNAPS

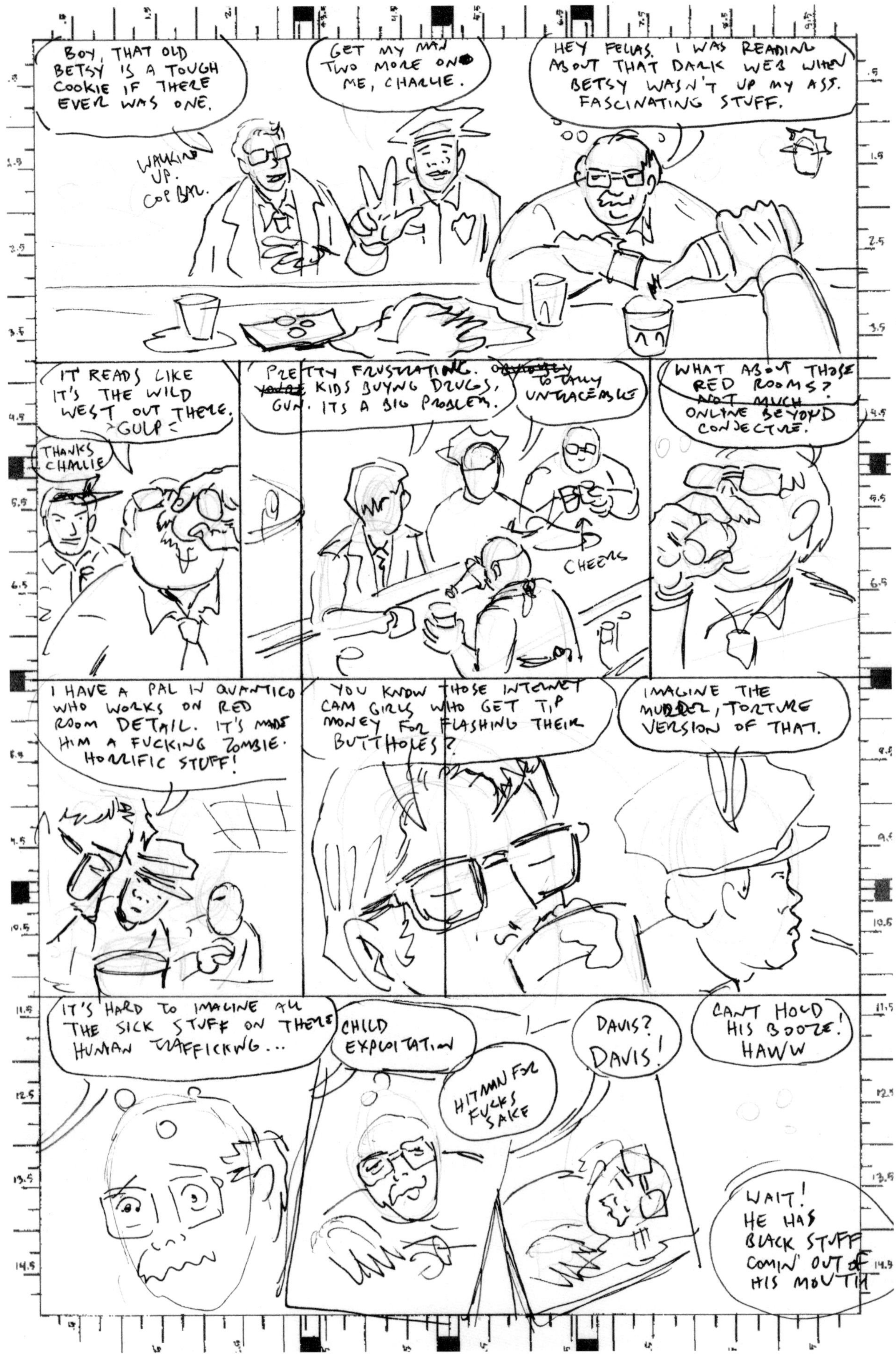
BOY, THAT OLD BETSY IS A TOUGH COOKIE IF THERE EVER WAS ONE.
WAKING UP. COP BAR.
GET MY MAN TWO MORE ON ME, CHARLIE.
HEY FELLAS. I WAS READING ABOUT THAT DARK WEB WHEN BETSY WASN'T UP MY ASS. FASCINATING STUFF.
IT READS LIKE IT'S THE WILD WEST OUT THERE.
GULP
THANKS CHARLIE
PRETTY FRUSTRATING. KIDS BUYING DRUGS, GUN. ITS A BIG PROBLEM.
TOTALLY UNTRACEABLE
CHEERS
WHAT ABOUT THOSE RED ROOMS? NOT MUCH ONLINE BEYOND CONJECTURE.
I HAVE A PAL IN QUANTICO WHO WORKS ON RED ROOM DETAIL. IT'S MADE HIM A FUCKING ZOMBIE. HORRIFIC STUFF!
YOU KNOW THOSE INTERNET CAM GIRLS WHO GET TIP MONEY FOR FLASHING THEIR BUTTHOLES?
IMAGINE THE MURDER, TORTURE VERSION OF THAT.
IT'S HARD TO IMAGINE ALL THE SICK STUFF ON THERE HUMAN TRAFFICKING...
CHILD EXPLOITATION
HITMAN FOR FUCKS SAKE
DAVIS? DAVIS!
CAN'T HOLD HIS BOOZE! HAWW
WAIT! HE HAS BLACK STUFF COMIN' OUT OF HIS MOUTH

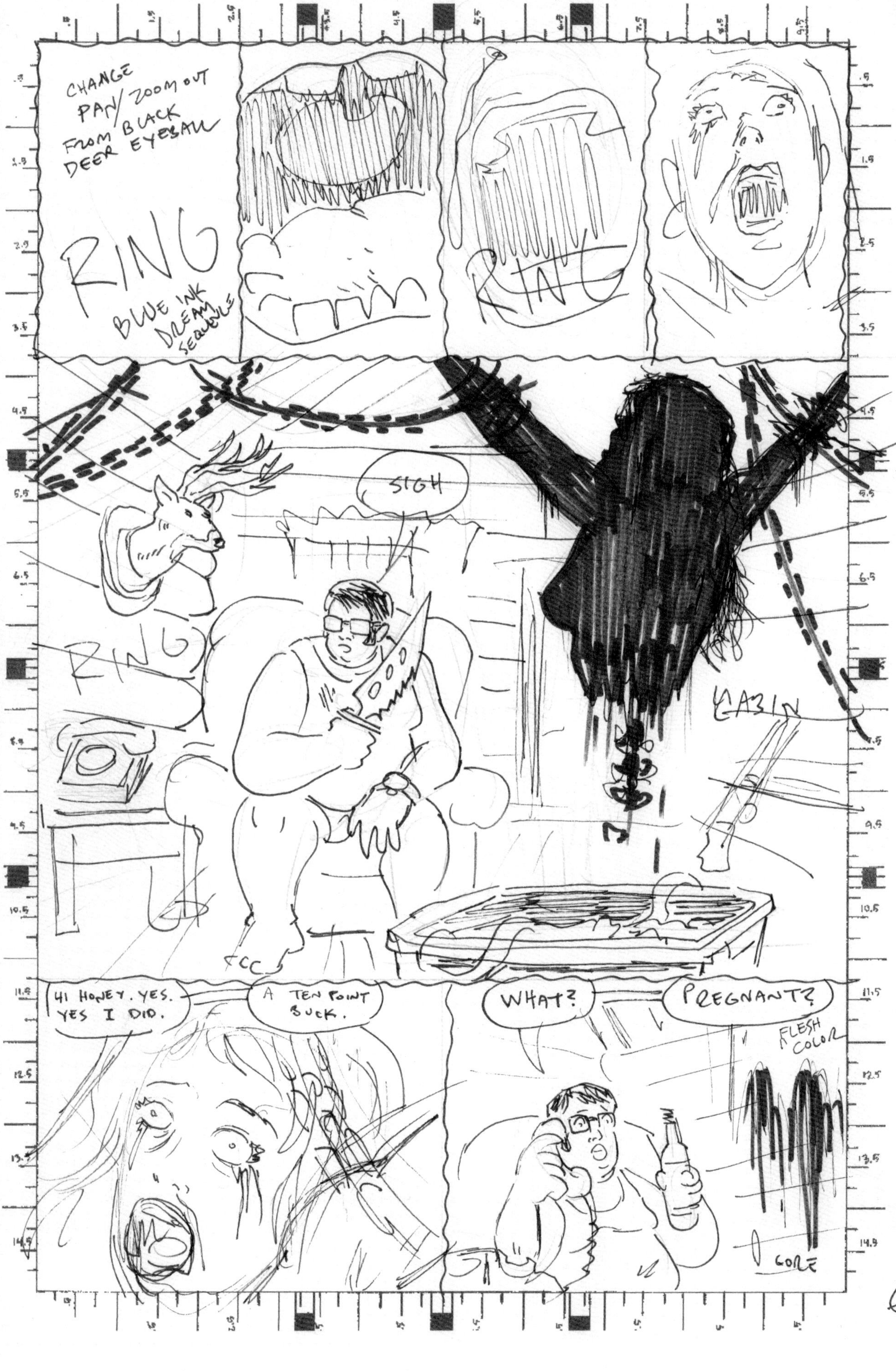
CHANGE PAN/ZOOM OUT FROM BLACK DEER EYEBALL
RING
BLUE INK DREAM SEQUENCE
RING
SIGH
RING
CABIN
HI HONEY. YES. YES I DID.
A TEN POINT BUCK.
WHAT?
PREGNANT?
FLESH COLOR
GORE

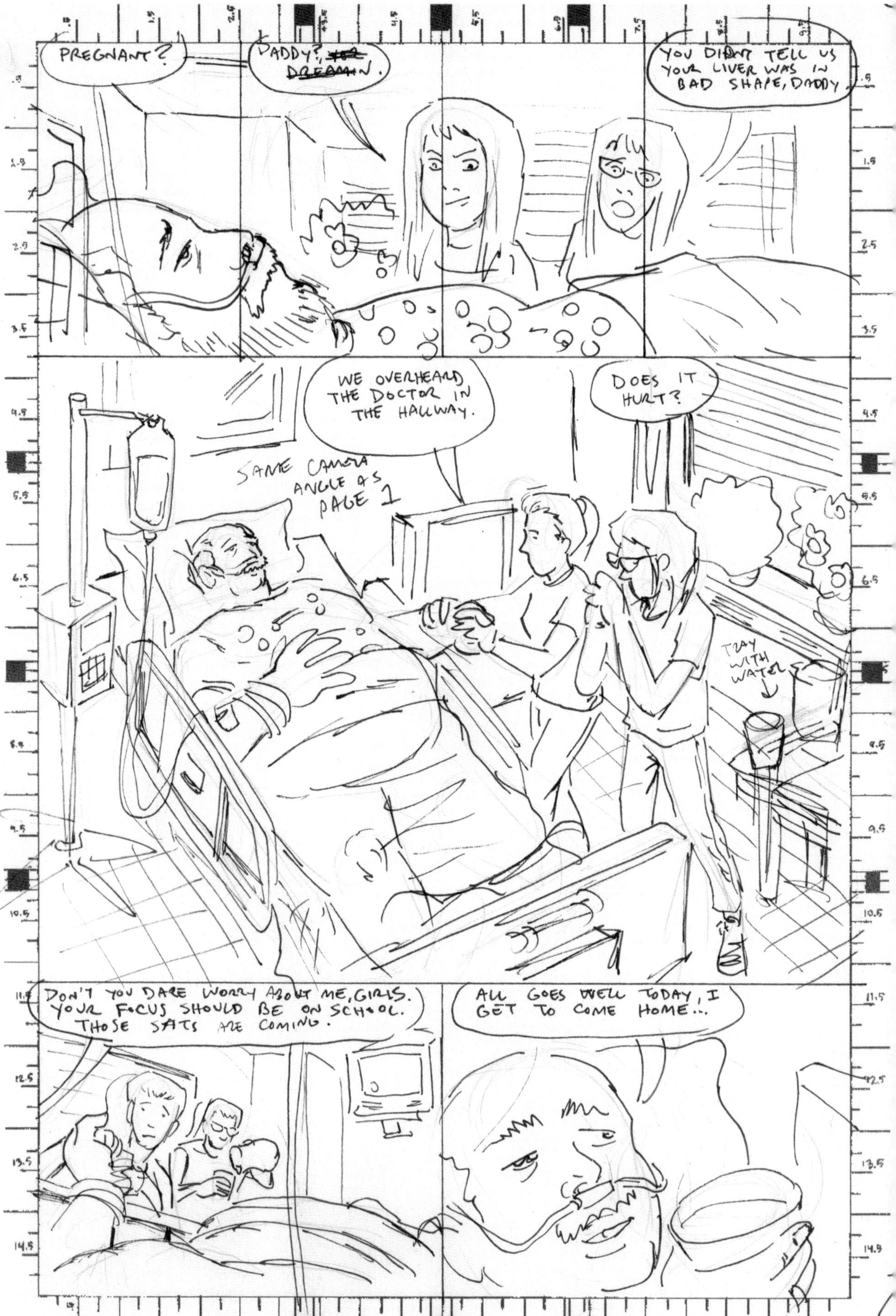
PREGNANT?
DADDY?, DREAMIN.
YOU DIDN'T TELL US YOUR LIVER WAS IN BAD SHAPE, DADDY.
WE OVERHEARD THE DOCTOR IN THE HALLWAY.
DOES IT HURT?
SAME CAMERA ANGLE AS PAGE 1
TRAY WITH WATER
DON'T YOU DARE WORRY ABOUT ME, GIRLS. YOUR FOCUS SHOULD BE ON SCHOOL. THOSE SATS ARE COMING.
ALL GOES WELL TODAY, I GET TO COME HOME...

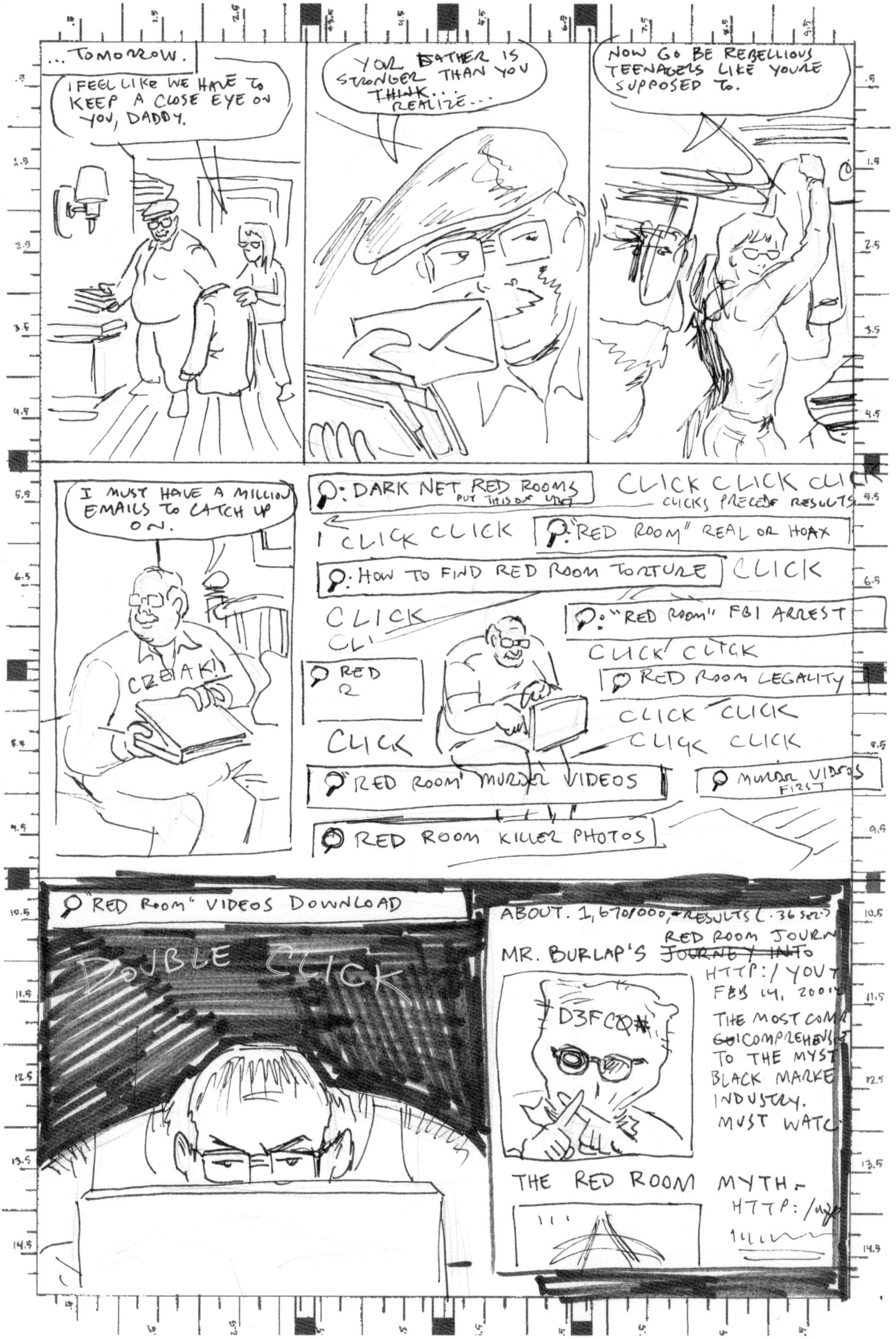
... TOMORROW.
I FEEL LIKE WE HAVE TO KEEP A CLOSE EYE ON YOU, DADDY.
YOUR FATHER IS STRONGER THAN YOU THINK... REALIZE...
NOW GO BE REBELLIOUS TEENAGERS LIKE YOU'RE SUPPOSED TO.
I MUST HAVE A MILLION EMAILS TO CATCH UP ON.
CREAK!
DARK NET RED ROOMS
PUT THIS OUT LEFT
CLICK CLICK CLICK
CLICKS PRECEDE RESULTS
CLICK CLICK
"RED ROOM" REAL OR HOAX
HOW TO FIND RED ROOM TORTURE
CLICK
CLICK
"RED ROOM" FBI ARREST
CLICK CLICK
RED R
RED ROOM LEGALITY
CLICK CLICK
CLICK
CLICK CLICK
"RED ROOM" MURDER VIDEOS
MURDER VIDEOS
FIRST
RED ROOM KILLER PHOTOS
"RED ROOM" VIDEOS DOWNLOAD
DOUBLE CLICK
ABOUT. 1,670,000 RESULTS (.36 SEC)
MR. BURLAP'S RED ROOM JOURN
HTTP:/ YOUT
FEB 14, 2001
D3FCQ#
THE MOST COMP COMPREHENSIVE TO THE MYST BLACK MARKE INDUSTRY. MUST WATC
THE RED ROOM MYTH -
HTTP:/

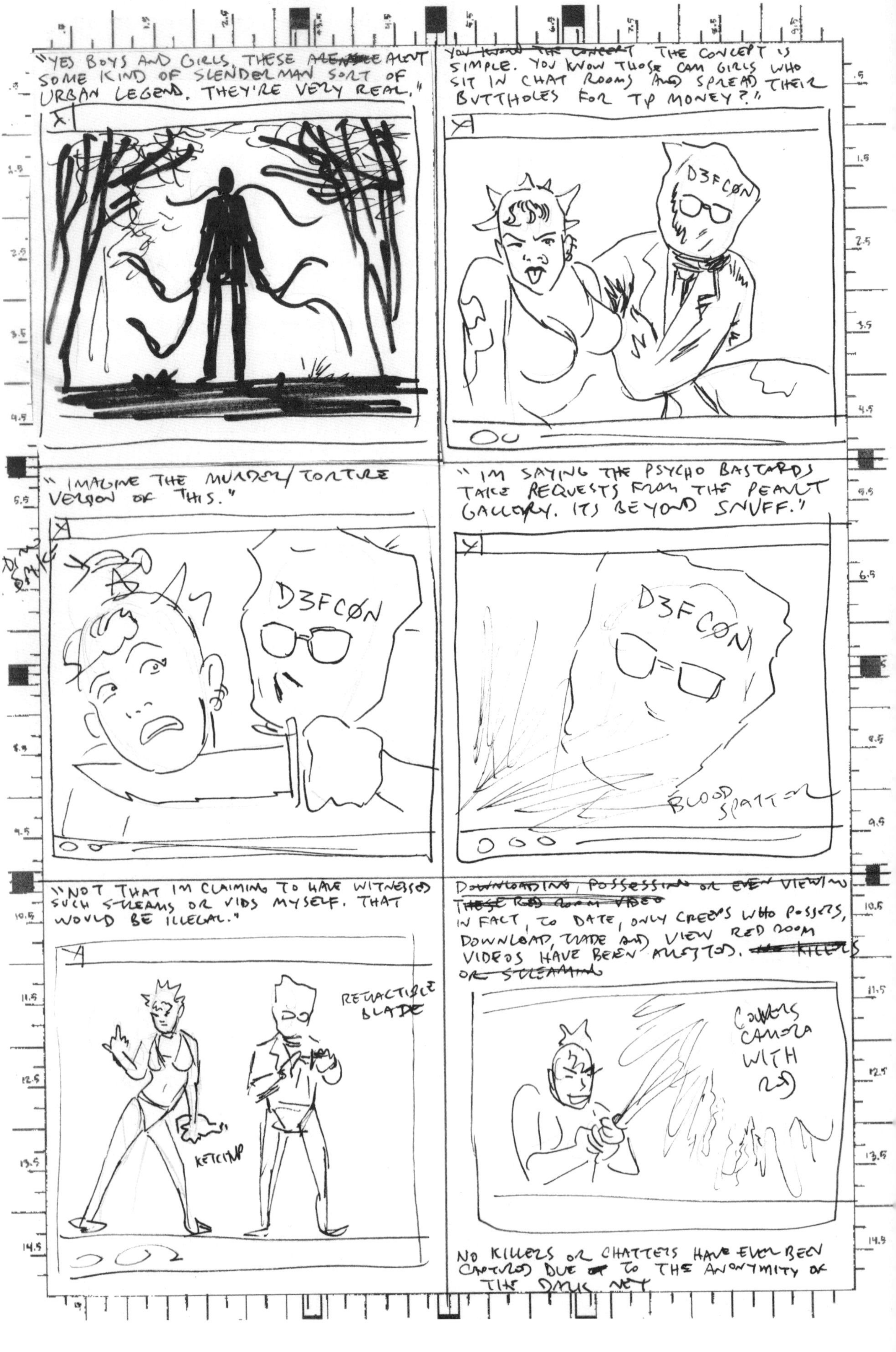
"YES BOYS AND GIRLS, THESE AIN'T SOME KIND OF SLENDERMAN SORT OF URBAN LEGEND. THEY'RE VERY REAL."
THE CONCEPT IS SIMPLE. YOU KNOW THOSE CAM GIRLS WHO SIT IN CHAT ROOMS AND SPREAD THEIR BUTTHOLES FOR TIP MONEY?"
D3FCON
"IMAGINE THE MURDER/TORTURE VERSION OF THIS."
D3FCON
"IM SAYING THE PSYCHO BASTARDS TAKE REQUESTS FROM THE PEANUT GALLERY. ITS BEYOND SNUFF."
D3FCON
BLOOD SPATTER
"NOT THAT IM CLAIMING TO HAVE WITNESSED SUCH STREAMS OR VIDS MYSELF. THAT WOULD BE ILLEGAL."
RETRACTIBLE BLADE
KETCHUP
IN FACT, TO DATE, ONLY CREEPS WHO POSSESS, DOWNLOAD, TRADE AND VIEW RED ROOM VIDEOS HAVE BEEN ARRESTED.
COVERS CAMERA WITH RED
NO KILLERS OR CHATTERS HAVE EVER BEEN CAPTURED DUE TO THE ANONYMITY OF THE DARK NET

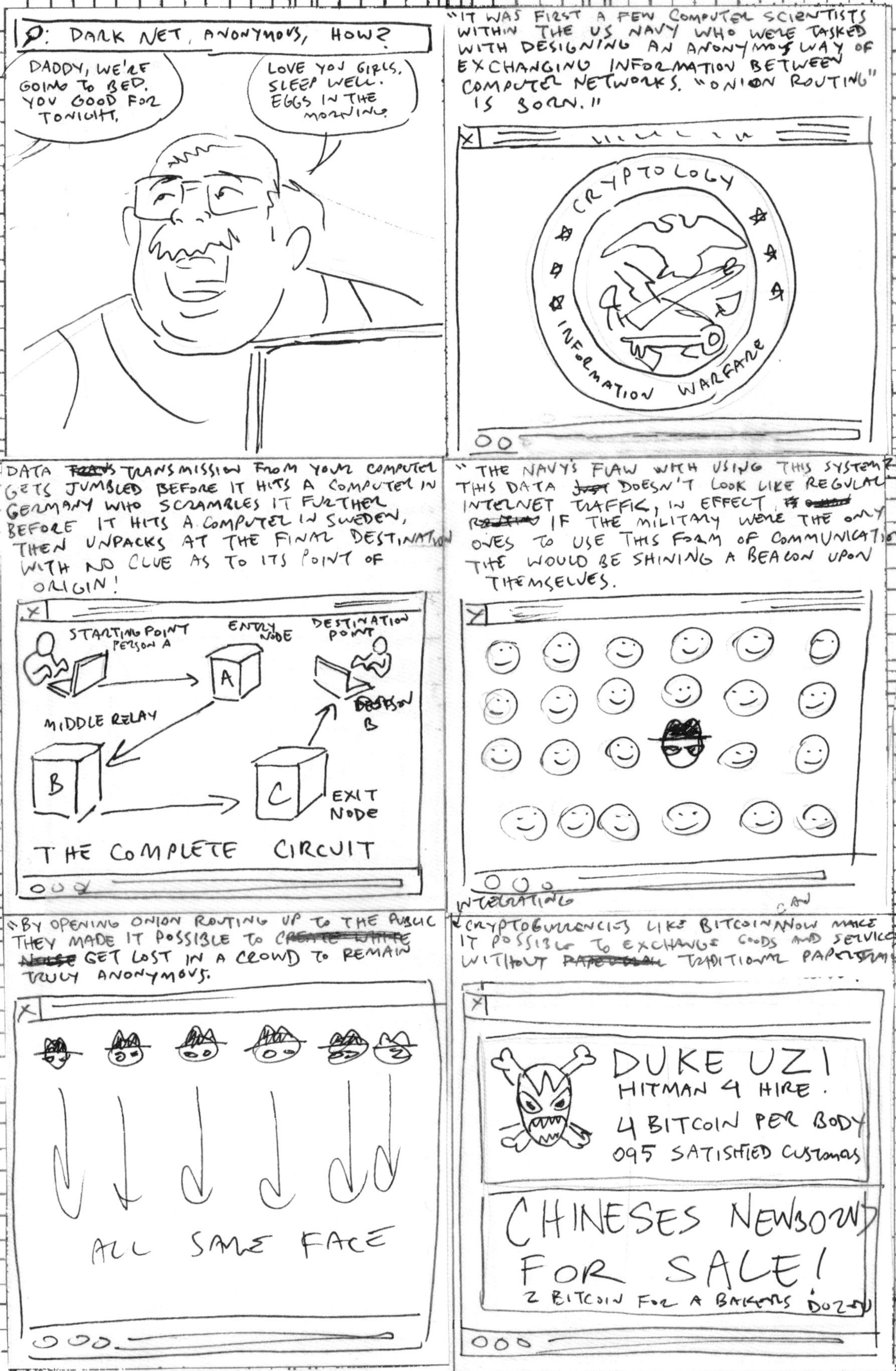
Q: DARK NET, ANONYMOUS, HOW?
DADDY, WE'RE GOING TO BED. YOU GOOD FOR TONIGHT.
LOVE YOU GIRLS. SLEEP WELL. EGGS IN THE MORNING.
"IT WAS FIRST A FEW COMPUTER SCIENTISTS WITHIN THE US NAVY WHO WERE TASKED WITH DESIGNING AN ANONYMOUS WAY OF EXCHANGING INFORMATION BETWEEN COMPUTER NETWORKS. "ONION ROUTING" IS BORN."
CRYPTOLOGY
INFORMATION WARFARE
DATA TRANSMISSION FROM YOUR COMPUTER GETS JUMBLED BEFORE IT HITS A COMPUTER IN GERMANY WHO SCRAMBLES IT FURTHER BEFORE IT HITS A COMPUTER IN SWEDEN, THEN UNPACKS AT THE FINAL DESTINATION WITH NO CLUE AS TO ITS POINT OF ORIGIN!
STARTING POINT PERSON A
ENTRY NODE
DESTINATION POINT
A
PERSON B
MIDDLE RELAY
B
C
EXIT NODE
THE COMPLETE CIRCUIT
"THE NAVY'S FLAW WITH USING THIS SYSTEM? THIS DATA DOESN'T LOOK LIKE REGULAR INTERNET TRAFFIC, IN EFFECT, IF THE MILITARY WERE THE ONLY ONES TO USE THIS FORM OF COMMUNICATION THE WOULD BE SHINING A BEACON UPON THEMSELVES.
INTEGRATING
"BY OPENING ONION ROUTING UP TO THE PUBLIC THEY MADE IT POSSIBLE TO GET LOST IN A CROWD TO REMAIN TRULY ANONYMOUS.
ALL SAME FACE
"CRYPTOCURRENCIES LIKE BITCOIN CAN NOW MAKE IT POSSIBLE TO EXCHANGE GOODS AND SERVICES WITHOUT TRADITIONAL PAPERTRAILS.
DUKE UZI
HITMAN 4 HIRE.
4 BITCOIN PER BODY
095 SATISFIED CUSTOMERS
CHINESES NEWBORNS FOR SALE!
2 BITCOIN FOR A BAKERS DOZEN

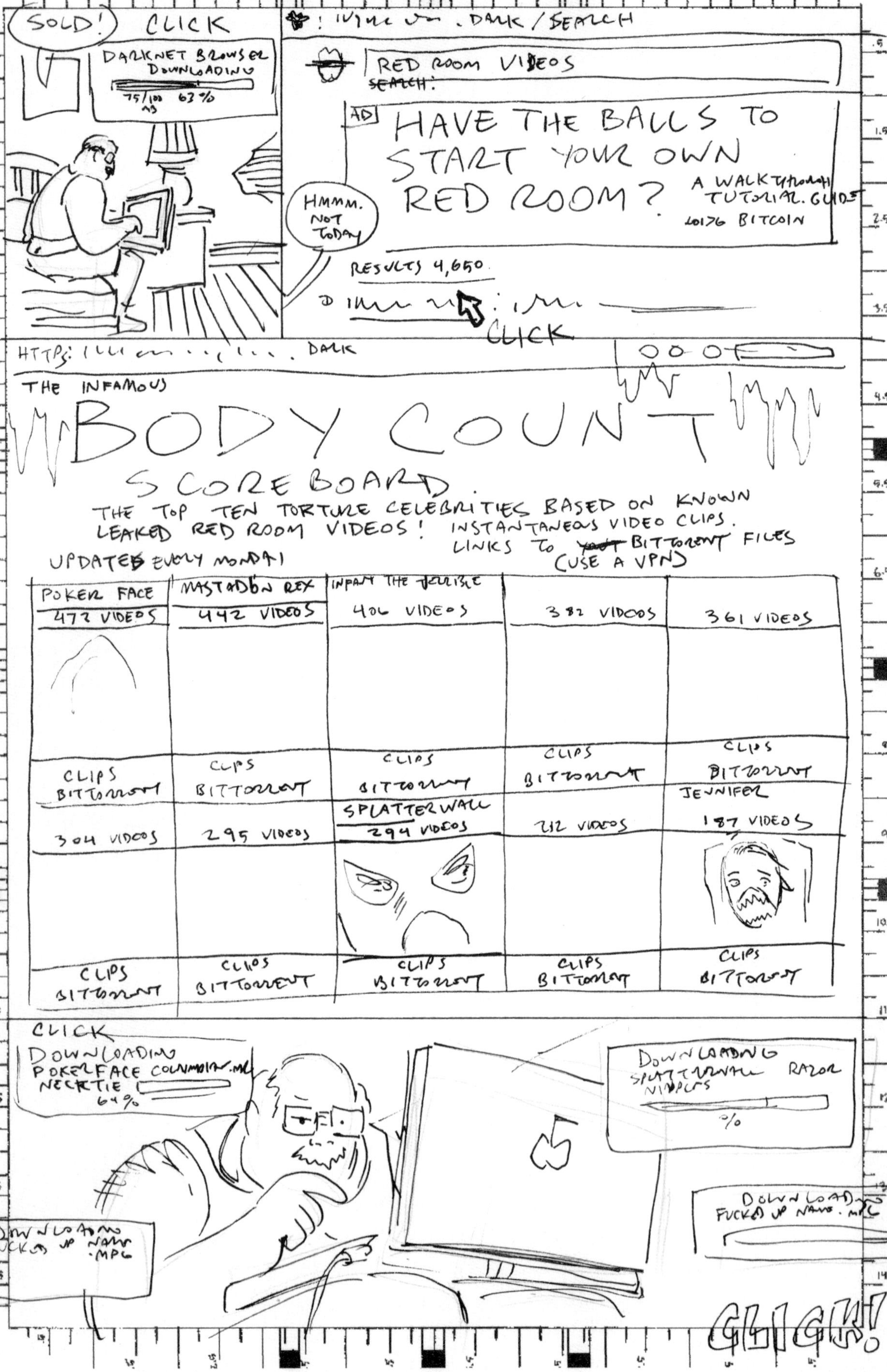
SOLD!
CLICK
DARKNET BROWSER DOWNLOADING
75/100 MB 63 %
. DARK / SEARCH
RED ROOM VIDEOS
SEARCH:
AD
HAVE THE BALLS TO START YOUR OWN RED ROOM?
A WALKTHROUGH TUTORIAL GUIDE
.0176 BITCOIN
HMMM. NOT TODAY
RESULTS 4,650
CLICK
HTTPS: . DARK
THE INFAMOUS
BODY COUNT
SCOREBOARD.
THE TOP TEN TORTURE CELEBRITIES BASED ON KNOWN LEAKED RED ROOM VIDEOS!
INSTANTANEOUS VIDEO CLIPS. LINKS TO BITTORRENT FILES (USE A VPN)
UPDATED EVERY MONDAY
POKER FACE
472 VIDEOS
MASTADON REX
442 VIDEOS
INFANT THE TERRIBLE
406 VIDEOS
382 VIDEOS
361 VIDEOS
CLIPS BITTORRENT
CLIPS BITTORRENT
CLIPS BITTORRENT
CLIPS BITTORRENT
CLIPS BITTORRENT
304 VIDEOS
295 VIDEOS
SPLATTERWALL
294 VIDEOS
212 VIDEOS
JENNIFER
187 VIDEOS
CLIPS BITTORRENT
CLIPS BITTORRENT
CLIPS BITTORRENT
CLIPS BITTORRENT
CLIPS BITTORRENT
CLICK
DOWNLOADING POKERFACE COLUMBIAN NECKTIE
64%
DOWNLOADING SPLATTERWALL RAZOR NIPPLES
%
DOWNLOADING FUCKED UP NAME.MPG
DOWNLOADING FUCKED UP NAME.MPG
CLICK!

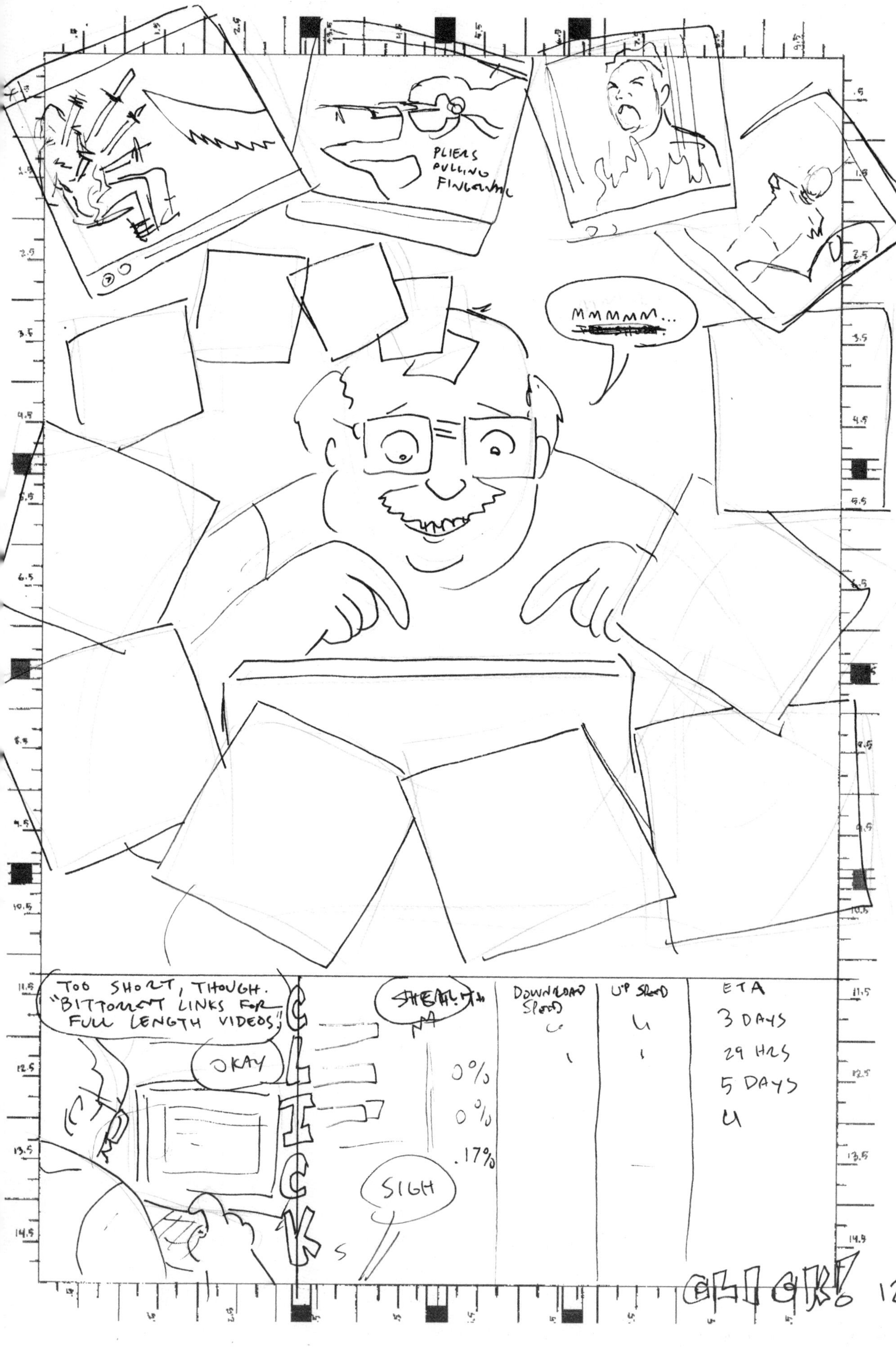

PLIERS PULLING FINGERNAIL
MMMMM...
TOO SHORT, THOUGH. "BITTORRENT LINKS FOR FULL LENGTH VIDEOS"
OKAY
CLICK
DOWNLOAD SPEED
UP SPEED
ETA
3 DAYS
29 HRS
5 DAYS
0%
0%
.17%
SIGH
CLICK

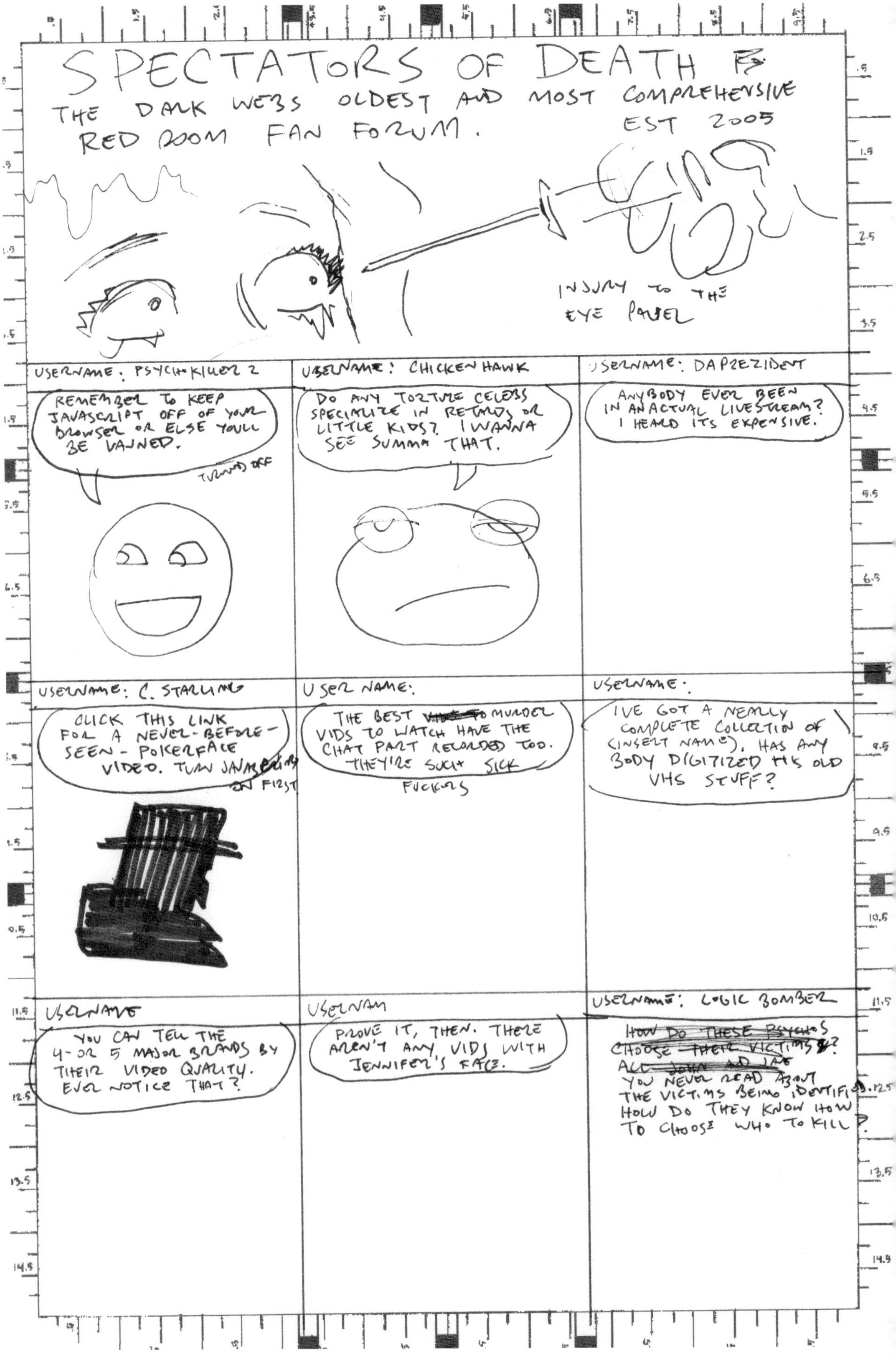
SPECTATORS OF DEATH
THE DARK WEBS OLDEST AND MOST COMPREHENSIVE RED ROOM FAN FORUM.
EST 2005
INJURY TO THE EYE PANEL
USERNAME: PSYCHOKILLER 2
REMEMBER TO KEEP JAVASCRIPT OFF OF YOUR BROWSER OR ELSE YOU'LL BE PWNED.
TURNED OFF
USERNAME: CHICKENHAWK
DO ANY TORTURE CELEBS SPECIALIZE IN RETARDS OR LITTLE KIDS? I WANNA SEE SUMMA THAT.
USERNAME: DAPREZIDENT
ANYBODY EVER BEEN IN AN ACTUAL LIVESTREAM? I HEARD ITS EXPENSIVE.
USERNAME: C. STARLING
CLICK THIS LINK FOR A NEVER-BEFORE-SEEN-POKERFACE VIDEO. TURN JAVASCRIPT ON FIRST
USERNAME:
THE BEST VIDS TO MURDER VIDS TO WATCH HAVE THE CHAT PART RECORDED TOO. THEY'RE SUCH SICK FUCKERS
USERNAME:
I'VE GOT A NEARLY COMPLETE COLLECTION OF (INSERT NAME). HAS ANY BODY DIGITIZED HIS OLD VHS STUFF?
USERNAME
YOU CAN TELL THE 4-OR 5 MAJOR BRANDS BY THEIR VIDEO QUALITY. EVER NOTICE THAT?
USERNAM
PROVE IT, THEN. THERE AREN'T ANY VIDS WITH JENNIFER'S FACE.
USERNAME: LOGIC BOMBER
HOW DO THESE PSYCHOS CHOOSE THEIR VICTIMS? ALL JOHN AND JANE
YOU NEVER READ ABOUT THE VICTIMS BEING IDENTIFIED. HOW DO THEY KNOW HOW TO CHOOSE WHO TO KILL?

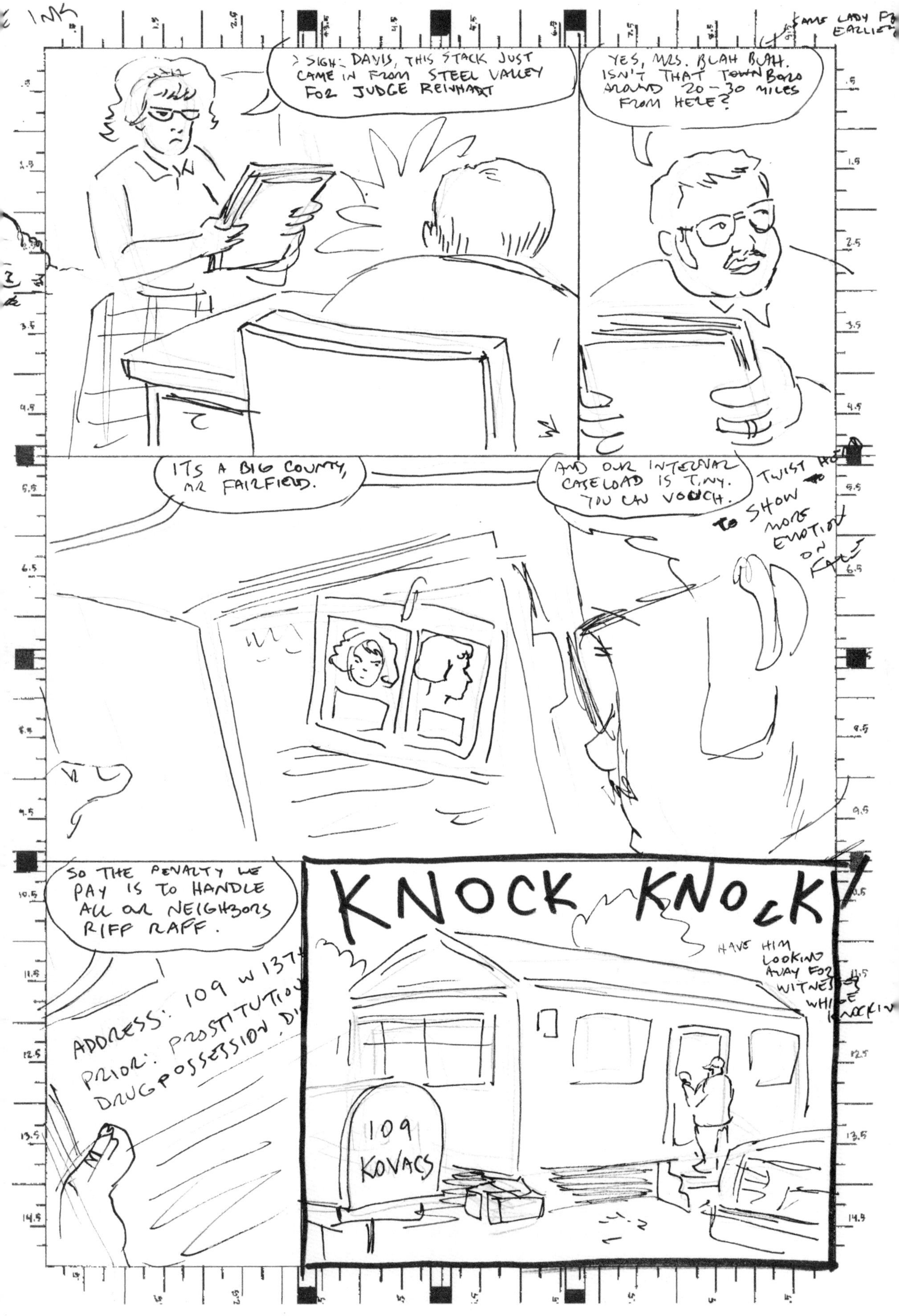
INK
SAME LADY FROM EARLIER
SIGH DAVIS, THIS STACK JUST CAME IN FROM STEEL VALLEY FOR JUDGE REINHART
YES, MRS. BLAH BLAH. ISN'T THAT TOWN BORO AROUND 20-30 MILES FROM HERE?
ITS A BIG COUNTY, MR FAIRFIELD.
AND OUR INTERNAL CASELOAD IS TINY. YOU CAN VOUCH.
TWIST HEAD TO SHOW MORE EMOTION ON FACE
SO THE PENALTY WE PAY IS TO HANDLE ALL OUR NEIGHBORS RIFF RAFF.
ADDRESS: 109 W 137
PRIOR: PROSTITUTION
DRUG POSSESSION
KNOCK KNOCK
HAVE HIM LOOKING AWAY FOR WITNESS WHILE KNOCKING
109
KOVACS

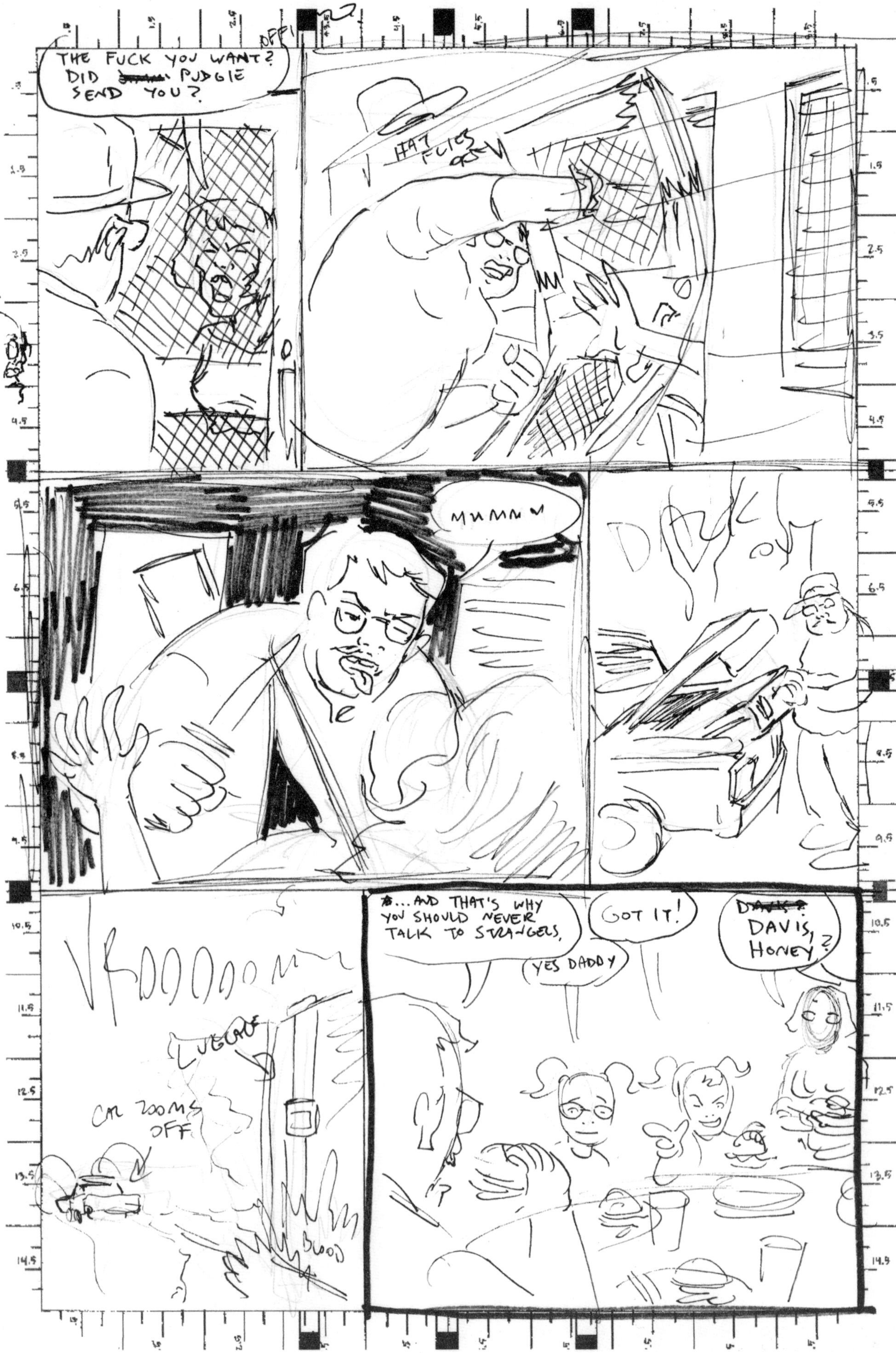
THE FUCK YOU WANT? DID PUDGIE SEND YOU?
OFF!
HAT FLIES OFF
MUMMM
VROOOOOOM
LUGGAGE
CAR ZOOMS OFF
BLOOD
...AND THAT'S WHY YOU SHOULD NEVER TALK TO STRANGERS.
GOT IT!
YES DADDY
DAVIS, HONEY?

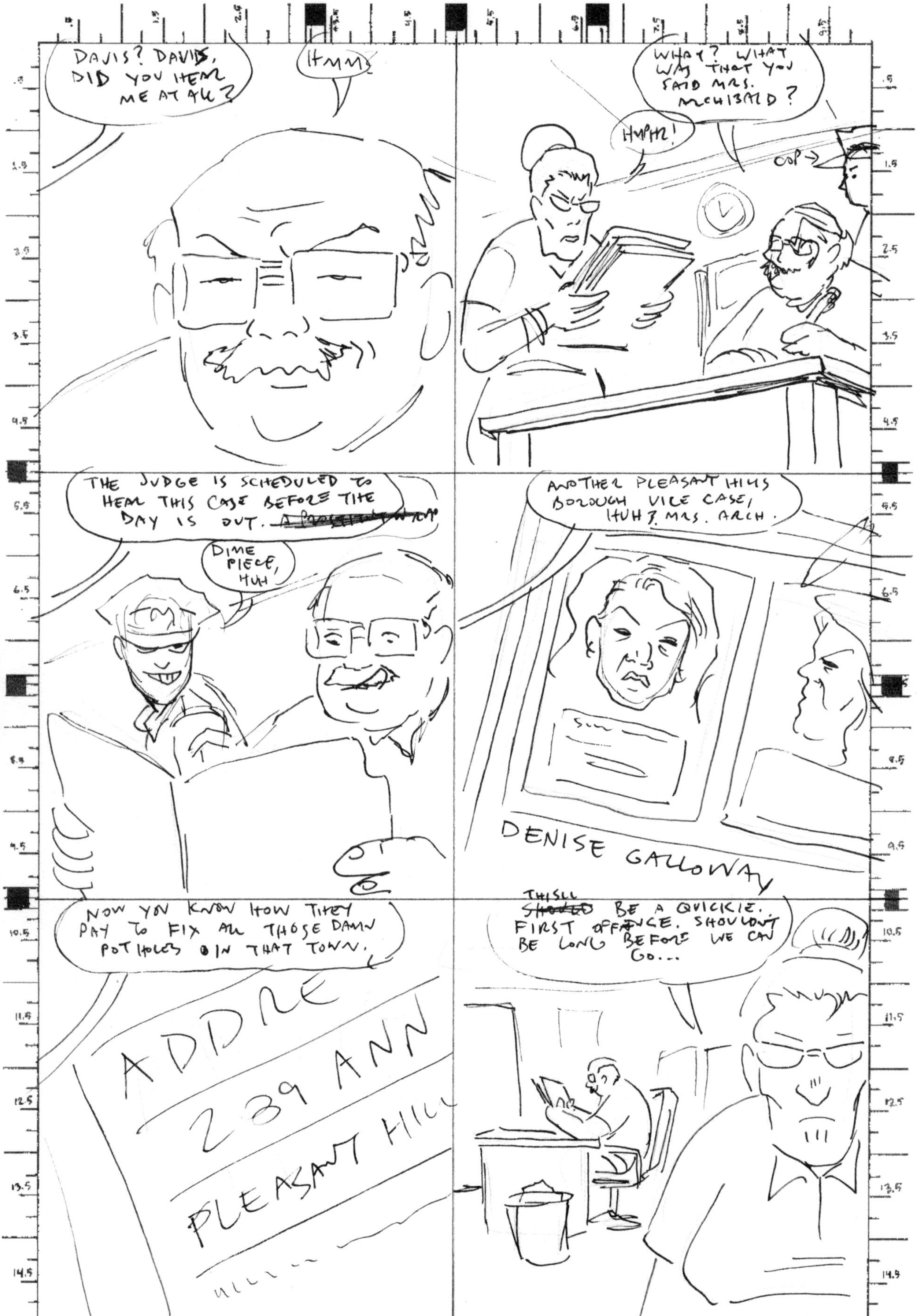
DAVIS? DAVIS, DID YOU HEAR ME AT ALL?
HMM?
WHAT? WHAT WAS THAT YOU SAID MRS. ARCHIBALD?
HMPH!
COP →
THE JUDGE IS SCHEDULED TO HEAR THIS CASE BEFORE THE DAY IS OUT.
DIME PIECE, HUH
ANOTHER PLEASANT HILLS BOROUGH VICE CASE, HUH? MRS. ARCH.
DENISE GALLOWAY
NOW YOU KNOW HOW THEY PAY TO FIX ALL THOSE DAMN POTHOLES IN THAT TOWN.
ADDRE
239 ANN
PLEASANT HILL
THIS'LL BE A QUICKIE. FIRST OFFENCE. SHOULDN'T BE LONG BEFORE WE CAN GO...

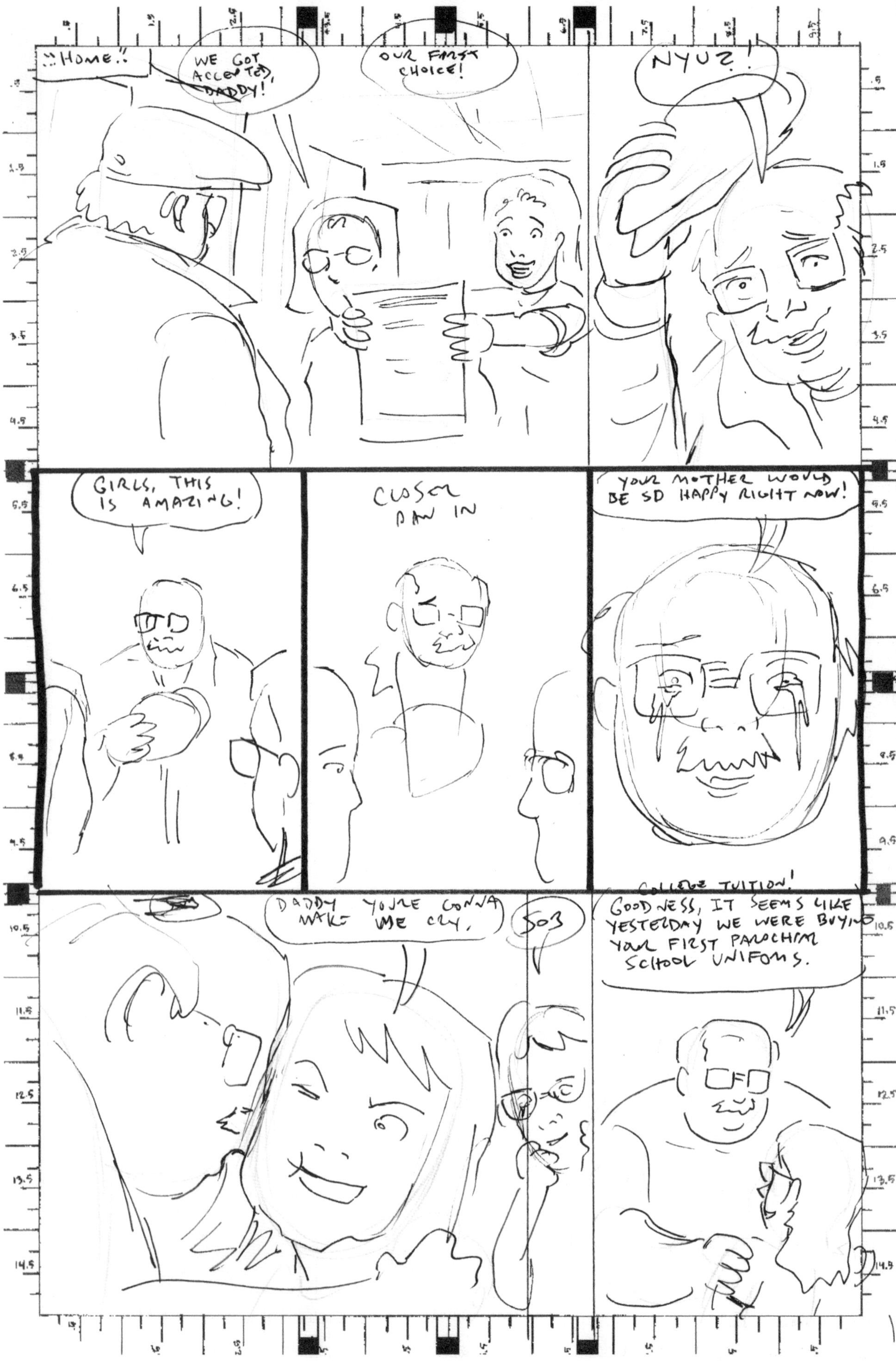

!!HOME!!
WE GOT ACCEPTED, DADDY!
OUR FIRST CHOICE!
NYU2!
GIRLS, THIS IS AMAZING!
CLOSER PAN IN
YOUR MOTHER WOULD BE SO HAPPY RIGHT NOW!
DADDY YOU'RE GONNA MAKE ME CRY.
SOB
COLLEGE TUITION!
GOODNESS, IT SEEMS LIKE YESTERDAY WE WERE BUYING YOUR FIRST PAROCHIAL SCHOOL UNIFORMS.

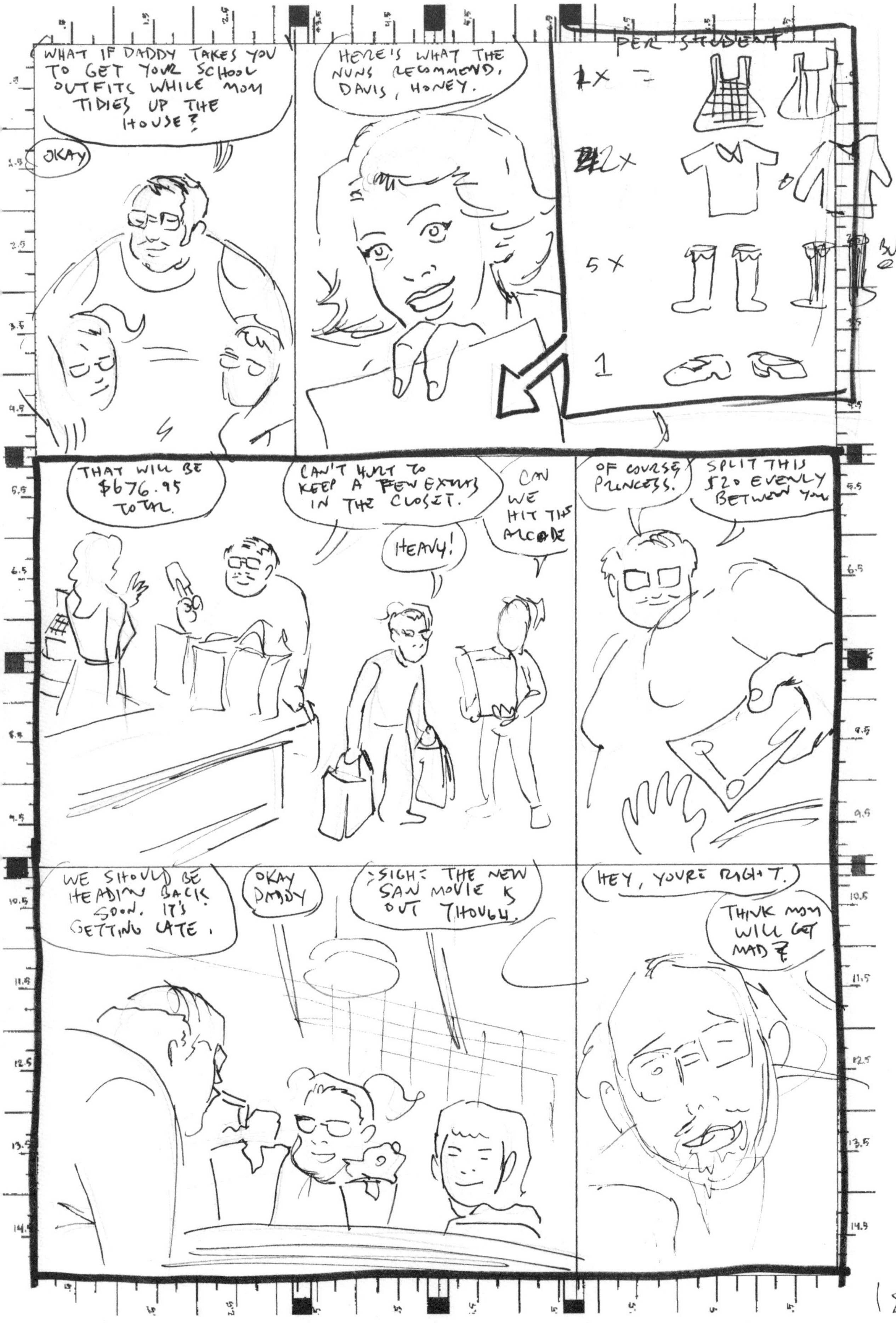
WHAT IF DADDY TAKES YOU TO GET YOUR SCHOOL OUTFITS WHILE MOM TIDIES UP THE HOUSE?
OKAY
HERE'S WHAT THE NUNS RECOMMEND, DAVIS, HONEY.
PER STUDENT
1X
2X
5X
1
THAT WILL BE $676.95 TOTAL.
CAN'T HURT TO KEEP A FEW EXTRAS IN THE CLOSET.
HEAVY!
CAN WE HIT THE ARCADE
OF COURSE PRINCESS.
SPLIT THIS $20 EVENLY BETWEEN YOU
WE SHOULD BE HEADING BACK SOON. IT'S GETTING LATE.
OKAY DADDY
:SIGH: THE NEW SAN MOVIE IS OUT THOUGH.
HEY, YOU'RE RIGHT.
THINK MOM WILL GET MAD?

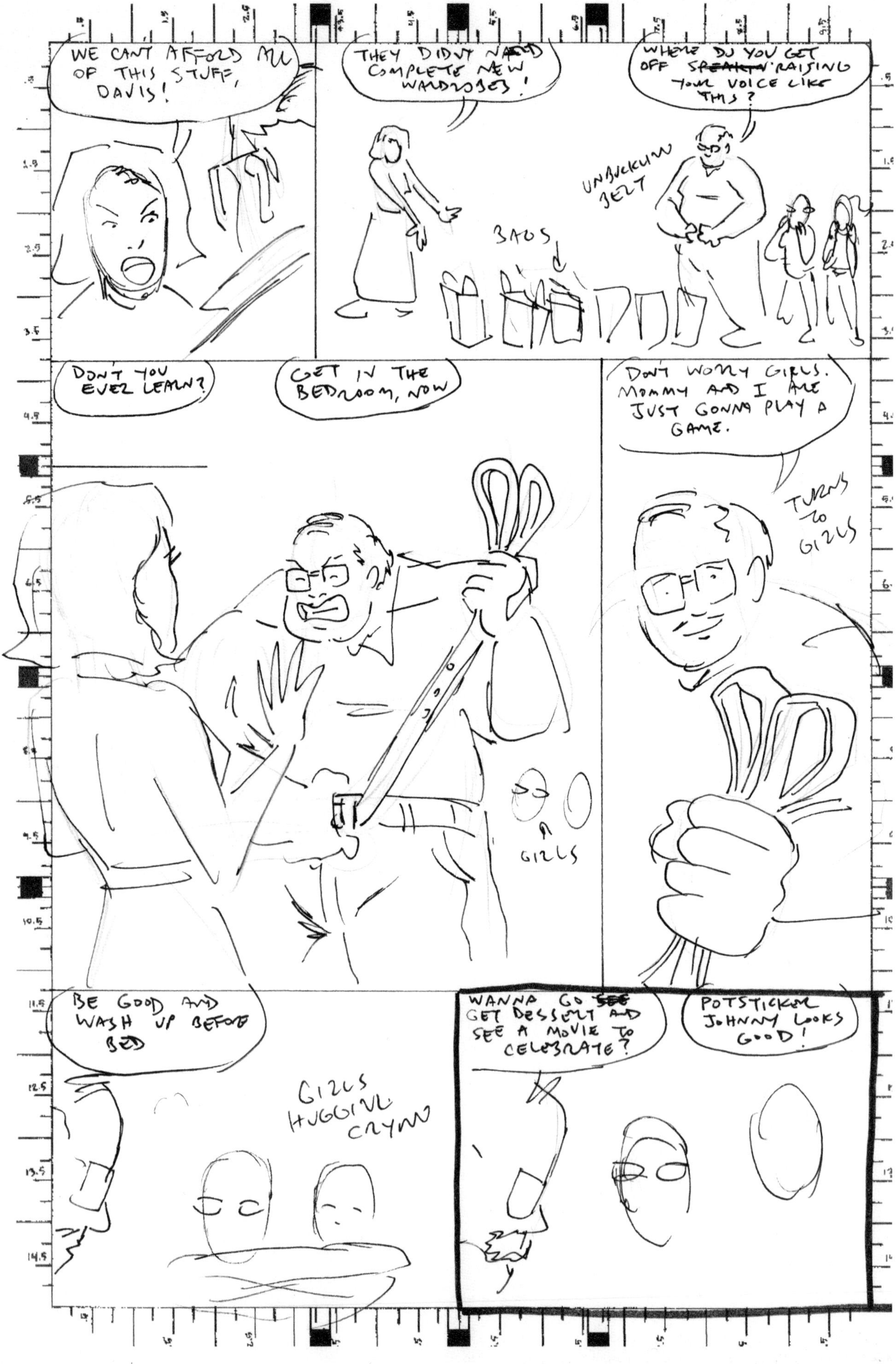
WE CANT AFFORD ALL OF THIS STUFF, DAVIS!
THEY DIDNT NEED COMPLETE NEW WARDROBES!
WHERE DO YOU GET OFF ~~SPEAKIN~~ RAISING YOUR VOICE LIKE THIS?
UNBUCKLIN BELT
BAGS
DON'T YOU EVER LEARN?
GET IN THE BEDROOM, NOW
GIRLS
DON'T WORRY GIRLS. MOMMY AND I ARE JUST GONNA PLAY A GAME.
TURNS TO GIRLS
BE GOOD AND WASH UP BEFORE BED
GIRLS HUGGING CRYING
WANNA GO ~~SEE~~ GET DESSERT AND SEE A MOVIE TO CELEBRATE?
POTSTICKER JOHNNY LOOKS GOOD!

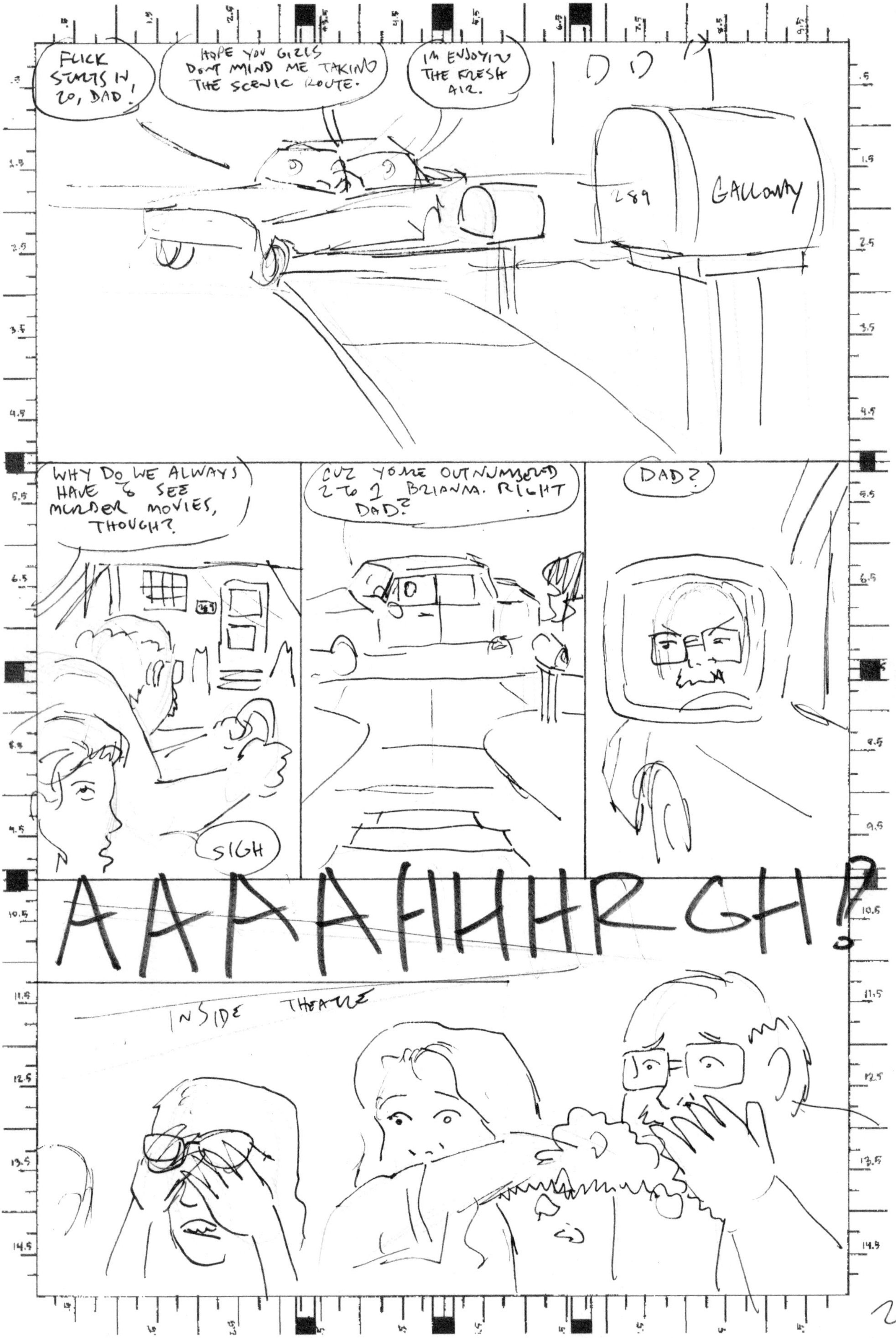
FLICK STARTS IN 20, DAD!
HOPE YOU GIRLS DONT MIND ME TAKING THE SCENIC ROUTE.
IM ENJOYIN THE FRESH AIR.
289
GALLOWAY
WHY DO WE ALWAYS HAVE TO SEE MURDER MOVIES, THOUGH?
SIGH
CUZ YOURE OUTNUMBERED 2 TO 1 BRIANNA. RIGHT DAD?
DAD?
AAAAHHHRGH!?
INSIDE THEATRE

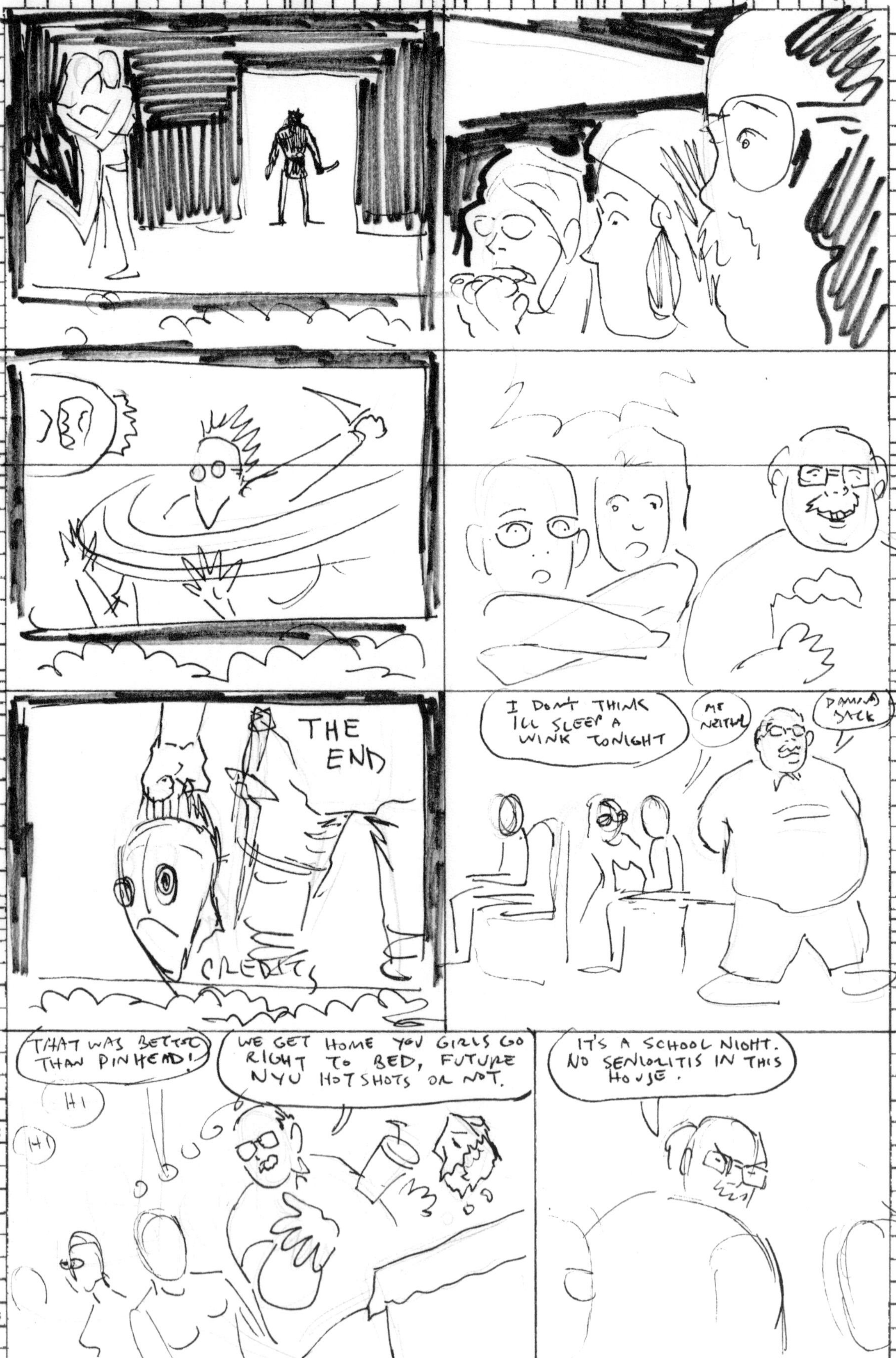

THE END
CREDITS
I DON'T THINK I'LL SLEEP A WINK TONIGHT
ME NEITHER
DAMN JACK
THAT WAS BETTER THAN PINHEAD!
HI
HI
WE GET HOME YOU GIRLS GO RIGHT TO BED, FUTURE NYU HOTSHOTS OR NOT.
IT'S A SCHOOL NIGHT. NO SENIORITIS IN THIS HOUSE.

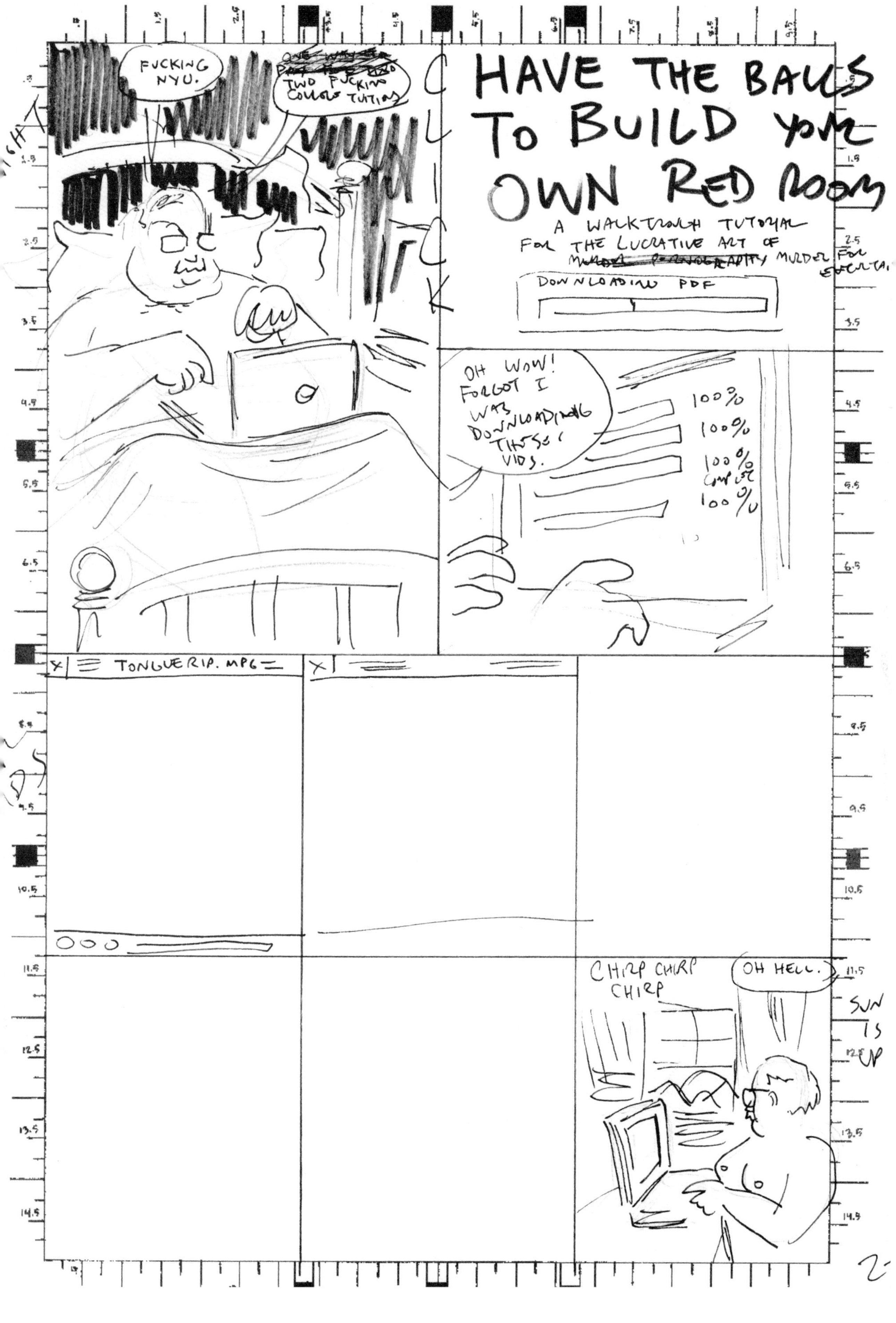
FUCKING NYU.
TWO FUCKING COLLEGE TUITIONS
CLICK
HAVE THE BALLS TO BUILD YOUR OWN RED ROOM
A WALKTHROUGH TUTORIAL FOR THE LUCRATIVE ART OF MURDER FOR ENTERTAI
DOWNLOADING PDF
OH WOW! FORGOT I WAS DOWNLOADING THESE VIDS.
100%
100%
100% COMPLETE
100%
TONGUERIP.MPG
CHIRP CHIRP CHIRP
OH HELL.
SUN IS UP

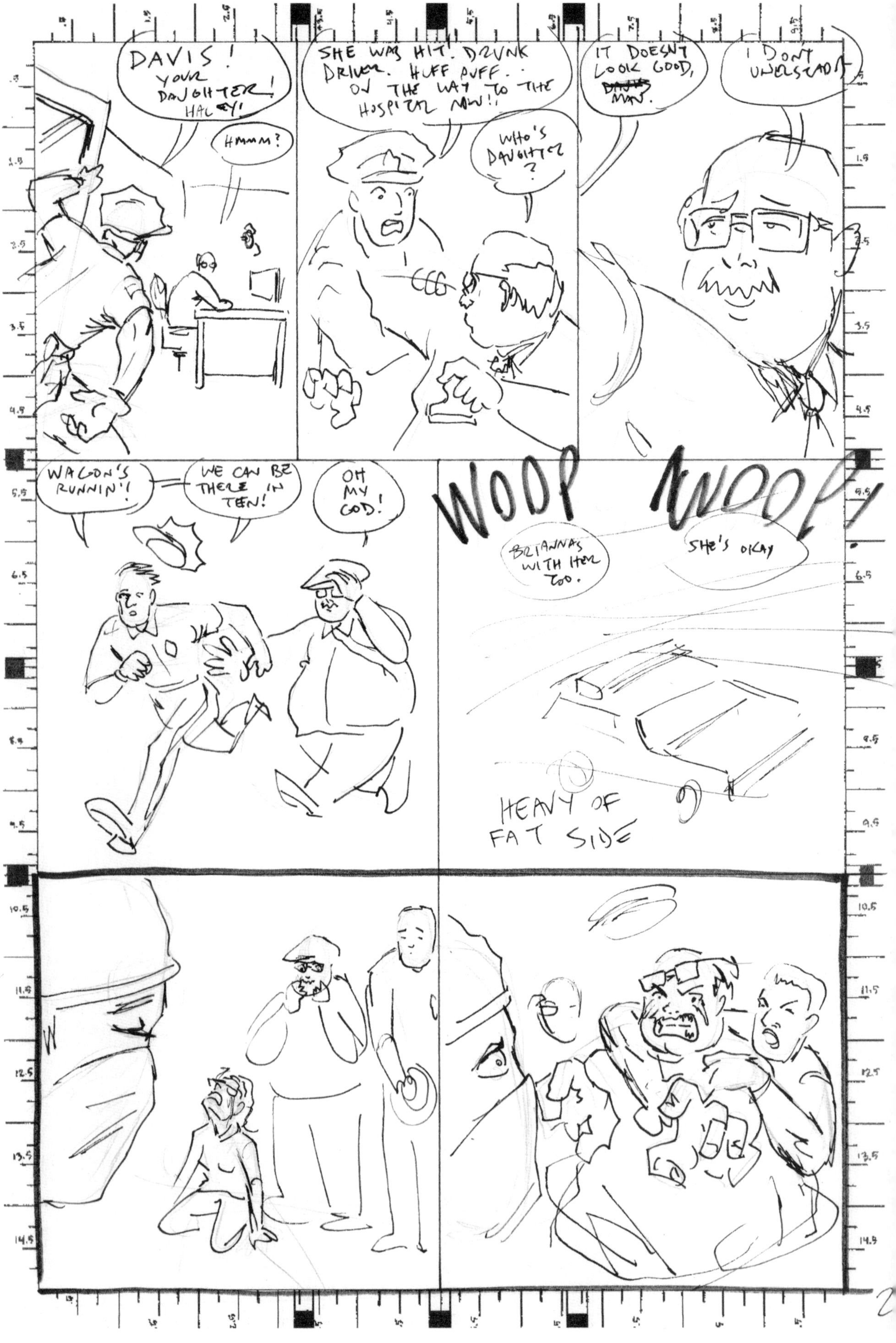
DAVIS! YOUR DAUGHTER! HALEY!
HMMM?
SHE WAS HIT! DRUNK DRIVER. HUFF PUFF.. ON THE WAY TO THE HOSPITAL NOW!!
WHO'S DAUGHTER?
IT DOESN'T LOOK GOOD, ~~DAVIS~~ MAN.
I DONT UNDERSTAN
WAGON'S RUNNIN'!
WE CAN BE THERE IN TEN!
OH MY GOD!
WOOP WOOP!
BRIANNA'S WITH HER TOO.
SHE'S OKAY
HEAVY OF FAT SIDE

2

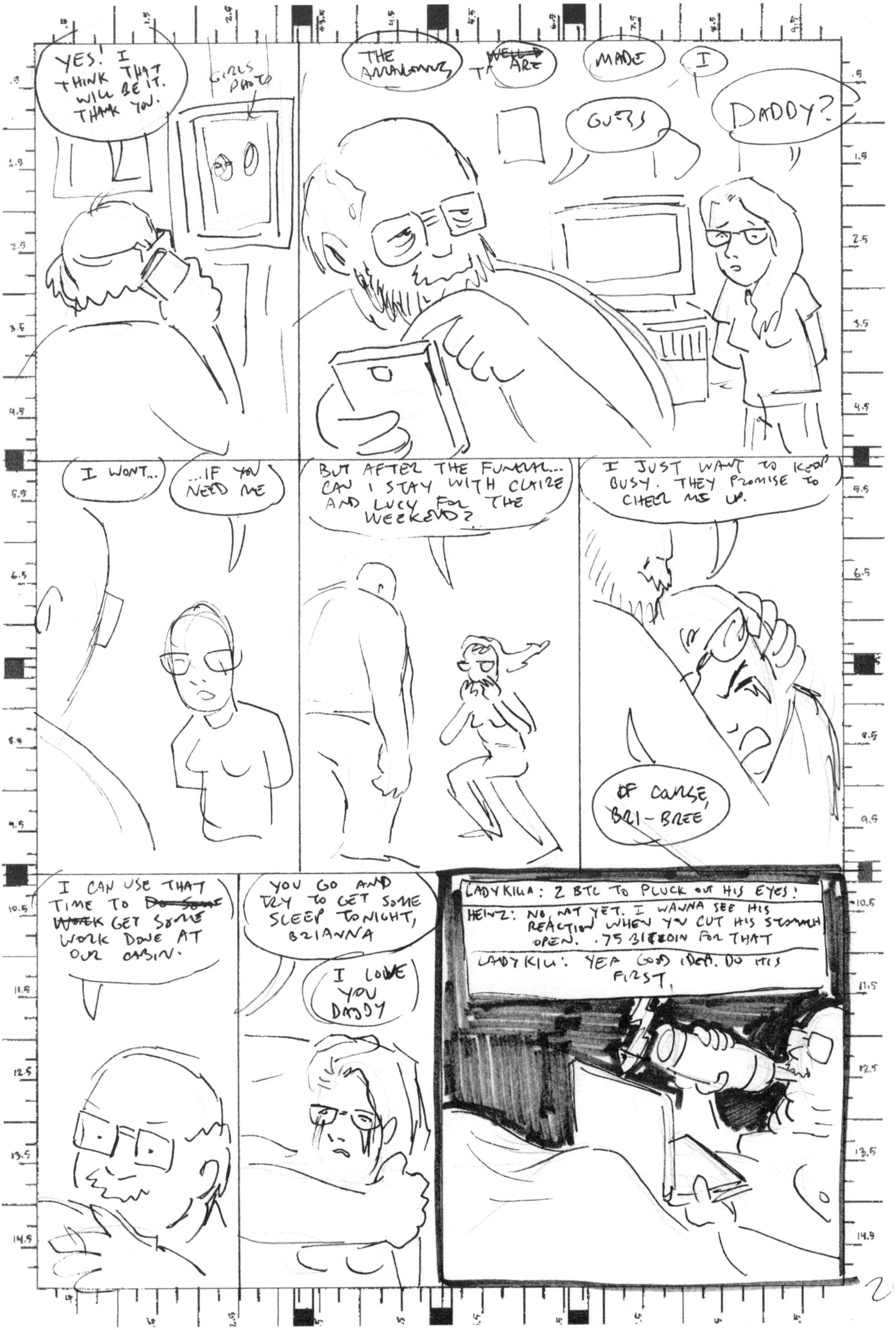
YES! I THINK THAT WILL BE IT. THANK YOU.
GIRLS PHOTO
THE
ARE
MADE
I
GUESS
DADDY?
I WONT...
...IF YOU NEED ME
BUT AFTER THE FUNERAL... CAN I STAY WITH CLAIRE AND LUCY FOR THE WEEKEND?
I JUST WANT TO KEEP BUSY. THEY PROMISE TO CHEER ME UP.
OF COURSE, BRI-BREE
I CAN USE THAT TIME TO GET SOME WORK DONE AT OUR CABIN.
YOU GO AND TRY TO GET SOME SLEEP TONIGHT, BRIANNA
I LOVE YOU DADDY
LADYKILLA: 2 BTC TO PLUCK OUT HIS EYES!
HEINZ: NO NOT YET. I WANNA SEE HIS REACTION WHEN YOU CUT HIS STOMACH OPEN. .75 BITCOIN FOR THAT
LADYKILLA: YEA GOOD IDEA. DO HIS FIRST
2

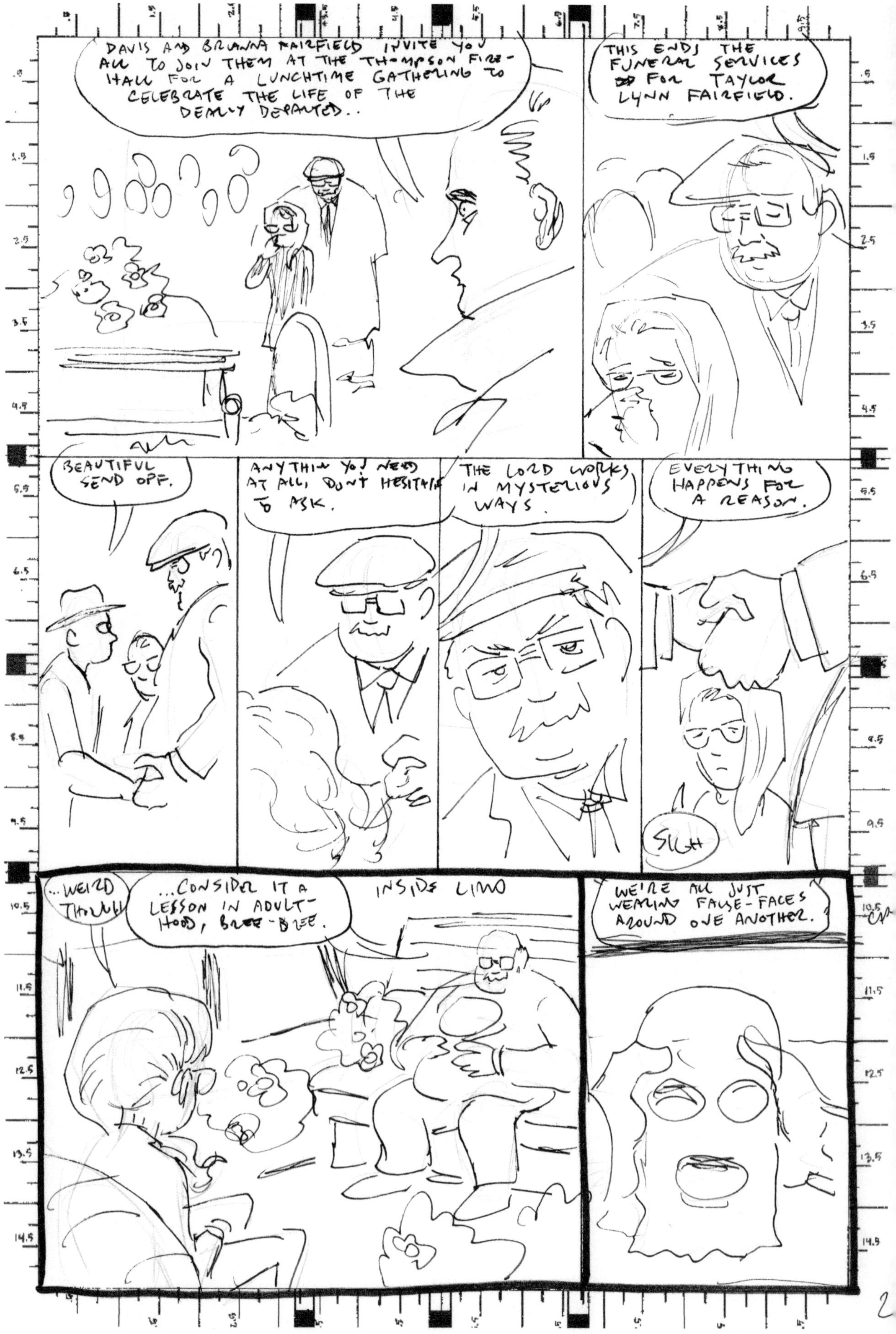
DAVIS AND BRIANNA FAIRFIELD INVITE YOU ALL TO JOIN THEM AT THE THOMPSON FIRE-HALL FOR A LUNCHTIME GATHERING TO CELEBRATE THE LIFE OF THE DEARLY DEPARTED..
THIS ENDS THE FUNERAL SERVICES FOR TAYLOR LYNN FAIRFIELD.
BEAUTIFUL SEND OFF.
ANYTHIN YOU NEED AT ALL, DONT HESITATE TO ASK.
THE LORD WORKS IN MYSTERIOUS WAYS.
EVERYTHING HAPPENS FOR A REASON.
SIGH
...WEIRD THOUGH
...CONSIDER IT A LESSON IN ADULTHOOD, BREE-BREE.
INSIDE LIMO
WE'RE ALL JUST WEARING FALSE-FACES AROUND ONE ANOTHER.

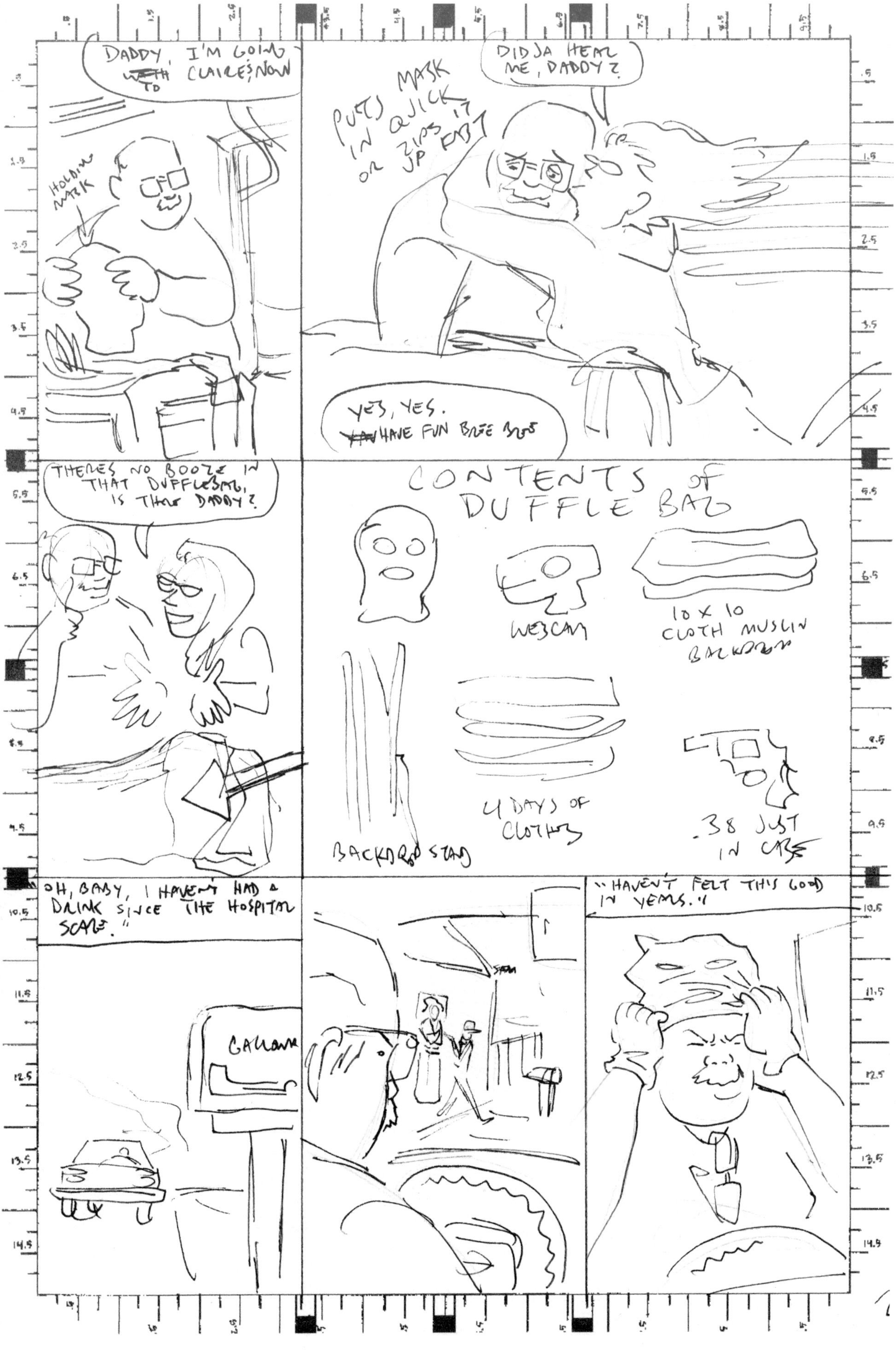
DADDY, I'M GOING TO CLAIRE'S NOW
HOLDING MASK
PUTS MASK IN QUICK OR ZIPS IT UP FAST
DIDJA HEAR ME, DADDY?
YES, YES. HAVE FUN
THERE'S NO BOOZE IN THAT DUFFLEBAG, IS THERE DADDY?
CONTENTS OF DUFFLE BAG
WEBCAM
10 x 10 CLOTH MUSLIN BACKDROP
BACKDROP STAND
4 DAYS OF CLOTHES
.38 JUST IN CASE
"OH, BABY, I HAVEN'T HAD A DRINK SINCE THE HOSPITAL SCARE."
"HAVEN'T FELT THIS GOOD IN YEARS."

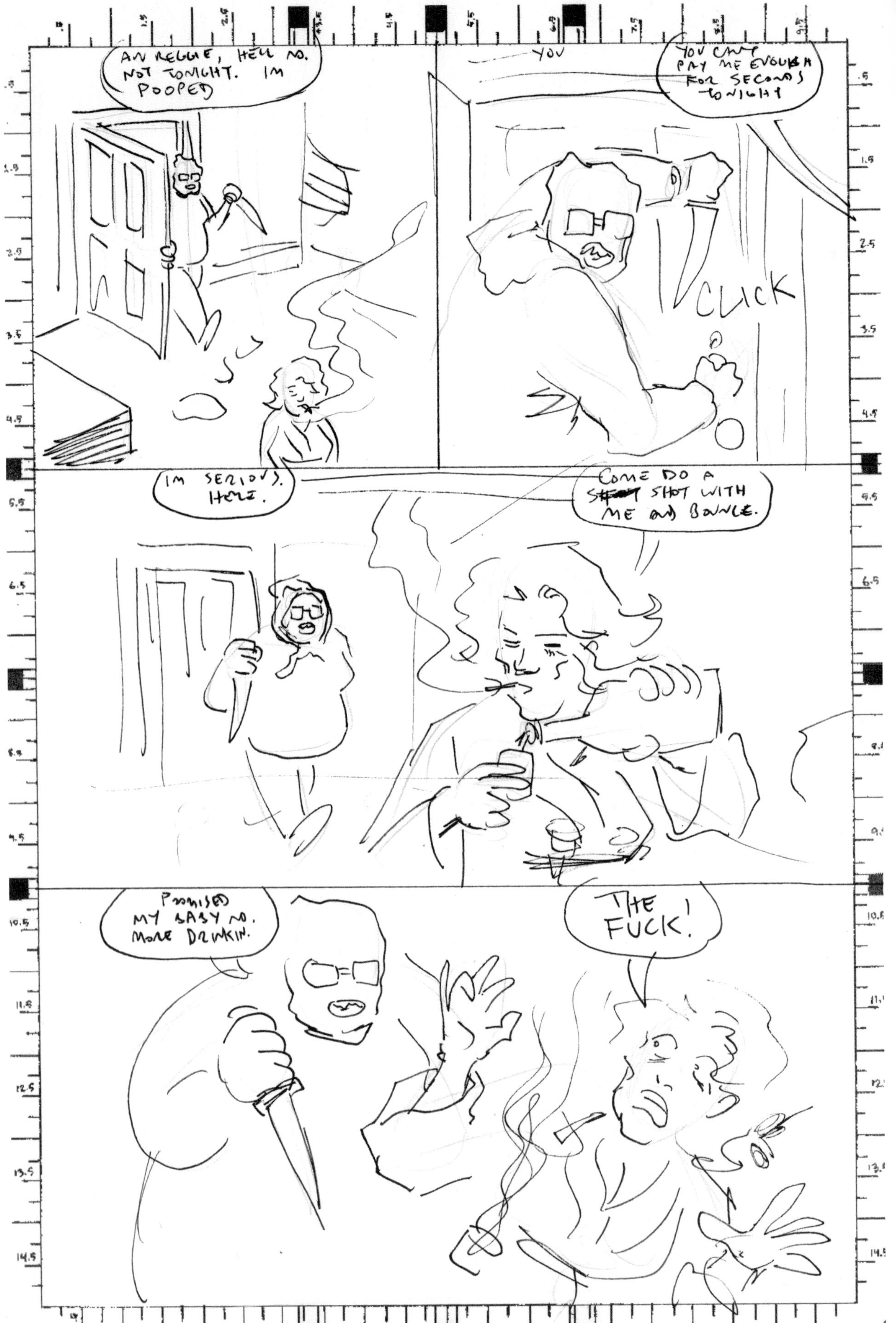
AW REGGIE, HELL NO. NOT TONIGHT. IM POOPED
YOU
YOU CANT PAY ME ENOUGH FOR SECONDS TONIGHT
CLICK
IM SERIOUS. HERE.
COME DO A SHOT WITH ME AND BOUNCE.
PROMISED MY BABY NO MORE DRINKIN.
THE FUCK!

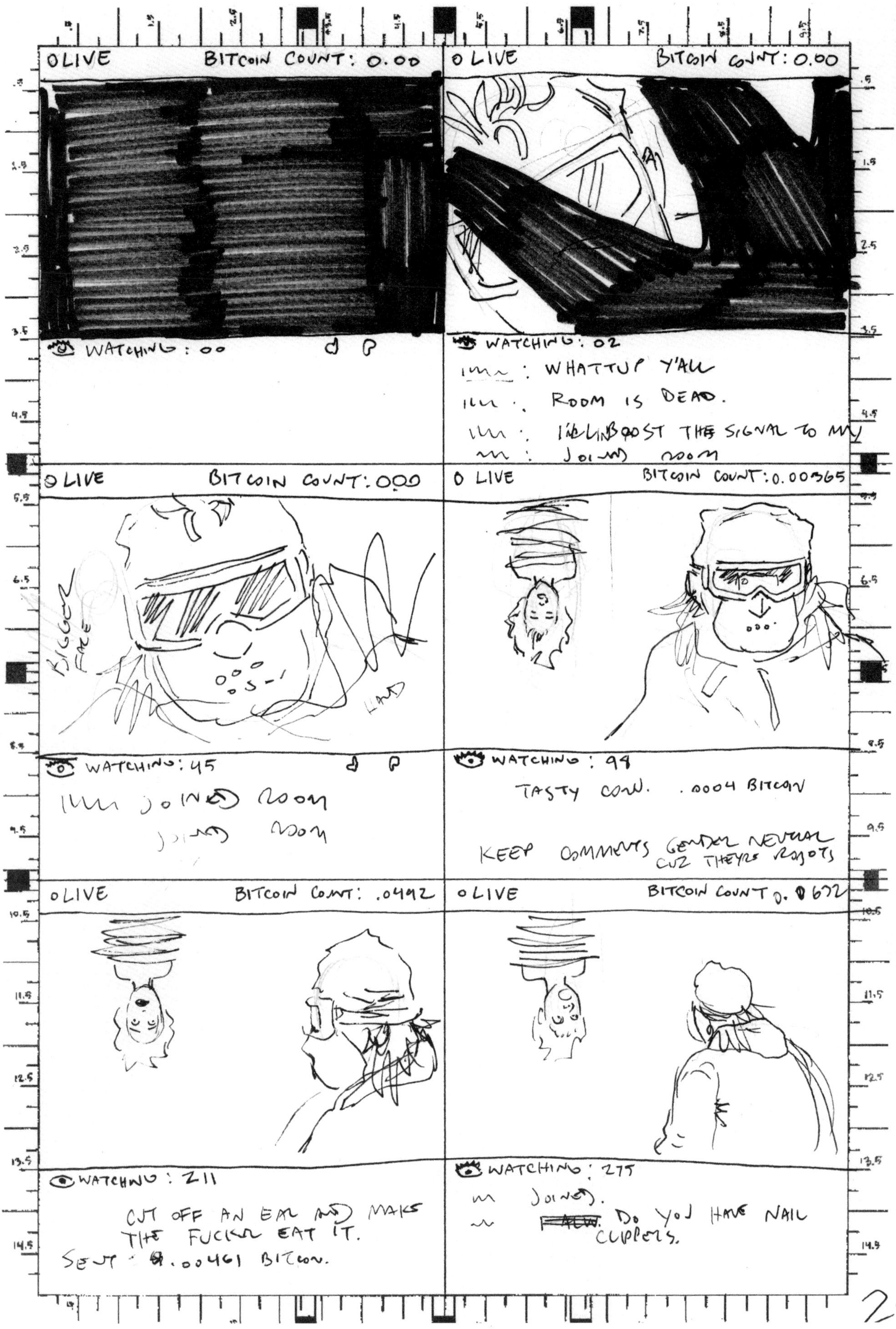
OLIVE
BITCOIN COUNT: 0.00
WATCHING: 00
OLIVE
BITCOIN COUNT: 0.00
WATCHING: 02
WHATTUP Y'ALL
ROOM IS DEAD.
BOOST THE SIGNAL TO MY
JOINED ROOM
OLIVE
BITCOIN COUNT: 0.00
BIGGER FACE
HAND
WATCHING: 45
JOINED ROOM
JOINED ROOM
OLIVE
BITCOIN COUNT: 0.00365
WATCHING: 99
TASTY COW. .0004 BITCOIN
KEEP COMMENTS GENDER NEUTRAL CUZ THEYRE ROBOTS
OLIVE
BITCOIN COUNT: .0492
WATCHING: 211
CUT OFF AN EAR AND MAKE THE FUCKER EAT IT.
SENT .00461 BITCOIN.
OLIVE
BITCOIN COUNT
WATCHING: 275
JOINED.
DO YOU HAVE NAIL CLIPPERS.

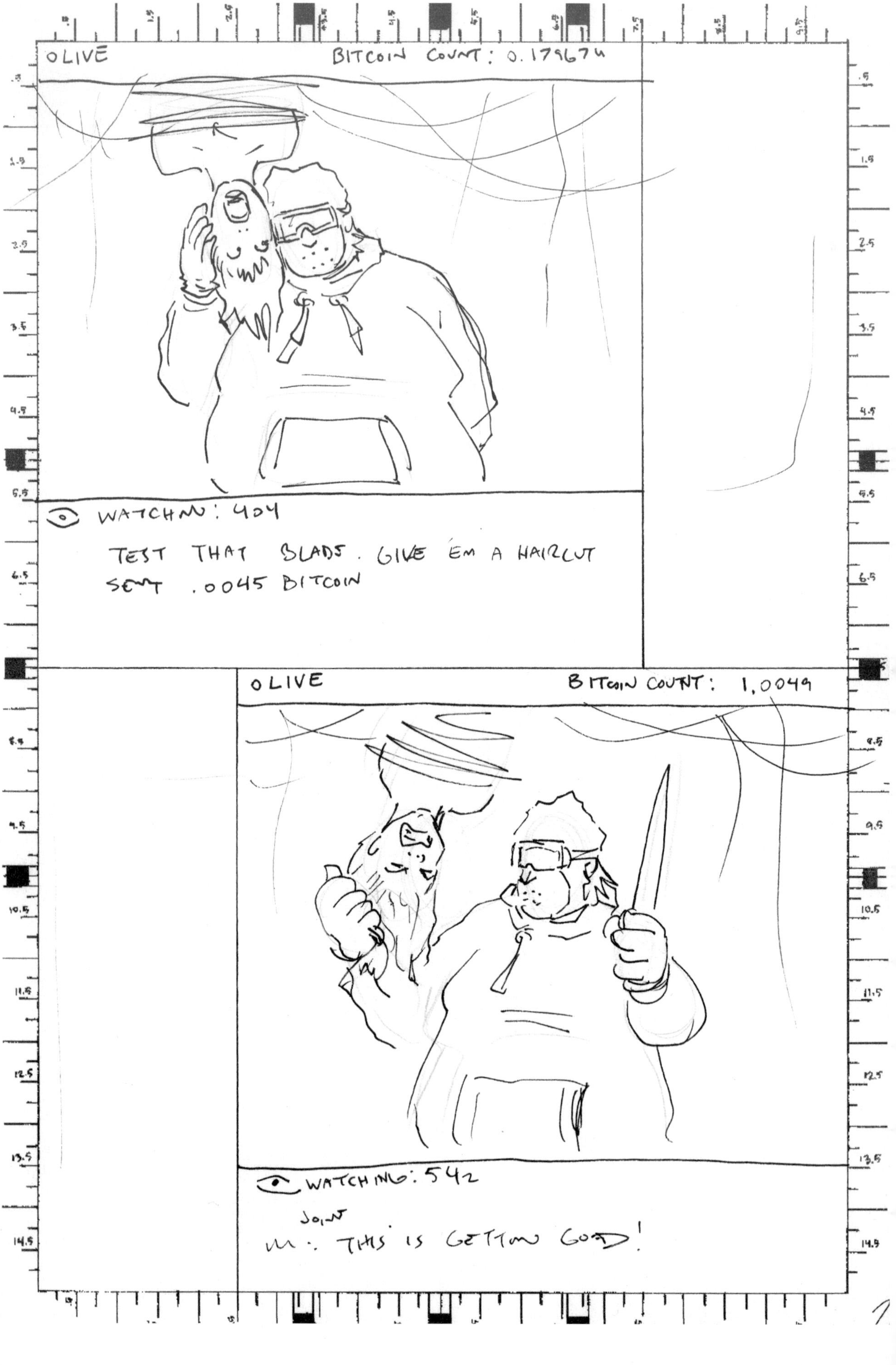
OLIVE
BITCOIN COUNT: 0.179674
WATCHN: 404
TEST THAT BLADE. GIVE 'EM A HAIRCUT
SENT .0045 BITCOIN
OLIVE
BITCOIN COUNT: 1,0049
WATCHING: 542
JOIN
M: THIS IS GETTIN GOOD!

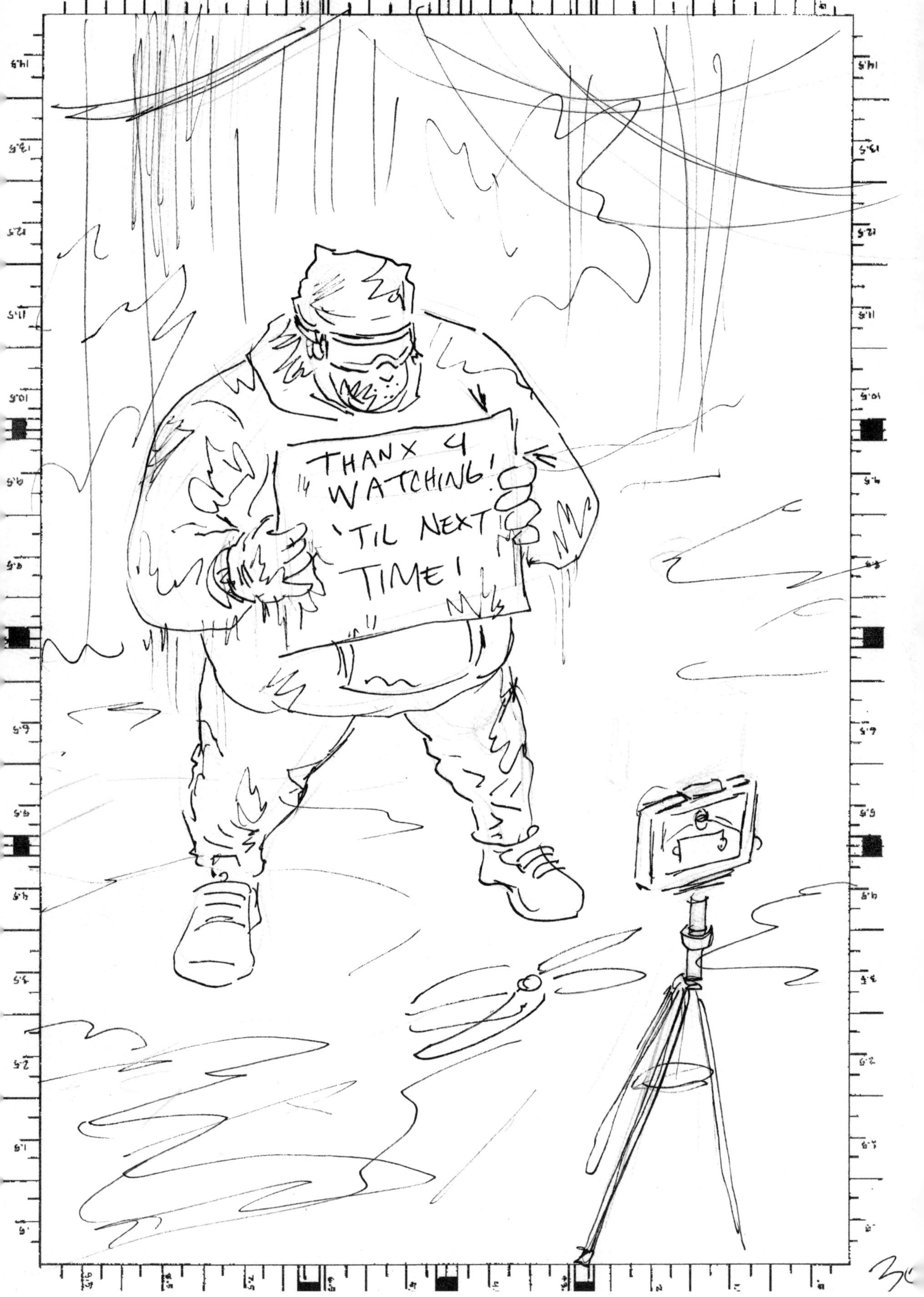
THANX 4 WATCHING! 'TIL NEXT TIME!

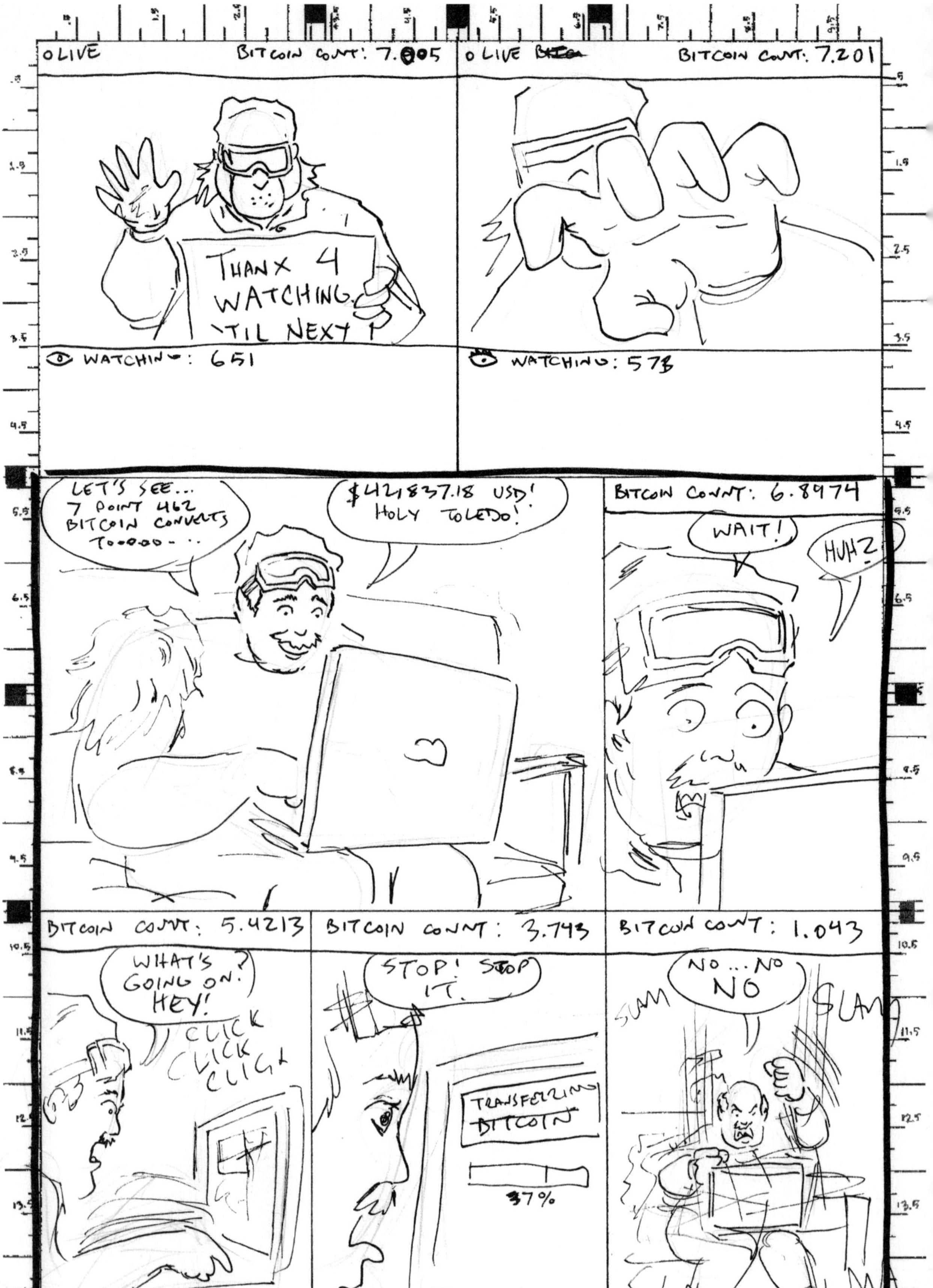

LIVE
BITCOIN COUNT: 7.?05
THANX 4 WATCHING. 'TIL NEXT T
WATCHING: 651
LIVE
BITCOIN COUNT: 7.201
WATCHING: 578
LET'S SEE... 7 POINT 462 BITCOIN CONVERTS TOOOOO-..
$421837.18 USD! HOLY TOLEDO!
BITCOIN COUNT: 6.8974
WAIT!
HUH?
BITCOIN COUNT: 5.4213
WHAT'S GOING ON? HEY!
CLICK CLICK CLICK
BITCOIN COUNT: 3.743
STOP! STOP IT.
TRANSFERRING BITCOIN
37%
BITCOIN COUNT: 1.043
NO...NO NO
SLAM
SLAM

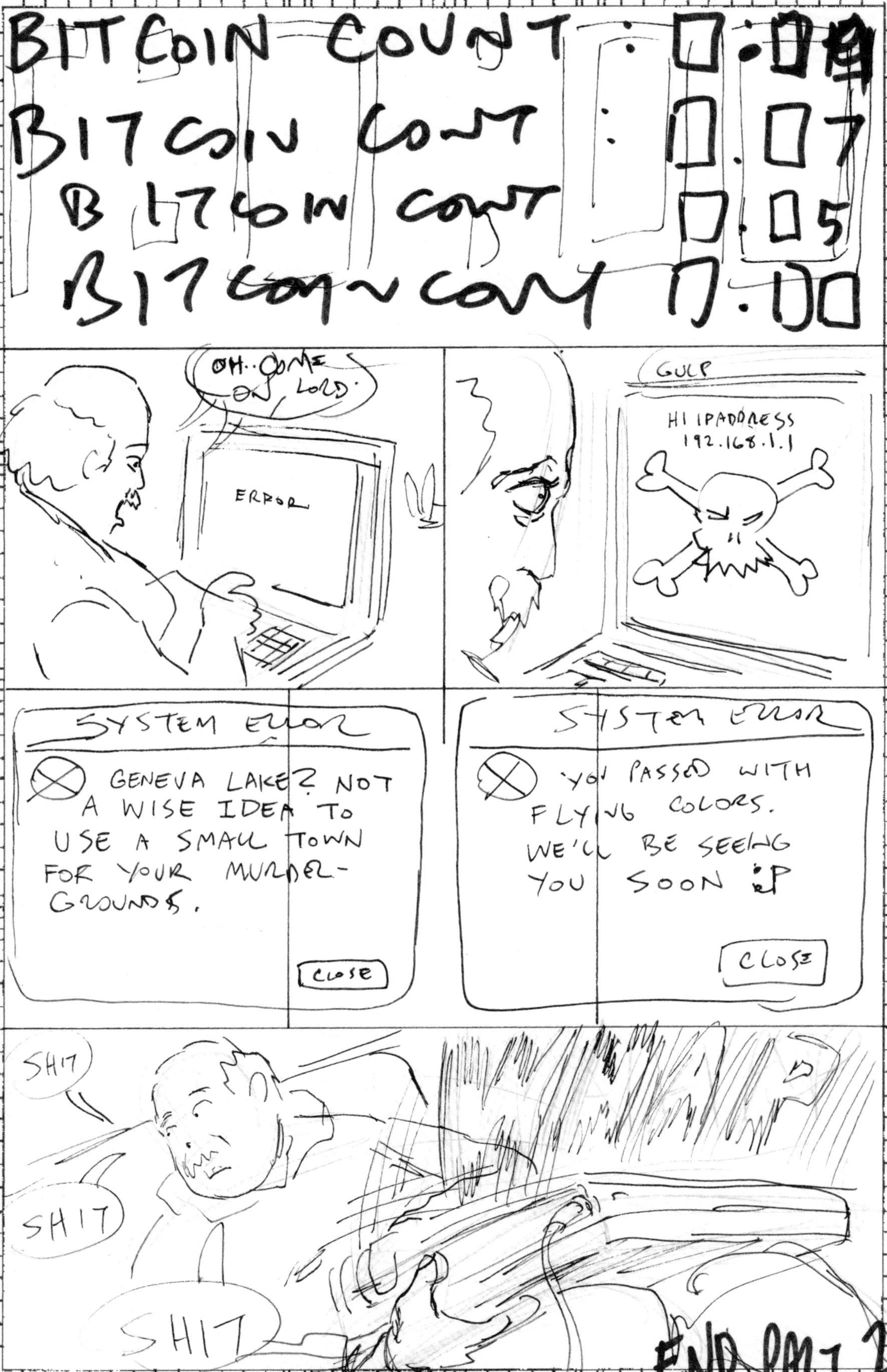
BITCOIN COUNT : 0.09
BITCOIN COUNT : 0.07
BITCOIN COUNT 0.05
BITCOIN COUNT 0.00
OH.. COME ON, LORD.
ERROR
GULP
HI IPADDRESS 192.168.1.1
SYSTEM ERROR
GENEVA LAKE? NOT A WISE IDEA TO USE A SMALL TOWN FOR YOUR MURDER-GROUNDS.
CLOSE
SYSTEM ERROR
YOU PASSED WITH FLYING COLORS. WE'LL BE SEEING YOU SOON :P
CLOSE
SHIT
SHIT
SHIT
END PART 1

DIRECTOR'S COMMENTARY

A GLIMPSE INTO THE MIND OF A MANIAC

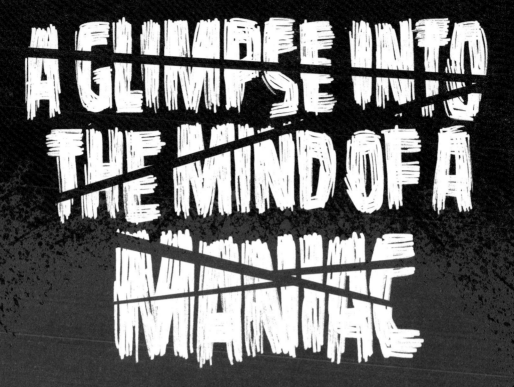

"BLOODY BAPTISM"

Pages 1–64

PAGE 3: I did lots of research into the mind of your common serial killers because, guess what, it's hard to try and figure out motivations to commit cold blooded murder. Discovering the FBI profiling works of John E. Douglas, of *Mindhunter* fame, it was scary to see all the clear similarities between many of the killers he's examined. Lots of Douglas's groundwork was used to build the Davis Fairfield character. I'll explain clearly as we go.

PAGE 4: Serial killers often have a fascination for law enforcement, if only for self-preservation reasons. They rarely could make the cut as police officers, but they sometimes can be found having close associations or jobs that give them some modicum of power. Think about BTK Dennis Rader working as a code enforcement officer in his hometown. Our guy, Davis, is a mere clerk of the local municipal court system. It puts him in close contact with the jakes, and he rarely gets the respect that he'd like.

PAGE 5: There are often inciting reasons for serial killers to act. They don't just wake up and decide that today's a good day for a kill. I chose to take the bulk of Davis's family away from him. Having this abrupt change in life would be a shock to anyone's system. The normal soul would mourn. Davis is a good actor, once again, for the sake of self-preservation.

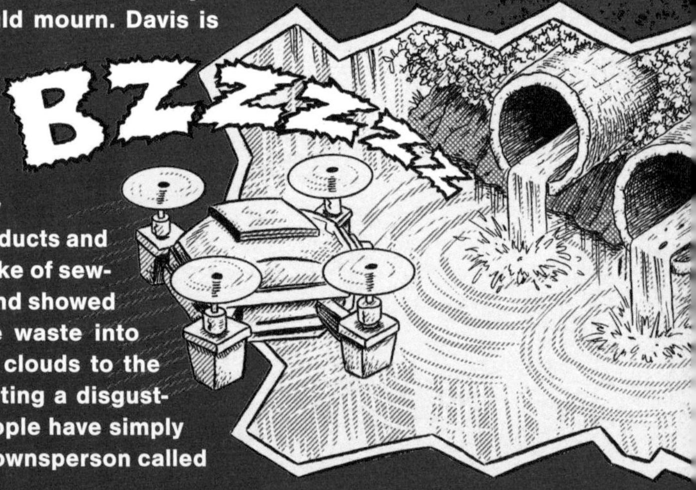
BZZZZZ

PAGES 6-7: I saw some drone footage online where someone flew a camera over a factory farm that specialized in pig products and highlighted this gross, giant lake of sewage that had similar culverts and showed the water jets that shoot the waste into the atmosphere, carrying the clouds to the neighboring town, and generating a disgusting smell that all the townspeople have simply gotten used to. Maybe a new townsperson called our bloggers into action?

PAGES 8-9: Reading up on the dark net and hidden sites, it seems that they need to be extremely lightweight when it comes to their coding so that they leave as few vectors for hacking and viruses as possible. That's the reason for these stripped down, almost 1984 Macintosh-looking user interfaces. Can't get ornate with the aesthetics of these chatrooms or else the FBI might be able to find a backdoor to deanonymize the users.

Security is the name of the game when it comes to the business of red rooms. The conversation on this page shows how much the bad actors care. Not only do they not want one piece of skin to show on a killer, but they don't even want the feds to be able to figure out the weather outside for fear that it would narrow the law enforcement investigation even a little bit.

PAGES 10-11: This speaks more to the security-consciousness of the Pentagram fam. Even their security guards are in the dark and expendable. I thought it would be a cool idea to show the Mistress's hair in different colors and styles each time so that you never know the real deal. The house is tricked out like an extra paranoid Winchester Mansion.

PAGE 12: *Sigh*. That middle tier can be called my "death pet peeves": selfishness, gossip, clichés, and platitudes.

PAGES 13-14: Middle tier on 13, I like the bold black shapes of our main guy and how young Brianna is just floating in that pool of black (still recovering from the car accident).

Last panel on 13 to 14 is one of those classic Alan Moore transition sequences where one page leads into the next using a trigger word. I'm such a sucker for this convention and I don't doubt that it was fresh in my mind from reading Moore's essays on writing comics from 1986.

The tattoo artwork was done on a separate piece of paper and made fairly transparent when married with the true line art to give it that faded impression. This is around where I got way more comfortable using white media on top of the hair textures to add some more frizz and split ends. Very effective, looking back on it.

PAGE 15: I never really know what the gore will be until I sit down and draw the pages in an almost Marvel Method approach. The task is simple: before I draw a fresh sequence, I daydream until something really grosses me out, and then it gets committed to paper.

PAGE 16: Davis has to get the girl out of the house asap. Gotta establish the existence of the cabin as a remote location that gives Davis ultimate privacy, and I like the setting-as-character here, where it's up to your interpretation: did they always live under these conditions, or has the house quickly gotten out of control after the death of the matriarch?

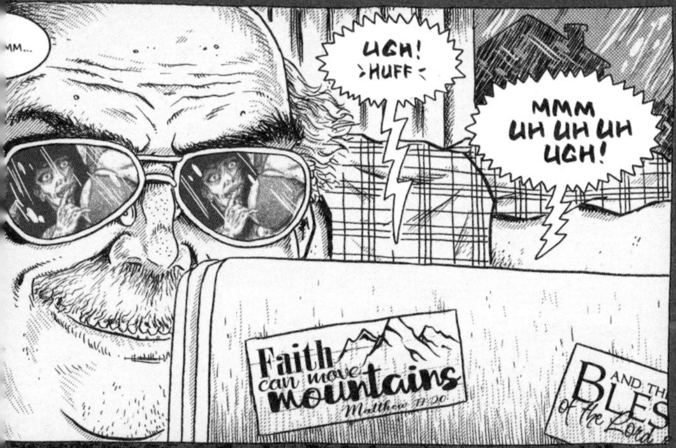
UGH! HUFF
MMM UH UH UH UGH!
Faith can move mountains

PAGE 17: I drew three versions of this page. The other two were tipping the hand too much and giving the reader way more info than needed in the moment. Gotta let the stories unfold a bit. If you didn't catch it the first time, pay attention to the reflection in Davis's glasses in that last panel. We'll see a better glimpse at the complete image later.

PAGE 18: Another one of those Alan Moore transitions; this time, the porno sounds carry us from one setting to another. This lawyer character is a bit inspired by that "pharma bro" guy who was in the news for skyrocketing the price of his company's HIV medication. The people in *Red Room* are all big scumbags. No heroes in the lot.

PAGE 19: The lawyer uses discovery evidence to leak to Mistress Pentagram, so that they can build a better, more secure infrastructure to operate their red room business.

PAGES 20-21: Even the hired hands of the Pentagram red rooms have to go through rigorous strictures in order to perform their function. The idea of using these killers as products themselves was amusing to me, so the refrigerator cartons filled with packing peanuts made a lot of sense to me and provide some fun visuals, which is the name of the game if you make comics correctly.

PAGE 22: My Cartoonist Kayfabe brother-at-arms, Jim Rugg, suggested the eyeball up to the face in the last of that four-panel sequence. He's a sicko when he wants to be.

PAGE 23: There's often a sexual component to serial killing and Hazzard suggesting that he wishes there were a better pool of victims suggests his lack of satisfaction.

PAGE 24: The dialogue here of the Pentagrams' observations came to me by thinking of red room killers as porn stars of sorts. I'd imagine that the viewing audience would burn out on them rapidly if they don't keep coming up with new tricks. Then the question becomes, what do you do with the washed-up stars?

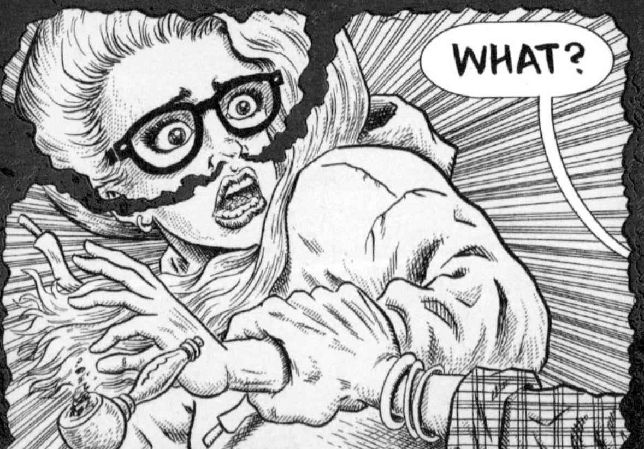
WHAT?

PAGES 25-26: I guess Brianna is the nicest character in the series, but I also wanted her to have her own secrets that she keeps from her dad.

PAGE 27: The only people who really get into legal entanglements from red rooms are the rubes who trade in secondhand videos from the

internet. I've read all the big articles about dark web sting operations in drugs and exploitation porn and it always seems that the amount of people who use the platforms far dwarfs the few people who end up ultimately getting arrested for participating. The masterminds rarely, if ever, get caught in real life, so that is mimicked in *Red Room*.

PAGES 28-29: I mentioned in the foreword that *Red Room* is a world building exercise. Here's an opportunity to throw some stuff up in the air for future story fodder. Remember the reflection in Davis's glasses from page 17? The full image is that panel of Sarah Jane Payne. I've yet to tell her story as of this writing, but it's going to be pretty hardcore when I get to it. Fair warning.

PAGES 30-31: When we first saw the lawyer interacting with Mistress Pentagram, there was talk of a trojan horse they were planning on deploying on the dark web. Looks like they caught some bait.

PAGES 32-33: John E. Douglas, the famous FBI profiler, discovered that lots of sickos would frequent cop bars and would often become friendly with the detectives and patrolmen. They'd also be aficionados of salacious true crime magazines, hence Davis riffing on serial killers, though he inaccurately says that the Zodiac Killer was in LA; that'd be Richard Ramirez.

PAGE 34: Worth mentioning the dialogue bubbles of the Pentagram/Thelema family. I knew you'd never get to see their faces, so I needed each family member to have their own distinct dialogue balloons so that you can tell them apart.

PAGE 35: That black page is a Frank Miller stroke from *That Yellow Bastard*. Remember when Harti-

RELAX!

RELAX.

RELAX.

THAT'S A GOOD BOY.

OSIRUS.

YEAH, PULL THE TRUCK AROUND.

AND GET A **CRATE** READY.

A REFRIGERATOR CARTON WON'T DO FOR **THE WHITE WHALE.**

gan is hanging and loses consciousness in the last issue? That shit was dope!

PAGE 36: Hartigan, "No!" Loved that Miller sequence.

PAGE 37: Here we go from Frank Miller to Uncle Todd McFarlane in one of his most notorious splash pages from *Spawn* (#5), when Billy Kincaid is strung up in chains with popsicle sticks and ice cream scoopers impaling him.

PAGE 38 ONWARD: I think I really started to hate the rectangle box of the standard grid so at this point I'm looking at a lot of McFarlane, Hewlett, and Sam Keith for inspiration when it comes to page layout.

PAGE 39: The Uzi in the nose comes from looking at the *G.I. Joe* issue that both Marshall Rogers and Todd McFarlane drew. They drew the same comic with almost the same amount of panels, and I wanted to do my own Uzi/nose piece.

PAGES 40–41: I think this is the part where I listened to enough Stephen King audiobooks to see that he had so many characters who were writers and it made me want to inject more comics culture into my stuff. The world of *Red Room* is a world where the dominant form of mainstream entertainment is comics. This convention setting is pretty similar to the Pittsburgh Comicons of my youth.

PAGE 42: The first shot of Mistress Pentagram! I was reading about how Starbucks baristas were instructed to write customers' names incorrectly so that they'd take photos of the faux pas and post them online as a kind of viral advertising for the brand. I think I

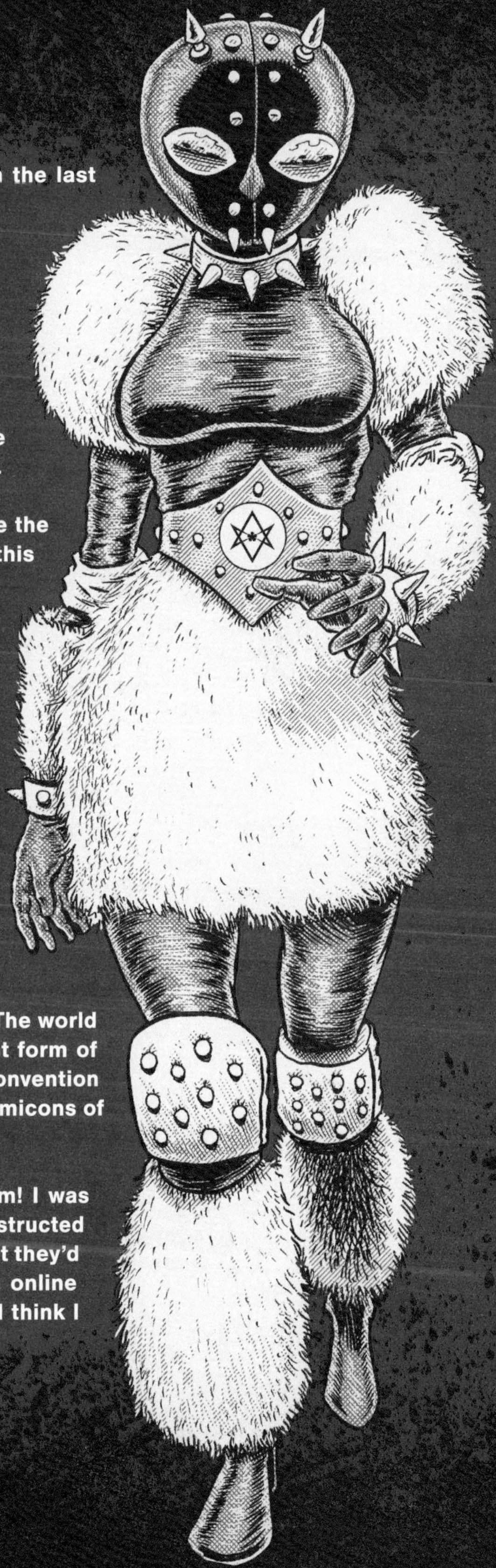

might have been too subtle with my own stab at it, because as of this writing none of my peanut gallery has helped promote *Red Room* by posting the symbol on her belt and roasting me for having Mistress Pentagram wearing a hexagram design.

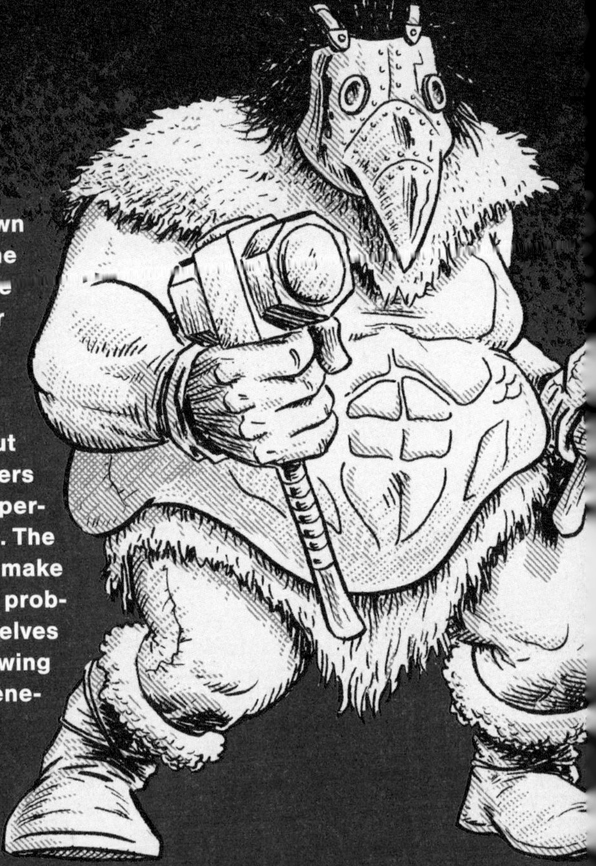

PAGES 44–47: I was reading online about rumors of red rooms where U.S. soldiers got hold of ISIS terrorists and would perform deadly torture on video, for a price. The rumors probably aren't true, but it did make me think about how some people would probably be able to make peace with themselves and enjoy watching such atrocities, knowing that the acts were being performed on enemies of the state.

PAGE 48: Mistress Pentagram and the Thelema family literally ushering Davis into the world of red rooms.

PAGE 51: More of that world building stuff, suggesting that the history of red rooms has existed far longer than the emergence of TOR and the dark web. This piece sparked the idea for the Donna Butcher story because I began thinking a lot about what the VHS era of red room snuff might have looked like.

PAGE 52: The pit. I saw the French flick *Martyrs* after making this issue and was pleased that there was a deep, dark, sub-basement sequence. I also did this sequence before reading some of Jack Ketchum's work, where he also referred to his human fodder as "cows." When I started to absorb these outside works, it became scary to realize how in tune I was with these other creators.

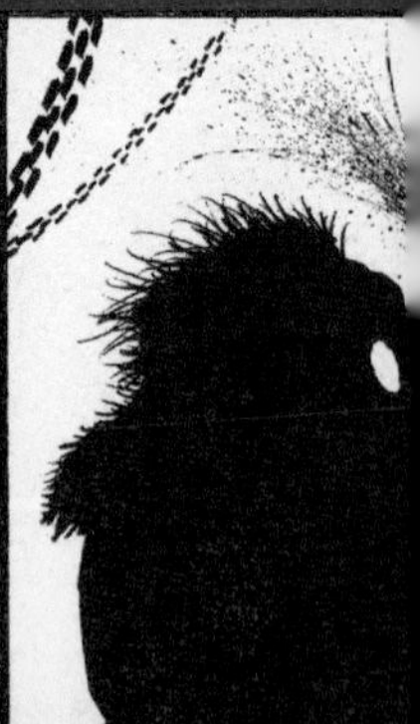

PAGE 53: Prions! The root of Mad Cow Disease. At this point I was generating lots of ideas for *Red Room* #2 and I was going to launch into a story where one of these inbreeds caught a cold, and then Covid-19 happened and I didn't wanna spend too much time making a plague comic. I can pick that thread up again now, I suppose.

PAGE 56: I think that's where the plague doctor mask came from. From my plague story. The rest of his outfit is inspired by Giant Gonzales's outfit from the WWF in the early 1990s. You gotta look it up.

PAGES 57-60: Davis needed to be seen as a veteran in the killing game. Also, this might be the only thing he's really good at and I like the idea of him taking pride in his work. So much of the Type "A" stuff that comes out of the killers' mouths across the issues could almost be pulled verbatim from conversations with my comic book making brethren.

PAGE 61: I remember on this page that I began getting way more comfy drawing backgrounds without pencilling. I would pencil in the perspective grids to make sure everything lined up but I was in such a flow state that I could just draw the backgrounds straight in ink. I might have switched from Micron pens to Copic fine liners around this point, too.

PAGES 62-64: We end the first big story on a domestic note. A nice moment between dad and daughter with some underlying darkness in between. Note the silhouette panel at the bottom-right of page 63 and its similarity to the bottom red room panel on page 58. I never wanted you to really think the daughter was in danger, but I do want you to recall that the same guy hugging up his daughter is doing it with the same hands that brutalized that inbred fucker a few pages prior.

END NOTE: This first issue comprises of what was going to be two issues of a four-issue story arc that I would have then collected into one big work, until I realized that it would be lame as fuck to do things the way everybody else does. *Stray Bullets* was my favorite comic when it was first coming out and I loved the way Lapham would do these character studies for the first couple years and the point-of-view would jump around so much. That's become a crucial element to what I wanted to do with the *Red Room* series.

"FRESH MEAT"
Pages 65–88

PAGE 67: I think there are some good rules to keep in mind with the standard comic format. One, gotta start that shit off strong. Two, the Jim Shooter mandate: every comic is someone's first comic. The little title box that would be at the top of the 1970s Marvel comics was a perfect summary to get newbs into the title. I hope the big two comics still have some version of this.

PAGE 70: When I look at these pages, I feel like everything I'm focusing on is clearly apparent. This page I was thinking about ways to incorporate lettering into the whole design of a page. The part where the dead girl's butt emerges from the water is ripped off from either Corben or *Little Annie Fannie*... maybe both?

PAGE 71: That far off shot from above the church really sells the hopelessness of the situation for our poor guy.

PAGE 72: I got the idea of procuring red room victims via natural disasters from, I think, just a passing sentence that was uttered by some rando in the first season of *True Detective*. That seems like such a perfect way to disappear a body without much investigation and that is precisely the conditions that any proper red room business would need to operate securely.

PAGE 73: I have a whole backstory to these Poker Face people. I think it could work as a good issue of *Red Room*. One part of it is that the Poker Face killers all suffer from various stages of CTE from their past vocations.

PAGE 75: Bottom tier, I was thinking about the sniper sequences in the *Golgo 13* video game for the NES, when the crosshair moves and juts all over as you try and take your precise shot.

PAGE 76: Sigh, I was drawing this page when there was all kinds of talk about ventilator shortages in the news, due to increased covid-19 cases. It felt so eerie that I considered shelving this particular issue for a bit, just so to get my mind off the plight we were all enduring.

PAGE 77: This piece was extra sick to me. Makes you wonder how they got hold of the doctor, doesn't it? I might make that one into an issue at some point.

PAGE 78: Selling the doctor a little bit beforehand, showing the family on video, and ending with the visual of him being chained to a radiator is some of my favorite storytelling in this issue.

PAGE 79: Part of my thinking is that this mysterious red room owner guy with the laptop is like a Stan Lee analog. The only difference is that in my universe, comics authors are as successful as J.K. Rowling. He must own 1,000 buildings like that walkup.

PAGE 80: I really do make my comics in a vacuum and it's hard for me to tell how this stuff plays sometimes. Do readers know what's gonna happen? I just don't know. To this day I still don't have people to test the stuff on for objective feedback. I'm saying this because as of this writing, this particular issue is a week from hitting the stands and I'm curious to see what some people think about the flow.

PAGE 81: The doctor's only saving grace was knowing that his family was okay, and this video just twists that knife. Sometimes, for the good of the comic, you have to be a sadist with your characters. If you knew his backstory, though, you wouldn't mind his turmoil.

PAGE 82: I was really thinking of drawing some annoying celebrity portrait here. Justin Bieber or someone. I opted not to out of laziness, because I knew I'd have to draw the schmuck at least five more times

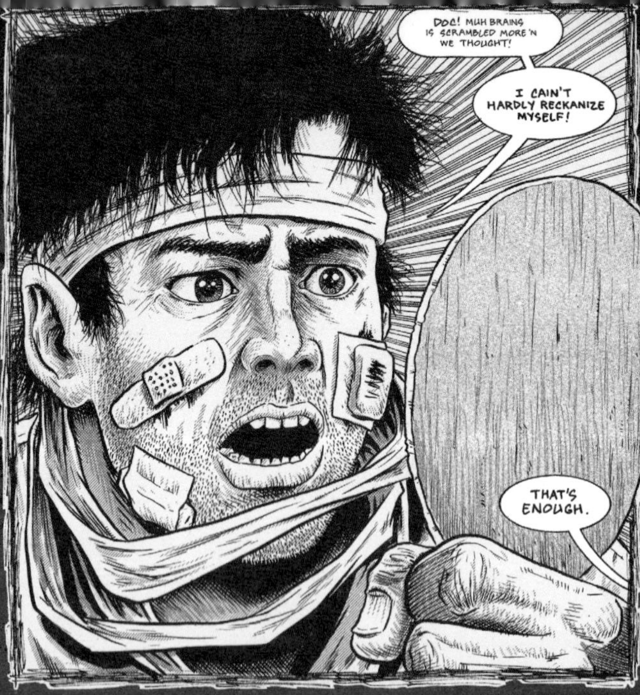
DOC! MUH BRAINS IS SCRAMBLED MORE 'N WE THOUGHT!
I CAIN'T HARDLY RECKANIZE MYSELF!
THAT'S ENOUGH.

or so. Still, dig the facial expression in the splash. Kinda like a Frank Castle with the headband and stubble.

PAGE 84–87: I said it before but it's worth saying again: I never know what the gore situation is going to be until it's time to get to drawing. I would have a page count in mind for the sequence and the entire time I'm making the comic leading up to the red room moment, I'm playing different scenarios in my mind. Usually I never settle on something by the time I get to draw the sequence. I might have to take a whole day or two and keep away from the drawing table until I come up with something sufficiently disgusting to me. This piece takes the cake. The challenge after this kind of thing, though, is to continue to try and top it, because that's how those red room businesses operate. They're competing with one another for the buying dollar (bitcoin) of very wealthy patrons. Gotta keep upping the ante.

"UNINTENDED CONSEQUENCES"

Pages 89–112

The genesis of this story comes from thinking about the genesis of TOR (The Onion Router) itself, and the dark web in general, and also the emergence of the prominent dark web black market website the Silk Road and its creator Ross Ulbricht (currently serving a multiple life sentence as of this writing). I was thinking about how the people involved with these creations didn't necessarily have ill intentions with their inventions, but the platforms have been misused all the same. How would one reconcile themselves

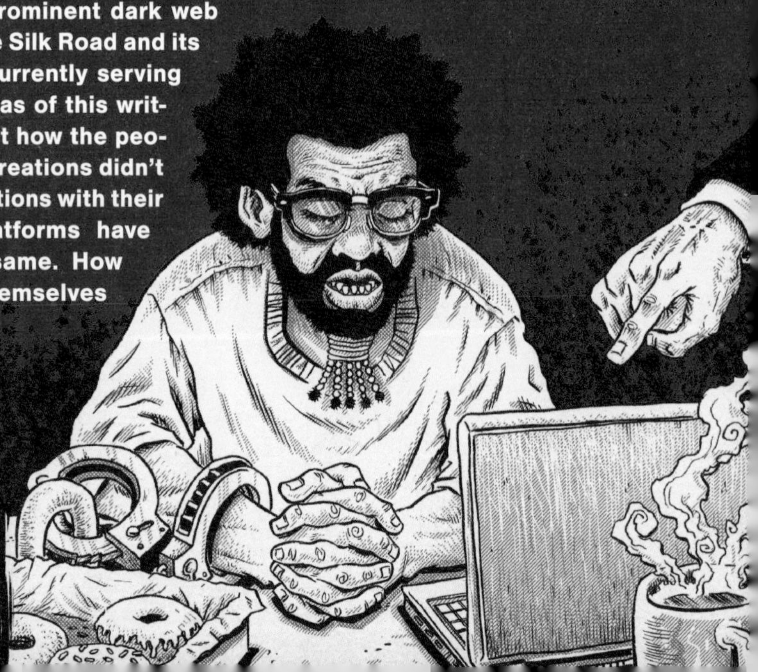

with such a catastrophe, knowing that great harm was coming from their genius? How deep would the guilt go? There's a really good book about Ross Ulbricht and the plight of the Silk Road that I highly recommend, *American Kingpin: The Epic Hunt for the Criminal Mastermind Behind the Silk Road*, by Nick Bilton, which gave me lots of key insights for this story's main character, Levee Turks. Some of it made it on the page, lots of it didn't. There's more story to tell with him in the future.

PAGE 91: The Rambo introduction of Levee Turks. Instead of pounding rocks with a chain gang as the colonel appears, our protagonist this issue is being wooed by the feds in an appeal to help unmask red rooms. Even though he's guilty of a nerdy crime, it was important to show the armed guards up front to imply that he isn't in one of those white collar prison camps.

PAGES 92-93: I took a month-long tour through Japan and it was a geek quest the entire time. This spread probably wouldn't have turned out this way without that influence fresh in my mind. More than just the speed lines, the excessiveness is something I'd routinely see in the works that spoke most to me while on my manga hunts. I was also drawing this story closer to manga original art size.

SCARAB BLOODSHED OUTLAW MASTERPIECE

PAGE 94: When I posted this Scarab video screen on social media people thought it was a way more vulgar piece than what's really here. Cunnilingus was mentioned by several people when they first saw the thumbnail image.

PAGE 95: Took a day to figure out a good excuse to let this guy off the hook without arousing too much suspicion. I also clearly remember watching Scarface recently when drawing this and I think that affected the hair on our girl here, which is similar to Tony Montana's little sis.

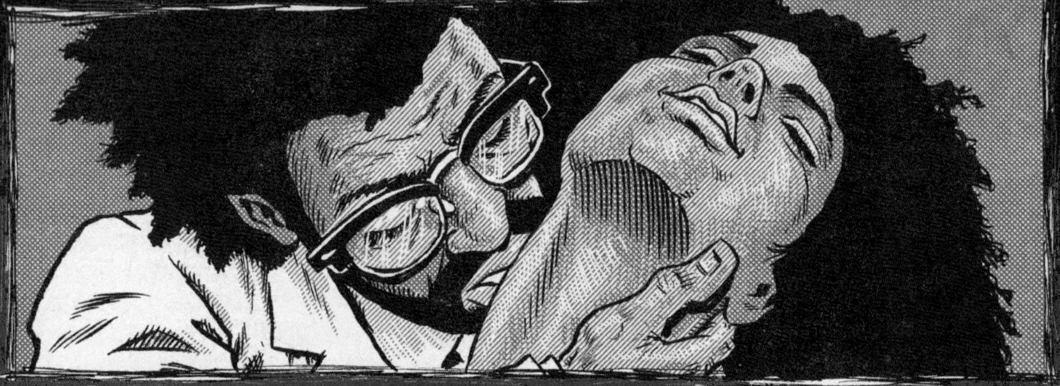

PAGE 96: Want motion in your cars? Get the wheels off the ground. The discerning reader will recognize the mansion as Hugh Hefner's old digs.

PAGES 98–99: This is pretty much the first sex scene I ever drew. In the world of red rooms, I imagine the carnography is more sexually gratifying than the carnality.

PAGES 105: This page was drawn in May of 2020 after months of not seeing another soul as the onslaught of Covid-19 plagued the country. When I put pen to paper on the last stroke of this page, scanned it, and got it print-ready, I couldn't pick up a pencil again for two months. I needed to see friends and family by any means necessary. I needed to have enough physical activity to calm my nerves. Quickly started a regime of 20-mile bicycle rides each morning which did wonders for my mental health.

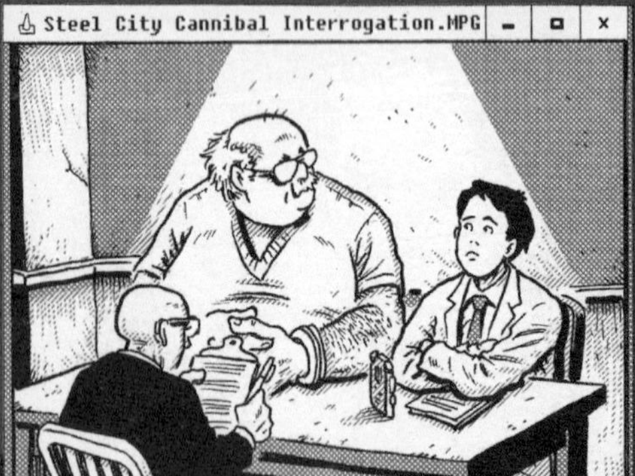
Steel City Cannibal Interrogation.MPG

PAGES 106–107: I knew I would have this sequence to ease me back into drawing the strip and I haven't looked back since (as of this writing). I like these kinds of scenes with a static camera angle and lots of body language to sell the conversation. *Red Room* operates like early *Stray Bullets* or *Sin City* comics where each issue takes place at different points in time to flesh out the world. Here, Davis Fairfield is incarcerated but we don't get to see how he got captured. It's also not clear that he's a red room killer, either. That's all for another story/issue!

PAGE 108: Replace the computer hacking and the "clicks" with a drawing board and the sounds of pencil scratching and you have an autobiographical comic right here.

PAGES 109-112: From the beginning, the actual people who patronize red rooms were always meant to be the 1%, "for the man or woman who has everything." Earlier we saw that the Pentagram lawyer was a fan of the subculture, but I wanted to give another glimpse at a user who might have flown under the radar. I had to create the impression that anybody can be a red room fan if they have enough money to buy-in.

The last balloon where she says "you gotta fuckin' save me..." is to imply an addiction to the subculture. Very sordid stuff.

"DONNA BUTCHER"

Pages 113–136

This is the issue I can honestly say I began finding my groove. I had a few goals narratively and formally that I wanted to explore with this comic. For one, I wanted to tell a red room story that existed from a time before the dark web. I'm a product of the VHS era and I wanted to explore what a red room would look like from that era.

While listening to Stephen King's 1981 *Danse Macabre* audiobook he made mention of snuff flicks that have been leaking out on video from South America and that could be easily corroborated these days with the amount of snuff that hits the internet from the Brazilian cartels who rule with iron grips and use the videos to put fear in both their enemies and subordinates.

The other parameter that I had in my mind was to, perhaps, try and make an EC style comic where all the smaller stories with O. Henry endings are a part of one bigger tale. Instead of the slavish structure and page count of the EC stuff, I opted for 3 stories instead of 4 and to keep them loosely tied to their specific "act" in the narrative.

PAGES 115-116: I started things off with a Feldstein-ian amount of EC verbosity but I just couldn't sustain it.

Last panel on page 116: I read about victims of child exploitation videos who are awarded restitution if creeps are caught with their videos and it seemed

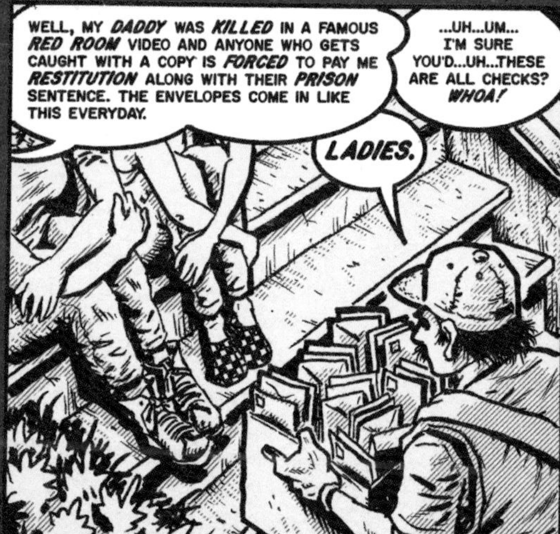

WELL, MY DADDY WAS KILLED IN A FAMOUS RED ROOM VIDEO AND ANYONE WHO GETS CAUGHT WITH A COPY IS FORCED TO PAY ME RESTITUTION ALONG WITH THEIR PRISON SENTENCE. THE ENVELOPES COME IN LIKE THIS EVERYDAY.
...UH...UM... I'M SURE YOU'D...UH...THESE ARE ALL CHECKS? WHOA!
LADIES.

like a logical piece to add to *Red Room*. Built into the legal aspects of *Red Room* is the illegality of the videos on the grounds that they promote the continuation of the black market enterprise. The only people who ever seem to get in trouble are the lowest rung traders and swappers rather than the creators and propagators.

PAGE 117: With all that info in mind from the previous paragraph it did make me wonder, "would the courts be lenient on the victim who downloaded material about themselves?" That was a big springboard for this story to unravel.

Last panel: I'm a sucker for a comic book action montage sequence.

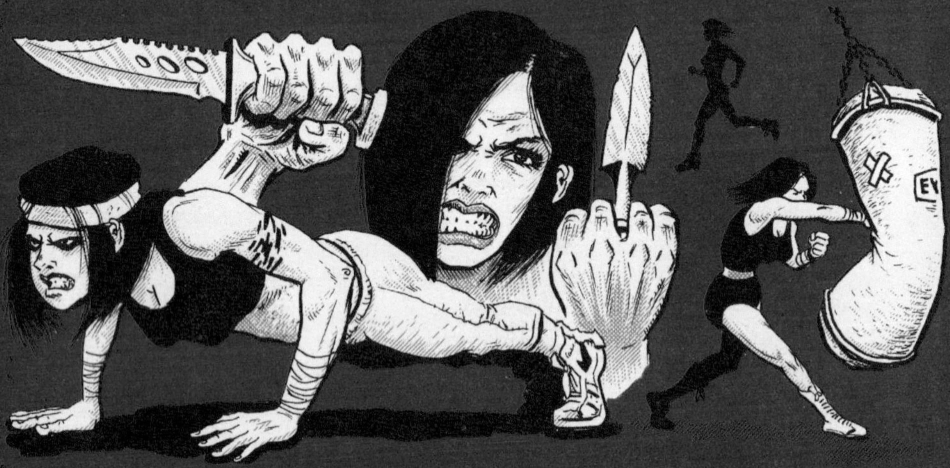
EV

PAGE 119: Getting Raina to shave her head was a timing device for a future page as much as it's a character piece to sell her caption in that second-to-last panel.

PAGE 120-121: Here it is, some VHS snuff. Had to download a specific font for that perfect digital type style that was built into all our camcorders at the time. On page 121 I wanted to pull a bit of a swerve, since I knew there was going to be a second look at the guy in the liquid. If the reader initially thought he was being dissolved in acid, that would make me happy.

PAGE 122: Here's what I meant by Raina's hair as a timing device. Rather than say "two months later" or whatever, the time it takes for the feds

WE ALL KNOW A FEW JERKS AND ASSHOLES, BUT WE RARELY RUN INTO AN OUTLIER OF CHAOS AND DESTRUCTION, FOR IF WE DID IT WOULD CERTAINLY MEAN OUR DOOM... OR INCARCERATION, AT THE VERY LEAST. I'M TALKING ABOUT THAT 1% OF THE WORLD'S POPULACE WHO NEED NO PARTICULAR MOTIVATION TO EXHIBIT...
PURE EVIL!
DONNA BUTCHER JUST HAPPENS TO BE ONE SUCH INDIVIDUAL CURSED WITH THE RARE BURDEN OF ACUTE PSYCHOPATHY. IS THERE SOME SIMPLE EXPLANATION FOR THE MENTAL CONDITION? NATURE? NURTURE? NEITHER! LET'S DIVE DEEP AND SEE WHAT MADE DONNA BUTCHER THE QUEEN OF THE RED ROOMS IN THE VHS DAYS OF YORE BEFORE SARAH JANE PAYNE TOOK THE CROWN.
No_Hedz_Better_Than_One.WMV

GREETINGS, BOILS AND GHOULS! WELCOME ONCE AGAIN TO THE MAGAZINE VOTED, "I'D MOST LIKE TO BE SHIPWRECKED ON A DESERT ISLAND WITH, IF MARILYN MONROE WERE ALONG TOO!" HMMM! THERE MUST BE AN HONOR IN THAT SOMEWHERE. ANYWAY, IT'S YOUR CRYPT-KEEPER AGAIN, WELCOMING YOU TO ANOTHER SLIMY SESSION OF SICKENING SELECTIONS STARTING WITH THIS SCREAM-STORY GUARANTEED TO DRIVE YOU NOTES! IT'S A MASTERPIECE OF MUSICAL MORBIDITY... A FAVORITE OF MINE! I CALL THIS DISGUSTING DELVING INTO DELIRIUM...
CONCERTO for VIOLIN and WEREWOLF
SACHA BARAK, THE FAMED CONCERT VIOLINIST, CLUTCHED HIS PRECIOUS STRADIVARIUS PROTECTIVELY TO HIS BREAST AND CURSED SOFTLY TO HIMSELF AS THE OLD COACH RUMBLED AND BUMPED OVER THE RUTTED ROAD THROUGH THE ROUMANIAN COUNTRYSIDE. THE OLD COACH HAD BEEN THE ONLY MEANS OF TRANSPORTATION AVAILABLE TO SACHA. TAXI DRIVERS HAD LOOKED AT HIM WIDE-EYED AND TURNED AWAY WHEN HE TOLD THEM HIS DESTINATION. SO HE'D CLIMBED INTO THE ANCIENT VEHICLE, WITH ITS TIGHT-LIPPED DRIVER, AND NOW HE WAS BEING WHIPPED AND JOSTLED ABOUT AS IT THUNDERED INTO THE NIGHT...
BLAST! THESE CONFOUNDED TRANSYLVANIAN HIGHWAYS ARE EVEN WORSE THAN I REMEMBER THEM. IF IT WEREN'T TO SEE VASILE IORGA, I WOULD NEVER EVEN ATTEMPT SUCH A JOURNEY!
1

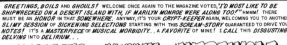

ABOVE: The splash page for "Concerto for Violin and Werewolf," drawn by Jack Davis and appearing in EC's *Tales From the Crypt* #42, June–July 1954.

to finally kick in her door is exactly the time it takes for a person's hair to grow from zero to that length.

PAGE 123: "Pure Evil," the Donna Butcher origin story. It's yet another place where I dig into my John E. Douglas FBI profiler bag of tricks to build our killer girl.

PAGE 124: Had to give our girl the serial killer trifecta on top of the abuse of a shitty home life. Little Evie wets the bed, plays with fire, and has a penchant for playing god with helpless animals.

PAGE 125: Discovering that there is a subgenre of porn out there where ladies step on little animals was a queasy revelation but lends well to the makeup of a future *Red Room*er.

PAGE 126: I mentioned it early without realizing I so much as say it in the comic, but I read about how those drug cartel videos are motivational tools for the underlings and warnings to rivals. Had to put some of that into the comic.

PAGE 127: This was a page I couldn't wait to draw. VHS red rooms complete with time-specific TVs and VCRs. We continue the same video we

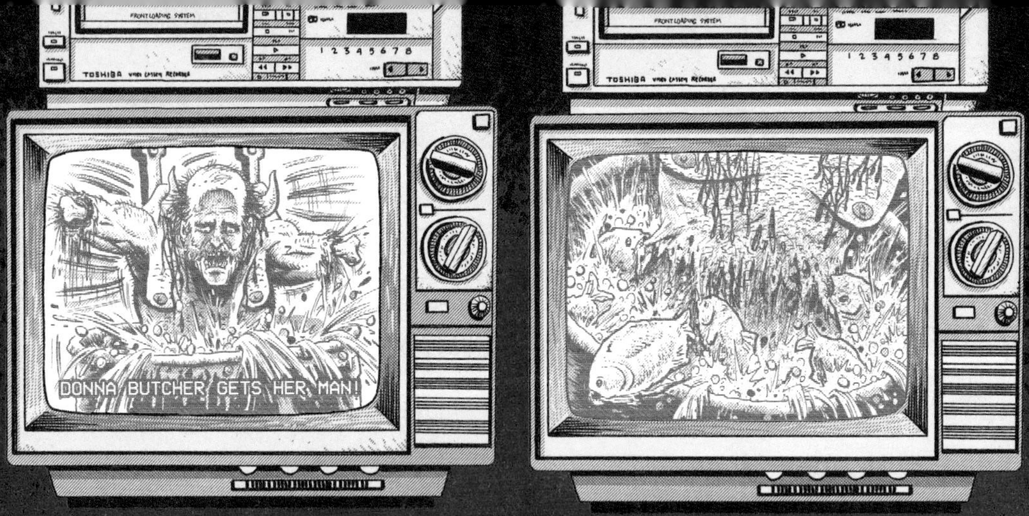
DONNA BUTCHER GETS HER MAN!

saw before to reveal that it's not acid the guy is being dunked into, but a vat of man-eating fish.

PAGES 128–129: Even on the previous pages, beginning with little Evie's dog head-on-spike panel, I wanted to have open panels, with each page showing the evolution of the character as she got older. Slowly the open panels would expand until we see her in her vastly different final form. Remember those old "Got Milk?" ads from the early 1990s? That was the thought in mind. Also, I liked the idea of Donna Butcher becoming overripe and spoiled in her final, prison inmate iteration.

PAGE 131: Our girls are together! This last part of the story was helped by a tried and true reference book that I've gone back to a few times called *Prisoners' Inventions* by Angelo, which highlights all the makeshift stuff one can create while in a penitentiary to improve the quality of life. I first discovered the book while working on *Wizzywig* and it's proving once again to be a valuable resource. The tattoo gun is made from a shaving kit motor and there was mention that one could use a garbage bag full of water to lift weights or dispatch enemies by dropping it on their heads from a level above.

PAGE 132–133: Not sure exactly how clear the bag full of water gimmick is visually but I tried my best. Lots of sketchbooking to get to the final boards.

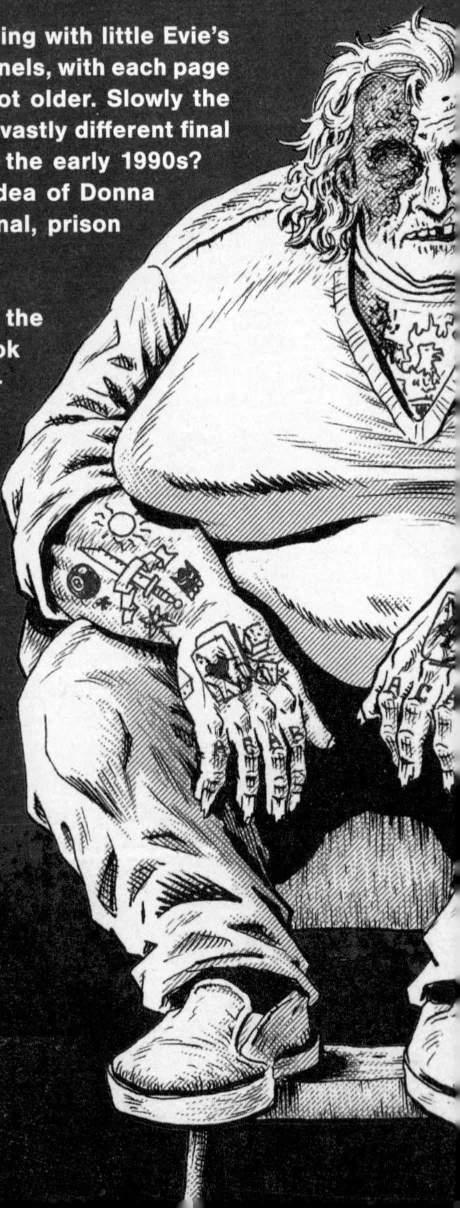

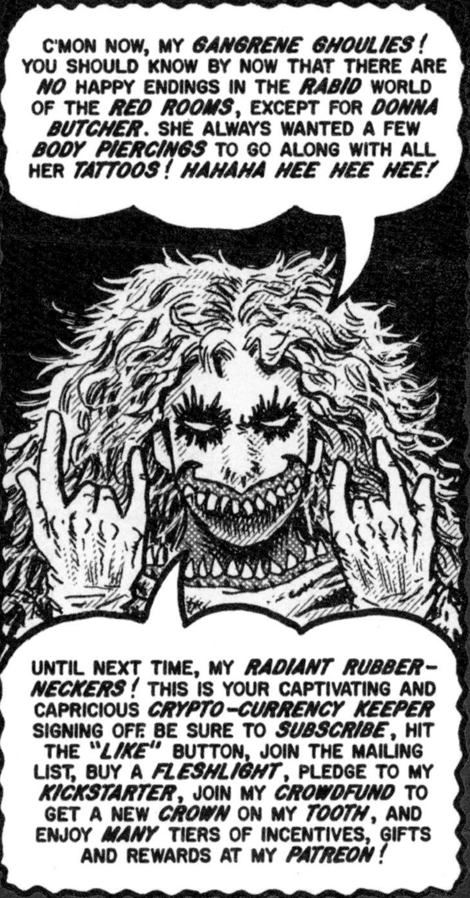
C'MON NOW, MY *GANGRENE GHOULIES!* YOU SHOULD KNOW BY NOW THAT THERE ARE *NO* HAPPY ENDINGS IN THE *RABID* WORLD OF THE *RED ROOMS*, EXCEPT FOR *DONNA BUTCHER*. SHE ALWAYS WANTED A FEW *BODY PIERCINGS* TO GO ALONG WITH ALL HER *TATTOOS! HAHAHA HEE HEE HEE!*
UNTIL NEXT TIME, MY *RADIANT RUBBER-NECKERS!* THIS IS YOUR CAPTIVATING AND CAPRICIOUS *CRYPTO-CURRENCY KEEPER* SIGNING OFF. BE SURE TO *SUBSCRIBE*, HIT THE *"LIKE"* BUTTON, JOIN THE MAILING LIST, BUY A *FLESHLIGHT*, PLEDGE TO MY *KICKSTARTER*, JOIN MY *CROWDFUND* TO GET A NEW *CROWN* ON MY *TOOTH*, AND ENJOY *MANY* TIERS OF INCENTIVES, GIFTS AND REWARDS AT MY *PATREON!*

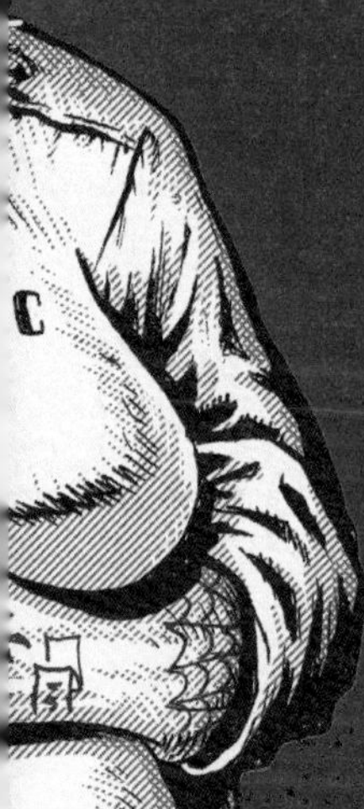

PAGE 134: Chekov's Jolly Rancher. You don't show the Jolly Rancher stick on the first page of "Snuff Said" without having some sort of payoff in the end.

PAGE 135: I remember thinking of killing Raina really late in the making of this story, and I don't doubt that I settled on it the second it was time to draw this page. The ending could have gone a different way, but this seemed to make the most sense and it creates a new kind of red room possibility within the subculture...

PAGE 136: The found-footage, exclusive, newsworthy red room video. One can imagine that this would be a hot selling item once the word spread on the dark web.

Speaking of the word spreading, I want to thank you all for your time and support for *Red Room*. For as pulpy as the stories are, there is still a lot of work that goes into their making and I pledge to keep doing my best for future issues. Wait 'til you see what's in store!

Ed Piskor
Dixmont State Hospital
for the Criminally Insane

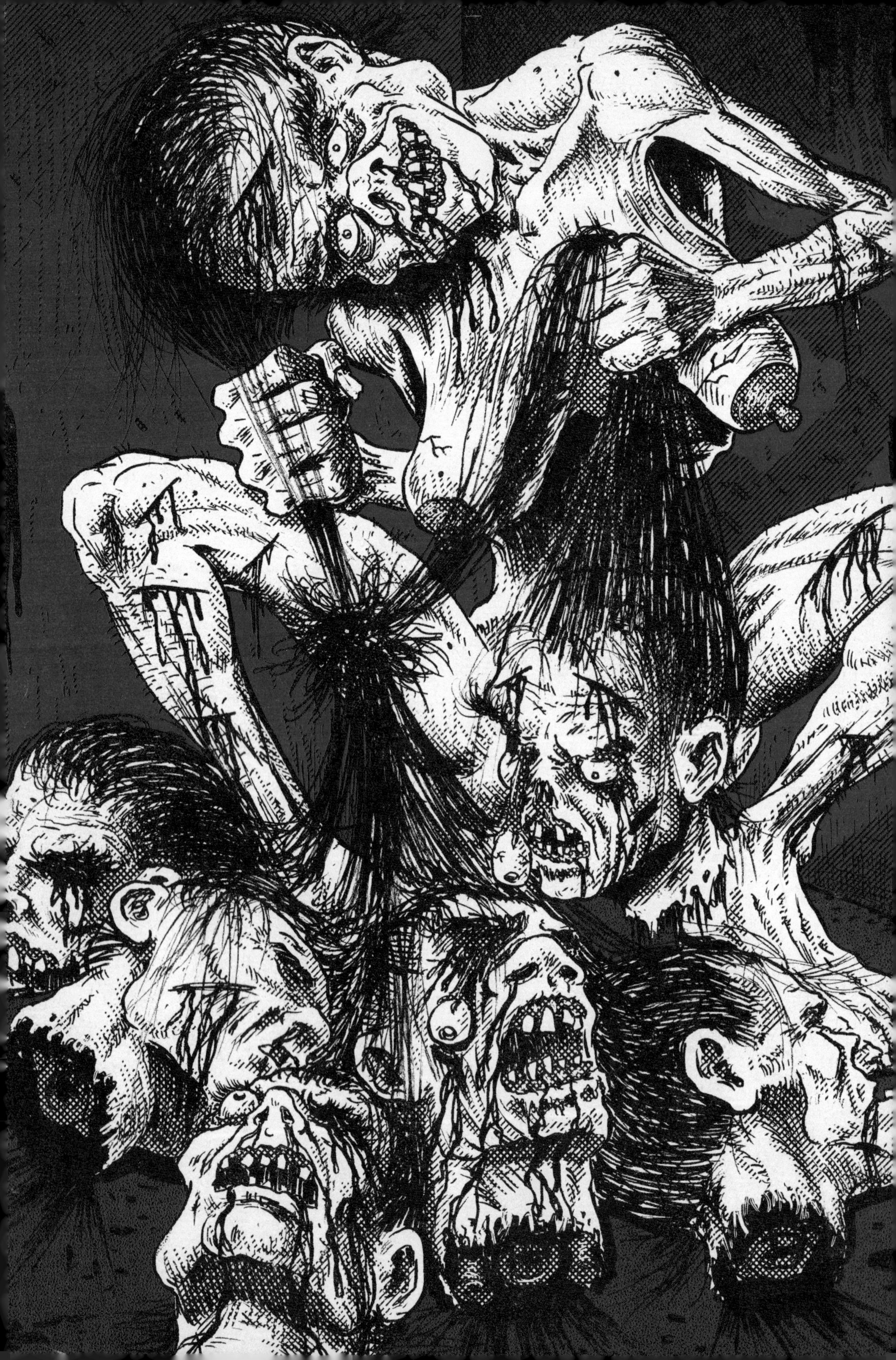